WordPerfect, Lotus 1-2-3®, dBASE®:

Tutorial and Applications

Anita Thompson
Ben Davis High School
Indianapolis, IN

South-Western Publishing Co.

Editor-in-Chief: Robert E. First
Acquisitions Editor: Janie Schwark
Developmental Editor: Dave Lafferty
Production Editor: Shannon O'Connor
Coordinating Editor: Lisa McClary
Senior Designer: Jim DeSollar
Associate Photo Editor/Stylist: Fred M. Middendorf
Marketing Manager: Brian Taylor
Consulting Editor: Rick Sullivan

ISBN: 0-538-62094-3

6 7 8 BC 99 98 97 96 95

Printed in the United States of America

PREFACE

INTRODUCTION

This text-workbook was written to make learning software applications an enjoyable and rewarding experience. This learning experience includes basic features of the three major software packages—WordPerfect® 5.1[1], Lotus® 1-2-3 versions 2 and 3[2], and dBASE® III and IV[3], as well as basic DOS commands and microcomputer vocabulary. The desired results are: creation of numerous types of documents using the software packages, performance of everyday DOS tasks, and effective communication about computers.

Although written for secondary and postsecondary students, these materials have also been used successfully with adult learners. Most people prefer concise, straight-to-the-point information when they are learning a new skill. This also makes the book ideal as a reference in other computer classes, while completing personal computer work, when "boning up" for a job interview, or when using a computer on the job.

ABOUT THIS BOOK

Many features have been included in this book that can aid in learning and retention. It is written in a workbook format that allows one to record answers, jot notes, and highlight text. Frequent screen captures show how the document should look after using particular features. A separate Command Summary for each of the software programs and DOS is added at the back of the book for ready reference.

Evaluation techniques for each section include two or three on-computer Review Exercises and Reinforcement Activities and a short true/false quiz. Comprehension is evaluated every few pages with Quick Questions that test knowledge of what was recently read or done; these can form the basis for class discussion. Where possible, information is personalized to each particular computer environment.

[1] WordPerfect is a registered trademark of WordPerfect Corporation.

[2] Lotus and 1-2-3 are registered trademarks of Lotus Development Corporation.

[3] dBASE III and dBASE IV are registered trademarks of Borland International, Inc.

A Template disk and Solution disks are available to aid the student or instructor. The Template disk has basic documents and can be used to reduce keying. The Solution disks contain files for all projects completed throughout the book. The Solution disks can be used if the student erases a file, makes a critical error, or is absent when a file is created. The instructor can also project the solution with a computer projector so the document can be discussed. The Template and Solution disks are not required to use this book, but they are highly recommended to save time for the instructor and the student. A comprehensive Teacher's Manual is also available with many tips and explanations.

A very unique Integration unit gives detailed instructions for importing a worksheet into WordPerfect and dBASE, a WordPerfect document into dBASE and Lotus, and a dBASE file into both Lotus and WordPerfect. It is ideal for an advanced topic or can be delegated to the bright student who needs a challenge.

USING THIS BOOK

This book has been developed to include all areas of computer experience usually presented in a beginning Computer Applications course. In order of inclusion in the book, these areas are:

- Unit 1 - Vocabulary of microcomputers (3 sections)
- Unit 2 - Basics of DOS (3 sections)
- Unit 3 - Basics of using the WordPerfect 5.1 program (10 sections)
- Unit 4 - Basics of using the Lotus 1-2-3 program (8 sections)
- Unit 5 - Basics of using the dBASE program (8 sections)
- Unit 6 - Integration of software files (4 sections)

It is recommended (but not mandatory) that the units be completed in this order. For example, microcomputer terms will be used in later units, and using DOS commands may simplify using dBASE commands. Unless files are obtained from the Solution disk, the Integration unit must be completed after the WordPerfect, Lotus, and dBASE units because it uses files created in those units. It is not necessary to complete all units or all of the sections within a unit, as any files needed for later activities may be obtained from the Solution disk.

An attempt has been made to clearly identify what to key, what to do, and what to read. Everything that is to be done on the computer has a line above and below and is preceded by a symbol that clarifies the action. The symbols and their actions are:

KEY: Key a word or words.

DO: Perform an action on the keyboard, such as key a command.

[.] Used only in the dBASE section, key a dot prompt command.

▭ Press a key, such as (Shift).

File names and often field names are shown in caps, but do not need to be keyed in caps.

ACKNOWLEDGMENT

Thanks go, first of all, to my Computer Applications colleagues, Scott Williams, Debbie Richhart, and Doug Opel, who have offered praise and encouragement, as well as suggestions for improvement. Special thanks go to Nancy Kisling, the best Department Chairperson ever, who has always supported me 150%! I am grateful that I teach for the MSD of Wayne Township, which offers its teachers many opportunities for professional growth.

I am very impressed with the South-Western editors. They are all enthusiastic and supportive. Thank you, Janie, for having blind faith in a teacher who had never written professionally. Rick, I can't praise you enough for your editorial skill and technical knowledge, but most of all for your ultimate patience in assisting me to complete this book. Dave, thank you for your information and guidance.

I especially want to thank Grace Runyan, my student-teacher-turned-editor, for her belief in me and for her careful proofreading of my manuscript. Thank you most of all to my computer students, who make teaching a challenge and a joy, especially to Dennis and Gary for your concern and words of encouragement.

WHERE TO GO FROM HERE

When you complete some or all of this book you will know a lot more about computers than most people. But that isn't enough! You have learned only the basic features of the software packages covered in this book. There are many advanced applications not covered here, such as macros, desktop publishing, statistical analysis, presentation graphics, and more. Challenge yourself by taking more computer classes or learn on your own using books like this. Many computer magazines on the market can help keep you informed. Part of the excitement of using computers is the constant change, always with new things to learn!

CONTENTS

8 GRAPHS L82

UNIT 5
Using dBASE

1 GETTING ACQUAINTED dB2

2 THE BASICS dB6

3 CREATE A DATABASE dB12

4 DATA ENTRY dB24

APPENDIX
Command Summaries

UNIT 1

Using Computers

1

HARDWARE

OBJECTIVES

- Define computer, computer program, computer system, data, and information.
- List the functions of input, process, output, and storage components of a computer.
- Identify microcomputer, minicomputer, and mainframe.
- Describe the input, process, output and storage hardware in a computer system.
- Define input-, process-, output- and storage-related terms.
- Compare the main types of printers for quality, price, and features.
- List specifications of the classroom printer(s).
- Identify the parts of diskettes, proper handling procedures, and specifications.
- Compare floppies, hard drives, cd-rom, and interactive videodisc.
- Recognize modems as common telecommunications devices.
- Identify the parts of stand alone and networked computer systems.

As you work through this book, you will learn to use the computer as a tool to complete many projects. Besides being able to use the computer, you must also be able to communicate about computers. This unit is designed to help you understand how computers function and to become familiar with the vocabulary of microcomputers.

COMPONENTS OF A COMPUTER SYSTEM

A **computer** is an electronic device that is programmed to receive data, change the data to information, present the information, and store the information. A **computer program**, through a series of instructions telling the computer what actions to take, determines how the computer will change data into information. **Data** is raw facts entered into a computer, whereas **information** is the result of data processing.

A **computer system** includes the computer and all of its devices. The functions and components of a computer system are: send data (**input**) → change the data to information (**process**) → present the information (**output**) → store the information (**storage**.)

The diagram below (UC1.1) shows how the four components of a computer system relate to each other.

FIGURE UC1.1
The Components of a Computer System

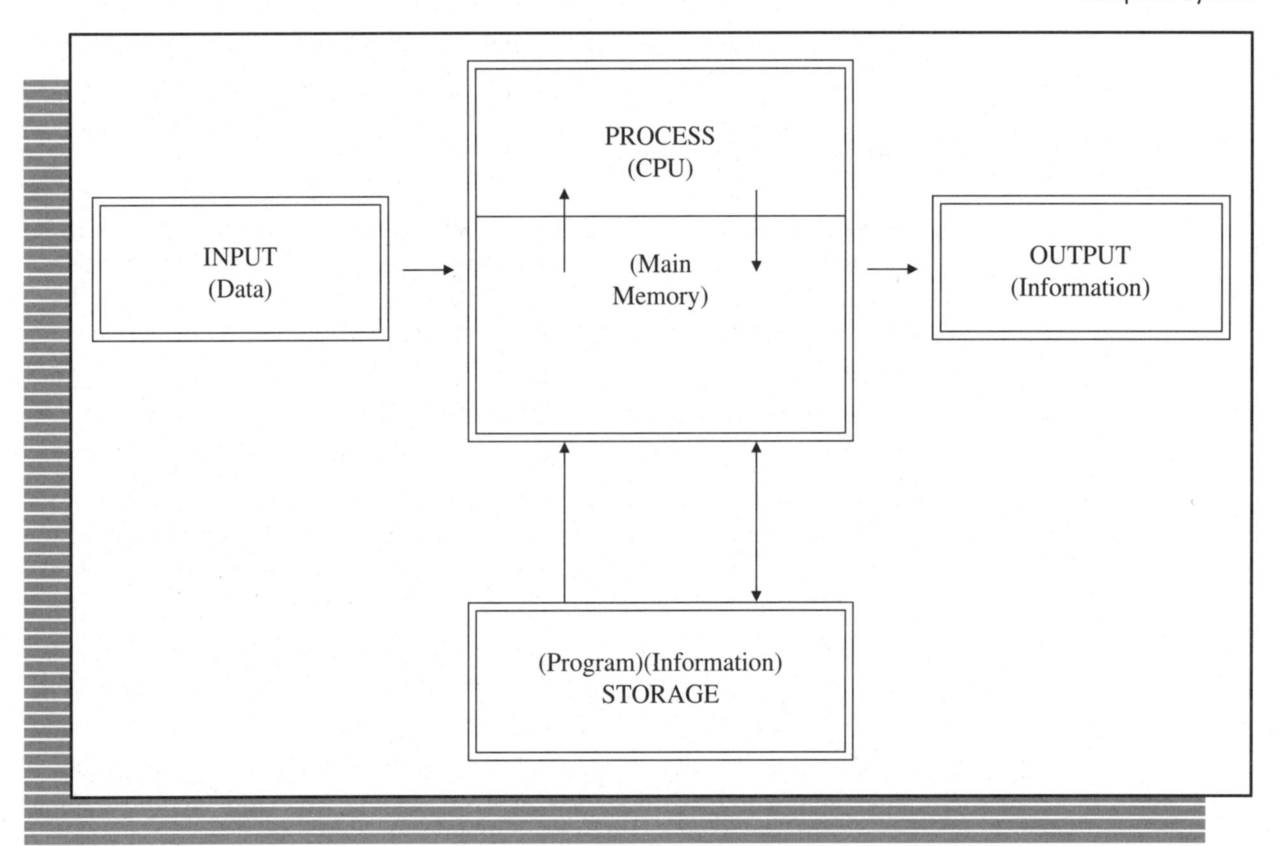

Main Memory, the storage unit inside the computer, performs the following actions:

1. accepts a *Program* from storage and *Data* input for processing
2. sends *Program Instructions* and *Data* to the CPU as requested for processing
3. receives processed *Information* from the CPU and sends it to output and/or storage
4. receives a *Program* and *Information* from storage when updating is needed

The **Central Processing Unit (CPU)**, also called the **processor**, is inside the computer. The CPU follows the instructions of a computer program to process or change the incoming data to the desired output. This change to data can be achieved through **arithmetic** calculations like adding and dividing. Data can also be changed through **logical** operations, where the computer determines if a character is greater than, less than, or equal to another character. Sometimes data is simply arranged in a useful way.

SIZES OF COMPUTERS

Computer systems are available in several sizes to accommodate different needs, including number of users, amount of data to be processed, required processing speed, number of attached devices, and cost. The focus in this book is on microcomputers.

Microcomputers, also called PCs (personal computers), are small enough to sit on a desktop and are controlled by tiny CPUs called microprocessors. Microcomputers also include laptops, PCs that are small enough to be portable.

Minicomputers, mid-sized computer systems, have powerful processors (CPUs) that may be accessed through keyboard-and-screen non-processing terminals that look like computers.

Mainframes are the largest computer systems, and they usually are made up of one or more large processors, many terminals, and several large storage devices.

The classification of a particular computer system into one of the three sizes can be difficult because small computers are becoming more powerful and may be linked together to share devices.

QUICK QUESTIONS

1. What is a computer?
2. What is a computer program?
3. Compare data and information.
4. What is a computer system?

5. Write the function of the following components:
   a) input
   b) process
   c) output
   d) storage
6. List the four actions of Main Memory:
   a)
   b)
   c)
   d)
7. What is the purpose of the CPU in a computer?
8. List two different operations a CPU can perform to change data:
   a)
   b)
9. List the three sizes of computers, from the largest to the smallest:
   a)
   b)
   c)
10. From memory, draw a diagram that shows the interrelationship of the components of a computer system. Draw arrows and label all parts.

VOCABULARY

Computer
Computer Program
Data
Information
Computer System
Input
Process
Output
Storage
Main Memory
Central Processing Unit
CPU
Processor
Arithmetic Calculations
Logical Operations
Microcomputer
PC
Microprocessor
Laptop
Minicomputer
Mainframe

COMPUTER HARDWARE

The functions of the computer system components—input, process, output, and storage—are performed by specific devices. Computers and their related devices are known as **hardware**. Each device except the CPU and Main Memory is considered **peripheral hardware**.

PROCESS HARDWARE

Process hardware, which changes data into information, is contained in the **System Unit**. The System Unit of a PC is usually a horizontal, rectangular unit on the desktop, but can be a vertical "tower" placed on the floor. The System Unit includes storage devices, a power supply, and expansion slots for upgrading the system, but most importantly, its **motherboard** contains the chips that control the computer. **Chips** are tiny wafers with electronic circuits. The motherboard, the main circuit board, contains Main Memory, called RAM; ROM; and the CPU, called a microprocessor.

RAM, an abbreviation for random-access memory, is used for storage of your active computer program and the data you create with it. RAM is erased when you turn off the computer. **ROM**, read-only memory, contains special programs that power up the computer. The programs in ROM remain when the computer is off. The **microprocessor** regulates the functions of RAM and the peripheral hardware. The peripheral hardware, such as a mouse, printer, or keyboard, attaches to the CPU through **ports**, sockets in the System Unit.

What brand and model of computer will you be using? __________

INPUT HARDWARE

Input Hardware sends data to RAM (Main Memory.) Common input devices include keyboards, mice and trackballs, and various scanners.

Can you name an additional input device that would send data to an electronic game or other computerized machine? ______________

KEYBOARDS. The most widely used input device is the keyboard. Most computers have either the **standard** keyboard (UC1.2) or the **enhanced** keyboard with additional keys (UC1.3.)

Which type of keyboard will you be using? ______________

FIGURE UC1.2
Standard Keyboard

FIGURE UC1.3
Enhanced Keyboard

Computer keyboards include not only letters, numbers, and characters, but also special keys that simplify using computer programs. Using the picture of your keyboard (UC1.2 or UC1.3), show where the following keys are located. Draw arrows and write the name of the key or group of keys.

FIGURE UC1.4
Mouse

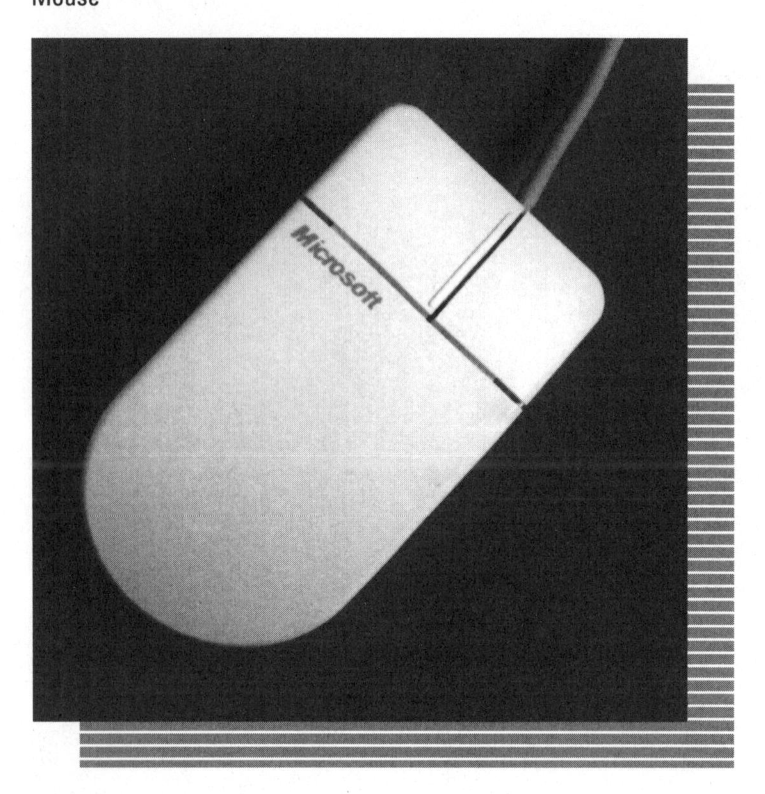

FIGURE UC1.5
Trackball

HELPFUL KEYS.

Cursor keys (→ ← ↑ ↓) and the special keys *Home, End, Page Up,* and *Page Down* allow easy movement around the computer screen.

Insert, Delete, Backspace perform editing functions.

Alt, Ctrl, Shift, used in combination with other keys, perform commands that differ in use from one computer program to another.

Function keys are used to perform commands that vary among computer programs.

Esc (Escape) is used in many computer programs to cancel an instruction or to exit from a menu or the program.

Num Lock must be activated for the **numeric keypad**, the pad of numbers at the right of the keyboard, to display numbers.

Print Screen (PrtSc) can be used in any program to print the entire contents of the computer screen onto paper in the printer.

MICE. A **mouse** (UC1.4) is an input device that is used to select options from a program menu or to draw on the computer screen. A similar device is a **trackball** (UC1.5.) Both hardware items move the cursor by means of a rolling ball. Will you be using a mouse or trackball?

SCANNERS. A **scanner** is hardware that can "read" data and send it to RAM, eliminating the need for human entry of data. Scanners are widely used; you have probably seen them in department stores and grocery stores.

QUICK QUESTIONS

1. What is hardware?
2. What is peripheral hardware?
3. What is the purpose of process hardware?
4. Name four items contained in the System Unit of a PC.
   a)
   b)
   c)
   d)
5. What is a motherboard?
6. Describe each item on the motherboard.
   a) RAM
   b) ROM
   c) microprocessor
7. What is the purpose of input hardware?
8. What is the most widely used input device?
9. Which key is often used to cancel instructions or to exit from menus or programs?
10. What key must be activated for the numeric pad to display numbers?
11. Which input device is used to select options on a menu or to draw on the computer screen?
12. Which input device reads data, eliminating human entry of data?

VOCABULARY

Hardware
Peripheral Hardware
Process Hardware
System Unit
Motherboard
Chip
RAM
ROM
Microprocessor
Port
Input Hardware
Keyboard
Cursor Keys
Function Keys
Numeric Keypad
Mouse
Trackball
Scanner

OUTPUT HARDWARE

Output hardware receives information from RAM and usually presents it in a readable form, either on a computer screen or on paper.

COMPUTER SCREEN. Also known by other names such as **CRT**, **monitor**, and **display**, the screen displays data entered from the keyboard as well as instructions and information from the computer program.

Computer screens are either **color** or **monochrome**. Monochrome screens display in a single color, white, black, green, amber, or orange, against a contrasting background. Computer screens also differ in their **resolution**, sharpness of image. What brand and model of screen will you be using? ______________________________

Is it color or monochrome? ______________________________

PRINTER. The printer displays information on paper, known as a **hard copy** or **printout**. Printers are usually divided into **impact** and **nonimpact** types.

Impact Printers strike the printer paper with an inked ribbon. This makes them noisy, but essential for printouts that include carbon copies. The most common printer in this category is the dot matrix printer. An inexpensive printer, the **dot matrix** prints text and graphics as a series of dots. It is widely used in homes and schools, and in business firms for draft copies.

Another impact printer, the **daisy wheel**, prints much like an electronic typewriter; it has a print wheel and can only print text.

Nonimpact Printers include ink jet and laser printers. An **ink jet** printer has a nozzle that sprays ink onto paper in the shape of a character or design. The quality of print is relatively high, and some ink jet printers can print in color.

The most popular nonimpact printer is the **laser** printer. A laser printer uses a version of the reproduction technology of copy machines to fuse text and graphic images to the page. Laser printers are expensive, but they are very fast and the print quality is excellent. In addition, laser printers offer many **font** options, which means you can vary the size and appearance of the printed characters.

What printer(s) will you be using? ______________________________

____

QUICK QUESTIONS

1. What is the purpose of output hardware?
2. What does a CRT do?
3. What is the correct name for a monitor that displays in black and white?
4. What word refers to the sharpness of the image displayed on a computer screen?
5. What is a hard copy?
6. Which type of printer strikes the paper with an inked ribbon?
7. Name two impact printers and describe how they print.
   a)
   b)
8. Which impact printer is most popular for home and school use?
9. Name two nonimpact printers and how they print.
   a)
   b)
10. In the chart below, indicate type, print quality, and price, and write something special about each printer. Base your answers on the information given to you and your own opinions.

Printer	Type I=Impact N=Nonimpact	Quality H=High M=Moderate L=Low	Price H=High M=Moderate L=Low	Special Feature
Dot matrix				
Daisy wheel				
Ink jet				
Laser				

11. List below any information you can gather about the printer(s) you will be using. Obtain the information from the printer itself, the printer manual, or your instructor.
    a) What is the brand? What is the model?
    b) What kind of printer is it?
    c) Does it have a narrow or a wide carriage?
    d) How is the paper fed (sprocket or sheet fed)?
    e) How fast does it print?
    f) What fonts are available?

Output Hardware
Computer Screen (CRT, Monitor, Display)
Monochrome Screen
Resolution
Hard Copy
Printout
Inpact Printer
Dot Matrix Printer
Daisy Wheel Printer
Nonimpact Printer
Ink Jet Printer
Laser Printer
Font

STORAGE HARDWARE

Storage hardware is often called **auxiliary storage**. Auxiliary storage devices receive information from RAM and store it, making it available if a computer program recalls it at a future time. The most common auxiliary storage devices are **floppy drives** and **hard drives**.

Floppy Disk Drives record data to and read data from **diskettes,** small plastic storage disks. Every computer must have at least one floppy disk drive so programs can be used or installed. Diskettes may be 5¼-inch in diameter sealed in a thin, easily bent plastic jacket or 3½-inch in diameter sealed in a rigid plastic case. Both types of diskettes are called **floppies** because the recording surface inside the jacket or case is a flexible magnetic plastic, similar to cassette tape material. Diskettes are used to store programs as well as information.

HANDLING DISKETTES. Both sizes of diskettes can be damaged without the following precautions:

- Keep away from magnetic items.
- Keep away from intense heat.
- Do not touch the recording surface.
- Do not remove diskette when drive light is on.

Because the 3½-inch diskettes are in a rigid protective case, they are more difficult to damage. The 5¼-inch diskettes, however, require additional precautions:

- Do not bend or place heavy objects on the diskette.
- Store the diskette in its protective envelope when not in use.
- Always handle carefully.

The 5¼-inch diskette has a **write protect notch**, and the 3½-inch diskette has a **write protect switch**. (See UC1.6.) To record on the diskette, a 5¼-inch write protect notch must be uncovered, and a 3½-inch write protect switch must be closed (no opening above the switch.) When you desire to protect a diskette from being written on, wrap tape across the write protect notch so it is no longer notched or flip the write protect switch so there is an opening above the switch.

FIGURE UC1.6
5¼-inch Diskette, 3½-inch Diskette

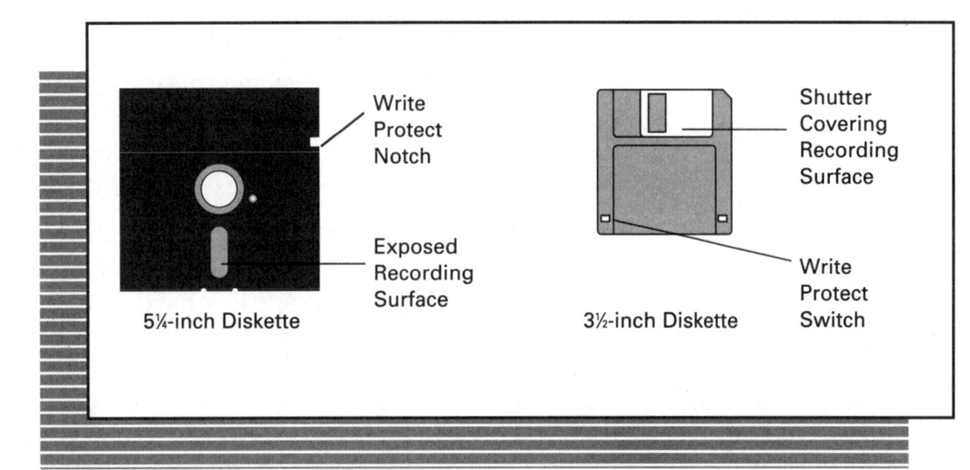

As you can see in UC1.6, the recording surface on a 5¼-inch diskette is exposed when the protective envelope is removed. Be careful not to touch or scratch the diskette. The metal **shutter** on a 3½-inch diskette is opened by the disk drive so it can access the recording surface. You should never open the shutter yourself, as you could damage the disk.

STORING ON DISKETTES. The amount of information a diskette can store is measured in thousands of characters called **Kilobytes (K)** or millions of characters, **Megabytes (MB).** Figure UC1.7 shows the maximum **bytes** (characters) various diskettes can hold.

The following chart illustrates that the capacity of a diskette depends on other factors in addition to diskette size. Almost all diskettes today are **double sided**, meaning data can be recorded on both the top and bottom surface of the diskette. Earlier computers could record data on only one surface, making the diskettes **single sided**.

FIGURE UC1.7
Diskette Capacities

Diskette Size	Density	Capacity
5¼ inch	Double sided, Double density (DS, DD)	320 -360K
5¼ inch	High capacity, Double density	1.25MB
3½ inch	Double sided, Double density (DS, DD) or (2DD)	720K
3½ inch	Double sided, High density (2HD)	1.44MB

Diskettes are also measured according to **recording density**. Density refers to how much data can be "packed" on a diskette. **High-density** diskettes pack more data per inch than double-density diskettes. It is important to know the density of a diskette because double-density disk drives cannot read or write to high-density diskettes.

Another factor that determines the capacity of a diskette is the **number of tracks** on which data is stored, 40 or 80, depending on the disk drive. Figure UC1.8 shows how a diskette is divided into circular **tracks** and pie-shaped **sectors**. The tracks and sectors are established when a new disk is **formatted**, or prepared for use. When processed information, called a **file**, is stored on a disk, it takes the number of sectors on a track it needs, according to the length of the file.

Information is stored as **magnetic spots** on the tracks of the diskette. The first track on the diskette, the **directory**, keeps a record of each file's position by logging the track number and sector number of each file. This is how a disk drive can find and access a file.

HARD DISK DRIVES. Disks in hard disk drives are permanently located, or fixed, inside a computer's system unit; they are not removed like floppy diskettes. A **hard disk** is made of one or more metal platters that pack data so tightly that hard disks hold from 10MB (10 million bytes) to more than 100MB. As with a floppy disk, data is recorded as magnetic spots on tracks within sectors. Because a hard drive is so large, many programs and files can be stored on it.

FIGURE UC1.8
Data Storage on Diskette, Hard Disk

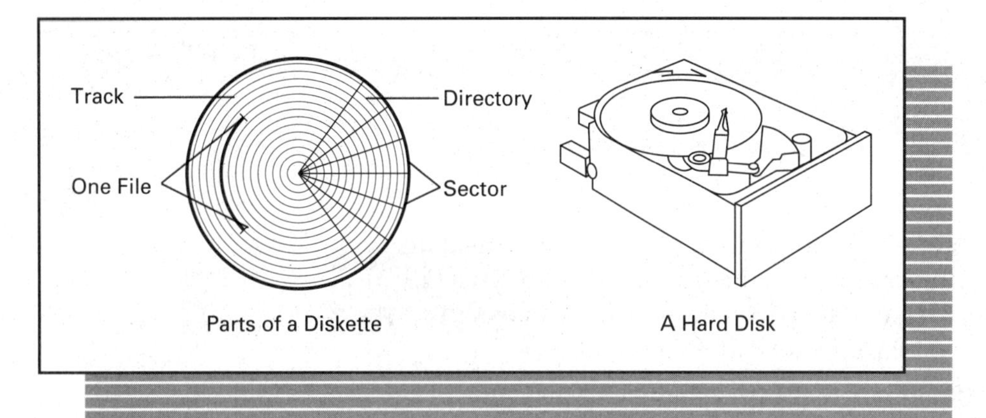

READ-ONLY STORAGE DEVICES. Some special devices use disks that are purchased with data already on them; the user cannot record on them. These include compact disks and interactive videodiscs.

A **compact disk**, also known as **CD-ROM** or **Optical Disk**, has data stored as microscopic pits and smooth areas that create different reflective properties. A laser beam detects reflections and translates them into digital data that the computer can use. Compact disks hold immense amounts of data—up to 650MB! You can buy encyclopedias on CD-ROM.

Interactive videodiscs are designed for the storage of images, including still pictures and continuous video, that can be input to RAM from a videodisc player.

What types of auxiliary storage will you be using? ______________

QUICK QUESTIONS

1. What is the purpose of storage hardware?
2. What are the most common auxiliary storage devices?
3. Why are diskettes called floppies?
4. Why does a 5¼-inch diskette require special handling?
5. Can you record on a 3½-inch diskette if you see an opening above the write protect switch?
6. Why is it important to leave the shutter closed on a 3½-inch diskette?
7. How many characters will a 1.44MB diskette hold?
8. Name four factors that determine the amount of data a diskette can hold:
   a)
   b)
   c)
   d)
9. Which holds more data, a high-density diskette or a double-density diskette?
10. What is the word that refers to preparing a disk for use by establishing tracks and sectors?
11. What is a file?
12. What form does data take when it is stored on a diskette?
13. How does a disk drive find and access a file?
14. What is the name for a large auxiliary storage device that is fixed inside a system unit?
15. Name two read-only auxiliary storage devices.
    a)
    b)
16. In front of each item, write **FD** for Floppy Disk, **HD** for Hard Disk, **CD** for Compact Disk, or **IV** for Interactive Videodisc. Some items will have more than one answer.

    _________ cannot store user data

    _________ holds 10MB or more

    _________ a circular material

    _________ can be carried in a shirt pocket

    _________ very high density

    _________ user may store data or programs

    _________ every computer must have one

    _________ used for images only

    _________ data is recorded as magnetic spots

    _________ uses laser technology

Storage Hardware
Auxiliary Storage
Floppy Disk Drive
Diskette
Floppy
Write Protect Notch
Write Protect Switch
Shutter
Kilobyte (K)
Megabyte (MB)
Double-Sided Disk
Recording Density
High-Density Diskette
Double-Density Diskette
Track
Sector
Format
File
Magnetic Spots
Directory
Hard Disk Drive
Hard Disk
Read-Only Storage Device
Compact Disk (CD-ROM) (Optical Disk)
Interactive Videodisc

TELECOMMUNICATION HARDWARE

Telecommunication has advanced the sending of information into instantaneous transmission around the world. Telecommunication requires a sending device that will change data into telephone signals, a receiving device that will change the telephone signals back into the original data, and a telephone line linking the two. Most devices can act as either sender or receiver. (See UC1.9.)

FIGURE UC1.9
Telecommunication

Sending Device		Receiving Device
Data Changed To Telephone Signals	Telephone Line	Telephone Signals Changed To Data

The most commonly used telecommunication device for microcomputer systems are **modems**. Modems send data from one computer to another and can be located outside the computer or inside the System Unit. The sending modem converts data in RAM or on a disk into telephone signals to be converted back into data by a modem on the other end of the telephone line. To use a modem, you must purchase special telecommunications software in addition to a computer, modem, and telephone line.

QUICK QUESTIONS

1. What word refers to the technology of transmitting information via sending and receiving devices that are linked by a telephone line?
2. What is the name of a device that sends data from one computer to another?
3. Name the four items necessary to send a modem message.
   a)
   b)
   c)
   d)

Telecommunication

Modem

COMPUTER SYSTEM CONFIGURATIONS

Information on the components of a computer system and the descriptions of hardware you have studied referred mainly to stand alone microcomputer systems, such as the one shown in UC1.10. With stand alones, the user has complete control over his/her hardware, and one malfunctioning computer does not affect other computers.

Label the parts in UC1.10. If your system is a stand alone, include your brand and model names with the labels.

FIGURE UC1.10
Stand-Alone Computer System

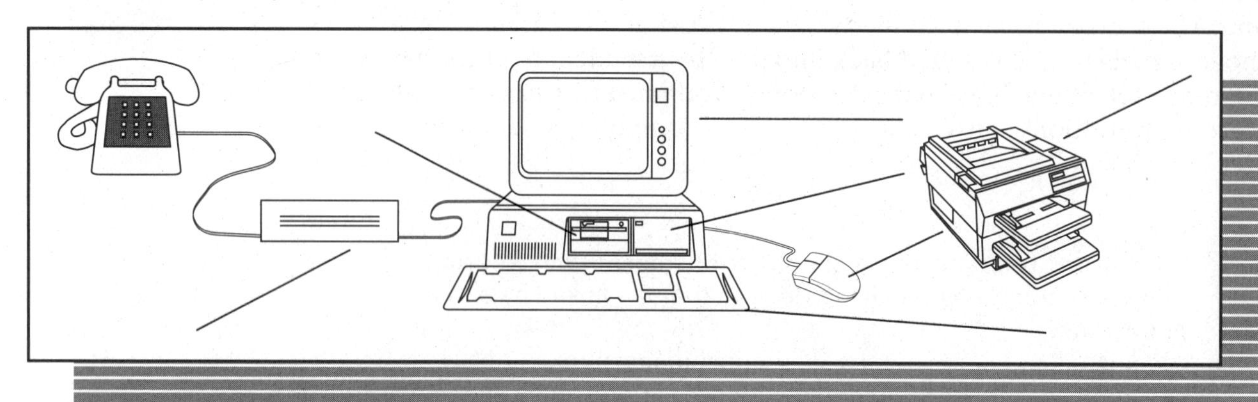

Instead of stand alones, many classroom computer systems use a **Local Area Network** or **LAN**. A LAN links computers within a limited area so users can exchange information, share hardware such as printers, and use a massive hard disk on a special computer called a **file server**. The file server's disk can hold over 100MB of programs and data. A LAN system may resemble UC1.11, but it could include any number of computers. If your computer system is networked and similar to UC1.11, label the hardware with your brands and models.

FIGURE UC1.11
Networked Computer System

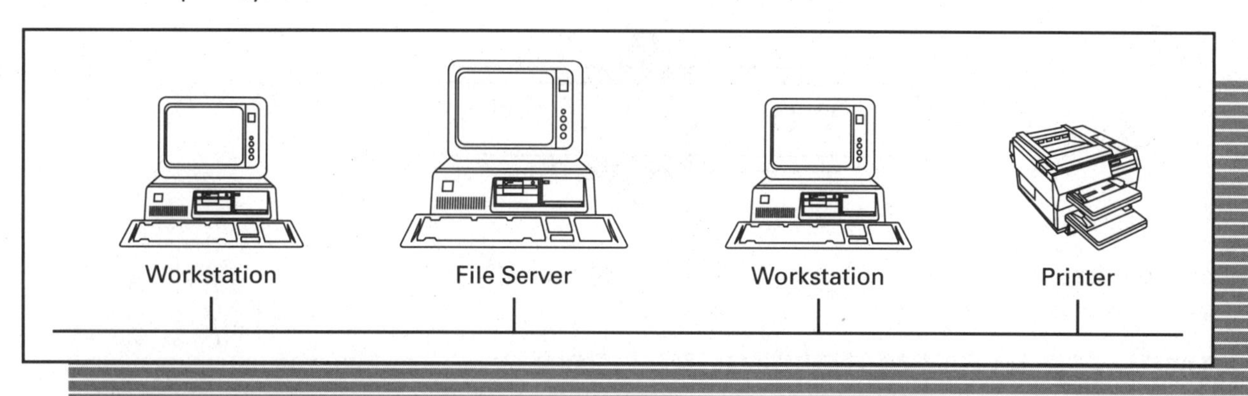

USING HARDWARE CROSSWORD PUZZLE

ACROSS

1 May be 5¼-inch or 3½-inch in size
7 Hardcopy
8 A laser beam detects data
9 Single-color display
14 Device that allows computers to telecommunicate
16 Sending data across phone lines
17 Portable microcomputer
18 Prepare a disk for use
21 Stores active program and data
23 Computer devices
24 Programmable electronic device
25 Processes data to desired output
26 Prevents saving to or erasing a disk
27 Large drive on a LAN
28 Processed data, output

DOWN

1 Stored as magnetic spots on disk
2 Pie-shaped area on a diskette
4 Printer that sprays ink
5 Set of instructions to a computer
6 Computer compares characters
10 A name for the computer screen
11 Sockets to attach hardware to CPU
12 Regulates actions of the computer
13 Appearance of printed characters
15 Receives information from RAM
19 A million characters of data
20 Another name for diskette

2

SOFTWARE

OBJECTIVES

- Conclude that software instructs the computer through sequential instructions.
- Contrast system and application software.
- Determine that operating system programs are necessary for computer operation.
- Differentiate ROM, operating system, and utility software.
- Define DOS, shell, user interface, menu, Windows, and GUI.
- Identify the main types of application programs and their functions.
- Define electronic mail, bulletin board, and on-line data service.
- Identify leisure activity and special purpose software.
- Compare full- and limited-feature software.
- Identify several sources of software.
- Compare commercial, shareware, and public domain software.
- Describe virus, program installation, documentation, and foreign files.

COMPUTER SOFTWARE

As you learned in the Hardware section, a computer is an electronic device that is programmed to receive data, change the data to information, present the information, and store the information. A **computer program** is a series of instructions telling the computer what actions to take. A computer must have a computer program, or **software**, to coordinate the components so it can complete user tasks. Software you will use includes DOS, WordPerfect, Lotus 1-2-3, and dBASE.

Software is necessary to **boot up** the computer, to get it ready to be used. Then an **application program** that will obtain the desired output is placed in RAM from auxiliary storage. The application program will then regulate the flow of data into RAM, change the data through arithmetic calculations and/or logical operations, and send the resulting information to the output device and/or auxiliary storage. The illustration on the next page, UC2.1, shows how software controls the operations of a computer system.

FIGURE UC2.1
Software Controls the Operations of a Computer System

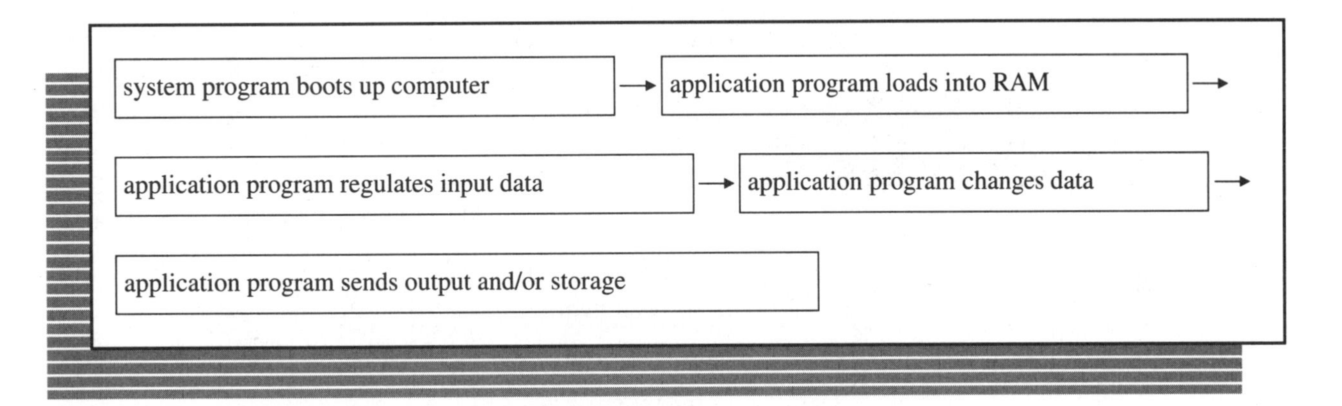
system program boots up computer
application program loads into RAM
application program regulates input data
application program changes data
application program sends output and/or storage

Software instructions must be arranged in a logical sequence so the computer components will function properly to achieve the desired result. The hardware will do what the program tells it to do, whether correct or not. Figure UC2.2 shows the step-by-step instructions of a simple application program to add two numbers.

FIGURE UC2.2
A Simple Application Program

Desired Result: Add two numbers input by a student and display the sum	
Program Instruction Sequence	Component(s) Involved
1. Clear memory	Main memory
2. Load calculating program	Auxiliary storage → Main memory
3. Input first number	Input → Main memory
4. Input second number	Input → Main memory
5. Add the numbers	CPU
6. Display the sum	Main memory → Output

QUICK QUESTIONS

1. What is a computer program?
2. Why is software essential to the operation of a computer?
3. What does it mean to "boot up" the computer?
4. What is an application program?
5. Why must the steps in a program be in a logical order?
6. Arrange the steps below in the proper *logical* order, as they would be written within a computer program. Number them from 1 to 8, with 1 being the first step and 8 the last step. The desired result: Find the average of three test scores and print the average on the printer. (Use Figure UC2.2 as a guide.)

    ________ Add the three test scores.

    ________ Input the second test score.

    ________ Print the average.

    ________ Input the third test score.

    ________ Clear the memory.

    ________ Load the calculating program.

    ________ Divide the total of the three numbers by three.

    ________ Input the first test score.

Computer Program

Software

Boot Up

Application Program

TYPES OF SOFTWARE

The two types of software needed for computer operation are system software and application software. **System software** works "behind the scenes" to boot up, operate, and maintain the computer system and make application programs work. **Application software**, what the user sees, performs useful tasks like printing mailing labels or keeping a list of baseball cards. System software tells the computer how to use application software.

SYSTEM PROGRAMS

System software is essential to the operation of a computer, as it "tells" the computer how to perform all tasks. The user can control many of the system software functions. In the unit on DOS in this book, you will learn some ways to manipulate your computer hardware using system software commands.

System software is divided into ROM, operating system, and utility programs.

ROM SOFTWARE. **ROM** (read-only memory) **software** resides in computer when the unit is purchased and is necessary to begin the boot up of a computer.

OPERATING SYSTEM SOFTWARE. An **operating system** program, the manager of the computer, completes the boot up procedure. When boot up is completed, control of the computer passes to the user. The operating system software remains in RAM to be used as needed.

When the computer user takes control of the computer system, he or she usually loads an application program to perform a specific task. A program is **loaded** when it is retrieved from auxiliary storage and placed in RAM. The operating system program already in RAM works with the application program to coordinate the components of the computer system. The user need only concentrate on completing his or her task.

UTILITY SOFTWARE. Before, after, or while using some application programs, the user may want to perform some housekeeping tasks with the computer, known as **utilities**. Utilities include, among many other tasks, formatting new disks, erasing files, looking at the names of files on disk, and copying files or copying disks.

Figure UC2.3 shows the three types of system software.

FIGURE UC2.3
Types of System Software

SYSTEM PROGRAMS	
Program	Purpose
ROM	Starts boot up procedure
Operating System	Completes boot up Resides in RAM to be used as needed by user or application program
Utility	Loaded into RAM as needed to do housekeeping tasks

USING OPERATING SYSTEM PROGRAMS

The actual operating system program used varies with the type and brand of computer. Minicomputers and main frames may run under the UNIX operating system. Apple microcomputers use ProDOS, and

IBM-compatible microcomputers use MS-DOS. Some computers will run under several operating systems.

As an IBM-compatible computer user, you will be using **MS-DOS** operating system software. It is called MS-DOS because it was written by Microsoft Corporation (MS), and it is a Disk Operating System. It is usually just called **DOS**.

MS-DOS traditionally has been a command-driven program. For example, to copy a file called FILE1 from one floppy to another, the user would have to recall and key exactly the following command: *copy a:file1 b:*

In an attempt to be more user-friendly and avoid memorization of complicated commands, DOS sometimes has a user interface called a **shell**. A **user interface** is a bridge between the user and the operating system; it is designed to make using a computer easier. With the shell, the user can choose from a **menu**, or list of options on screen (UC2.4).

FIGURE UC2.4
A DOS Shell Menu

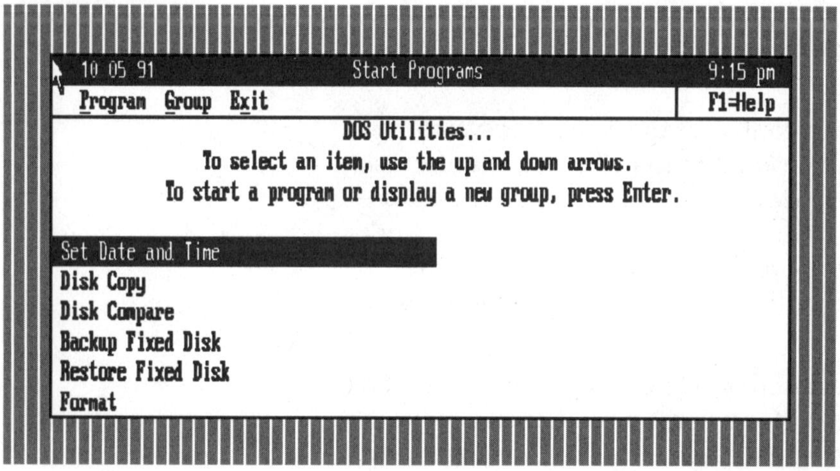

Another product that makes using DOS easier is **Windows**. The Windows program provides a **GUI, graphical user interface**. A graphical user interface shows pictures of user options. For example, a picture (icon) of a trash can may symbolize "throw away" or "delete." GUIs like Windows may include helpful features such as an on-screen clock, calendar, and calculator.

What operating system will you be using? ____________________

Will you use the shell? ________ Will you use Windows? ________

QUICK QUESTIONS

1. Contrast system software and application software.
   system software *application software*
2. Tell whether the following functions would be completed by system (S) or application (A) programs.

________ save a file to disk

________ input data to RAM

________ prepare a Treasurer's Report

________ print a document

________ create a birthday card on computer

________ play Space Invaders

3. Why is system software essential to the operation of the computer?
4. What is meant by "loading" a program?
5. Tell whether each function is completed by ROM (R), operating system (OS), or utility (U) programs.

 _________ does housekeeping tasks

 _________ starts the boot up procedure

 _________ resides in RAM until needed

 _________ used to copy files and disks

 _________ resides in the computer when you buy it

 _________ last program in boot up

 _________ bridge between the user and the application program

6. What is MS-DOS?
7. What is a shell?
8. Describe user interface.
9. What is a menu?
10. Name a benefit of using Windows.
11. What is a GUI?
12. What are some extra features GUIs like Windows may include?

System Software
Application Software
ROM Software
Operating System Software
Load
Utility Software
MS-DOS
DOS
Shell
User Interface
Menu
Windows
Graphical User Interface (GUI)

APPLICATION PROGRAMS

Application software completes tasks for people. What kinds of tasks do people want computers to do for them?

ARRANGE AND PRINT TEXT. Printers attached to computers leave typewriters in the dust! The hand-written page is even more rare! Sometimes people want to print page after page of very complicated information without human intervention. This information can include numerous type styles and sizes, graphic images, and different paper forms. Common printing jobs consist of letters, memos, reports, and mailing labels. Computers and printers are especially good at preparing **merge letters**. Merge letters, personalized for each receiver, are produced through an application program that will alternate the body of the letter with the personal data of each receiver of the letter.

The type of application program most commonly used to arrange and print text is **word processing**. Word processing, as its name implies, uses the computer to process or change words. Therefore, word processing packages are used to arrange text in an attractive, easily read form. Word processing is the most widely used type of application program because people in all walks of life need to prepare printed matter. As a result, there are many brands of word processing packages on the market. In this book you will learn to use the most popular one, WordPerfect.

Another type of application program that enhances printing is **desktop publishing**. Desktop publishing software arranges text and graphics to produce flyers, brochures, and newsletters. Although not considered professional desktop publishing programs, sign and banner programs also unite text and graphics. Desktop publishing and banner programs are not covered in this book.

CALCULATE. Computers can perform as extremely fast calculators. People often want computers to do *number crunching*, calculations of many types and complexities. The type of application program most commonly used to calculate is a **spreadsheet**.

Spreadsheet packages not only calculate, but they automatically update figures. If one value is changed on a spreadsheet, all dependent figures are recalculated. This feature allows users to play "What if?;" entering a new value gives new information to aid in decision making. Spreadsheets also produce **graphics**, pictorial illustrations of the data in a spreadsheet. These graphics take the form of scattergrams and line, bar, and pie charts.

The spreadsheet you will learn to use in this book is Lotus 1-2-3, the business standard.

ORGANIZE AND RETRIEVE DATA. Using a computer to organize data can eliminate the inconvenience of having to refer to written documents to find data each time it is needed. A **database** program enables a person to enter data, arrange it alphabetically or numerically, select only certain pieces of data, and print the data in the desired form.

Database packages are very useful for keeping data at one's fingertips. For example, if you call the telephone company about an error on your phone bill, the person you speak with will pull up on his or her computer screen a record of your phone charges from the customer database. A database helps a business maintain and quickly locate information on customers.

Many home computer users also put important data in databases. Coin collectors, for example, may want to keep accurate data about their coins. The data desired for each coin would probably resemble that shown in UC2.5.

The database program you will learn to use is dBase III or IV. It has many commands that permit the user to be very specific about tasks; you will learn the basics of the program.

SEND AND RECEIVE DATA. People sometimes want to communicate with distant computers. To transmit data between microcomputers, the sender and the receiver must have a modem, a telephone line, and software that tells the computer how to use the modem. This type of software is called **communications software**. Computers on a LAN (local area network) also have communications software that sends signals to the workstations.

FIGURE UC2.5

COIN COLLECTION DATABASE

Type of Coin
Date Minted
Rarity
History of Coin
Condition
Date Purchased
Purchase Price
Seller
Date Sold
Sale Price
Purchaser

Electronic mail, bulletin boards, and on-line data services have all evolved due to the ease of using a microcomputer and modem. **Electronic mail, E-Mail**, is the sending of text to another computer, which stores the message until the user "reads" his or her mail. A **bulletin board system (BBS)** is often set up by a computer hobbyist so other hobbyists can send and receive messages and software, especially games and helpful computer hints. Subscribers to **on-line data services** can access information from computers with very large storage devices. Subscribers may access news and stock reports, research encyclopedia entries, and make airline reservations, among other services.

PROVIDE LEISURE ACTIVITIES. Many software programs are available to help people relax or pursue hobbies. Of course, everyone knows about the many computer games that are available. There are also programs that allow users to store recipes, design quilting patterns, manage plants, read palms, plan diets, relieve stress, and create a family tree.

MEET SPECIAL NEEDS. Some people have special software needs and purchase application programs written just for those needs, as you can see from some of the leisure activity software above. Much special-purpose software, however, is written for specific types of businesses. A few of the many businesses that use special-purpose software are airlines, car rental agencies, hospitals, and grocery stores.

QUICK QUESTIONS

1. List the five main tasks people want computers to do for them.
   a)
   b)
   c)
   d)
   e)
2. Which type of software is designed to arrange and print text?

3. What are merge letters?
4. Describe desktop publishing.
5. Name three functions of spreadsheet programs.
   a)
   b)
   c)
6. Name the four main functions of a database program.
   a)
   b)
   c)
   d)
7. What type of software tells the computer how to use a modem?
8. What is E-Mail?
9. Explain the purpose of a bulletin board.
10. What are some services provided by on-line data services?
11. What are some uses of leisure activity software?
12. What is special-purpose software?

Merge Letters
Word Processing
Desktop Publishing
Spreadsheet
Graphics
Database
Communications Software
Electronic Mail (E-Mail)
Bulletin Board System (BBS)
On-Line Data Service
Special-Purpose Software

USING APPLICATION PROGRAMS

As you have seen, people use computers to perform a number of functions. Many software companies, as well as individuals, write and sell programs that will perform those functions. People who write computer programs are called **programmers**.

OBTAINING PROGRAMS. At work and at home, most people use off-the-shelf programs, called **commercial software packages**. Software packages can be full-feature programs like the ones you will use in this book, or they can be limited-feature programs. **Full-feature programs**

like spreadsheets can perform numerous operations, take hours to learn, and are expensive.

Limited-feature programs like tax preparation programs are easy to use and inexpensive because they perform only a few operations. Examples of the many limited-feature programs are ones that write wills, create resumes, print mailing labels, print name tags, and keep student grades for teachers.

Commercial software packages can be purchased from computer stores, from software companies, and from mail-order houses. When you purchase a program, you will receive a contract, usually called a **lease agreement**, from the programmer or the company that wrote the program. The lease agreement will usually state that the program may be used on one computer only, that you are entitled to one **backup** (extra copy) of the program for emergencies, and that you may not transfer the program to another person. Software is subject to the same copyright laws as written documents.

Shareware programs are often, but not always, written by computer hobbyists who develop useful programs they want to share with others for a small registration fee. **Public domain software** has been written by professional or amateur programmers who want to share their products with others for no charge whatsoever. Both shareware and public domain programs can be freely copied and distributed. Shareware and public domain programs may be acquired from bulletin boards and mail-order companies.

One danger of shareware and public domain programs is that they may be infected by a **virus**. A virus is a computer program that will "spread" by copying itself. Once the virus gets in the RAM of a computer, it will contaminate any diskette put into that computer. There are many strains of computer viruses; each is designed to cause unusual problems for the computer user. They are usually written by amateur programmers who like to "surprise" unsuspecting computer users. Unfortunately, some of them cause a great deal of trouble.

When you buy a software package, it will usually have a **version number** and **release number**. For example, you will be using WordPerfect 5.1, Version 5, Release 1 of the WordPerfect program. When a program enters the market, it is Version 1.0. As it is improved or expanded, *major* changes increase the number on the *left* of the period. *Minor* changes increase the number on the *right* of the period. WordPerfect has had four major revisions (5.), and the latest major revision has been slightly modified once (.1).

USING A NEW PROGRAM. When you obtain a new program, you must complete several tasks before using it. *First*, make a backup of the program. If the original program becomes faulty for any number of reasons, you are protected.

Second, install the program according to the **documentation** that came with the program. Documentation includes the manual, instructions, and reference information that accompany the program. Documentation can take the form of printed or on-screen assistance. Part of the **installation** procedure will involve identifying the hardware that the program will use. This often consists of brand and model information for the monitor, mouse, keyboard, drives, and printer. Installation may include copying the program to a hard disk or a file server.

When you have completed these one-time tasks, you are ready to use the program. To use a program you must load it into RAM. Your documentation will also tell you how to load the program. It often involves keying several characters at the on-screen prompt. If you are using a LAN or a menu program in the classroom, you will simply select the name of the program you desire.

CREATING PROGRAM FILES. When you create a file using a software program, you must load that software program every time you want to use the file. For example, if you create a database using dBase IV and save it on your disk today, you must first load dBase IV before you can print the file tomorrow. Although it is possible to import **foreign files**, files created in a program other than the current one, it should be avoided until you know more about file formats. You will learn later in this book how to import foreign files into WordPerfect, Lotus 1-2-3, and dBase.

QUICK QUESTIONS

1. What is a programmer?
2. Compare full-feature software to limited-feature software.
   full-feature *limited-feature*
3. List the tasks performed by several limited-feature software packages.
4. Explain lease agreement and why you think software companies use them.
5. What is a backup?
6. Compare commercial, shareware, and public domain software.
7. List four places where you can acquire software.
   a)
   b)
   c)
   d)
8. What is a computer virus?
9. How many major and minor changes has Lotus 1-2-3, Ver. 3.1 had?
10. What is the first computer task you should complete when you purchase a new program?
11. Why is documentation for a program important?
12. Describe the installation of a program.
13. What is a foreign file?

Programmer
Commercial Software Package
Full-Feature Program
Limited-Feature Program
Lease Agreement
Shareware Program
Public Domain Software
Virus
Version Number
Release Number
Documentation
Installation
Foreign File

USING SOFTWARE CROSSWORD PUZZLE

ACROSS

4 Software that performs user tasks
7 Shows pictures of user options
8 Provides on-line information
10 Operating system software for IBM compatibles
11 Software for computer housekeeping tasks
14 DOS user interface with menus
17 Program that calculates
18 Get a computer ready to use
20 Combines text and graphics
22 Personalized letter
23 Number of major software change
24 Task that prepares software for use
25 Off-the-shelf software
26 Computer program

DOWN

1 Program for a specific type of business
2 A GUI with pictures of options
3 Disk operating system
5 Program that organizes data
6 List of options on screen
7 Popular type of leisure software
9 Send mail to another computer
13 Person who writes programs
15 Bridges user and operating system
16 Agreement for software purchaser
19 File created in another package
21 Software that regulates computers

3

DATA

OBJECTIVES

- Trace the flow of data through the computer system.
- Describe how data can be processed by the Arithmetic-Logic Unit.
- Define input, process, output, and stored data.
- Explain binary number and ASCII code.
- Explain bits and bytes.
- Categorize data size as to byte, word, field, record, file, database, and DBMS.

DATA

Computer hardware and software exist primarily to change input *data* into output *information*. It is common practice, however, to use the term "data" when referring to input, process, output, or storage. We have followed this practice in a limited way in this section to simplify explanations. For example, the UC3.1 diagram shows data in each component of the computer system.

INPUT DATA. Input data can take many forms: numbers, letters, symbols, a drawing, keys pressed for a game, or UPC bars on a price tag, among others. As you learned in the Hardware unit, there are many devices that will input data to RAM.

PROCESS DATA. When RAM receives data, it is stored there until the program instruction in the CPU calls for it. When called for processing, the data is moved to the **arithmetic-logic unit** (ALU), a part of the CPU. If the data is numeric, the program often calls for the ALU to calculate with it by adding, subtracting, multiplying, or dividing.

When instructed by the program, the ALU can also arrange data in alphabetic or numeric order by comparing characters to determine whether each is greater, less than, or equal to other characters. The action of comparing characters and arranging them in order is referred to as using the logic function of the ALU.

Sometimes the program tells the ALU to move the data through without processing so it can simply be printed and/or saved on disk. An example of this is printing mailing labels. The names and addressees for the labels are input so they can be simply moved through the CPU to the printer and put on labels.

FIGURE UC3.1
Data in a Computer System

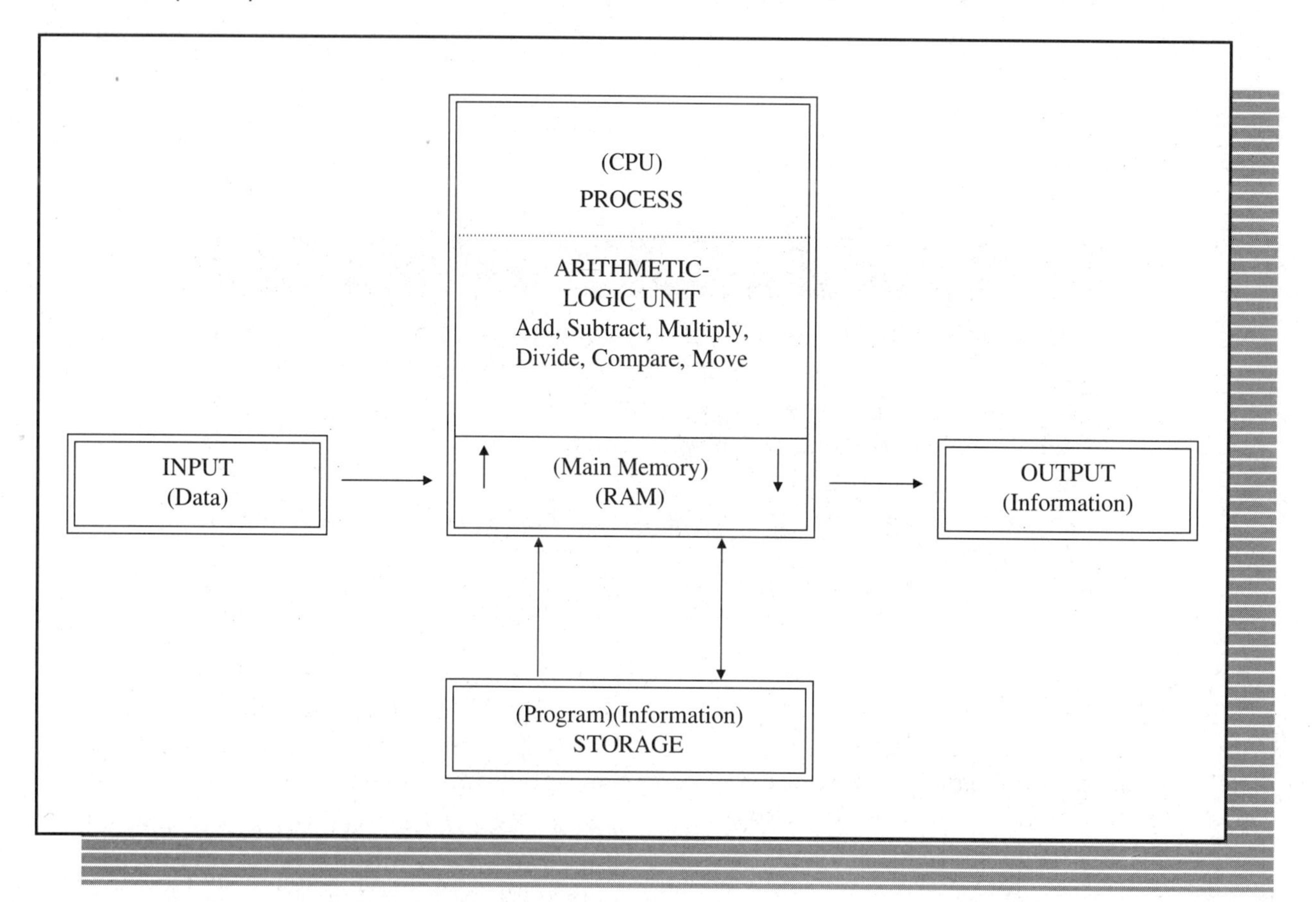

OUTPUT INFORMATION. Information, the result of data processing, is usually printed or displayed on a computer screen.

STORED DATA/INFORMATION. Both data and information can be stored on disk, making them available for use at any time. Data or information stored on disk is called a **file**.

QUICK QUESTIONS

1. What is the main reason for using computer hardware and software?
2. Name four forms of input data:
   a)
   b)
   c)
   d)
3. When does data move to the arithmetic-logic unit?
4. What types of calculations does the ALU do?
5. Name two functions of the ALU other than calculating.
   a)
   b)
6. Use logic (compare) to arrange the following data in numeric order. Write 1 beside the lowest value through 5 beside the highest value:

   _________ 88989788

   _________ 88899787

   _________ 88989878

   _________ 88899778

   _________ 88899788
7. What does the ALU do when it "moves" data?
8. What is information?
9. Which type of data is available for use at any time?

Arithmetic-Logic Unit (ALU)

File

DATA INSIDE THE COMPUTER

When data is input to RAM, it is no longer in the form of letters, numbers, or symbols. The microprocessor changes each input character into a set of eight signals; each signal is an electric current that is on or off. The on/off concept can be compared to a light switch. When a light switch is turned on, an electric current flows to the lamp. When the light switch is turned off, there is no electric current. The computer knows that a certain sequence of on/off electric currents represents a specific character.

For example, when the letter "K" is pressed on the keyboard, the microprocessor changes it to electric signals in the following pattern: on, off, off, on, off, on, on. Humans can see this better when it is represented by the **binary code** 1001011, where 1 is a signal on and 0 is a signal off. Binary means composed of two parts; the binary code is a series of only two digits, 0 and 1.

The specific set of seven signals or digits for each character is assigned according to the **ASCII code**. The ASCII code is a standardized coding system among computers. This coding system shows only seven digits or **bits** because the eighth is a **parity bit** the computer uses for data accuracy. The parity bit is always on or off for a particular computer. Figure UC3.2 shows several characters and their **bit pattern** or binary code equivalents.

RAM is designed to store each character in a **byte** of memory. Each byte is composed of the eight electric circuits or bits needed to represent a character. The number of bytes a specific computer can hold at once depends on the RAM size of the computer.

FIGURE UC3.2

ASCII CODES FOR SOME CHARACTERS				
Character	Bit Pattern		Character	Bit Pattern
$	0100100		5	0110101
D	1000100		R	1010010

What is the RAM size of your computer? ______________________

How many bytes of data will it hold? ______________________

Below is an illustration of how the character "S" is stored in a byte of RAM. The shaded circuits (bits) are on, and the white circuits (bits) are off. It is more convenient for us to think of the letter "S" as the binary number 1010011. (The eighth bit is a parity bit).

A Byte of Memory Storing the Letter "S"

QUICK QUESTIONS

1. Explain how the microprocessor changes an input character so it can be stored in RAM.
2. What is the binary code?
3. How does the binary code relate to circuits that are on and off?
4. What is the ASCII code?
5. How many bits are needed to store one character?
6. What is a bit pattern?
7. How many bits are in a byte?
8. Looking at UC3.2, does the number "5" have more circuits on or more off when it is in RAM?

Binary Code
ASCII Code
Bits
Parity Bit
Bit Pattern
Byte

SIZES OF DATA

Because people who work with computers need to communicate effectively, data is often discussed in terms of size.

CHARACTER AND WORD. The smallest size of data is usually considered to be a byte or **character**, such as *s*. The next size, a related set of characters, is called a **word**; *street* is a word.

FIELD. A related set of words is known as a **field** or **data item**. Each field is given a **field name**. *324 Main Street* is a field; the name of the field could be *Address*. Fields can be alphabetic, numeric, or alphanumeric (both alphabetic and numeric).

RECORD. All related fields about an individual or an event are referred to as a **record**. Looking at chart UC3.3, the following is a record: *Ed Lopez 6621 E. Randolph Greenfield 46140 462-6569 3-7-45 Headache 6-17-91 Fair Ibuprofen*

The chart below (UC3.3) displays data that would be useful to a doctor. The fields of data are shown as horizontal rows; column one lists a name for each field. Columns two, three, and four each contain a record for one patient.

Is "Headache, Nausea" for Billy Lumkin a word, field, field name, or record? ____________________

FIGURE UC3.3
A File Containing Three Records

Field Name	Record #1	Record #2	Record #3
Name	Ed Lopez	Janeen Jenkins	Billy Lumkin
Address	6621 E. Randolph Greenfield 46140	236 S. Grand #20 Indianapolis 46241	3448 Hunters Path Fairland 46126
Phone	462-6569	637-2205	835-7571
Date of birth	3-7-45	4-25-22	10-10-38
Complaint	Headache	Lethargy	Headache, Nausea
Date of complaint	6-17-91	2-14-90	2-23-91
Prognosis	Fair	Excellent	Good
Prescriptions	Ibuprofen	Levothroid	Phenergan

Is all the information about Ed Lopez a word, field, field name, or record? ____________________

Is "Date of Complaint" a word, field, field name, or record? __________

FILE. All related records, about a specific group of people or events, is called a **file**. If the doctor using the data in UC3.3 only had three patients in his or her practice, the illustration would show the doctor's entire patient file. The file might be given the name *Patients*.

The doctor might have a different file called *Accounts Payable* made of records of debts he or she owed. Another file could be *Accounts Receivable*, records of money owed to the doctor. Most businesses have many files, but each file contains only records that have the same fields of data.

DATABASE. A **database** is a collection of related information about a subject organized in a useful manner that provides a foundation for retrieving information and making decisions. A database may be on a computer, on index cards or a Rolodex, or in file folders.

DBMS. A **Database Management System**, or **DBMS**, is an application program with data storage, organization, and retrieval capabilities for multiple databases. A full-feature database program like dBASE is considered a DBMS.

The chart below shows a database for a school of ten students. If it is on computer and uses a full-feature application program, what is it called? __________

Label the shaded parts of the database with the following terms: **WORD, FIELD, FIELD NAME, RECORD, FILE:**

1 ____________________

2 ____________________

3 ____________________

4 ____________________

5 ____________________

STUDENT LOCKER ASSIGNMENTS

1	Locker #	Student #	Student Name
	4565B	7810250	Akers, Connie
2	5570B	6971022	Bradbury, Eugene
	7824A	3675363	Brown, Alex
3	9785C	8512050	Douglas, Elizabeth
	5893B	3662421	Ellis, Tabitha
4	6996C	7640085	Ladd, Willis
	7912A	4597542	Masters, Mary Elaine
5 →	8780C	3207587	Moore, Aaron
	6822B	9648288	Truett, Dawn
	4241C	2434891	Vestal, Johnny

QUICK QUESTIONS

1. Why is it important for a computer user to know the different sizes of data?
2. Arrange the sizes of data from 1 for smallest to 6 for largest:

   _________ field

   _________ database

   _________ byte

   _________ DBMS

   _________ file

   _________ record
3. What term refers to a related set of characters?
4. What word refers to related fields about an individual or an event?
5. What term is used to refer to a related set of words?
6. What type of characters can be contained in a field?
7. What word refers to all related records about a group of people or an event?
8. What word is used to refer to an application program with data storage, organization, and retrieval capabilities for multiple databases?
9. What term is used to describe a collection of related information about a subject organized in a useful manner for retrieving information and making decisions?

Character (Byte)
Word
Field (Data Item)
Field Name
Record
File
Database
DBMS

USING DATA CROSSWORD PUZZLE

ACROSS

4 Smallest size of data
5 Computer unit that calculates
6 All related fields about a person
7 Memory for one character
9 A system of zeros and ones
10 Data that has been processed
11 A related set of characters
13 Data that will be processed
14 Related records
17 Name given to data items
19 Data sent to the storage device

DOWN

1 Organized collection of data
2 Data in the Arithmetic-Logic Unit
3 Processed data
8 Computer coding system
9 Binary code equivalents
12 Binary digits
15 A related set of words; field
16 A related set of words; data item
18 A full-featured database program

UNIT 2

Using DOS

1

DOS BASICS

OBJECTIVES

- Recall that DOS commands are used to perform common computer tasks.
- Describe the purpose of boot up and the procedure for a **cold** and a **warm boot.**
- Use the **system prompt** to determine **current drive.**
- **Log** to various drives.
- Display and change the **date** and **time.**
- **Clear the screen.**
- Display the **version** of DOS being used.

WHAT IS DOS?

Every computer needs system software in order to operate. System programs not only manage the system hardware, but they also manage the operation of application programs. Your IBM-compatible computer uses a system program called DOS. Although DOS is an abbreviation for disk operating system, DOS does more than handle disk drives. In this unit you will learn how to use DOS commands to perform common tasks required by computer users.

Beginning with DOS 4.0, a user interface called the DOS Shell has been added to the program to make it more *user friendly*. This is done with menus from which commands can be chosen. Since the shell can vary among computers, we will use the standard method of directing DOS, the command prompt.

BOOT UP

A computer cannot do anything until system programs are loaded into RAM. This process is called **booting up** the computer. After you boot up your computer with DOS, the computer is ready to accept your commands. Boot up is necessary before you can use application programs like WordPerfect, Lotus 1-2-3, or dBASE.

You may perform two types of DOS boot up. If the computer is off and you turn it on so it can activate DOS, you perform a **cold boot**. If the computer is on and you hold down (Ctrl)-(Alt) while you tap (Delete) or (Del), you perform a **warm boot**. A warm boot is gentler to your hardware, so it is preferred.

DOS may be found on a hard disk, a floppy diskette, or a file server. The following steps will probably boot your computer. If not, follow the directions of your instructor.

1. *Using a floppy disk:*
   a) Insert the DOS diskette into Floppy Drive A.
   b) If the computer is *on*, hold down (Ctrl) and (Alt) while you tap the (Delete) or (Del) key (warm boot).
   c) If the computer is *off*, turn it on (cold boot).
   d) If the DOS Shell appears, select *Command Prompt*.
   e) The *command prompt* A:\> appears.
2. *Using a Hard Disk:*
   a) If the computer is *on*, hold down (Ctrl) and (Alt) while you tap the (Delete) or (Del) key (warm boot).
   b) If the computer is *off*, turn it on (cold boot).
   c) If the DOS Shell appears, select *Command Prompt*.
   d) The *command prompt* such as: C:\> appears.
3. *Using a File Server:*
   a) Insert the network boot diskette into your floppy drive.
   b) If the computer is on, hold down (Ctrl) and (Alt) while you tap the (Delete) or (Del) key (warm boot).
   c) If the computer is off, turn it on (cold boot).
   d) Select *DOS* from the menu (or follow instructor directions).
   e) If the DOS Shell appears, select *Command Prompt*.
   f) The *command prompt* appears, but its appearance varies.

DRIVE SPECIFICATION AND PROMPT

DRIVE SPECIFICATION. The drive where DOS resides becomes your **current drive** by default when you boot up. DOS will perform all commands on the current drive unless you specify otherwise.

What is your default current drive? ____________ What type of drive is it? ____________

SYSTEM PROMPT. DOS lets you know when it is ready for your command by displaying the **system prompt**. (DOS "prompts" you for a command). The system prompt displays the current drive and usually has a > sign after it. The following are examples of system prompts: A> and B:\>. The system prompt may include the current directory, as in C:\DOS>. Any command you give DOS must be keyed *right next to the system prompt*. Although shown in upper case in this book, commands and file names may be keyed in upper or lower case.

What does your default system prompt look like? ______________

LOG DRIVES. If you want a command to affect another drive, **log** onto the other drive by keying right beside the system prompt the letter of the drive followed by a colon.

To log on to drive B, next to the system prompt key the following command.

KEY: B: (Enter)

If you have a hard drive, log on to drive C.

KEY: C: (Enter)

Log on to your default drive.

KEY: the characters that will log you on to your default drive

---

CORRECTING INVALID COMMANDS. If you make a keying error that DOS can't understand, you can cancel the command and return to the system prompt by pressing (Ctrl)-(Pause/Break). Remember, you must have a system prompt to give a command.

QUICK QUESTIONS

1. What system program is used by IBM-compatible computers?
2. Why are DOS commands used?
3. How is the DOS Shell made more user friendly?
4. What is meant by "booting up"?
5. What must be done before you can use an application program?
6. How do you perform a cold boot?
7. How do you perform a warm boot?
8. Why is the current drive important to DOS?
9. How do you know DOS is ready for your command?
10. What does your default system prompt look like?
11. What should you key to log to drive B?
12. What should you press to cancel a faulty command?
13. Should commands be keyed in upper or lower case?

DATE, TIME

Most computers today have an internal battery-operated clock that will keep the date and time correct, even if the computer is turned off. However, you may use an older computer that has no battery or a computer with a battery that is depleted. In these instances, it is important to set the correct date and time because files you create or update are marked with the date and time of day you store them. In some instances, the date will help you find a file if you forget its name. The date can also tell you if a file has been updated recently.

DATE. Use the **Date** command to see if your computer has the correct date. Next to the system prompt, key the following command.

KEY: DATE (↵Enter)

The screen shown below is displayed (DS1.1).

FIGURE DS1.1

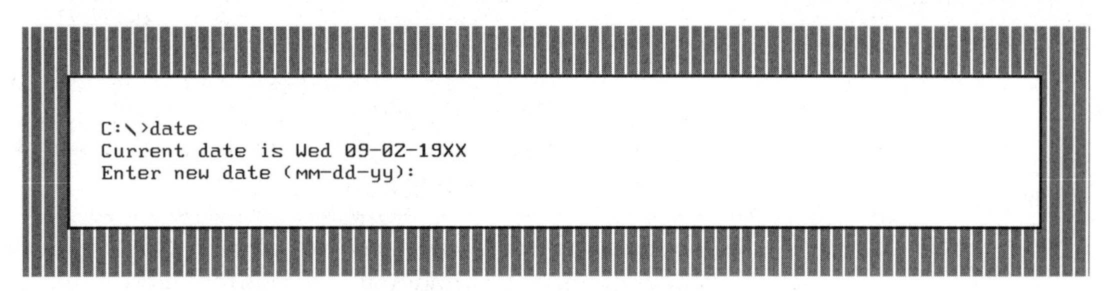

C:\>date
Current date is Wed 09-02-19XX
Enter new date (mm-dd-yy):

Below the command you entered, you see the system message, *Current date is* ____________, which is the current day of the week and date according to the clock. Below that message you see a second message, *Enter new date (mm-dd-yy)*:

KEY: Next to the colon, key today's date in this sequence: month-day-year (↵Enter) using numbers separated by hyphens. If you get an error message, try it again until you get it correct. Use (Ctrl)-(Pause/Break) if necessary to rekey the command.

KEY: DATE (↵Enter)

See what day of the week Christmas falls on this year.

KEY: 12-25-*current year* (↵Enter)

KEY: DATE (↵Enter)

What day does it fall on? ______________________________

See what day of the week your next birthday falls on.

KEY: DATE (↵Enter)

KEY: the month, day and year of your next birthday (↵Enter)

Set the clock so the date is correct before going on.

KEY: DATE (↵Enter)

KEY: today's date (↵Enter)

TIME. Use the **Time** command to set the correct time.

KEY: TIME (↵Enter)

FIGURE DS1.2

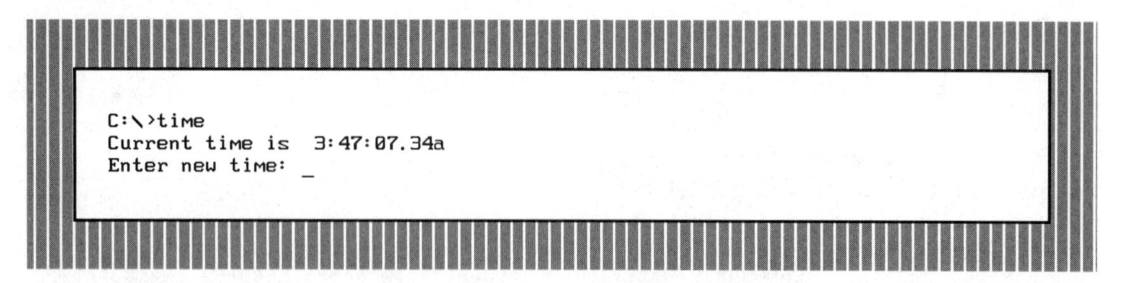

C:\>time
Current time is 3:47:07.34a
Enter new time: _

Below your command, you see the system message, *Current time is —:—:—.—*, which is the current time according to the clock. Below that message is a second message, *Enter new time.*

KEY: Next to the colon, key the current time in 24-hour format. To use 24-hour format, simply key in the current time in the morning, such as 9:43:26; add 12 hours to the current time if it is after noon, as in 13:47 (1:47 + 12) for 1:47 p.m.
(You do not have to enter seconds or hundredths of seconds.) Use numbers only, separated by colons. If you get an error message, try it again until you get it correct. Be sure the time is correct before continuing.

If your computer does not keep the correct date and time, always set them before you begin using the computer each day. If the correct date or time is shown when you use the Date or Time commands, just press (↵Enter) to accept it.

CLEAR THE SCREEN

When you have given DOS several commands, your screen becomes cluttered. To clear it, use the **Cls** command.

KEY: CLS (↵Enter)

Use the Cls command whenever you feel you would like to clear your screen.

VERSION

It is important to know which version of DOS you are using when you purchase software because each software package is written to work under specific versions of DOS. In addition, some DOS commands can be used by certain versions of DOS only.

Each version of DOS has a **version number** and a **release number**, such as DOS 4.0. The digit to the left of the period is the version number, and the digit to the right of the period is the release number. (See the Software section for more information on version and release numbers.)

To find which version of DOS you are using, use the **Ver** command. At the system prompt:

KEY: VER (↵Enter)

Which version of DOS are you using? ________________________

QUICK QUESTIONS

1. If your computer has a battery-operated clock, why should you know how to use the date and time commands?
2. Why is it important for your computer to have the correct date and time?
3. What command can you use to see on which day of the week a special occasion falls?
4. What data should you enter when using the Time command?
5. When should you use the Cls command?
6. Why is it important to know which version of DOS you are using?
7. What is the version and release number of Lotus 1-2-3, 3.1?
8. What command will display the version of DOS you are using?

REVIEW EXERCISE

As a review of this section, key a command that will complete each request below. Use the section as a reference if needed. Write the command you used in the space following the request. Commands are repeated for more practice.

1. Key the command that will show the version of DOS you are using.
2. Display the current date and change it if it is incorrect.
3. Clear the screen.
4. Display the current time and change it if it is incorrect.
5. Log on to Drive C (if possible).
6. Log on to Drive A (if possible).
7. Log on to Drive B (if possible).
8. Log on to your default drive.
9. Clear the screen.
10. Display the time.
11. Display your version of DOS.
12. Log to Drive A (if possible).
13. Display the date.
14. Log on to your default drive.

DIRECTORIES

OBJECTIVES

- Compare directories to a paper filing system.
- Distinguish between the **root directory** and **subdirectories.**
- Identify the **current directory** and its importance.
- Identify the directories to be used in this book.
- Use the **prompt** command to identify the current drive and directory.
- Change to and from the root directory and subdirectories.
- Use **Dir** with **/P** and **/W** to list files and directories and gather file information.
- Identify common file extensions and their types of files.
- Use **wildcards** to list groups of file names.

DIRECTORIES

Fixed disks, often called **hard disks** or **hard drives**, are used in many computers because of their large storage capacity for programs and data. Because they are so large, it is essential that program files and data files be well organized for retrieval. To achieve this organization, files are stored in **directories** and **subdirectories**.

A directory is a major storage area, much like a drawer in a file cabinet. Just as the file drawer may contain many documents, a directory may contain many files and even other directories, known as subdirectories. (See DS2.1).

The main directory on a disk is known as the **root directory**, as it is the source of all other directories and files. The root directory can be thought of as the file cabinet that holds the directory drawers.

The root directory of a hard drive may be designated as C:\. The inverted slash (\) beside a drive letter indicates the root directory of that drive.

In Figure DS2.2, four program directories (C:\DOS, C:\WP51, C:\LOTUS, and C:\DBASE) are subdirectories of the root directory, C:\. A **subdirectory** is a secondary directory within a primary directory. The root directory is shown as the primary directory by the C:\ that precedes the name of each subdirectory. The WordPerfect directory is the primary directory of a subdirectory called LEARN. This is designated as C:\WP51\LEARN.

If you have a hard drive, it may be set up similar to Figure DS2.2.

When a computer is set up with directories, you often have to tell DOS the path to follow through the directories to store or find a particular file. A **path** includes the drive letter followed by directory, subdirectories, and file names. For example, to find a file called PRINT.HLP in the LEARN subdirectory of the WP51 directory on drive C, the path would be: C:\WP51\LEARN\PRINT.HLP.

FIGURE DS2.1

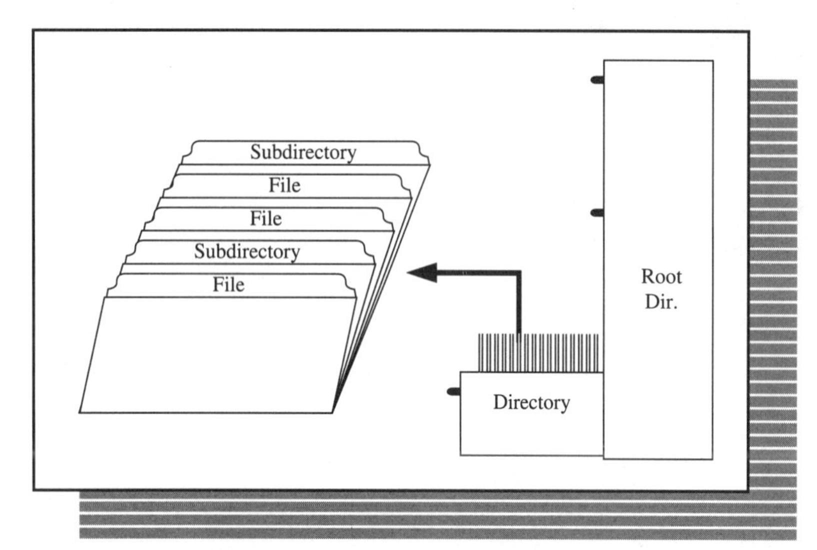

CURRENT DIRECTORY. Before using the directory commands, be certain that your system prompt displays not only the current drive, but also the desired **current directory**. The current directory is the one in which DOS will perform all commands unless you specify otherwise.

FIGURE DS2.2

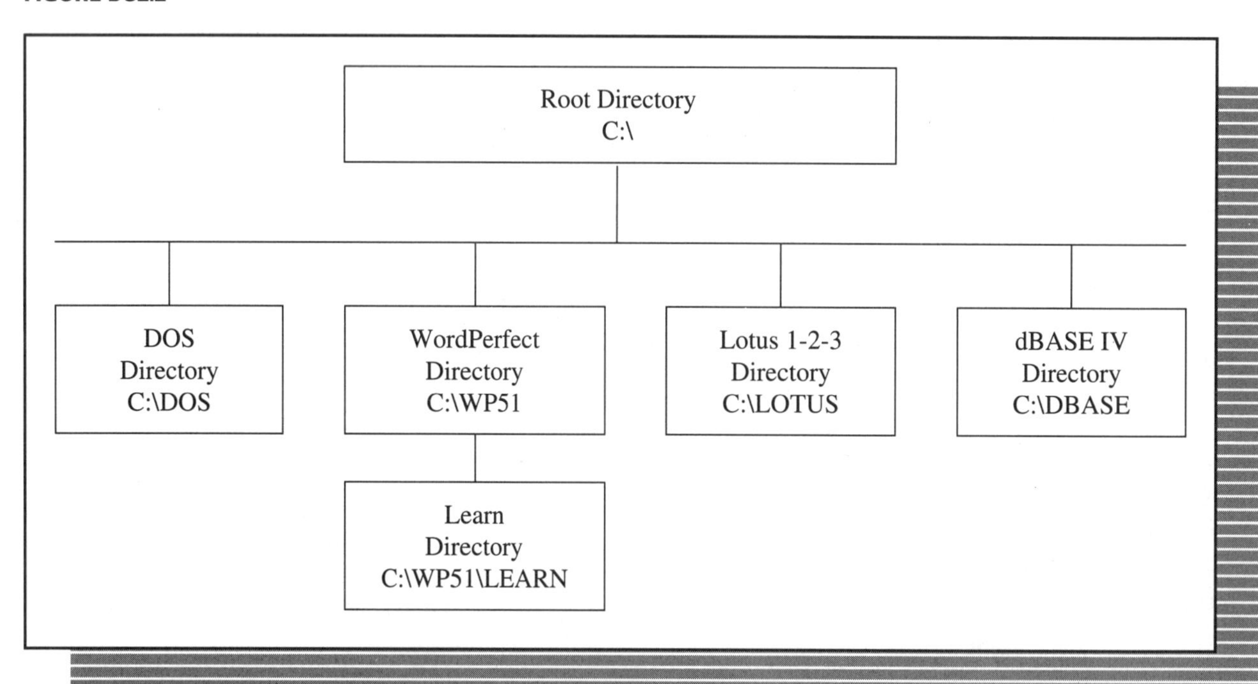

PROMPT. The **Prompt** command allows you to design the appearance of the system prompt. Including the $P (Path) and $G (Greater-Than Sign) parameters in the Prompt command will display the current drive and directories. **Parameters** are qualifiers that make a command more precise.

KEY: PROMPT PG (Enter)

DOS should now keep you informed of your position as you move from directory to directory. Watch your system prompt to see that it reflects the correct path as you continue.

CHANGE DIRECTORIES. Ask your instructor the name of your directories for DOS, WordPerfect, Lotus, and dBASE. Write them below.

DOS Directory ____________ WordPerfect Directory ____________

Lotus Directory ____________ dBASE Directory ______________

When given a directory name in the commands that follow, key in your directory name as you wrote it on the line above. As with commands and file names, directories may be keyed in upper case, lower case, or a combination.

DO: Log on to the drive that contains the directories shown above. Be sure you are in the *root directory* of that drive.

The command to change directories is **Cd**. The Cd command, however, must include the directory you wish to change to. Change to the Lotus directory.

KEY: CD\LOTUS (↵Enter) (or substitute the directory name you wrote earlier, if different)

Return to the root directory. You can change to another directory only by returning to the root directory, just as you must go to a file cabinet to retrieve another document.

KEY: CD\ (↵Enter)

Check your prompt to see if you are at the root directory (A:\, B:\, C:\ or similar prompt).

Change to the WordPerfect directory.

KEY: CD\WP51 (↵Enter) (or substitute the directory name you wrote earlier, if different)

Does your prompt reflect the new directory (similar to A:\WP51, B:\WP51, or C:\WP51)?

Change to the dBASE directory by returning to the root directory first.

KEY: CD\ (↵Enter)

KEY: CD\DBASE (↵Enter) (or substitute the directory name you wrote earlier, if different)

Does your prompt reflect that you are in the dBASE directory?

Return to the root directory and then to the Lotus directory in one command.

KEY: CD\LOTUS (↵Enter)

Return to the root directory.

KEY: CD\ (↵Enter)

DO: Remain in the root directory for the next activity.

QUICK QUESTIONS

1. Why is it an advantage to have a hard drive in a computer?
2. What is the purpose of using directories and subdirectories?
3. Compare the root directory and subdirectories to a paper filing system.
4. What is the name for the main directory on a disk?
5. What directory are you in if the system prompt shows C:\?
6. What is a subdirectory?
7. What is contained in a path, and why is a path used?
8. Why is the current directory important to DOS?
9. What does $P do when used as a parameter with the Prompt command?
10. What is the purpose of the Prompt command?
11. What command should you key to go from the root directory to the DOS directory, both on drive C?

Listing Directories and File Names

DIRECTORY. You have learned how to go to a specific directory. Once in the root or any other directory it is often helpful to see what files or subdirectories are in that directory. Use the Dir command to see a list of files and subdirectories of your root directory.

KEY: DIR (↵Enter)

If you have a large number of files and subdirectories in a directory, part of the listing will scroll off the screen. Adding **/P** (Pause) to the Dir command will pause the listing at a screenful. Press any key to continue.

KEY: DIR/P (↵Enter)

When you use the Dir command at the root directory, you see a listing similar to DS2.3.

FILE INFORMATION. As you can see in Figure DS2.3, each *directory* is marked with brackets, as in DBASE <DIR>. Each *file* has several columns of information about the file.

FIGURE DS2.3

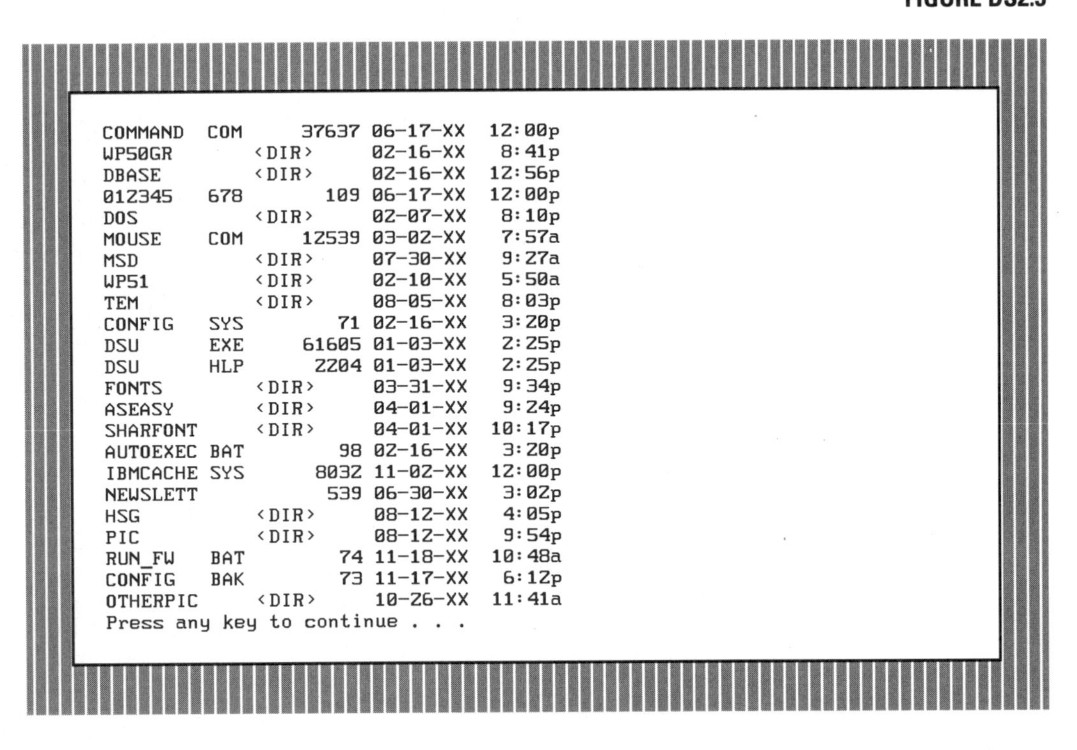

```
COMMAND  COM      37637 06-17-XX  12:00p
WP50GR       <DIR>       02-16-XX   8:41p
DBASE        <DIR>       02-16-XX  12:56p
012345   678        109 06-17-XX  12:00p
DOS          <DIR>       02-07-XX   8:10p
MOUSE    COM      12539 03-02-XX   7:57a
MSD          <DIR>       07-30-XX   9:27a
WP51         <DIR>       02-10-XX   5:50a
TEM          <DIR>       08-05-XX   8:03p
CONFIG   SYS         71 02-16-XX   3:20p
DSU      EXE      61605 01-03-XX   2:25p
DSU      HLP       2204 01-03-XX   2:25p
FONTS        <DIR>       03-31-XX   9:34p
ASEASY       <DIR>       04-01-XX   9:24p
SHARFONT     <DIR>       04-01-XX  10:17p
AUTOEXEC BAT         98 02-16-XX   3:20p
IBMCACHE SYS       8032 11-02-XX  12:00p
NEWSLETT            539 06-30-XX   3:02p
HSG          <DIR>       08-12-XX   4:05p
PIC          <DIR>       08-12-XX   9:54p
RUN_FW   BAT         74 11-18-XX  10:48a
CONFIG   BAK         73 11-17-XX   6:12p
OTHERPIC     <DIR>       10-26-XX  11:41a
Press any key to continue . . .
```

1. The first column contains the file name, often followed by a file extension. For example, COMMAND is a file name followed by COM, an extension.
2. The next column shows the size of the file in bytes. For example, COMMAND.COM has 37,637 bytes (characters).
3. The date column shows the date the file was created or last changed.
4. The time column shows the time of day the file was created or last changed.

In Figure DS2.3, find MOUSE.COM. How many bytes in the file? __________ What date was it created or last changed? __________ What time of day was it created or last changed? __________

Using Figure DS2.3, answer the following questions. Is MSD a file or a directory? __________ Is DSU.HLP a file or a directory? __________ What is the size in bytes of CONFIG.SYS? __________ What date was AUTOEXEC.BAT created or last changed? __________

DO: If prompted to do so, press a key to continue the listing until you return to the system prompt.

List the files in the WordPerfect directory.

KEY: CD\WP51 (Enter) (or substitute the directory name you wrote earlier, if different)

KEY: DIR/P (↵Enter)

Pause the screen as needed to answer the following questions. Name a file extension shared by at least ten files. __________ If possible, name two subdirectories of the WP51 directory. __________ and __________

When the system prompt reappears, return to the root directory.

KEY: CD\ (↵Enter)

Another way to view a listing of files is with the Dir **/W** (Wide) command.

KEY: DIR/W (↵Enter)

Notice that the listing of files and subdirectories is displayed horizontally, showing more file and directory names at once. However, less information is given about each file, and directories are not marked.

When would it be better to use the Dir/P command rather than the Dir/W command?

____

When would using the Dir/W command be better than using the Dir/P command?

____

COMMON FILE EXTENSIONS. Use the Dir/W command once more to observe some common file extensions.

KEY: DIR/ W (↵Enter)

Here are some common file extensions you probably see: .COM (Command File), .EXE(Executable File), and .BAT (Command Batch File). These three file extensions are used in many programs to designate files that DOS can execute easily. They should be avoided as file extensions for files you name.

Look for these common file extensions in the DOS directory.

KEY: CD\DOS (↵Enter)

KEY: DIR/ W (↵Enter)

Name two files that have a COM extension. __________ and __________

Can you find a BAT extension? __________

DO: Return to the system prompt and remain in the DOS directory.

WILDCARDS. To enable a computer user to perform actions on a group of files at once, wildcards are used. The two wildcards are * and ?. The asterisk is used to represent any number of characters. The question mark is used to represent one character.

To see a list of all files in the DOS directory that have any file name with the extension .COM, use the asterisk to represent any file name (any number of characters). When keying filenames and extensions, no spaces are allowed between them.

KEY: DIR *.COM (↵Enter)

A list of all the .COM files appears.

Display a list of all files in the DOS directory that have any file name with the .EXE file extension.

KEY: DIR *.EXE (↵Enter)

Name the last two files that have an .EXE extension. __________ and __________

What could you key to see a list of all files in the DOS directory with a .MOS extension?

____

Display a list of all files that have the .SYS extension.

KEY: DIR *.SYS (↵Enter)

To display a list of all DOS file names that begin with the letter D, place the wildcard where all characters except D could appear.

KEY: DIR D*.* (↵Enter)

Display a list of all DOS file names with the file extension .COM and the file name BASIC followed by one character. Use the question mark to represent the character.

KEY: DIR BASIC?.COM (↵Enter)

DO: Return to the root directory of your default drive.

QUICK QUESTIONS

1. What command is used to see a list of files and subdirectories?
2. What does /P do when used with the Dir command?
3. How can you identify a directory name when looking at a list of files and directories?
4. What four types of information about files can you get when using the Dir command?
   a)
   b)
   c)
   d)
5. What is the purpose of /W when used with the Dir command?
6. If you see the file extension .COM, what can you assume about the type of file?
7. What is the purpose of using wildcards?
8. What command could you use to see a list of all file names called TYPE with various file extensions?
9. What command could you use to see a list of all file names that begin with TYPE followed by a single digit and any file extension?
10. What command could you use to see a list of all files that have any file name and any extension?

As a review of this section, key a command to complete each request below. Use the section as a reference if needed. Write the command you used in the space following the request. Many commands are repeated for more practice.

1. Key the command that will show you a list of all files in the root directory of your default drive.
2. Show a list of all files in the Lotus directory, pausing at a screenful.
3. Use a command that will allow you to see how large the files are in the WordPerfect directory.
4. Show a horizontal list of all files in the root directory.
5. Use a command that will show the date each WordPerfect file was created or last changed.
6. Show all files in the DOS directory that are .EXE files.
7. Show all files in the DOS directory that begin with the letter D.
8. Show all files in the WordPerfect directory that are .WPG files.
9. Show all files in the Lotus directory that are .WK1 files, using a horizontal display.
10. Show all files in the dBASE directory that begin with D and have 5 letters or less.

3

USEFUL DISK COMMANDS

IMPORTANT: Specific directories and file names are needed to complete this section. All are available on the Template disk.

OBJECTIVES

- **Format** or know how to format new diskettes.
- **Copy** files from directory to directory and disk to disk.
- **Rename** files.
- **Erase** files.

FORMAT

When new diskettes are purchased, they cannot be used in a computer until they have been formatted. Formatting a diskette prepares it to be used by a particular type of disk drive. When the **Format** command is used, electronic boundaries are placed on the disk so it can store files. The format command not only prepares a new disk; it also *erases all files* on a used disk.

Because it could accidentally erase an entire disk, even a hard disk, the Format command must be used very carefully! Use this command to prepare a new disk only under the guidance of your instructor. Ask your instructor if you will be formatting a diskette; if so, follow your instructor's directions.

The command to format a new diskette is **Format A:** if it is in Drive A. Use **Format B:** if your diskette is in Drive B. The Format command *must* include the drive letter A or B.

COPY FILES

Files may be copied from one disk to another. Also, files may be copied to the same disk under a different name or into a different directory. Use the **Copy** command to make copies of files. In the following activities, you will include two parameters with the Copy command: the path and file name of the *sending* file, and the path and file name of the *receiving* file. The sending file is the file to be copied, and the receiving file is the new file that will exist when the copy is complete.

Use a template disk for the following commands. The directory names given in these activities are not actual program directories; they are just directories made to be used for practice. When keying the commands, use the letter of your drive containing the template disk if it is different from Drive A.

Copy a file from the DOST directory to the root directory, using the same file name.

KEY: COPY A:\DOST\MORE1.COM A:\ (↵Enter)

Copy a file from the DOST directory to the root directory, using a different file name.

KEY: COPY A:\DOST\MORE1.COM A:\EXTRA.COM (↵Enter)

Copy a file from the root directory to the LOTUST directory, using the same file name.

KEY: COPY A:\MORE1.COM A:\LOTUST (↵Enter)

Copy a file from the WP51T directory to the LOTUST directory, using the same file name.

KEY: COPY A:\WP51T\FILE1 A:\LOTUST (↵Enter)

What command could you use to copy a file called FILE1 in the WP51T directory to the root directory, using the same file name? Write it below, and then try it on your computer.

What command could you use to copy a file called FILE2 in the WP51T directory to the LOTUST directory using a different file name of LOTFILE? Write it below, and then try it on your computer.

RENAME

Occasionally a computer user will want to change the name given to a file. This occurs because of keying mistakes or simply because a person decides on a better name for the file. Use the **Rename** command to change a file name on disk. Include the *current* file name and the *new* file name in the command. (Include a path if the file is not in the current directory.)

Rename the MORE1.COM file in the DOST directory to NEWFILE.COM.

KEY: RENAME A:\DOST\MORE1.COM A:\DOST\NEWFILE.COM (↵Enter)

After renaming the file, change to the receiving directory and display the file names to see if NEWFILE.COM is listed.

KEY: CD\DOST (↵Enter)

KEY: DIR/P (↵Enter)

Rename the FILE1 file in the WP51T directory to FILE0.

KEY: RENAME A:\WP51T\FILE1 A:\WP51T\FILE0

What command could you use to rename the FILE1 file in the LOTUST directory to FILE8? Write it below and then try it on your computer.

____

Erase, Del

To delete a file you no longer want, use the **Erase** or **Del** command. These commands must include the file name of the file you want to delete. To delete a file called OLDFILE in the root of Drive A, you would use the command: ERASE A:\OLDFILE (↵Enter) or DEL A:\OLDFILE (↵Enter).

A *group* of files can be erased using wildcards. To delete all files with the file extension .BAD in the root of Drive A, you would use the command: ERASE A:*.BAD (↵Enter) or DEL A:*.BAD (↵Enter).

Computer users must be careful using the Erase and Del commands. When the command is entered, the file is erased instantly. It is important to think carefully *before* using the command.

Erase the NEWFILE.COM file in the DOST directory very carefully.

KEY: ERASE A:\DOST\NEWFILE.COM (↵Enter)

Erase MORE1.COM from all directories.

DO: Change to each directory (root, DOST, LOTUST, WP51T). When in each directory, list the files first using DIR/P to see if MORE1.COM is in the directory. If it is, then carefully use the Erase or Del command to delete it. Then list the files in that directory once more to see that MORE1.COM has been deleted.

QUICK QUESTIONS

1. What must be done to a new diskette before it can be used to store files?
2. Why must one be very careful when using the Format command?
3. What is the command to format a diskette in Drive A?

4. Name the two ways you can copy a file to the same disk.
   a)
   b)
5. What two parameters should you use with the Copy command?
6. What command would copy a file called REPORT from A:\LOTUST to the root directory of Drive A?
7. What command would change the name of a file called OOPS to LETTER, both in the root of Drive A?
8. Do the Erase and Del commands differ?
9. What should you always do before erasing a file?
10. What two commands would erase a file called OBSOLETE on A:\?
    a)
    b)
11. What command would erase all .WK1 files in the LOTUST directory on a disk in Drive A?

As a review of this section, key a command to complete each request below. Use the section as a reference if needed. Write the command you used in the space following the request. All commands apply to Drive A (or the drive containing the template disk).

1. Key the command that will copy the DOST file called KEYA.COM to the root directory.
2. Copy the KEYA.COM file from DOST to the root directory but change its name to PRAC.COM.
3. Rename the PRAC.COM file to PRAC2.COM.
4. Rename the KEYA.COM file in the root directory to PRAC1.COM.
5. Copy the DOST file called GRATABL.COM to the WP51T directory.
6. Rename the WP51T GRATABL.COM file to PRAC3.COM.
7. Erase the file named PRAC1.COM in the root directory.
8. Carefully use wild cards to erase all files with PRAC as a part of the file name, any extension, that are in the LOTUST, DOST, or WP51T directories.

UNIT 3

Using WordPerfect 5.1

1

GETTING ACQUAINTED

OBJECTIVES

- Define word processing.
- Recognize type of keyboard to be used.
- Use the template correctly.
- Load the WordPerfect program.
- Recognize the blank typing screen and the status line.
- Understand how to follow instructions in this unit.

WORD PROCESSING

Word processing is using your computer as a "typewriter" to create attractive and easily readable text, usually in the form of sentences and paragraphs. Unlike a typewriter, the computer also enables you to save your work on disk to be used later and provides resources like help, spell checking, and a thesaurus. Word processing can also use the computer to do complex tasks like merging form letters and sharing files with other types of programs.

WordPerfect, the most popular word processing program, has sold more copies worldwide than any other word processing package. You will use WordPerfect to prepare letters, memos, tables, reports, and other text documents.

THE KEYBOARD

Several keyboards are available. (See the Using Computers unit, Hardware section, for an illustration of standard and enhanced keyboards.) The keys on an enhanced keyboard are described first, but the keys on a standard keyboard are included. If you have an enhanced keyboard, using the special key pad located between the alphabetic keyboard and the numeric keypad will save you time. It is a closer reach from the alphabetic keyboard where you do most of your keying, freeing the numeric pad for numbers.

FUNCTION KEYS AND THE TEMPLATE

WordPerfect 5.1 users have two methods of selecting commands, using the function keys or using the pull-down menus. For those who prefer using the function keys, a template is available so that the commands can be seen at all times. The template, a strip of material on which the WordPerfect commands are printed, is positioned above or around the function keys for quick reference. (See templates below, WP1.1 and WP1.2). This visual reminder of the commands is one of the reasons WordPerfect has become so popular.

WP1.1 WordPerfect 5.1 Template - Enhanced Keyboard

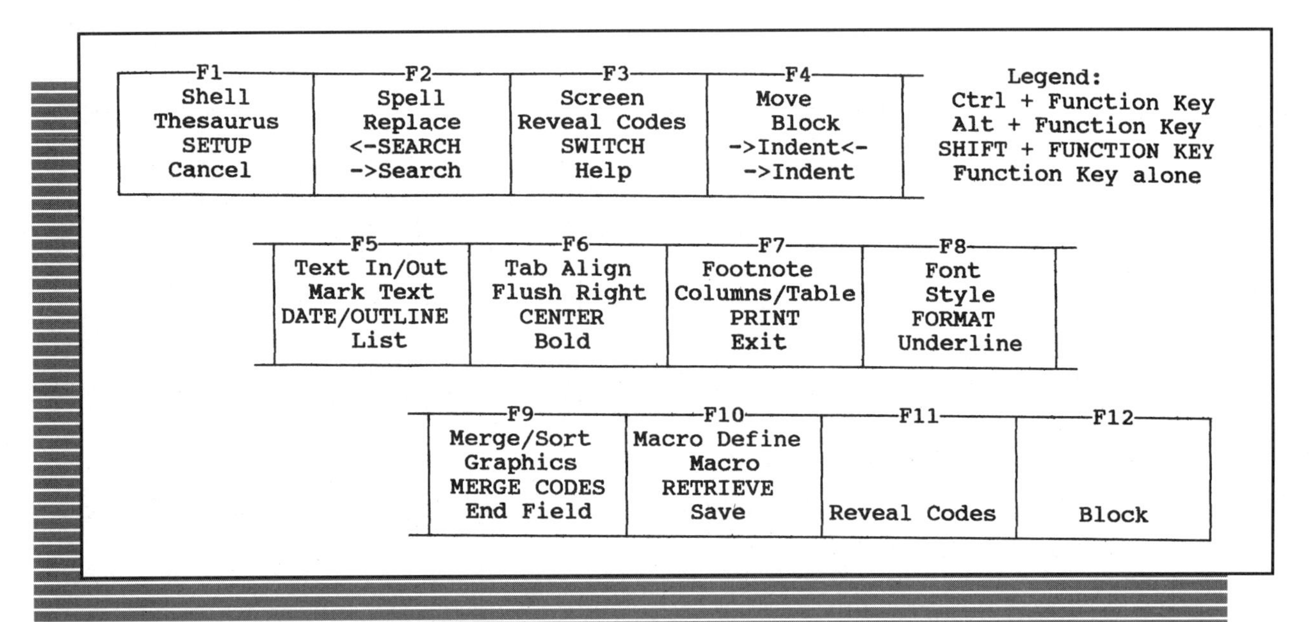

F1	F2	F3	F4
Shell	Spell	Screen	Move
Thesaurus	Replace	Reveal Codes	Block
SETUP	<-SEARCH	SWITCH	->Indent<-
Cancel	->Search	Help	->Indent

F5	F6	F7	F8
Text In/Out	Tab Align	Footnote	Font
Mark Text	Flush Right	Columns/Table	Style
DATE/OUTLINE	CENTER	PRINT	FORMAT
List	Bold	Exit	Underline

F9	F10	F11	F12
Merge/Sort	Macro Define		
Graphics	Macro		
MERGE CODES	RETRIEVE		
End Field	Save	Reveal Codes	Block

Legend:
Ctrl + Function Key
Alt + Function Key
SHIFT + FUNCTION KEY
Function Key alone

WP1.2 WordPerfect 5.1 Template - Standard Keyboard

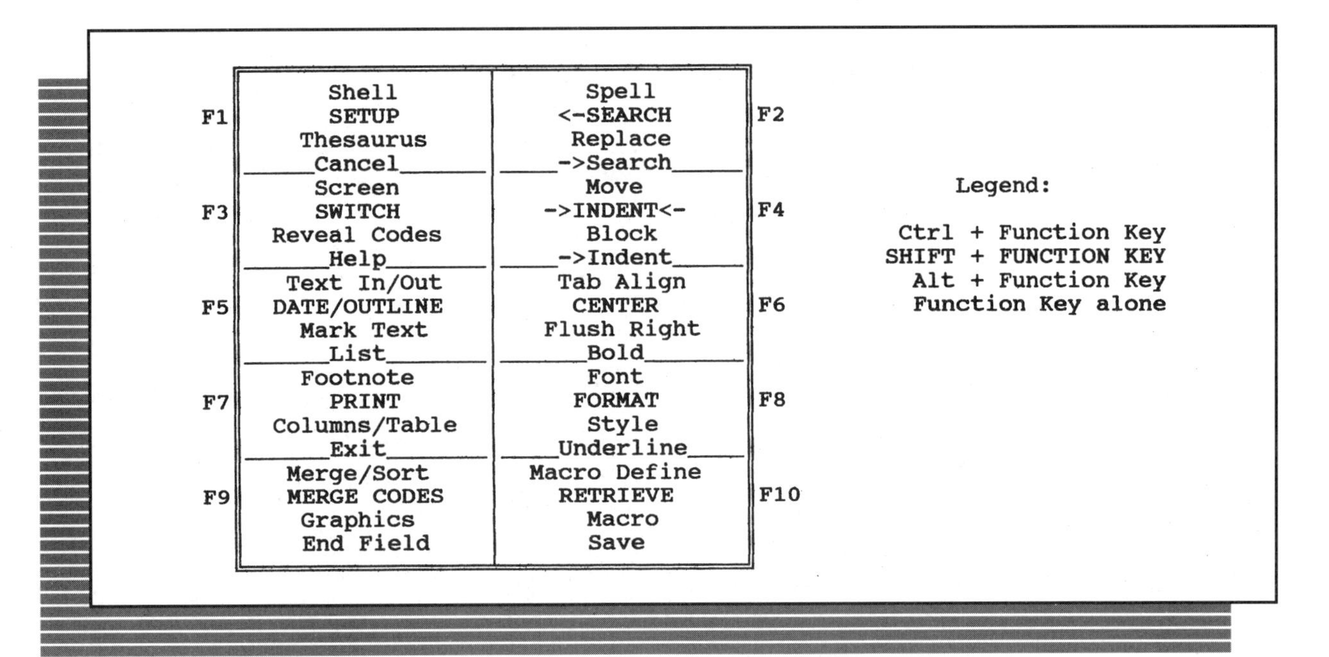

F1	Shell SETUP Thesaurus Cancel	Spell <-SEARCH Replace ->Search	F2
F3	Screen SWITCH Reveal Codes Help	Move ->INDENT<- Block ->Indent	F4
F5	Text In/Out DATE/OUTLINE Mark Text List	Tab Align CENTER Flush Right Bold	F6
F7	Footnote PRINT Columns/Table Exit	Font FORMAT Style Underline	F8
F9	Merge/Sort MERGE CODES Graphics End Field	Macro Define RETRIEVE Macro Save	F10

Legend:

Ctrl + Function Key
SHIFT + FUNCTION KEY
Alt + Function Key
Function Key alone

Looking at the template and legend for your type of keyboard, each function key (except F11 and F12 on enhanced keyboards) is responsible for four commands. For example, the F1 function key controls the Shell, Thesaurus, Setup, and Cancel commands. Each of the four commands on a function key is activated by pressing Ctrl, Shift, or Alt with the function key or by pressing the function key alone.

The top command shown for each function key on the template (F1-Shell, F2-Spell, F3-Screen, F4-Move, F5-Text In/Out, F6-Tab Align, F7-Footnote, F8-Font, F9-Merge/Sort, and F10-Macro Define) is obtained by holding down Ctrl *while* pressing the appropriate function key. To get the Font function, for example, hold down Ctrl while pressing the F8 function key.

Commands in the second row are obtained by holding down Alt while pressing the appropriate function key on enhanced keyboards and by holding down Shift on standard keyboards. Commands on the third row are obtained by holding down Shift while pressing the function key on enhanced keyboards and by holding down Alt while pressing the function key on standard keyboards. For the bottom row of commands, press the function key only.

THE MOUSE AND PULL-DOWN MENUS

WordPerfect Version 5.1 is the first version that supports a mouse, which can be used to access the pull-down menus, on-screen lists of commands. Section Four of this unit has instructions for using a mouse with WordPerfect. From that point on, those who have a mouse and prefer to use it will be given the mouse command for new features, indicated by ⊎. The pull-down menus may also be accessed or eliminated with Alt-=. Use the cursor keys to move throughout the menus and ↵Enter to select commands.

LOADING WORDPERFECT

One of the following procedures may load the WordPerfect program for you. If not, your instructor will tell you how to load it in your particular situation.

1. *Using two disk drives:*
   a) Start DOS.
   b) Insert the WordPerfect Disk 1 in Drive A.
   c) Insert your data disk in Drive B.
   d) Key **B:** ↵Enter to set Drive B as the default for files.
   e) Key **A:WP** ↵Enter to start WordPerfect.
   f) When prompted, replace Disk 1 in Drive A with WordPerfect Disk 2.
2. *Hard disk:*
   a) At the DOS prompt, key **CD\WP51** ↵Enter (or the name of the directory where the WP.EXE file is located).
   b) Insert your data disk in the floppy drive.
   c) Key **WP** ↵Enter

3. *Networked system:*
   a) Log on to the computer system.
   b) Select WordPerfect from the menu (or follow instructor directions).

THE SCREEN AND STATUS LINE

After WordPerfect is loaded, the typing screen, called the **editing screen**, appears (WP1.3). It is clear or "clean" except for the lower right corner, where the Status Line is located. Refer to the **Status Line** as you use the program; it will keep you informed of several important conditions:

- **Doc** (Document) should display "1" (you actually have two document screens).
- **Pg** (Page) tells you which page your cursor is on.
- **Ln** (Line) tells how many inches your cursor is from the top of a sheet of paper (your screen should be thought of as a sheet of paper).
- **Pos** (Position) tells how many inches your cursor is from the left edge of a sheet of paper.

When you load WordPerfect, you will key text on the clean screen as if it were a sheet of paper.

FIGURE WP1.3
The WordPerfect Editing Screen

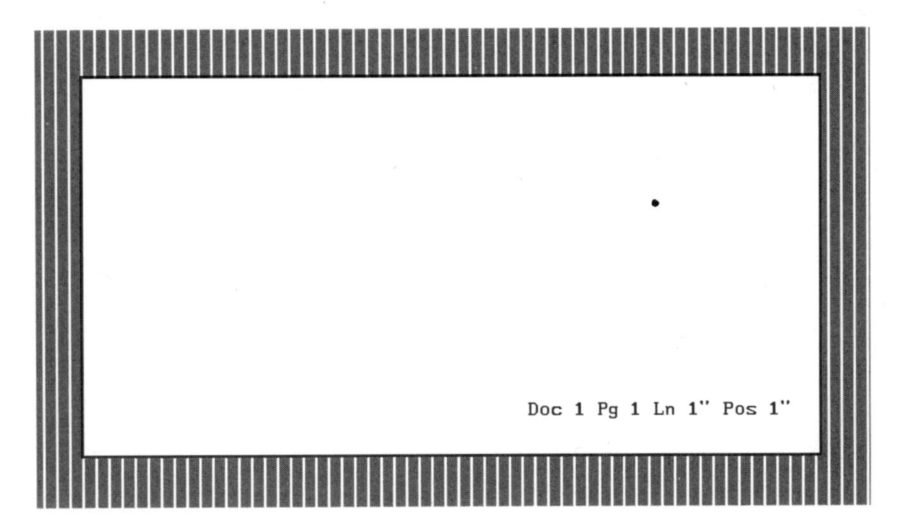

FOLLOWING INSTRUCTIONS

Throughout this book, student actions such as data to be keyed, commands to be activated, or options to be chosen will be between double lines and marked specially:

- **Data to be keyed** will be indicated by the word *KEY*.
- **Keyboard actions other than keying data** will be indicated by the word *DO*.
- **Keys** to press are shown inside key caps: (Insert). If a key is to be held down while pressing another key, the keys will be "locked" together like this: (Ctrl)-(F2). If keys are to be pressed separately in sequence, they will be shown as: (F7) (N) (N); this means press (F7), then press (N), then press (N).
- **File names** are shown in caps, but don't need to be keyed in caps.

Special directions that you will see in the WordPerfect section are:

- **A shaded box** with the caption *WPKey*, followed by the number of the section and the number of the keying assignment, indicates a quantity of text to be keyed.
- **An unshaded box** with the caption *WPCheck* provides a picture of the WordPerfect screen so you can check your work for accuracy.
- **Mouse** selection and keyboard access of the pull-down menus is shown with ⛎.

QUICK QUESTIONS

1. What is word processing?
2. Do you have a standard or an enhanced keyboard?
3. What is a WordPerfect 5.1 template?
4. Looking at your template, what is pressed to use the Bold feature?
5. What is pressed to use the Help feature?
6. Will you have a mouse available?
7. Write the steps you will use to get WordPerfect started each time you use it:
8. What is the name of the screen part that keeps you informed about your cursor position?
9. What is the purpose of the *Pos* (Position) indicator?
10. What does the notation Alt-F6 mean you should do?
11. What does ↵Enter mean?

Practice using the WordPerfect template. Use your own template or the picture of keyboard templates on page WP3. In the chart below, show the keys that would be pressed to obtain the features.

Place a check mark in the appropriate column if Ctrl, Alt, or Shift would be used. In the Function Key column, write the function key that would be pressed. The first one has been done as an example.

Feature	Ctrl	Alt	Shift	Function Key
Spell	✓			F2
Flush Right				
Thesaurus				
Format				
Block				
List				
Cancel				
Retrieve				
Help				
Graphics				
Move				
Save				
Replace				
Merge/Sort				

2

THE BASICS

OBJECTIVES

- Erase unwanted text with the **backspace** key.
- Use **cursor keys** to move in a document.
- Erase unwanted text with the **delete** key.
- Use **wordwrap.**
- **Insert** text and **type over** existing text using the insert key.
- **Clear** the screen.
- Use **caps lock**, **underline**, and **bold.**
- **Reveal codes** to see beginning and ending codes.
- **Exit** the program without saving.

LOAD THE PROGRAM

If you have not loaded WordPerfect, do so according to the steps listed on pages WP4-5 or the direction of your instructor. The WordPerfect editing screen appears, ready for text to be entered.

BACKSPACE (← Backspace)

The Backspace key erases to the *left* of your cursor. It may be held down to repeat erasing to the left.

KEY: Key the text *in the shaded box* (WPKey 2.1):

FIGURE WPKEY2.1

```
This is practice for backspace.
```

DO: Carefully backspace until you have erased the period and the words *for backspace.* (Rekey any words/letters you erase accidentally.)

CURSOR KEYS (→) (←) (↑) (↓)

These keys have arrows on them and move the cursor up, down, left, and right. You cannot move the cursor through a *clear* part of the screen.

DO: Cursor with the left arrow to the capital *T* in *This.*

DELETE (Delete) OR (Del)

The Delete key erases the character your cursor is on. When held down, it erases to the right of your cursor.

DO: Delete all remaining words on your screen.

WORDWRAP

DO NOT PRESS ENTER AT THE RIGHT END OF EACH KEYED LINE. Always let WordPerfect end lines for you, called **wordwrap**. (If you edit text or change format settings later, wordwrapped text will adjust automatically). Press (↵Enter) only at the end of a paragraph, a short line, or where you want a blank line.

KEY: Key the following paragraph (WPKey 2.2). If you make errors, use (←Backspace) to erase to the left or (Delete) to erase the character your cursor is on and to the right. Do NOT press Enter to end each line; let wordwrap end lines.

FIGURE WPKEY2.2

```
The WordPerfect screen is just like a piece of paper in
a typewriter. It is ready for you to type right on it.
Standard margins and single spacing are already set for
you, and you will be using them for a while.
```

DO: Use the cursor (arrow) keys to move your cursor around as you make the following changes. When you get to the appropriate character, use (Delete) or (←Backspace). (Erase extra spaces as well as the words; rekey any words you accidentally erase.) If you make a "drastic" mistake, just press (↵Enter) a few times and begin again.

DO: Erase *just*.

DO: Erase the words *right on it*.

DO: Erase *already*.

DO: Check your work for accuracy with the display below, WPCheck2.1.

FIGURE WPCHECK 2.1

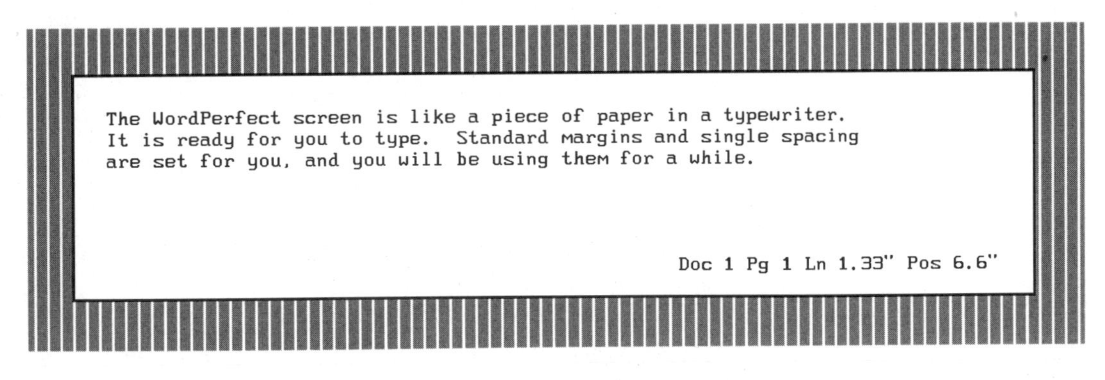
The WordPerfect screen is like a piece of paper in a typewriter.
It is ready for you to type. Standard margins and single spacing
are set for you, and you will be using them for a while.
Doc 1 Pg 1 Ln 1.33" Pos 6.6"

QUICK QUESTIONS

1. Which key erases the character your cursor is on?
2. To erase three characters to the left of your cursor, which key should be pressed three times?
3. Can you move the cursor through a clear part of the screen?
4. What is the name of the feature that frees you from making line-ending decisions?
5. List three occasions when you should press (↵Enter) in WordPerfect.
   a)
   b)
   c)
6. Which key should you press to move to the right in text (keyed words)?
7. Can you move the cursor from Line 1 to Line 5 by pressing the Down Arrow key if nothing has been keyed on your screen?

INSERT/TYPEOVER (Insert) OR (Ins)

The Insert key does the OPPOSITE of what it sounds like. WordPerfect inserts by default. As you key new words in existing text, the previous words "move over" to make room for the new ones.

Press (Insert) when you want to TYPE OVER existing text. While Typeover is in effect, the word *Typeover* appears in the lower left corner of the editing screen. Press (Insert) a second time to end Typeover. Typeover should only be used when necessary.

DO: For the text you just keyed, WPKey2.2, press the (Insert) key on and off to make the following changes while you watch for the *Typeover* message. Insert a (Space) where needed. Use (←Backspace) and (Delete) when helpful. (You will notice the screen moves to *adjust* as you key.)

DO: Insert *display* before *screen.*

DO: Typeover *piece* with *sheet.*

DO: Typeover *single* with *double.*

DO: Insert *not* before *set.*

DO: Insert the word *little* and insert a space before *while.*

DO: Check your work with WPCheck2.2.

FIGURE WPCHECK 2.2

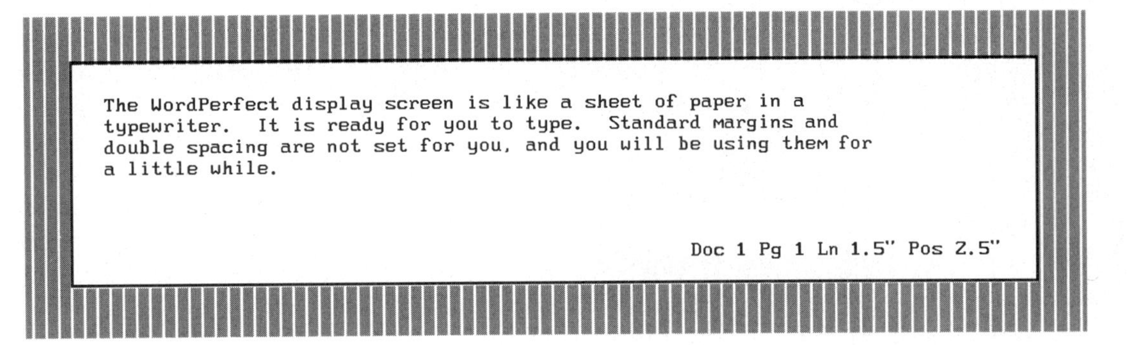
The WordPerfect display screen is like a sheet of paper in a
typewriter. It is ready for you to type. Standard margins and
double spacing are not set for you, and you will be using them for
a little while.

Doc 1 Pg 1 Ln 1.5" Pos 2.5"

CLEAR THE SCREEN (F7) (N) (N)

When you simply want to clear your display screen and not save your work, press this sequence of keys:

1. Press (F7), *Exit*.
2. Press (N), *No* you don't wish to save the document.
3. Press (N), *No* you don't wish to exit the program—you want to do some more work in WordPerfect.

DO: Press (F7) (N) (N). Your screen is blank and ready for the next feature. ALWAYS have a clean screen before starting a new document in this unit.

CAPS LOCK

This key makes alphabetic characters capitalized; it does not affect numbers or symbols. Like (Insert), this key is a toggle. A **toggle** is an on/off feature. Press a toggle key once to begin it, and press it a second time to end it.

The Status Line always shows Caps Lock is on by displaying the Pos indicator in all caps: POS. On some keyboards, a green light in the upper right corner of the keyboard also indicates that Caps Lock is on.

KEY: Key the text in WPKey 2.3. Use (Caps Lock) for keying the first sentence; use (Shift) to key uppercase letters in the second sentence. Correct keying errors. When done, leave the text on your screen.

FIGURE WPKEY2.3

```
THIS IS IN ALL CAPS. This Is In Initial Caps Only.
```

UNDERLINE (F8)

The **Underline** command, another toggle, puts a line under characters. Complete these steps when you want to underline:

1. Press (F8) to begin underlining.
2. Key the words to be underlined.
3. Press (F8) to end underlining.

Depending on how your program is set up and the type of display you have, underlined text and the *Pos* indicator on the Status Line will either be underlined, shown in a contrasting color, or have a lightened background.

Key: Space two times and then add the text in the box below (WPKey 2.4) to the text already on your screen. Press (F8) to toggle Underline on and off where shown. Leave this on your screen.

FIGURE WPKEY2.4

```
This text is underlined. This text is not.
```

BOLD (F6)

The **Bold** command, a toggle, makes characters darker than normal. Complete these steps when you want to make text bold:

1. Press (F6) to begin Bold.
2. Key the words to be bolded.
3. Press (F6) to end Bold.

Depending on how your program is set up and the type of display you have, bolded text and the *Pos* indicator in the lower right corner of the display will either be a different color or bright white.

Key: Space two times and then add the text in the box below (WPKey2.5) to the text already on your screen. Press (F6) to begin and end bold where shown.

FIGURE WPKEY2.5

```
This text is bold. This text is not.
```

FIGURE WPCHECK 2.3

Check your work with WPCheck2.3.

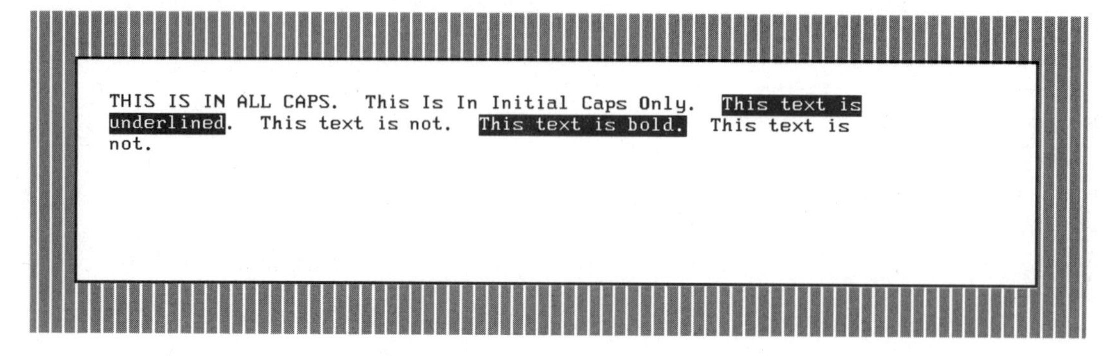
THIS IS IN ALL CAPS. This Is In Initial Caps Only. This text is
underlined. This text is not. This text is bold. This text is
not.

REVEAL CODES (F11) OR (Alt)-(F3)

As you select WordPerfect features, hidden codes are imbedded for them in your text. You do not see these codes because WordPerfect shows you on screen how the *printed* document will appear. Since codes will not appear when printed, they are not shown on the screen.

You may, however, look at the hidden codes at any time by *revealing* them with the **Reveal Codes** feature. Press F11 or Alt-F3 to toggle Reveal Codes on and off.

DO: Press F11 or Alt-F3 to reveal your codes. (See WP2.1). Look below the line which divides the screen into two parts for feature codes shown inside brackets.

The first code you see is **[UND]**. UND is the abbreviation for underline, and the uppercase letters indicate that underlining is *beginning*. Look for the **[und]** code. The lowercase letters indicate that underlining is *ended*. This means that the words between the [UND] and the [und] codes will be underlined when you print.

FIGURE WP2.1
Revealing Codes

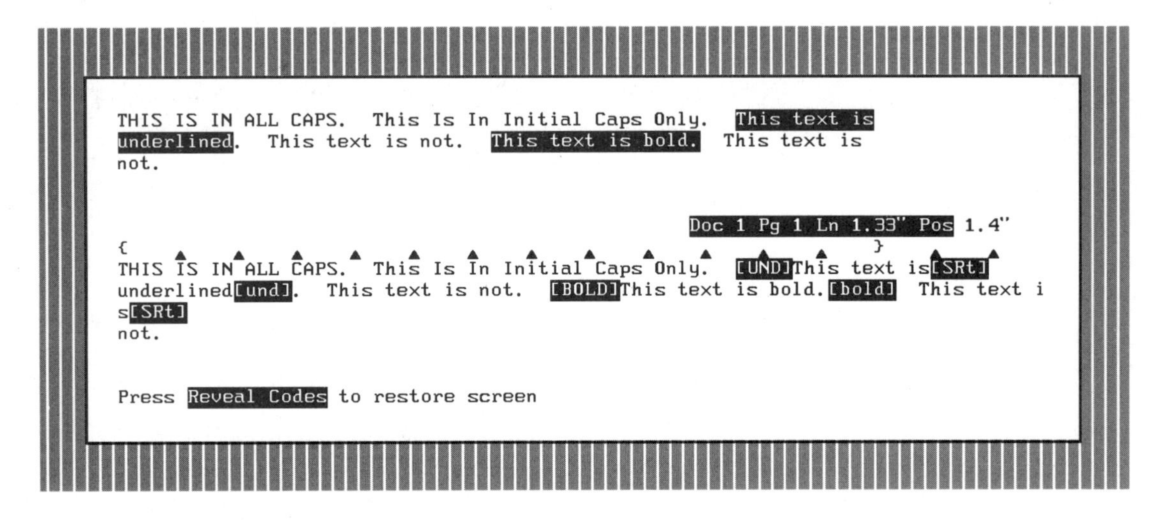
THIS IS IN ALL CAPS. This Is In Initial Caps Only. This text is
underlined. This text is not. This text is bold. This text is
not.
Doc 1 Pg 1 Ln 1.33" Pos 1.4"
THIS IS IN ALL CAPS. This Is In Initial Caps Only. [UND]This text is[SRt]
underlined[und]. This text is not. [BOLD]This text is bold.[bold] This text i
s[SRt]
not.
Press Reveal Codes to restore screen

DO: Exactly what words will be underlined when you print?

____

DO: What words do you think will be printed in *bold*?

____

DO: Find **[SRt], Soft Return,** codes. These codes show where wordwrap ended a line for you. The first [SRt] is after what word? __________

MONOCHROME DISPLAY. If you are using a monochrome display, the cursor in Reveal Codes may be "gray" when it is on a code and a darker background when it is on a character. (You may need to adjust your lightness/darkness and contrast dials on your display.) Ask your instructor what your cursor looks like in Reveal Codes.

COLOR DISPLAY. If you are using a color display, the cursor in Reveal Codes is a contrasting color. What is the color of your cursor in Reveal Codes? __________

DO: Be sure your cursor is at the end of your keying. Looking below the line that divides the screen, press (←) several times. Locate the cursor as you move left. Then move up, down, and right. If you have trouble locating your Reveal Codes cursor, find the cursor in the upper typing screen. Your lower Reveal Codes cursor is on the same character as your upper screen cursor.

DO: To *delete* a code, place your cursor on the code and press (Delete). With your cursor on either [UND] or [und], press (Delete). Can you see that both codes are gone, and underlining has vanished?

DO: Since Reveal Codes is a toggle, press (F11) or (Alt)-(F3) to turn Reveal Codes off.

DO: Clear your screen by pressing (F7) (N) (N).

You can key while in Reveal Codes. Then you can watch the codes being put in place.

DO: Press (F11) or (Alt)-(F3) to reveal codes. Press *Bold* (F6), key your first name, and then press (F6) to *end* Bold. Press (Space). Press *Underline* (F8), key your last name, and then press (F8) to *end* Underline. Press (↵Enter). Key your street address in bold and then key your city, state, and zip underlined.

DO: Clear your screen by pressing (F7) (N) (N).

QUICK QUESTIONS

1. Is Typeover used to insert one word between two other existing words?
2. Is Typeover used to key *more* over the word *need*?
3. Where should you look on the screen to see if you are in Typeover mode?
4. How do you end Typeover?
5. What three-key sequence is used to simply clear your screen without saving your document?
6. Is it all right to have the document you just finished on your screen when you begin a new document in this unit?
7. What is the name for any on/off feature or key?
8. Which key is the best to use to get a series of uppercase letters?
9. Will (Caps Lock) give you the symbols at the top of the number keys?
10. Which function key is pressed to start and stop underlining?
11. What does underlining look like on your screen?
12. Can you key the words first, and then go back and make them bold?

13. What feature should you use if you want to check codes to see if a word will print in bold?
14. What does [UND]Summary[und] mean in revealed codes?
15. What does the [SRt] code mean?

EXIT WORDPERFECT (F7) (N) (Y)

When you no longer wish to key documents in the WordPerfect program, this sequence of steps will return you to your system prompt or program selection menu *without saving your file*:

1. Press (F7), *Exit*.
2. Press (N), *No* you don't wish to save the document.
3. Press (Y), *Yes* you do wish to exit the program.

DO: Press (F7) (N) (N). You are at the system prompt or program selection menu and no longer able to key in WordPerfect unless you reload the program.

Load WordPerfect if necessary. Key the following review paragraph. Correct any keying errors with Backspace, Delete, and Typeover. Press the appropriate keys for Caps Lock, Underline, and Bold. Correct spacing and punctuation where needed. Do not press (↵Enter); use wordwrap. You may want to key in Reveal Codes to see that you are using the features correctly. Delete any incorrect codes. (If you have a major problem, clear your screen with (F7) (N) (N) and start again.)

Using CAPS LOCK, underline, and **bold** can help make text more attractive. They are used specifically to make **special items** stand out, to make certain the reader doesn't overlook important information, and to DIVIDE THE TEXT INTO LOGICAL PARTS. When erasing text containing underline and **bold** features, the lower left corner of your display will ask you to verify that you want to erase these feature codes AS WELL AS the **text**.

1. Delete *underline*, in the first sentence.
2. Insert *certainly* before *help* in the first sentence.
3. Type over *special* with *unusual* in the second sentence.
4. Type over *important* with *prominent* in the second sentence.
5. Delete *display* and insert *computer screen* in the last sentence.

After you are successful with the directions above, either clear your screen with F7 N N and go on to the Reinforcement Activity, or exit from WordPerfect with F7 N Y.

REINFORCEMENT ACTIVITY

Load WordPerfect if necessary. Key the following paragraph. Correct any keying errors with Backspace, Delete, and Typeover. Correct spacing and punctuation where needed. Use Caps Lock, Underline, and Bold where shown. Do not press ↵Enter; use wordwrap.

WORD PROCESSING is a common use of <u>computers</u>. Most people need to key text from **time to time**, whether for LETTERS, REPORTS, or NOTES. Some folks use **word processing** to key <u>recipes</u> or <u>journal entries</u>. Of course, **authors, poets**, and **news reporters** would be at a <u>loss</u> without a word processor. These people who are in the business of MANIPULATING WORDS use delete, bold, and underline to **highlight** important words and phrases. <u>Not only</u> can they save their work to be changed at any time, but they have MANY FEATURES available to make **their job** of keying words <u>easier</u> and <u>more pleasant</u>.

1. Insert *very* before *common* in the first sentence.
2. Delete *from time to time,* in the second sentence.
3. Insert *paper* after *news* to become *newspaper* in the fourth sentence.
4. Delete *at a loss* and insert *LOST* in the fourth sentence.
5. Insert the word *insert,* after *bold,* in the fifth sentence.
6. Typeover *words and phrases* with <u>*phrases and words*</u> in the fifth sentence.
7. Delete **their job** *of* in the sixth sentence.

After you are successful with the directions above, either clear your screen with F7 N N and go on to the next section, or exit from WordPerfect with F7 N Y.

3

FILE NAMES, SAVE, RETRIEVE

OBJECTIVES

- Use **file names** and extensions correctly.
- Use the proper **drive/path** for saving on a disk.
- Use **exit to save.**
- **Retrieve** a file with Shift F10.
- **Edit** a file.
- **Resave** a file.

FILE NAMES

In this section you will begin storing your documents on disk. A document created with a computer is called a **file**, and a file must be given a name, called a **file name**. It is important to use a file name correctly so you can retrieve the file when you want it.

Always follow these rules for file names regardless of the program you are using:

- May be up to eight characters in length
- Can be keyed in upper or lower case or a mixture
- May NOT have any spaces

Correct File Names	Incorrect File Names
letter	MERGELETTER (too many characters)
PAGE3	letter merge (space)
5Letters	Page 3 (space)

A file name may include an optional **extension** of 3 additional characters. The file name and the extension are separated by a period. There may NOT be any spaces ANYWHERE within the file name and extension.

Correct File Names/Extensions	Incorrect File Names/Extensions
letter.1	Letter1 env (no period before extension)
letter1.env	letter.five (more than a three-character extension)
	LETTER. ENV (space)

QUICK QUESTIONS

Examples of correct and incorrect file names are listed below. Place a "C" beside each correct file name. Beside each incorrect file name, tell what is wrong with it.

1. memorandum
2. A
3. MiXeD
4. game 5
5. partfive doc
6. partfour.doc
7. 3dog.a

A good file name will indicate the contents of the file. Look at the file names/extensions in the Quick Questions above. Does the file name "A" indicate its contents? How about "game5?" Is "partfour.doc" a descriptive name?

USING DISK DRIVES

You must know where to store your files. This could be on a floppy in Drive A or B, in a directory on Hard Drive C, or on a file server if you are networked. You may need to key a **path** for your file, telling WordPerfect which drive and/or directory should be used.

Ask your instructor how you should save a file. On the line below, write exactly what you would key to save a file named DEC25.MIN.

On the line below, write exactly what you would key to save a file named PRAC.3.

You will save all your documents in the manner you wrote above, including a path if needed. Although file names are shown in all caps in this book, *you may key them in lowercase letters.*

KEY: Key the text in the box below (WPKey3.1); the document will be stored on disk. Use wordwrap, of course. Correct any keying errors with Backspace, Delete, or Typeover. Use Reveal Codes when it is helpful. (If you make a lot of mistakes, clear your screen F7 N N and start again.)

FIGURE WPKEY3.1

It is IMPORTANT not just to be able to **create** documents, but also to be able to <u>save</u> them so they can be **printed** later or even <u>changed</u> if necessary. You will SAVE THIS DOCUMENT, retrieve it, **change** it, and save it again in its FINAL FORM.

EXIT/SAVE (F7) (Y) FILE NAME (↵Enter) (N) OR (Y)

There are two ways to store a document on disk in WordPerfect. The method you will use now not only *saves* the document you see on your screen, but it will *also clear the screen* so you are ready to begin a new document. (If you do not clear your screen, you will stack several documents together, which is not desirable at this time.) Use the **Exit** command to save your document and then clear the screen:

1. Press (F7), *Exit*.
2. Press (Y), *Yes* save document.
3. Key the file name of the document including a path if needed and then press (↵Enter).
4. Press (N), *No* do not exit WordPerfect.

The name of the file will be WPKEY3.1. Press the keys shown and key the file name (shown in all caps), including a path if needed. Press (↵Enter) when you see (↵).

DO: Press (F7) (Y) WPKEY3.1 (↵Enter) (N)

Your document is saved on disk, and your screen is clean, ready for another document. Before keying the last (N) to exit WordPerfect, you may press (F1) *Cancel* to stop the clearing of your screen and to keep your document on the screen if desired.

RETRIEVE A FILE (Shift)-(F10)

Always be sure you have a clean screen before you retrieve a file in this unit.

There are two ways to retrieve a document from disk in WordPerfect. The method you will use now is the best one when you know the name of the document you wish to bring to your screen. To use the **Retrieve** command, HOLD DOWN (Shift) WHILE you tap (F10). Key any required path in front of the file name WPKEY3.1.

DO: Press (Shift)-(F10) *Retrieve,* WPKEY3.1 (↵Enter)

The WPKEY3.1 document should appear on your screen. (If it doesn't, you probably keyed a part of the path, the file name, or the extension incorrectly. Try keying it again.)

You may now edit the document any way you wish. Remember, the WPKEY3.1 file is still on your disk; you have only brought a *copy* of it to your screen. You could clear your screen now without "losing" the document, but keep it so you can edit it.

EDIT A FILE

Use the cursor keys to move through your text to make the following changes:

DO: Insert *attractive* before *documents* in the first sentence.

DO: Delete *to be able* in the first sentence.

DO: Make ***change*** in the last sentence become ***edit***.

DO: Typeover *even* in the first sentence with *also*.

Use the figure below to check your work (WPCheck3.1).

FIGURE WPCHECK3.1

```
It is IMPORTANT not just to create attractive documents,
but also to save them so they can be printed later or also
changed if necessary. You will SAVE THIS DOCUMENT,
retrieve it, edit it, and save it again in its FINAL FORM.
```

RESAVE A FILE (F7) (Y) (↵Enter) (Y)

The WPKEY3.1 file has been changed, or *edited*, **on screen**, but the file **on disk** is still in its original form. When a file is retrieved and changed, you have two options:

To keep both versions by saving the edited version with a **different** name:

1. Press (F7) *Exit*, (Y) *Yes*. The name of the document you *retrieved to your screen* will be shown in the lower left Status Line.
2. Move the cursor to the file name and key the **new** name you desire over the old name. (Delete any unwanted characters.)
3. Press (↵Enter).

OR

To save the edited version only by giving it the **same** name as the original, with the result that the original version is overwritten:

1. Press (F7) *Exit,* (Y) *Yes.* The name of the document you *retrieved to your screen* will be shown in the lower left Status Line.
2. Press (↵Enter) to **accept** that file name.
3. WordPerfect will double check with the message: *Replace? No(Yes).* Press (Y) *Yes,* you do want to **replace** the old file with the new version.

Save the revised version of your document with the same name as the original, WPKEY3.1.

DO: Press (F7) *Exit,* (Y) *Yes,* (↵Enter) to accept the document name, (Y) *Yes* to replace.

DO: When asked *Exit WordPerfect?,* press (N) *No* if you have more time to work or (Y) *Yes* if it is time to quit WordPerfect.

QUICK QUESTIONS

1. What is the maximum character size for a file name?
2. How many characters may be added to a file name in the form of an extension?
3. Write a good name for a file that is page 3 of an annual report.
4. Must a file name be keyed in all caps?
5. Pressing (F7) will not only save a document, but also perform what other action?
6. Why is it usually important for you to have a clear screen before retrieving a document from disk?
7. What keys are pressed to begin the Retrieve command?
8. Will a document remain on your disk when you retrieve it to your screen?
9. When you resave a document, what are the two options for naming the file?
   a)
   b)
10. What is the purpose of the WordPerfect prompt *Replace (file name)? No(Yes)?*

Key the paragraph below using the keys and features you have learned.

The PURPOSE of **Section Two** was to <u>introduce</u> the beginning WORDPERFECT user to the most basic manipulation of text. As the student continues through this book, **many features will be learned** that will <u>enhance</u> a document and make it much more <u>readable</u>. ENJOY THIS JOURNEY; learning something new and wonderful can be <u>VERY EXCITING</u>!

1. After the document is keyed, use (F7) to save the file as WPREV3; do not exit from WordPerfect.
2. Use (Shift)-(F10) to retrieve the file and make the following changes to it:
   a. Insert *MAIN* before *PURPOSE.*
   b. Typeover *much* with *even.*
   c. Delete *and wonderful.*
   d. Add the sentence <u>*GOOD LUCK!*</u>
3. Save the edited document as WPREV3A. To do this, press (F7) *Exit,* (Y) *Yes* to save, cursor past WPREV3 and add A at the end, press (↵Enter). When asked *Exit WordPerfect?*, press (N) *No* if you have more time to work or (Y) *Yes* if it is time to quit WordPerfect.

ACTIVITY A - LETTER

After you key the following letter, use F7 to save it as WPRA3LR; do not exit from WordPerfect. Use Caps Lock, Bold, and Underline as shown. Press ↵Enter once to end short lines and paragraphs; press ↵Enter an additional time to obtain a blank line. (Press ↵Enter four times after the date.)

(Current Date)

Mrs. Sonia Perez
3821 Westhampton
Cincinnati, OH 45227

Dear Mrs. Perez

We received your letter today, and we were dismayed to hear that your hair dryer was **defective**.

As a long-time customer of ours, we know you realize that **quality of our prod-ucts** is NUMBER ONE with us! The fact of the matter is, we "goofed." Somehow the faulty hair dryer slipped through our extensive quality control.

We are not **only** sending you a replacement hair dryer, but also a free *electric comb*. We feel confident you will enjoy the electric comb, and it will give us a chance to prove to you that our products are not only innovative, but among the FINEST on the market.

We hope you will continue to use SUPERIOR hair care products.

Sincerely

Frances Cline
Vice President, Consumer Affairs

After saving the document as WPRA3LR, retrieve it and make the following changes. Save the final document as WPRA3LR2; do not exit if you have time to go to the next activity.

1. Delete *dismayed* and insert **disappointed**.
2. Remove the bold codes from *defective*.
3. Typeover *long-time* with *loyal* and delete extra characters.
4. Delete *free* and insert *complimentary*.

ACTIVITY B - MEMO

Key the following memo. Press (Tab) after the colons in the headings. Use Caps Lock, Bold, and Underline as shown. Save the document as WPRA3MO; do not exit WordPerfect. Press (↵Enter) once to end short lines and paragraphs; press (↵Enter) an additional time to obtain a blank line.

MEMORANDUM

TO: (Tab) (Tab) <u>Supervisor, Accounting Department</u>

FROM: (Tab) <u>Supervisor, Computer Center</u>

DATE: (Tab) <u>March 27, 1991</u>

SUBJ: (Tab) <u>Payroll Deadline</u>

In response to your communication, I have assigned a **study group** to determine how we can expedite the processing of **payroll.** I am aware that our present procedures are inadequate and that your department is "under the gun" to complete your payroll activities prior to data processing.

The study group should have suggestions for **improvement** no later than next <u>Friday, April 5</u>. After I have met with them, I will contact you so we can discuss their findings. I know we can work together to modify our present policy in a way that everyone benefits.

Retrieve WPRA3MO. Make the following changes and then save the edited memo as WPRA3MO2. Either exit WordPerfect or go on to the next section.

1. Insert *three-member* before *study group* in sentence one.
2. Type over *inadequate* with *insufficient.*
3. Change *under the gun* to *pressured* (remove quotes).
4. Change *data processing* to *computer processing.*
5. Delete *next* in the second paragraph.
6. Type over *modify* with *change.*
7. Type over *everyone benefits* with *will benefit everyone.*

4

USING A MOUSE

Note: If you do not have a mouse to use, this section may be omitted.

OBJECTIVES

- Use a **mouse** for cursor **movement.**
- Use a **mouse** to select **features** and **their options.**

USING A MOUSE IN WORDPERFECT

Although WordPerfect supports a mouse, it is only used for three operations:

- to move the cursor
- to select features and their options
- to block text

When you have installed a mouse correctly, it is activated by simply moving it slightly. The mouse pointer is a "box" that looks like ■ ; it is reverse video on monochrome screens and a contrasting color on color screens. When it is not being used, it is not visible.

The mouse itself is used in three ways:

- click - press a button
- double click - click two times in quick succession
- drag - press and hold a button while moving the mouse

CURSOR MOVEMENT

You can use the mouse to move the cursor through existing text.

1. Move the mouse pointer to where you want the cursor positioned.
2. Click the left mouse button (LMB).
3. The WordPerfect cursor moves to that position.

***Note:** The practice exercises in this chapter, marked as **DO:**, can only be completed if a mouse is installed.*

DO: Use Shift-F10 to retrieve WPRA3MO2 from your disk. Press Home Home ↓.

DO: Move your mouse until the mouse pointer is on the first *c* in *communication* in the first sentence. Click LMB, the left mouse button. (Press LMB a second time if you get the Block message.) The WordPerfect cursor moves to the position you indicated.

DO: Move the mouse so that the mouse pointer is on the first *s* in *suggestions* in the first sentence of the second paragraph. Click LMB. Insert the words *some timely*.

DO: Move the mouse to the *p* in *present* in the last sentence. Click LMB. Press (Insert) to type over *present* with *current*.

DO: Keep the document on your screen for more mouse practice.

FEATURE AND OPTION SELECTION

WordPerfect commands may be selected by using the Menu Bar, a pull-down listing of commands. Access the Menu Bar with RMB (right mouse button) or (Alt)-(=).

FIGURE WP4.1
The Mouse Menu Bar

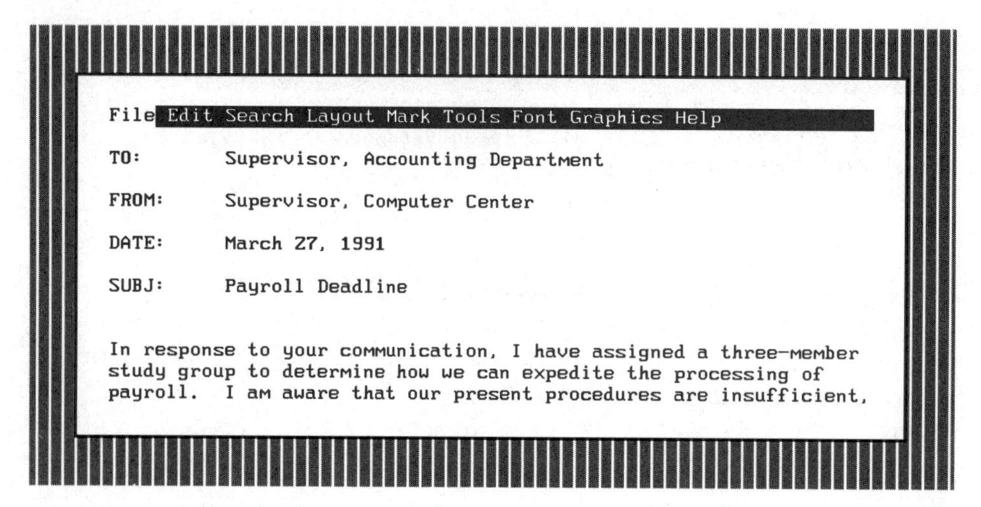

File Edit Search Layout Mark Tools Font Graphics Help
TO: Supervisor, Accounting Department
FROM: Supervisor, Computer Center
DATE: March 27, 1991
SUBJ: Payroll Deadline
In response to your communication, I have assigned a three-member study group to determine how we can expedite the processing of payroll. I am aware that our present procedures are insufficient,

DO: Press RMB. The Menu Bar appears at the top of the screen. (See WP4.1.)

DO: To reveal codes, click LMB on *Edit* to pull down the options. (See WP4.2.) Click LMB on *Reveal Codes.* The screen is divided, and codes are revealed.

DO: To end Reveal Codes, use the mouse buttons to display the Menu Bar and select *Edit.* Then click on *Reveal Codes* again.

Begin to save the document using the mouse menu.

DO: Display the Menu Bar. Click LMB on *File.* Click LMB on *Save.*

Cancel options using the mouse.

DO: When you see the name of the current document, WPRA3MO2, cancel the command. To cancel, press and hold either button, click the other button, and then release the first button. Try this until it "feels right."

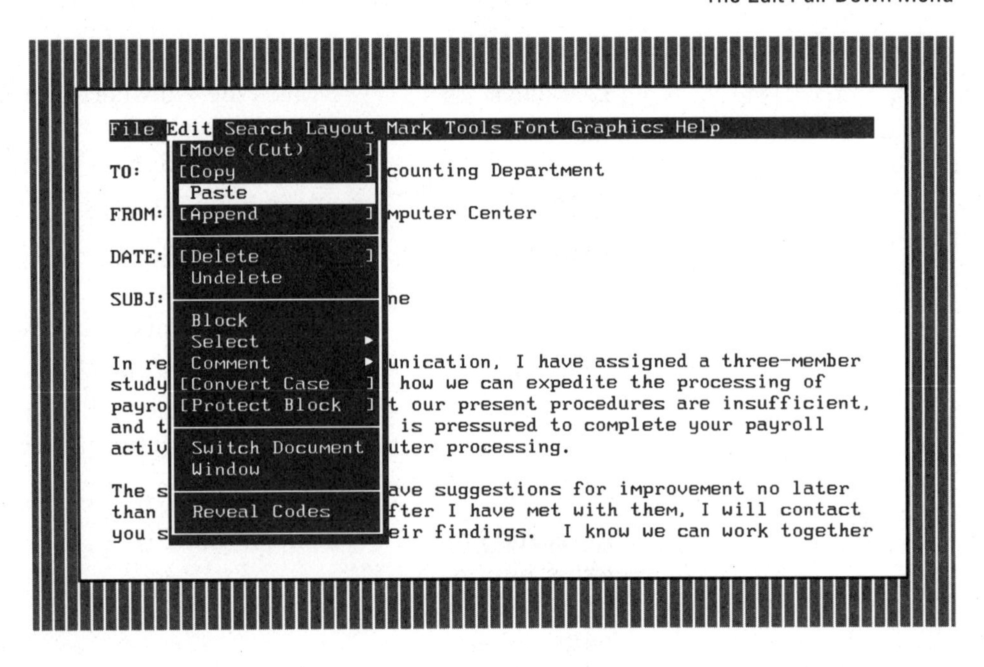

FIGURE WP4.2
The Edit Pull-Down Menu

Save the document.

DO: Display the Menu Bar. Click LMB on *File*. Click LMB on *Exit*. For *Save Document?*, click on *Yes*.

KEY: WPMOUSE1

DO: Press RMB, which functions as (↵Enter) when in menus and other options. For *Exit WP?*, you decide. If you have time to go to the next section, click RMB on *No*. If your computer time is up, click RMB on *Yes*.

MOUSE OPERATIONS

If you are not using the mouse, it becomes "dormant" (inactive), and you do not see the mouse pointer. When you touch the mouse in any way, it becomes activated, and the mouse pointer appears on your screen. The mouse pointer becomes dormant again when you press any key.

When an entire document cannot be seen on the screen at once, the mouse can be used to scroll the screen. **Scrolling** moves the display so a distant part of the document can be viewed. To do this, press the right mouse button (RMB) and *drag* the mouse in the direction you want to scroll.

The last operation for a mouse, blocking text, will be explained later in this unit.

Shown below is a list of efficient ways of using the mouse. From this point on, use the mouse instead of, or along with, your keyboard keys when you wish. Mouse selections are indicated with ⊎.

Mouse Action	Result
LMB click	Moves the WordPerfect pointer to the mouse pointer location Selects an option on any menu
LMB drag	Highlights a block
LMB double click	Selects an option on any menu and follows with Enter Accepts the default in a Status Line prompt
RMB click	Displays/Cancels the Mouse Menu Bar Exits from a menu Performs the Enter function for decisions
RMB drag	Scrolls the screen in a large document
Press and hold either button, click the other button, then release the first button	Cancels (like F1)

5

HELP, SPELL, THESAURUS

OBJECTIVES

- Use **Help.**
- Use **Spell.**
- Use **Thesaurus.**

HELP (F3) HELP

As with most good programs, WordPerfect has on-line help to provide information about its many features. Use **Help** within any menu to get a summary of each option; many times this is all the help you need. When you are confused, try the Help command—it is always there and only a few keystrokes away!

ON-SCREEN TEMPLATE. If your keyboard template is unavailable and you need to check the keystrokes to issue a command, use the on-screen template. Press (F3) twice for enhanced keyboard commands; press (F3) twice, followed by (1) for standard keyboard commands; or *Help, Template* when using a mouse.

DO: Press (F3) *Help* (F3) *Help* (followed by (1) for standard keyboards).

The *legend* on the right of the screen shows that the on-screen template is set up like the keyboard template. The *only* way to exit from the on-screen template is by pressing (↵Enter) or (Space).

DO: Press (↵Enter) to return to the normal editing screen.

HELP COMMAND LIST. When you press (F3) for Help, the first screen says to either press the letter(s) of the desired command and then the key shown for that command, or press a function key. Find out what the Shell feature is.

DO: Press (F3) *Help,* (S) *Shell,* (S) more *S* commands.

DO: Find *Shell, Go To* in the Features list. The keystrokes are *Ctrl-F1,1.*

DO: Press (Ctrl)-(F1).

Reading the Help screen, what kind of management program is the Shell?

DO: Press (↵Enter) to exit Help.

DO: Use Help to find what keys to press for Margin Release and the purpose of that feature. Write your answers below.

Keystrokes ____________ Purpose ____________

____

HELP WITHIN A MENU. When you are in a menu of options and you want to know more about each one, press (F3) Help. Find out more about some of those strange-sounding options on the Print menu.

DO: Press (Shift)-(F7) *Print,* (F3) *Help,* (B) to locate a description of the *Binding Offset* option. Write that description below:

____

____

____

DO: Press (↵Enter) to return to the Print menu.

DO: Still in the Print menu, press (F3) and then the letter or number of an option of your choice. Write the option you chose. ____________

What is its purpose? ____________

DO: Press (↵Enter) (↵Enter) to exit Help.

QUICK QUESTIONS

1. Use Help to find what three keys (combination of keys) are pressed to use the Center Page command. What are they?
2. Use the Format command, (Shift) (F8). Use Help to find the purpose of Headers and Footers. What do they do?
3. Which key is pressed to exit from Help?

SPELL (Ctrl)-(F2) TOOLS, SPELL

Even those who aren't good spellers can look good by using the **Spell** feature. This feature identifies words that may be spelled incorrectly, double words, words with numbers, and some capitalization errors. The Spell feature cannot find every error, however, because it only locates words that are not in its 115,000-word dictionary. Although it is a helpful tool, the Spell feature does not free you from proofreading each document yourself.

DO: With a clean screen, key the heading and text shown below, WPKey5.1.

USING REVEAL CODES

Some people like to keep Reveal Codes on while they type, while others find the Reveal Codes to be confusing. Each person must make the decision for him or herself. It is a very good idea, however, to use Reveal Codes now until you become familiar with it.

WPKEY5.1

CHECK ONE WORD, ONE PAGE, OR ENTIRE DOCUMENT. With the document to be checked on your editing screen, use the Spell command.

DO: (If you are running WordPerfect from two disk drives, remove your data diskette from Drive B and insert the Speller diskette before continuing.)

DO: Go to the top of the document.

DO: Press Ctrl-F2 *Spell* or Tools, Spell.

A list of Spell options appears on the message line at the bottom of the screen, as shown in Figure WP5.1. You may spell check one word, one page, or the entire document, as well as perform several other actions.

FIGURE WP5.1
Spell Options

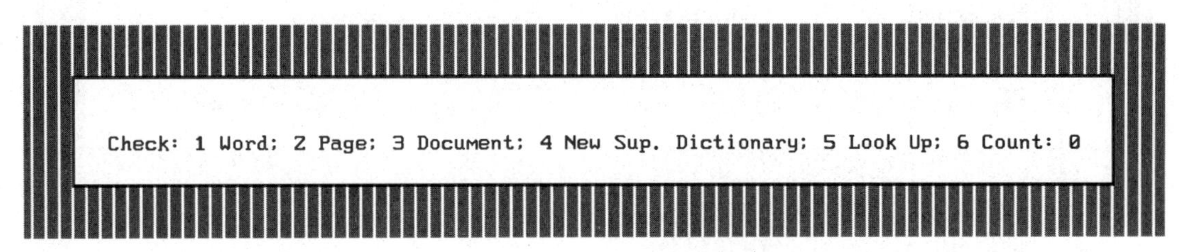

DO: Press W *Word.* The cursor skips over *Using* if it is spelled correctly; if it is not, the cursor will not proceed until the word is corrected or skipped. If you have an error, press 2 *Skip.* Press W several more times to see if the first few words of the document are spelled correctly; press 2 *Skip* for errors.

DO: Press P *Page.* **Your cursor can be at any position in a document when you spell check the entire page or document.** If you have a misspelled word, press 2 *Skip.* If you keyed everything correctly or skip misspelled words, the speller will display the following message at the bottom of the screen:
Word count: 50 Press any key to continue. Press any key. Press F7 to exit Spell.

Of course, if your document is only one page in length, either the Page or the Document option will check the entire document.

COUNT. To count all of the words in a document, choose the **Word Count** option.

DO: Looking at the Spell options, press (C) *Count.* After viewing the number of words in the document, press any key. Press (F7) to exit Spell. Clear your screen without saving.

Key: Key the text below (WPKey5.2); do *not* correct spelling.

FIGURE WPKEY5.2

```
Speel Cheking is a very very helpfil feeture to have
1. when you ar a poor speeler
2. when you ar typeing difficult material.
```

FIGURE WP5.2
Using Spell

DO: Press (Ctrl)-(F2) or Tools, Spell. Press (P) *Page.* See WP5.2.

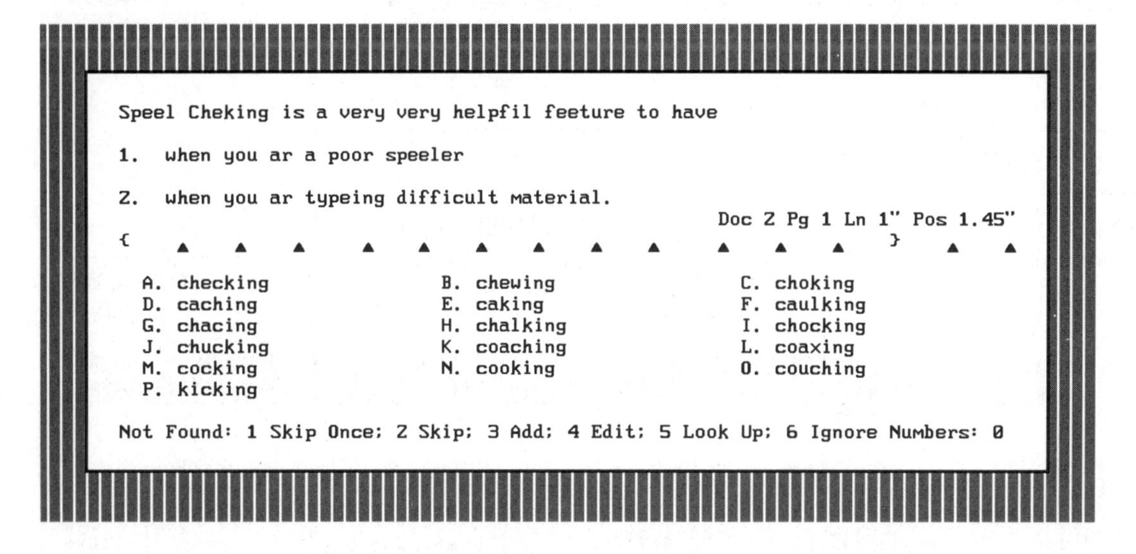

Caution: *Spellers vary because some learners accidentally add misspelled words to the Spell dictionary. As a result, your spell checking may vary from the directions below.*

DO: Notice *Speel* is skipped over. We know this word is misspelled here, but Spell will only locate words not in its dictionary. Speel, meaning *climb,* is in the dictionary; this shows why we must use our own judgment in each situation.

DO: *Cheking* is highlighted. The choices below the ruler include *A. checking,* the correct word. Press (A).

DO: *very very* is highlighted (a double-word combination). Press (3) for *delete 2nd.*

DO: *helpfil* is highlighted. Press (A) for *helpful.*

DO: *feeture* is highlighted. Press (A) for *feature.*

DO: *speeler* is highlighted. The correct choice is *speller*, so press (B).

DO: Notice *ar* is skipped over. We know this word is also misspelled, but there is such a word in the dictionary.

DO: *typeing* is highlighted. Press the letter of the correct word. Now the Speller is finished, because the message *Word count: 21 Press any key to continue* is displayed.

DO: Press (F7) once to exit the Speller.

LOOK UP. Use the **Look Up** option to look up words in the dictionary without moving your cursor to them and choosing the Word option. You can also look up words not even in your document.

DO: Let's do another check on the two misspelled words overlooked by the Speller. Use the *Look Up* option. Press (Ctrl)-(F2) or Tools, Spell. Press (L) *Look Up*. For the **word pattern**, key *speel* and (Enter). Notice there is such a word in the list.

DO: Key *ar* (Enter) for the next word pattern. Again, the word is in the list. Press any key to continue and/or press (F7) several times to exit the Speller.

DO: On your own, go to the words still misspelled, *ar* and *speel*, and edit them using typeover, etc. Be sure all words are correctly spelled, and then use (F7) to save the document as WPKEY5.2. (If you are using two disk drives, replace the Speller diskette with your data diskette before saving.) Clear your screen.

SPELLER PRACTICE. When the Speller highlights a word as being misspelled, you have several options: *1 Skip Once, 2 Skip, 3 Add, 4 Edit, 5 Look Up, 6 Ignore Numbers.* Several of these options are used frequently.

KEY: These words and symbols: *Use (F11) or (Alt)-(F3) to Reveal Codes.*

DO: (Insert the Speller diskette in Drive B if necessary.) Activate the Speller for the page by pressing (Ctrl)-(F2) (P). Notice, the word (F11) is highlighted. This is not in the Speller, but it is correct. You could either select *1 Skip Once, 2 Skip*, or *6 Ignore Numbers.* (If you select *2 Skip*, this word will be skipped every time it occurs in the document, not just this one time.) Press (2) or (6). Do the same for the word (F3). Exit Spell and clear your screen without saving.

Sometimes Spell will highlight a misspelled word and offer similar words that are incorrect or no similar words at all. When this occurs, press *4 Edit*, which activates the cursor so you can correct the error yourself, using another source for the correct spelling if necessary.

DO: On your clean screen key the words *Alldus PageMakker*. (This is a misspelling of a popular software package, Aldus Pagemaker.®) Activate the Speller for the page. *Alldus* is highlighted, and none of the choices are correct. Press (4) Edit. Delete the extra *l* in *Aldus* and then press F7. The speller does not recognize the corrected word, so press 2 *Skip*.

DO: Now *PageMakker* is highlighted, and there are no choices. Press 4 *Edit* and delete the extra *k* in *PageMaker*. Press F7. The speller still does not recognize the word, so press 2 *Skip*. Exit the Speller and clear your screen.

THESAURUS Alt-F1 ⏚ TOOLS, THESAURUS

The **Thesaurus** command is used to look up synonyms (words with a similar meaning) or antonyms (words with opposite meanings). This feature can help you choose precise and colorful words.

You can use the Thesaurus on words you have keyed or to look up words you haven't keyed.

DO: (If running WordPerfect from two disk drives, be sure your data diskette is in Drive B.) Retrieve WPKEY5.2 using Shift-F10. Be sure your cursor is at the top of the document.

DO: (If necessary, remove your data diskette from Drive B and insert the Speller/Thesaurus diskette.) Press Alt-F1 *Thesaurus* or ⏚ Tools, Thesaurus.

Spell, the word your cursor is on, is highlighted. The Thesaurus is looking up synonyms and antonyms for *spell*; they appear below a ruling dividing the screen into two parts, as shown in WP5.3.

FIGURE WP5.3
Using the Thesaurus

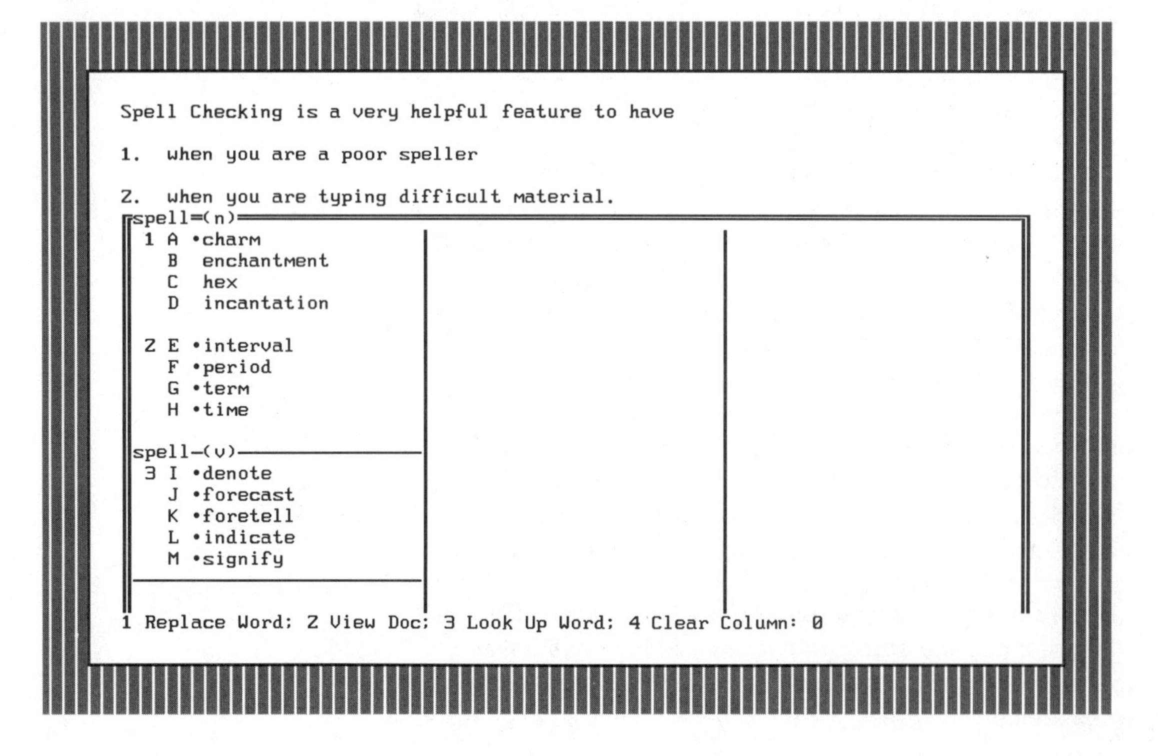

Notice *spell* is both a noun (n) and a verb (v). The first group of nouns are very similar in meaning and include words like *charm* and *enchantment*. The second group of nouns are very similar in meaning and include words like *interval* and *period*. The verbs include *denote* and *forecast*.

DO: Your choices on the message line at the bottom of the screen are: *Replace Word, View Document, Look Up Word,* and *Clear Column.* Press 1 for *Replace Word,* and then press J to replace *spell* with *forecast.*

DO: Move your cursor to the *h* in *helpful.* Press Alt-F1 or Tools, Thesaurus. Notice *helpful* is an adjective (a) only. This time, choose an antonym (opposite); Replace *helpful* with J for *useless.*

DO: Move to *poor.* Activate the Thesaurus. Replace *poor* with the adjective of your choice.

DO: Move to *difficult.* Activate the Thesaurus. The word *obstinate* is in group 7, but perhaps there is another word for *obstinate* that would be better. Press 3 for *Look Up Word.* Key *obstinate.* A new list of synonyms and an antonym for *obstinate* appears. Look up the word *obdurate; recalcitrant* is a synonym. Look up *recalcitrant.* Replace *difficult* with D *unmanageable.*

DO: (Remove the Speller/Thesaurus diskette if necessary and insert your data diskette.) Use F7 to exit WordPerfect, saving the document as WPKEY5.2A.

QUICK QUESTIONS

1. What are the four types of errors the Speller can find?
   a)
   b)
   c)
   d)
2. When using the Speller on a document, how are correct words indicated?
3. When using the Speller on a document, how are incorrect words indicated?
4. Your cursor must be moved to the top of the document when you use the Speller. T or F
5. Use the Speller now to look up the word *wiggle.* What are the words shown that have a similar word pattern?
6. Which Spell option should you select to see how many words your document contains?
7. When using Spell, can you be sure a word is spelled correctly if it is skipped over? Explain.
8. How can you check the spelling of a word not in your document?

9. What should you choose if the Speller finds a misspelled word but has no similar words to show you or shows similar words that are not correct?
10. What feature is very helpful in finding similar or opposite words?

Key the following document and then Spell check and correct any errors. Finally, use the Thesaurus to find and replace at least five different words. Save the document on your disk as WPREV5 and either exit WordPerfect or go on to the Reinforcement Activity with a clean screen.

Everyone needs to be amelierated in many instinces. WordPerfect is a sublyme program that works very ardously to rendar many benefecial atributes to its users.

Not only does WordPerfect offar a comprehenseiv Spell dictionary, but it also proffars a substancial thesaurus with many words to enable one to appear to have an unlimitted lexicon.

Other feetures include a hyphanation dictionery, silhoette feeture, and graphix. All of these toile together to dispense a maestro look to any manuscrept.

Key the following document and then Spell check and correct any errors. Finally, use the Thesaurus to find and replace at least five words to make the summary easier to understand. Save the document on your disk as WPRA5 and either exit WordPerfect or go on to the next section.

MICROCHIPS

Altho formaly designated as intergrated circet, the microchip is called simpley "chip." Although more diminutive than a fingernail, the scant flake of a lackluster, metalic essence called sillicon can garner or process infermation for a multiplicity of chores.

Contemporary chips can be found in video diversions, domicile appliences, and commerce operations. Chips have indubitably changed the world's gagets.

6

CANCEL, PRINT, LIST FILES

OBJECTIVES

- **Cancel** commands.
- **Restore** deleted text.
- **Print** using **Shift F7.**
- **View** a document.
- Observe information on the **List Files** screen.
- **Rename** a file.
- **Look** at a file.
- **Retrieve** using **List Files.**
- **Print** using **List Files.**

CANCEL F1

Since the keyboard is used so frequently in executing WordPerfect commands, a user may press the wrong key. No problem! Press F1, *Cancel*, to stop a command you have started but no longer want. Cancel is also used to recover text that has been deleted or to turn off a block. (Using blocks is practiced in Section 9.)

CANCEL COMMANDS. Use Cancel *instead of* Esc to discontinue commands in WordPerfect. Watch your screen as you practice canceling commands. Start several commands and then press F1 as many times as needed to return to your blank screen.

DO: Press Ctrl-F2 *Spell*, F1 *Cancel.*

DO: Press Alt-F2 *Replace*, N *No* to confirm, F1 *Cancel.*

DO: Press Shift-F8 *Format*, L *Line*, S *lineSpacing*, F1 *Cancel*, F1 *Cancel*, F1 *Cancel.*

RESTORE DELETED TEXT. If you want to reverse a decision you made to delete text, use F1 to **restore** (recover) any one of the last three portions of text you deleted.

KEY: Key the following sentence:

FIGURE WPKEY6.1

```
We will delete part of this sentence
and then restore it.
```

DO: Delete *sentence* (including the space) with the Delete key. Delete *then* (including the space) with the Delete key.

DO: Move your cursor to the *a* in *and.* Press F1 *Cancel.* See WP6.1.

FIGURE WP6.1
Restore Options

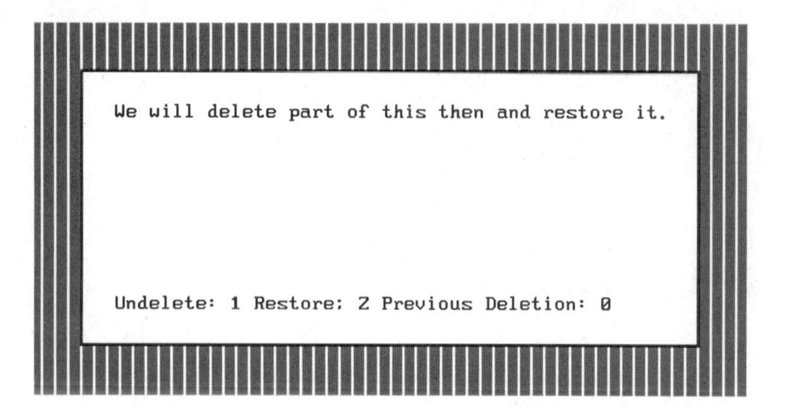

The left Status Line displays a message: *Undelete: 1 Restore; 2 Previous Deletion: 0*

1. If you press 1, the last text deleted will be restored at the cursor position.
2. If you press 2, the second to the last deletion will be restored at the cursor position.
3. If you press ↵Enter, you accept the default of 0 and nothing happens.

The **default** is always the option shown at the end of a message after the colon. Most features give a default choice, the one people tend to use most often. Just press ↵Enter to accept a default.

DO: Press 2 *Previous Deletion* to recover the first text deletion (sentence). Press 1 to *Restore* the deleted text.

DO: Move to the *r* in *restore.* Press F1 *Cancel,* 1 *Restore* to restore the last text deletion.

To get the first of three deletions, press 2 for Previous Deletion twice.

PRINT Shift-F7 FILE, PRINT

Printing, of course, copies a document onto paper. There are two methods of printing in WordPerfect, from screen or from disk. You will print from the screen the sentence you keyed in the previous exercise, WPKey6.1. After you press Shift-F7 *Print,* you will see the options on the Print menu. (See WP6.2.)

FIGURE WP6.2
Print Options

```
Print

     1 - Full Document
     2 - Page
     3 - Document on Disk
     4 - Control Printer
     5 - Multiple Pages
     6 - View Document
     7 - Initialize Printer

Options

     S - Select Printer                     HP DeskJet Plus
     B - Binding Offset                     0"
     N - Number of Copies                   1
     U - Multiple Copies Generated by       WordPerfect
     G - Graphics Quality                   Medium
     T - Text Quality                       Draft

Selection: 0
```

DO: Press Shift-F7 *Print.*

Ordinarily you will use only three or four of the Print options.

- **1 - Full Document.** This will be your choice 99% of the time. It will print the document on the screen, regardless of the number of pages. If it is five pages long, this option will print all five pages.

- **2 - Page.** This will print only the page *on which your cursor is positioned*. If your document is only one page in length, choose either Option **1** or **2**.
- **4 - Control Printer.** If you have printer difficulties of several types, your instructor may have you choose this option. It tells the status of the jobs sent to the printer; it is often used to stop document printing.
- **6 - View Document.** This shows you what the page your cursor is on will look like when it is printed. Use this often to check the document *before* sending it to the printer.

VIEW DOCUMENT.

DO: With the Print menu on your screen, press V *View* to see your document. Press 1 for *100%* to see the document at its actual size or 2 for *200%* to see it at twice its actual size. Press 3 for the *Full-Page* view.

DO: Press F7 *Exit* to return to your document screen.

From within a menu, F1 will usually take you back **one step**, but F7 will usually take you **completely** out of the menu.

The procedure for using the printer varies in each situation. Ask your instructor now for directions on printing your document. Write on the lines below any special directions from your instructor.

PRINT. Send your document, WPKey6.1, to the printer.

DO: Press Shift-F7 *Print*, F *Full Document*.

After printing, the document remains on your screen. Save it on your disk with the file name WPKEY6.1.

DO: Press F7 *Exit*, Y *Yes* save document, WPKEY6.1 ↵Enter N *No* don't exit.

Your screen is clear. Retrieve another document to print.

DO: Press F10 *Retrieve*, WPRA3MO2 ↵Enter.

DO: Press Shift-F7 *Print*, F *Full Document*, to print the full document.

DO: Press F7 N N to clear your screen.

QUICK QUESTIONS

1. List three uses for the Cancel command:
   a)
   b)
   c)
2. If you begin a command you no longer want, what key should you press to cancel it?
3. Should you use Esc to cancel commands in WordPerfect?
4. What is a **default** option?
5. If you have deleted text that you wish you had not, what can you press to restore it?
6. How many sets of deletions can you restore?
7. Which option(s) from the Print menu should you choose if your document is one page in length?
8. Which option(s) from the Print menu should you choose if your document is two pages in length and you want to print the entire document?
9. Which option(s) from the Print menu should you choose if your document is two pages in length and you want to print only page two?
   Where should your cursor be when you do this?
10. What keys are pressed to view your document prior to printing?
11. Should you press F1 or F7 if you want to get completely out of a menu?
12. Should you press F1 or F7 if you want to take one step back in a menu?

LIST FILES F5 FILE, LIST FILES

Because the **List Files** feature displays the names of all the files on your disk, it is a very handy way to retrieve, delete, rename, print, and copy files.

When you press F5 *List Files*, a message appears on the left Status Line: *Dir* followed by the default drive and file path. If this path is correct for your saved documents, press ↵Enter to accept it. If this path is not correct, reset the default: press = followed by the correct drive and path and then press ↵Enter. Ask your instructor exactly what you should do when you press F5 and see the *Dir* prompt. Write it on the line below:

____

DO: Press F5 and follow the directions you wrote on the line above.

A list of all files on your storage disk appears in *alphabetic* order from *left to right*. (See WP6.3.) If you have files listed that were created in other programs, keep in mind that in many cases you can only retrieve documents into WordPerfect that have been created using the WordPerfect program.

FIGURE WP6.3
The List Files Screen

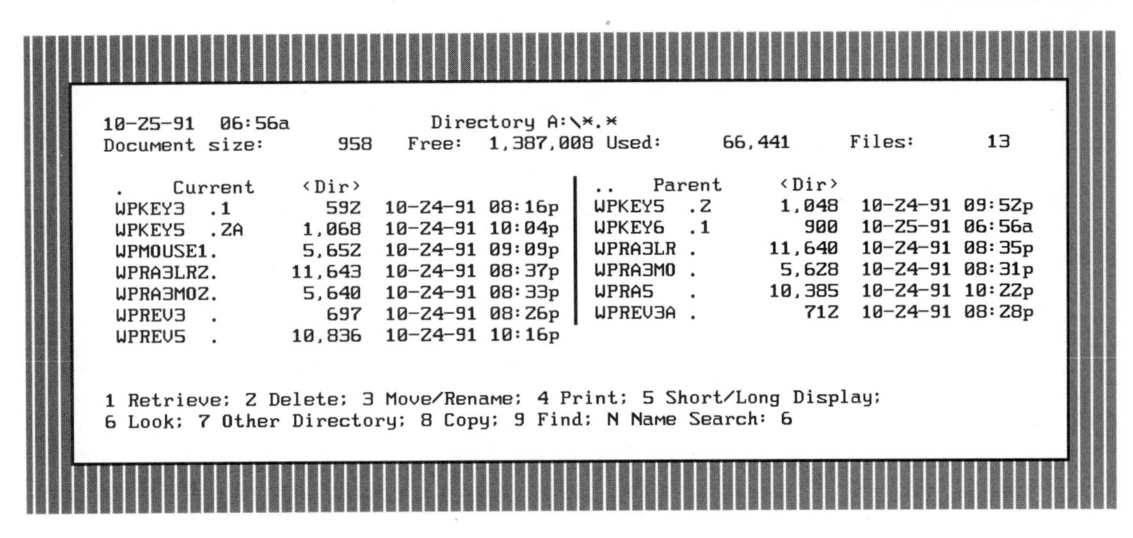

The documents you produced using this book are: WPKEY3.1, WPKEY5.2, WPKEY5.2A, WPKEY6.1, WPMOUSE1, WPRA3LR, WPRA3LR2, WPRA3MO, WPRA3MO2, WPRA5, WPREV3, WPREV3A, WPREV5. Notice that file extensions like .1 and .2A are separated from the file names with periods.

FILE INFORMATION. Each file name is followed by:

1. numbers showing the *size* of the file in *bytes* (characters)
2. the date the file was saved or last updated
3. the time of day the file was saved or last updated

(If you forget what you named a file, sometimes you can remember the date you saved it and locate the file name in that way.)

DO: Looking at the List Files screen, how many bytes in length is the WPREV3 file? ____________ What date and time of day did you save or last edit it? ______________________________

Two lines at the top of the List Files screen give you more information:

1. top line: today's date and time and the name of the directory you are in
2. second line: the size of any document currently *on your text screen*, the amount of disk space available (free) in bytes, the amount of disk space you have used already in bytes, and the number of files you have listed on the List Files screen

The bottom of the screen shows a list of options. (See WP6.3.) To select any option, **highlight** (using the cursor keys) the name of the **file** on which you want to perform the option. Then press the number or letter of the option.

RENAME. You may want to give a different name to a file you have saved.

DO: Still in List Files, use your cursor keys to move to the file WPREV3; this will highlight the file name. Press (M) *Move/Rename.*

The current path/file name appears on the message line. You will **rename** the file NEWNAME. (Don't be concerned that this option is also used for moving a file.)

DO: Carefully cursor over the drive path to where the file name begins. Hold down (Delete) until the file name is erased. Key NEWNAME. Press (↵Enter).

Search the list alphabetically for the file name NEWNAME. Now rename it to its original name.

DO: With NEWNAME highlighted, press (M) *Move/Rename.* Cursor past the path, press (Delete) repeatedly to erase NEWNAME, and key WPREV3 (↵Enter).

LOOK. From List Files you can merely "look" at a file to see if it is the one you actually want. Look at the WPKEY3.1 document:

DO: Use the cursor keys to highlight the name WPKEY3.1. Press (L) *Look* or (↵Enter). (The default is 6, so (↵Enter) accepts 6.)

Caution! *Most new users accidentally press (↵Enter) to retrieve a document once their file name is highlighted in the List Files screen. Pressing (↵Enter) does* ***not*** *retrieve; it only allows looking!*

The screen you see with Look is different from the normal document screen. When using Look you *cannot* edit, or work on the document. In this mode, you can **only** look! (The message line displays: *Look: 1 Next Doc; 2 Previous Doc: 0.* You will not use these options.)

DO: Press (F7) to exit from Look. Remain in List Files.

RETRIEVE. In Section Three, you learned to retrieve a document from disk by using (Shift)-(F10). When you know the exact name of a file, it is quicker to use (Shift)-(F10). When you're not sure about a file's name, use (F5) List Files to highlight the file name and retrieve it. Retrieve the WPREV3 file using List Files.

DO: Highlight the file name WPREV3. Press (R) for *Retrieve.*

The document appears on your screen, and you can edit it in any way.

DO: Clear your screen with (F7) (N) (N).

PRINT. Return to List Files and print directly from your disk. Be sure your printer is ready to accept your work.

DO: Press (F5) *List Files*, check the path in the left corner of the Status Line, and press (←Enter) when it is correct. Highlight WPKEY3.1 and press (P) *Print*.

You will get a message: *Page(s): (All)*. Pressing (←Enter) prints all; keying in certain page numbers allows you to print just portions of a long document.

DO: Press (←Enter) to accept *All*. When you return to the List Files screen, press (F1) to return to your working screen.

DO: If you have time to work, go on to the Review Exercise; if your time to work is at an end, exit WordPerfect with (F7) (N) (Y).

QUICK QUESTIONS

1. Should you retrieve using (F5) files created in other programs (like graphics or databases)?
2. In what order are file names listed in List Files?
3. What three types of information follows each file name and extension on the List Files screen?
4. When you are in List Files, what must you do first so you can perform an option on a particular document?
5. What can you do if you accidentally key the wrong file name for one of your documents when you save it?
6. What is the name of the List Files option that allows you to examine a document to see if it is the one you want?
7. List three ways to exit from the Look option:
8. Name two ways to retrieve a document.
9. List two ways to print a document.

Key the following text and then complete the actions listed below the text.

THE LIST FILES FEATURE

The List Files feature allows the WordPerfect user to do many convenient and handy functions. Although used most frequently for retrieving documents, List Files is also often used for printing from disk.

Other common tasks that can be accomplished with List Files include renaming and deleting files. In addition, the ability to "look" at a disk file can be very helpful. An experienced person can even copy files and search for the file that contains a particular word.

1. Print the document using (Shift)-(F7).
2. Edit the document by using your cursor keys to move around to delete the words *WordPerfect* and *and handy*.
3. Move to the proper place and restore *WordPerfect.*
4. Use (F7) to save the file with the name REVIEW6.
5. From List Files, rename the REVIEW6 file to WPREV6, replacing the original.
6. Print the document from List Files.
7. Press (F7) to exit the List Files screen. Either exit WordPerfect or continue to the Reinforcement Activities.

ACTIVITY A - MEMO

Key the following memo. Press (Tab) after the colons in the headings. Use Caps Lock, Bold, and Underline as shown.

MEMORANDUM

TO: (Tab) (Tab) Sally Moore, Information Systems Manager

FROM: (Tab) Nancy Alison, Vice President

DATE: (Tab) (Use current date)

SUBJ: (Tab) WordPerfect Instruction

I would like to meet with you on **Wednesday** to finalize plans for the WordPerfect training sessions for the clerical staff.

<u>Please bring the following materials to the meeting</u>:

1. topics to be covered and the dates for each

2. a copy of the training materials

3. a list of employees who have requested the training

I have completed a rental agreement with COMPUTERIZED SYSTEMS, INC. for ten net-worked microcomputers which will be delivered the day before the training sessions begin. That should give you an opportunity to set up your instructional plan and any other computer requirements you have prior to the actual training date.

After saving the memo as WPRA6MO, retrieve it and edit it:

1. Delete item three entirely. Delete *and any other computer requirements you have.*
2. Use View Document, (Shift)-(F7), to see that item three has been deleted.
3. Restore item three at the appropriate place.
4. Save the document, replacing the first WPRA6MO.
5. From List Files, rename the document MOOREMO and then print it and turn it in. Exit from List Files. Exit WordPerfect or continue to the next activity.

ACTIVITY B - LETTER

Key the following letter. Use Caps Lock, Bold, and Underline as shown. Spell check.

(Current date)

Mr. Alonzo Flowers
1242 Robson #20-B
Carlsbad, CA 92008

Dear Mr. Flowers

Thank you for your inquiry about our <u>lazer printer cartrige</u>. Our EZ-CARTRIGE can be used with any lazer printer, and it retales for only $99.95.

The EZ-CARTRIGE gives you not only the clearest, finest printing available, but it includes <u>25 different typefaces</u>! This is a product you just can't beat! And we are sure, Mr. Flowers, that you won't pass up this fantastic opportunity.

Just return the enclosed order card along with a check or charge card number and drop in the nearest mailbox. We will send you the EZ-CARTRIGE by return mail. We know you will be very happy with your new purchase. The cartrige will make your documents look very <u>professional</u>!

Yours truly

Donald Frump
President

1. Use F7 to save the letter as WPRA6LR.
2. Retrieve WPRA6LR using List Files.
3. Delete the sentence that begins *And we are sure, Mr. Flowers...*
4. Delete the sentence that begins *We know you will be very happy...*
5. Restore the sentence that began *And we are sure...* to its original position.
6. Use F7 to resave the edited file, replacing the original WPRA6LR.
7. Rename the file FLOWERS.LTR and then print it from List Files. Exit List Files. Then exit WordPerfect or go on to the next section.

7

MOVEMENT, LINE SPACE, CENTER, JUSTIFY

OBJECTIVES

- Use **cursor movement keystrokes.**
- Know the importance of **cursor position** when formatting.
- Set **line spacing.**
- **Center** a line.
- Set left, center, right and full **justification.**
- **Save** using F10.

CURSOR MOVEMENT

Up to this point your documents have been small, and it has been easy to move through the document with the four cursor keys. With longer documents, however, you will want quicker ways of moving from one place to another. There are at least 20 "shortcut" cursor movement keystrokes; listed below are some of the best to use.

KEYSTROKES	MOVEMENT
Home Home ↓	to bottom of document
Home Home ↑	to top of document after codes
Home Home Home ↑	to top of document in front of codes
Home Home ←	to left of the typing line
End	to right of the typing line
Ctrl-← or Ctrl-→	one word
Ctrl-Home *page #*	go to the specified page
- **on numeric pad**	up one screenful at a time
+ **on numeric pad**	down one screenful at a time

DO: Retrieve with Shift-F10 the document on your disk called WPREV3. (A document always retrieves with the cursor at the top.)

DO: Press Home Home ↓ to go to the bottom.

DO: Press Home Home ↑ to return to the top. This returns you to the first word in a document after any beginning codes.

DO: Hold Ctrl while you press →. Do this several times to "jump" one word at a time to the right.

DO: Press Home Home ← to return to the first character at the left of the current typing line. To return to the left in front of any codes, use (Home) (Home) (Home) (←).

DO: Press (End) to move to the right of the typing line.

DO: Do some more practice with the cursor movement shortcuts.

LINE SPACING (Shift)-(F8) (L) (S) ↵ LAYOUT, LINE, LINE SPACING

Your previously keyed documents have been single spaced, the default line spacing for WordPerfect. You can change the spacing to double, triple, or a fraction of those, such as 1.5, 2.33, 3.1, etc. **The *cursor position* is critical when changing line spacing, as well as other types of formatting.** Formatting commands put a format "code" at the cursor position, and the format is in effect *from that position forward.*

The **Line Spacing** command is located in the **Format** menu, option *1-Line*. (See WP7.1.)

Use the Line Spacing command to change a document from single spacing to 2.5 spacing.

DO: Use the WPREV3 file already on your screen. Press (Home) (Home) (↑) to return to the top of the document. Press (Shift)-(F8) *Format*, (L) *Line*, (S) *Line Spacing*

When you choose spacing, your cursor moves to the current line spacing number. Key right over that with the number you desire for spacing.

DO: Key 2.5 (↵Enter). Press (F7) to exit from the Format menu.

FIGURE WP7.1
The Line Format Menu

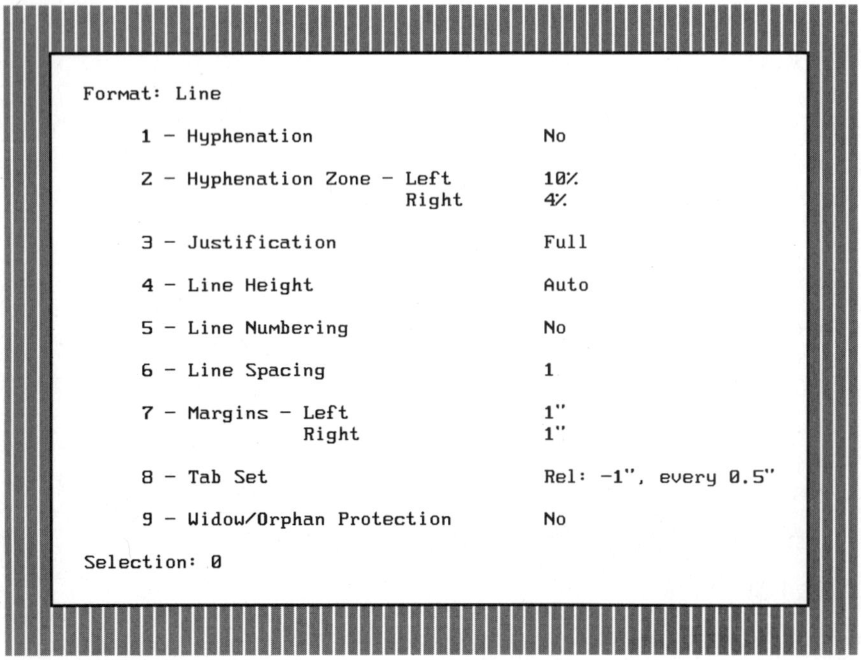

```
Format: Line

     1 - Hyphenation                        No

     2 - Hyphenation Zone - Left            10%
                            Right           4%

     3 - Justification                      Full

     4 - Line Height                        Auto

     5 - Line Numbering                     No

     6 - Line Spacing                       1

     7 - Margins - Left                     1"
                   Right                    1"

     8 - Tab Set                            Rel: -1", every 0.5"

     9 - Widow/Orphan Protection            No

Selection: 0
```

Notice your document appears with the new line spacing.

DO: Clear your screen (do not save). Retrieve the WPREV3 file again.

This time, we will see what happens if your cursor is not at the top of the document when you use a format command.

DO: Move your cursor to the first letter in the third line. Change the line spacing *from that position forward* to double spacing.

DO: Press Shift-F8 *Format*, L *Line*, S *Line Spacing*. Key 2 for double spacing ↵Enter. Press F7 to exit the menu.

The double spacing is in effect from where your cursor was when you issued the command.

DO: Press F11 or Alt-F3 *Reveal Codes*. Find the [Ln Spacing:2] code. Line spacing of 2, or double spacing, is in effect from the code's position.

DO: Place your cursor on the [Ln Spacing:2] code. Your cursor is on it when the code changes color or shade. Press Delete. When the code is gone, the line spacing returns to its previous setting.

DO: Clear your screen (do not save). When you clear your screen, formatting codes such as line spacing are cleared also; **however, formatting codes stay with the document in which they were created if it is saved on disk.**

QUICK QUESTIONS

1. What is pressed to move to the top of the document (in front of all codes)?
2. What is pressed to move to the bottom of the document?
3. What is pressed to move to the right of the line you are on?
4. What is pressed to move to the left of the line you are on, before any codes?
5. Use the Format Line commands, Shift-F8, L. Use Help for Line Spacing. What is Line Spacing?
6. Line Spacing is an option in which main command menu?
7. If you want an entire document to be triple spaced, where should your cursor be when you select Line Spacing?

CENTER Shift-F6 LAYOUT, ALIGN, CENTER

To center a single line such as a heading with the **Center** command, press Shift-F6, key the line, and press ↵Enter.

DO: Press Shift-F6 *Center*. Your cursor jumps to the middle of the screen.

KEY: THIS LINE IS CENTERED.

DO: Press ↵Enter. (Centering ends when you press Enter). Space down by pressing ↵Enter ↵Enter. Press Shift-F6 to start Center again.

KEY: THIS LINE IS LONGER, BUT IT IS STILL CENTERED ON THE PAGE.

DO: Press ↵Enter. Are both lines centered? Clear your screen. (Do not save).

PREPARING A COMPLETE DOCUMENT. Throughout this section, you will create the document that you see on page WP53, WPCheck7.1. Notice that the document is double spaced, and the heading is centered. You will learn how to *justify* the paragraphs to achieve their unusual appearance.

DO: Press (Shift)-(F8) *Format,* (L) *Line,* (S) *Line Spacing,* (2) (↵Enter) to set double spacing. Press (F7) to exit the menu. (Press Reveal Codes, (Alt)-(F3) or (F11), to see that you have entered a Line Spacing code for double spacing. Press (Alt)-(F3) or (F11) again to exit the Reveal Codes.)

DO: Press (Shift)-(F6) *Center* and key this line: EXAMPLES OF DIFFERENT TYPES OF JUSTIFICATION and then press (↵Enter) (↵Enter) (↵Enter) for two blank lines after the heading. (Keep this on your screen for additional keying.)

JUSTIFICATION (Shift)-(F8) (L) (J) LAYOUT, JUSTIFY

Justification is used to align a *group* of text lines (not just one line) at the left or right margins, at both margins, or centered between the margins.

The Help feature will give you more information on the four Justification options available: Left, Center, Right, and Full.

DO: Press (Shift)-(F8) *Format,* (L) *Line,* (J) *Justification.*

DO: Press (F3) *Help,* read the meaning of the four options, and record the definitions on the lines below. Finally, press (↵Enter) to exit Help.

Left Justification ____________________

____

Right Justification ____________________

____

Center Justification ____________________

____

Full Justification ____________________

____

DO: Add to the heading already keyed on your screen the following four paragraphs.

LEFT JUSTIFICATION.

DO: From the **Format: Line** menu with the **Justification** types at the bottom of the screen, press (L) *Left.* Press (F7) to exit the Line Format menu.

KEY: Key the text in the following paragraph (WPKey7.1).

FIGURE WPKEY7.1

This text is left justified. Left justified text is aligned on the left margin, but not on the right. This makes the right margin look jagged, but some people prefer this style.

DO: Press (↵Enter) to move the cursor to a new line.

CENTER JUSTIFICATION.

DO: Press (Shift)-(F8) *Format*, (L) *Line*, (J) *Justification*, (C) *Center*. Press (F7) to exit the Line Format menu.

KEY: Key the text in the following paragraph (WPKey7.2). Press (↵Enter) at the end of each *short* line.

FIGURE WPKEY7.2

This demonstrates how text can be centered between
the margins.
It is frequently used for lists, such as menus:
Fresh, Tender Sirloin Steaks
$9.98

DO: Press (↵Enter) to move the cursor to a new line.

RIGHT JUSTIFICATION.

DO: Press (Shift)-(F8) *Format*, (L) *Line*, (J) *Justification*, (R) *Right*. Press (F7) to exit the Line Format menu.

KEY: Key the text in the following paragraph (WPKey7.3). Press (↵Enter) only at the end of the paragraph and at the end of the last three *short* lines.

FIGURE WPKEY7.3

Text that is justified on the right is probably the least used of the different types. It is not very useful for paragraphs, but could be interesting for lists.
Jean Smith
5344 West Tenth Street
Indianapolis, IN 46214

SCROLLING. *Notice* the top of your document is no longer visible. Because your screen is only large enough to display about 24 lines, screen movement or *scrolling* takes place in long or wide documents so you can see what you are currently keying.

DO: Press (Enter) to move the cursor to a new line.

FULL JUSTIFICATION.

DO: Press (Shift)-(F8) *Format*, (L) *Line*, (J) *Justification*, (F) *Full*. Press (F7) to exit the Line Format menu.

KEY: Key the text in Paragraph WPKey7.4. **Full Justified text will not appear justified on the screen**; it is justified only when printed or on the View Document screen.

FLUSH RIGHT. To place a single short line rather than a paragraph at the right margin, use Flush Right (Alt)-(F6).

DO: Press (Enter). Press (Alt)-(F6) *Flush Right*. Press underline and then key your name. End underline.

FIGURE WPKEY7.4

shift + F8 → 1.3.4.

```
Text that has full justification will not appear even at
the right margin on the screen, but it will be justified
on both the left and right when it is printed. You will
print this document soon, so look for this document to
be justified at the left and the right.
```

SAVE (F10) FILE, SAVE

You already know how to save your document and clear your screen by using (F7) *Exit*. Sometimes, however, you will want to save your document and keep it on your screen for additional work by using the **Save** command. Saving in this way at short intervals can keep you from losing all of your work in case of electrical failure, accidentally clearing your screen, or other catastrophes.

To save using F10, follow these steps:

1. Press (F10) *Save*.
2. Key the path and file name and press (Enter).
3. If you get the question *Replace? No(Yes)*, key (Y) to replace the previous version of the document with the current version; key (N) and give the new version a different name if you want to keep the previous version.

DO: Press (F10) *Save*. Key the path if necessary and the file name WPKEY7.4 (Enter). The document remains on the screen, so you may continue working on it.

DO: Press (Shift)-(F7) *Print*, (F) *Full* to print the document. (Check your work with WPCheck7.1.)

DO: Clear your screen (the document is already saved).

FIGURE WPCHECK7.1

EXAMPLES OF DIFFERENT TYPES OF JUSTIFICATION

This text is left justified. Left justified text is aligned on the left margin, but not on the right. This makes the right margin look jagged, but some people prefer this style.

This demonstrates how text can be centered between the margins.It is frequently used for lists, such as menus:

Fresh, Tender Sirloin Steaks

$9.98

Text that is justified on the right is probably the least used of the different types. It is not very useful for paragraphs, but could be interesting for lists.

Jean Smith

5344 West Tenth Street

Indianapolis, IN 46214

Text that has full justification will not appear even at the right margin on the screen, but it will be justified on both the left and right when it is printed. You will print this document soon, so look for this document to be justified at the left and the right.

Your Name my name.

Alt +F6 = Full right

QUICK QUESTIONS

1. If you want to center a line, should you key it before or after using the Center command?
2. What key is pressed after the centered line is keyed?
3. Which of the four types of Justification will align text at the right margin only?

4. Which of the four types of Justification will align text at the right and left margins?
5. Which of the four types of Justification is often used for restaurant menus?
6. Justification is located in which main command menu?
7. What word refers to the movement of the text on the screen when you key long or wide documents?
8. About how many lines of text are visible on your screen at one time?
9. Which feature can be used to place a single short line at the right margin?
10. Does full justification look justified at both right and left margins on the editing screen?
11. What command is used to save a document and leave it on the screen so it can be completed?

Key the following short report. It should be double spaced. The first paragraph is left justified, the second is center justified, the third one is left justified, and the last four lines are right justified. Press ↵Enter at the end of each short right-justified line. Print the report and save as WPREV7.

WORDPERFECT'S POPULARITY

Although WordPerfect was originally written to be a popular word processing program for the law profession, its ease of use and wealth of advanced features has made it the program of choice for people in many professions.

W. E. "Pete" Peterson, Executive Vice President,
WordPerfect Corporation, comments:
"What makes WordPerfect attractive is that it gets
out of your way. It's like a
well-mannered house guest who is kind enough
not to disrupt your life or the way you do things."

WordPerfect's devotees have many reasons for using the program.

Their favorite features of the program include the following:

a clear typing screen uncluttered by menus or codes

an ever-increasing number of new features

support for a large number of printers

free and courteous customer support

ACTIVITY A - SUMMARY

Key the following short book summary. Use Flush Right, Alt-F6, for the right- justified lines. The body should be double spaced and left justified. Press Tab to indent the paragraphs. Print the report and save as WPRA7RPA.

WORDPERFECT DESKTOP PUBLISHING

Alice Lee-Williams

1991

Classy Publications, Inc.

This authoritative and very complete book covers not only using **WordPerfect** to key text in various styles and graphics techniques, but it also includes rules for basic publishing design.

Peppered throughout the edition are creative examples of newsletters, flyers, advertisements, magazine articles, catalog pages, stationery, and many other publications.

Besides a wealth of information on software applications and tips, the author clearly describes hardware suitable for desktop publishing. This is a tremendous help to the novice contemplating purchase of a new system.

I highly recommend this technical, yet easily understood and humorous book, to anyone using **WordPerfect** for desktop publishing on IBM or compatible computers.

ACTIVITY B - REPORT

Key the following report. Flush right, (Alt)-(F6), your name and the name of your class. Then use double spacing and full justification for the body. Press the (Tab) key to indent the paragraphs.

Your Name

The Name of Your Class

COMMUNICATION SKILLS

Communication, according to Webster's dictionary, is "a process by which information is exchanged between individuals through a common system of symbols, signs, or behavior."

Although we sometimes make contact with another person through facial expressions or other body signs, more frequently we use writing and speaking skills to communicate. When others communicate with us, we use reading and listening skills.

Some people assume that if a person is trained to read and write he or she will automatically develop competent speaking and listening skills. This is a fallacy.

Oral communication does not give us an opportunity to reread or rewrite for clarity. We have only a brief, timely opportunity to convey or receive the intended message.

1. **Print the document and use (F10) to save it as WPRA7RPB.**
2. **Edit the document to be left justified and single spaced.**
3. **Print the edited document and save it as WPRA7RPB.2**

Clerical Training Program

MEASUREMENT, MARGIN, TAB, TAB SET

OBJECTIVES

- Compare the screen to a sheet of paper.
- Compare **measurements** of a sheet of paper.
- Set **margins** and use **margin release** and **hang indent.**
- Use **tab, left indent**, and **double indent.**
- **Clear** and **set tabs.**
- Use **left** and **decimal** tabs.

THE SCREEN AS A SHEET OF PAPER

To format documents, it is necessary to understand the dimensions of a sheet of paper and how this relates to your computer screen.

WordPerfect, like many popular word processing programs, uses measurements in inches because of the widespread use of printers that handle proportional typefaces. With proportional typefaces, characters vary in size. For example, wide letters like "M" take more space than narrow letters like "I." The different sizes of letters can be measured by determining how wide they are in inches or portions of an inch.

The illustration on the next page (WP8.1) shows the size of a standard sheet of paper, 8.5 inches wide by 11 inches tall. Inside the sheet of paper are the **default** margins for WordPerfect. As you can see, the default margins are 1 inch on all sides—the top, bottom, left, and right. If you just begin keying on a clean screen, as you have been doing, you use the default margins. The margins, however, can be set at any size your printer can manage.

Think of your screen as a sheet of paper; use the *Status Line* to see where each character will appear when you print. When your screen is blank, the status line shows that your cursor is on *Ln 1"* (1 inch top margin) and *Pos 1"* (1 inch left margin). As you key, the *Ln* and *Pos* indicators change to show the cursor position.

DO: With a blank screen, press (Enter) six times. What line are you on according to the Status Line? ____________

DO: Now use the Center command, (Shift)-(F6). On what position is the cursor according to the Status Line? ____________

DO: Press (↵Enter) six more times. What line and position are you on?
Line ______________ Position ______________

FIGURE WP8.1

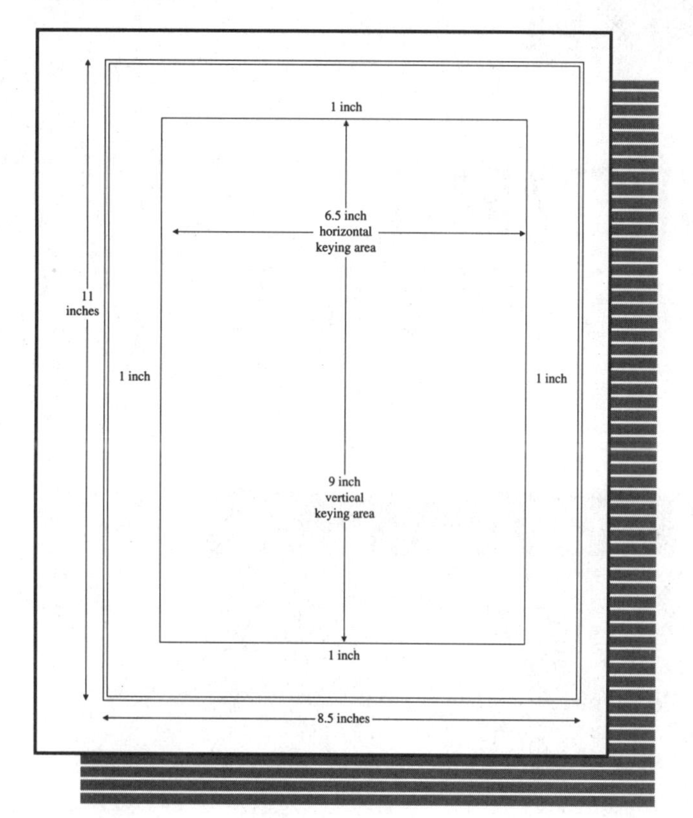

MARGINS (Shift)-(F8) (L) (M) ↵ LAYOUT

You may adjust any of the margins (top, bottom, left, right) to another size when desired by accessing the appropriate Format command option.

LEFT AND RIGHT MARGINS. The left and right margins may be changed by accessing the Format menu, option *1-Line*. (See WP8.2.)

Use the Format command to change both the left and right margins from 1 inch to 2 inches:

DO: Clear your screen. Press (Shift)-(F8) *Format*, (L) *Line*, (M) *Margins*. Key (2) (↵Enter) for the left margin. Key (2) (↵Enter) for the right margin. Press (F7) to exit.

DO: What is your cursor position? ______________

TOP AND BOTTOM MARGINS. The top and bottom margins may be changed by accessing the Format menu, option *2-Page*. (See WP8.2).

FIGURE WP8.2
The Format Menu

```
Format

     1 - Line
              Hyphenation                    Line Spacing
              Justification                  Margins Left/Right
              Line Height                    Tab Set
              Line Numbering                 Widow/Orphan Protection

     2 - Page
              Center Page (top to bottom)    Page Numbering
              Force Odd/Even Page            Paper Size/Type
              Headers and Footers            Suppress
              Margins Top/Bottom

     3 - Document
              Display Pitch                  Redline Method
              Initial Codes/Font             Summary

     4 - Other
              Advance                        Overstrike
              Conditional End of Page        Printer Functions
              Decimal Characters             Underline Spaces/Tabs
              Language                       Border Options

Selection: 0
```

Use the Format command to change the top margin from the default of 1 inch to 2.5 inches:

DO: Press (Shift)-(F8) *Format*, (P) *Page*, (M) *Margins*. Key 2.5 (↵Enter) for the top margin, press (↵Enter) for 1-inch bottom margin, and then press (F7) to exit.

DO: On what line is your cursor now? ____________

DO: Without moving your cursor, retrieve the WPREV3A file from your disk. Print it and then look at the margins. Are they larger than usual? Use a ruler to see if they are correct: 2 inches for each side and 2.5 inches for the top. Keep the document on your screen.

MARGIN RELEASE (Shift)-(Tab) LAYOUT, ALIGN, MARGIN REL

Margin Release is used to key into the left margin or to move already-keyed text into the left margin. Use Margin Release by pressing (Shift)-(Tab). The cursor or line will move left into the margin to a Tab Set, usually .5 inches, *each* time you press (Shift)-(Tab).

DO: With your cursor on the *T* at the beginning of the paragraph, press (Shift)-(Tab) twice. How many inches into the left margin is the line now? ____________

DO: Clear your screen.

Margin Release is often used with the Left Indent command, (F4), to **hang indent** paragraphs. As you can see in WPKEY8.1, when paragraphs are hang indented, all lines except the first are indented. Press (F4) (Shift)-(Tab) at the beginning of a paragraph to hang indent.

DO: Change both the right and left margins to 1.5 inches.

KEY: Key the following document (WPKey8.1), pressing (F4) (Shift)-(Tab) at the beginning of each paragraph. (Use Wordwrap, of course.)

FIGURE WPKEY8.1

```
This type of paragraph, where the first line is at
   the left and the others are indented, is called
   hanging indent.

Sometimes this is used instead of the traditional
   five-space paragraph indention. It gives a docu-
   ment a little variety.
```

DO: Clear the screen.

QUICK QUESTIONS

1. Why does WordPerfect 5.1 use measurements in inches?
2. What is the size of a standard sheet of paper?
3. What are the default margins for WordPerfect?
4. Where should you look to see the current line and cursor position?

5. If you are keying a word on Ln 5" according to the Status Line, how far will that word be from the top of the paper when it is printed?
6. If the Status Line says you are on Pos 3.3" when you begin keying a word, how far will that word be from the left edge of the paper when it is printed?
7. When using default margins, how wide is the *horizontal* keying area?
8. When using default margins, how tall is the *vertical* keying area?
9. After choosing the Format command, what option is selected to change the size of the left and/or right margins?
10. After choosing the Format command, what option is selected to change the size of the top and/or bottom margins?
11. What keys are pressed to hang indent a paragraph?

TAB (Tab)

Press the Tab key in WordPerfect to move to the next tab position, every .5 spaces when using default tab settings. Use Tab to indent the first line of a paragraph, the traditional means of indenting.

KEY: On a clear screen, key the following document (WPKey8.2), pressing (Tab) to indent each paragraph. Keep the document on your screen.

FIGURE WPKEY8.2

```
     Press Tab to indent paragraphs in reports of different
kinds and for business letters that have indented
paragraphs.

     If a report is double spaced, it will usually have
indented paragraphs so it is apparent where each
paragraph begins.

     Many business letters today do not have indented
paragraphs because pressing Tab to indent takes more time
than just typing at the left margin.
```

LEFT INDENT (F4) ⇆ LAYOUT, ALIGN, INDENT (→)

Left Indent is used to indent **all** lines of a paragraph from the left margin. Each time (F4) is pressed, it will indent .5 inches from the left (using default tab settings). Left Indent will remain in effect until you press Enter. Press (F4) after keying the period following the number in listings made up of items that are more than one line in length. (Left Indent is also used with Margin Release to hang indent a paragraph, as you did earlier in this section.)

KEY: Enter twice and add the following paragraphs (WPKey8.3) to your screen, pressing (F4) after the period following each number. Enter only after the period at the end of each item.

FIGURE WPKEY8.3

1. Left Indent is almost always used when keying numbered copy.

2. If you don't use (F4) after keying a number, the second line of an item and all others after it will go at the left margin under the number.

3. You can see that using Left Indent makes these items more attractive and easier to read.

DO: Print the document and save it on your disk as WPKEY8.3. Clear your screen.

DOUBLE INDENT (Shift)-(F4) LAYOUT, ALIGN, INDENT (→)(←)

Double Indent is used to indent *all* lines of a paragraph from *both* margins. (This feature is also called a Full Paragraph Indent.) Each time (Shift)-(F4) is pressed, it will indent an additional .5 inches from each margin.

KEY: Set the linespacing to 2 (double spacing). Key the following paragraph (WPKey8.4) *three* times on the same page. The first time, key it as you see it. The second time, press (Shift)-(F4) once before keying it. The third time, press (Shift)-(F4) *twice* before keying it.

FIGURE WPKEY8.4

Double Indent, or Full Paragraph Indent, is probably used most often in technical reports. Text that is indented from both margins calls attention to itself because it stands out from the rest of the text.

DO: Print the document. Save it as WPKEY8.4. Clear your screen.

TAB SET (Shift)-(F8) (L) (T) LAYOUT, LINE, TAB SET

For the practice exercises with Tab, Left Indent, and Double Indent, you used the default Tab Settings, every .5 inches. You can, however, set tabs where you desire with the **Tab Set** command.

DO: Press (Shift)-(F8) *Format,* (L) *Line,* (T) *Tab Set* to see the Tab Line. (See WP8.3.)

FIGURE WP8.3
The Tab Line

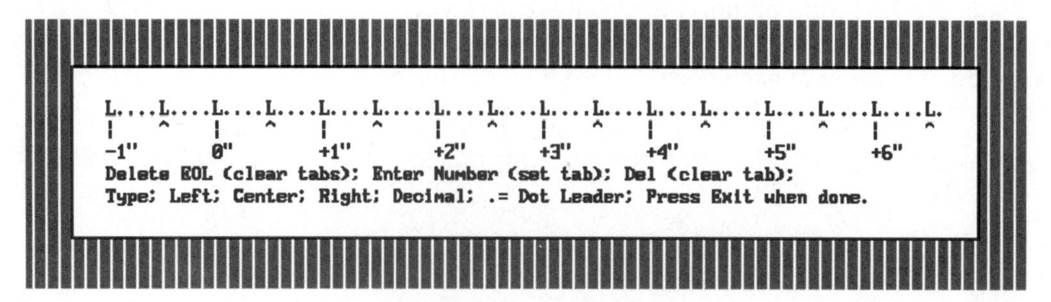

Notice, the **Tab Line** is like a ruler. Each *L* on the Tab Line is a *left* tab stop. It is called a left tab stop because characters begin at this tab position and print to the right.

DO: Your cursor is at position 0 inch. **The left margin is indicated by 0 inches on the Tab Line.** Find tab stop 1 inch. Find tab stop .5 inches, the first tab stop to the right of the left margin. (It looks like ^ and is between 0 inches and +1 inch.)

DO: Press Home Home ← so your cursor goes to the far left of the Tab Line. Find tab stop –1 inch and –.5 inch in the left margin. When you press Margin Release, these are the tab stops that are used; for that reason, you usually would not want to clear them.

CLEAR TABS Ctrl-End. The default tab stops can be changed. Before setting tabs, clear *all* of the current ones using Ctrl-End. To just clear some, cursor to them and press Delete.

DO: To clear *all* tabs, beginning at the left margin, place your cursor on the tab at the 0 inch position. Hold Ctrl while you press End. (See WP8.4.)

FIGURE WP8.4
Tabs Cleared From the Tab Line

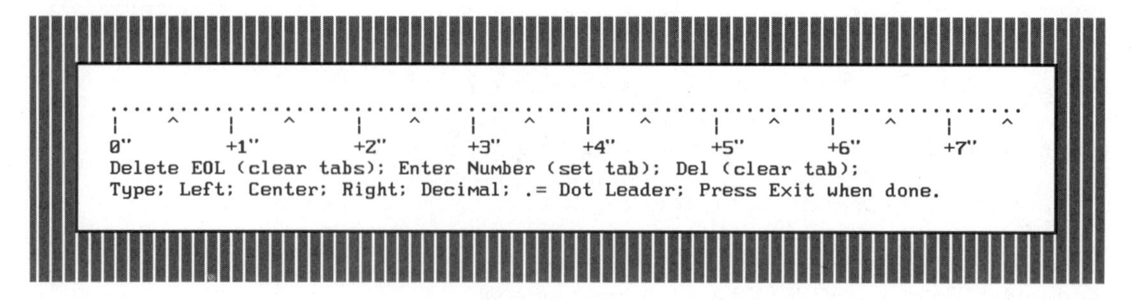

SET TABS. After tabs are cleared, key the position (in inches) from the left margin where you want the tab set.

DO: Set two tab stops, 1 inch and 2.5 inches from the left margin. (These tab stop positions are 2 inches and 3.5 inches from the left edge of the paper and will be shown as such on the Status Line). Key 1 and press ↵Enter. Key 2 . 5 and press ↵Enter. Press F7 to exit from the Tab Line.

KEY: Key the two columns shown in WPKey8.5. Press (Tab) and key **Column 1**. Press (Tab), key **Column 2**, and press (↵Enter). Follow this sequence, pressing (Tab) before each column and (↵Enter) at the end of each line. You must key each line *horizontally* when using tabs. Keep the document on your screen.

FIGURE WPKEY8.5

```
Column 1     Column 2
Line 2       Line 2
Line 3       Line 3
Line 4       Line 4
Line 5       Line 5
Line 6       Line 6
```

The tabs you used for WPKey 8.5 are Left Tabs, shown on the tab line with L's. Left Tabs align data on the left in each column. WordPerfect has several other types of tabs; one of these is the Decimal Tab.

DECIMAL TABS. A common type of business document is a table of figures with varying numbers of digits, including decimals. You can use Decimal Tabs to align the columns at the decimal points instead of aligning all figures on the left.

DO: Go to the end of the document: (Home) (Home) (↓). Press (↵Enter) twice.

DO: First, erase all tabs, beginning at position 0 inch on the Tab Line. To do this, press (Shift)-(F8) *Format*, (L) *Line*, (T) *Tab Set*, (Ctrl)-(End). Next, set tabs where the *decimals* will appear in the figures, 1 inch and 3 inches from the left margin (shown as positions 2 inches and 4 inches on the Status Line). Press (1) for one inch (↵Enter), (3) for three inches (↵Enter).

DO: Now move your cursor to each *L* and key a *D* right over it. ("D" is for "decimal" tab.) Press (F7) twice to exit and return to your keying screen.

KEY: Key the following table (WPKey8.6) in the same manner you did the previous exercise. Press (Tab) before each column including the first. Notice that when you press Tab, the lower left corner of your screen displays the message, *Align Character=*. This means that WordPerfect will align the numbers on the decimal point. (It can align on other symbols, such as ¢, %, $, #, etc.) Press (↵Enter) at the end of each line.

DO: Print the document and save it on your disk as WPKEY8.6. Clear your screen.

DO: Print the document and save it on your disk as WPKEY8.6. Clear your screen.

FIGURE WPKEY8.6

33.46	4.77
779.21	42.70
4.99	17.85
22.51	.99
634.44	7,922.32
10,225.89	65.61

QUICK QUESTIONS

1. What is used to indent the first line of paragraphs?
2. What type of tab is used to indent **all** lines of a paragraph from the *left* margin?

   What is pressed to get this type of tab?
3. What type of tab is used to indent **all** lines of a paragraph from *both* margins?

   What is pressed to get this type of tab?
4. How far apart are the default tabs?
5. What is the name of the ruler that shows where tabs are set?
6. How is the left margin shown on the tab line?
7. What is shown on the tab line to indicate left tabs?
8. On the tab line, what is the meaning of a negative number in relation to the left margin?
9. What keys are pressed to clear all tabs?
10. How do you clear just some tabs?
11. What do you key to set tabs at your desired locations?
12. What key is pressed to end an entry at one tab setting and move to the next tab setting on the line?
13. What is pressed at the end of each line of columns?
14. What is keyed over the "L" in left tabs to make them decimal tabs?
15. What does "Align Character" mean?

Key the document shown below, WPRev8. Use the tips given. (The position of the words on your screen may vary from the ones in the figure.)

1. Leave the left margin at 1 inch, but set the right margin at .5 inches.
2. Set the top margin at 2 inches.
3. Use any features necessary to make your document look like the one in WPRev8.
4. Read each paragraph in WPRev8 before keying it, and then complete the actions described to key it correctly. For example, the fifth paragraph tells you where to set tabs for the table that follows it.
5. When the document is complete, print it and save it as WPREV8.

FIGURE WPREV8

SETTING AND USING TABS

This document is a rather strange looking one, but its purpose is to illustrate several features. An attractive document would never have so many different formats on one page!

Use F4 Shift-Tab when beginning this paragraph to make it a hanging indent paragraph. This will indent all lines of the paragraph .5 inch except the first one.

Press Shift-F4 here so this paragraph will be indented from **both** margins.

Press Shift-F4 twice here so this paragraph will be indented twice, or one inch from **both** margins.

Key the following steps and then use them to set the tabs for the columns that follow:

1. Go to the tab line and erase all tabs.
2. Set new left tabs 1.5 inches and 3.5 inches from the left margin. Key each number followed by Enter.
3. "L"s will appear on the tab line. Exit the tab line and you will be ready to press Tab and key the first item.

<u>Entree</u>	<u>Side Dish</u>
pizza	salad
steak	mixed vegetables
coney	french fries
whitefish	slaw
chicken fillet	corn

For the next table, change the left tabs to decimal tabs.

5.50	1.25
12.95	.95
1.55	.85
1.99	.75
2.25	.89

ACTIVITY A - LETTER

Key the following letter. Set left and right margins at 1.5 inches. Use Shift-F4 for the paragraph that is indented from both margins. Although not the preferred letter style, press Tab to indent the paragraphs. Print the report and save as WPRA8LR.

(Current date)

Mrs. Jolie Rae
3341 West Tremont Street
Indianapolis, IN 46241

Dear Mrs. Rae

Thank you for your letter inquiring about our classes in Calorie Counting and Watching Cholesterol.

As you will note from the enclosed brochure and enrollment form, Calorie Counting is offered on the second Wednesday of the month, and Watching Cholesterol is offered on the third Tuesday of the month. Each class runs from 7 to 9:15 p.m.

Here is what one student told us:

> My husband, daughter, and I have all had health problems as a result of improper eating. I attended both Calorie Counting and Watching Cholesterol workshops. I have followed your clear and complete guidelines, and I am happy to tell you that in two months my family has lost a total of 32 pounds and all have lowered their blood pressure!

We hope to see you, Mrs. Rae, at our classes.

Sincerely

Pat Thomas
Registered Dietitian

ACTIVITY B - TABLE

Key the following table. Line spacing should be double. Set the top margin at 3 inches. Leave the side margins at 1 inch. Clear all tabs. Set left tabs at 0.5 inches and 1.5 inches and a decimal tab at 5 inches. Press (Tab) before keying each column. Underline the headings and key them at the left of each column (where (Tab) positions the cursor). Print the table and save as WPRA8TB.

PART NO	DESCRIPTION	PRICE
KG30549	Business Card Holder	4.25
HJ88735	Marker Board	23.25
LM2708	Strapping Tape	5.99
FN69932	Mahogany Executive Desk	599.99
FN13016	Connell Conference Table	199.99
FN25731	Executive Budget Chair	73.99
FN75491	1 inch Stack Chair	19.99
BW2795	Electric Pencil Sharpener	29.41
LK12223	Pentol Permanent Markers	7.96

ACTIVITY C - TEXT WITH A TABLE

Key the following text with table. Set the top margin at 2 inches, and left and right margins at 1.5 inches. Press (F4) (Shift)-(Tab) to hang indent the items. Triple space before keying the table at the bottom of the document. To key the table, clear all tabs and set left tabs at 1.5 inches and 3.25 inches. Underline and key the table headings. Before keying the table numbers, erase the left tab at 3.25 inches and set a decimal tab at 3.5 inches. Print the document and save as WPRA8SP.

PRICE SPECIFICATIONS
DESKTOP PUBLISHING BOOKS

Barta, Raymond, Revolutionary Publishing, Rooster Publications, 1990, 275 pages, #78-105.

Eagle, Juan, Dynamic Desktop Publishing, McLaughlin-Swain Publishing Co., 1991, 345 pages, #78-235.

Lin, Yang, Advanced Desktop Publishing, McLaughlin-Swain Publishing Co, 1990, 295 pages, #78-116.

Lyones, Darrel, Desktop Publishing Simplified, Twilight Publications, 1992, 245 pages, #78-400.

Wolff, Susanne, DTP Primer, Herndon Publishing, 1992, 325 pages, #78-340.

Pub. #	Price
78-105	22.95
78-116	24.95
78-235	25.99
78-340	22.50
78-400	18.95

9

SEARCH, REPLACE, BLOCK, MOVE

OBJECTIVES

- **Search** for all occurrences of a word or words.
- **Search and replace.**
- **Block** text and use bold, center, spell, delete, save, and print.
- Use **move** to move, copy, and delete a sentence.
- Use **move** to move and copy a block.

SEARCH (F2) ⇓ SEARCH, FORWARD

Sometimes you want to search a lengthy document for a particular word or words, either to verify their use or to replace them with other text. Simply look for words with the Search feature, or search for words to be replaced with the Search and Replace feature.

The **Search** command is normally used to search forward (beginning of document to the end), but you can also search backward (end of document to the beginning). *Cursor position* is important when Searching, because the search will begin at the cursor position!

The steps to search are:

1. Press (F2) *Search.*
2. At the (→) *Srch:* prompt, key the word(s) you want to search for. If you key the words in lower case, Search will find all occurrences of the word(s) in either upper or lower case. If you key any part of the word(s) in uppercase, Search will only find the occurrences that exactly match the uppercase characters.
3. Press (F2) *Search*, repeatedly if you desire to find all occurrences.

DO: Clear your screen. Retrieve WPREV8; your cursor is always at the top of a retrieved document.

DO: Search for the word "tab" in the document. Press (F2) and key *tab* in lowercase letters. A message on the lower left Status Line appears: (→) *Srch: tab.* (See WP9.1.)

DO: Press (F2) again. The cursor stops at the end of the first occurrence, which is *TABS* in the heading.

DO: Press (F2) repeatedly to search the rest of the document. Do it slowly enough that you can see the words where the search stops each time. The message * *Not found* * signals an end to the search and the document. Write on the line below any "strange" words that you did not expect to see in the search but did.

____

FIGURE WP9.1
Using the Search Feature

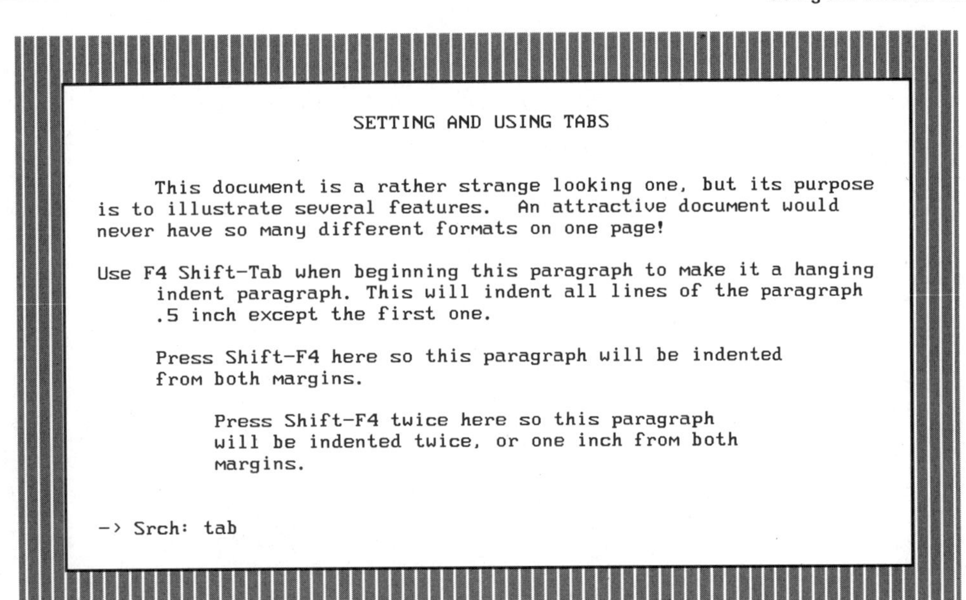

SETTING AND USING TABS

This document is a rather strange looking one, but its purpose is to illustrate several features. An attractive document would never have so many different formats on one page!

Use F4 Shift-Tab when beginning this paragraph to make it a hanging indent paragraph. This will indent all lines of the paragraph .5 inch except the first one.

Press Shift-F4 here so this paragraph will be indented from both margins.

Press Shift-F4 twice here so this paragraph will be indented twice, or one inch from both margins.

-> Srch: tab

Keying a word such as *tab* with no space before or after it in a search will find the letters t-a-b anywhere in a word.

DO: Try the same search, but this time key *tab* a little differently and see if the results are different. Press (F2), key (Space) tab (Space) and then press (F2) repeatedly. How was this search different?

____

SEARCH/REPLACE (Alt)-(F2) (F2) (F2) ↵ SEARCH, REPLACE

It is not uncommon for a word or words to be consistently misspelled throughout a document or for text to change at a later date. For example, you might spell Mr. Smythe's name as Smith throughout a document and later find your error. Or, a client may remarry and need to have a document updated with her new name. It is a simple matter to use the **Search and Replace** feature to Search for the incorrect surname and Replace it with the correct one.

In addition, you can often save time by keying initials for a company name or other lengthy phrase throughout a document. Then, when keying is complete, you can search for the initials and replace them with the full company name or phrase.

The steps to Search/Replace are:

1. Press (Alt)-(F2) *Replace.*

2. Answer the *Confirm?* question. If you answer No, the default, all occurrences will be replaced automatically. If you answer Yes, your cursor will stop at each occurrence and you will manually key (Y) *Yes* to replace or (N) *No* not to replace that occurrence.
3. At the (→) *Srch:* prompt, key the word(s) you want to search for (do not press (↵Enter)).
4. Press (F2) *Search* and at the *Replace with:* prompt, key the replacement word(s) (do not press (↵Enter)).
5. Press (F2) *Search,* to start the Search/Replace process.

KEY: Clear your screen. Key the text in the box below (WPKey9.1).

WPKEY9.1

```
(Current date)



Dear Mr. Smith:

This is just a quick note, Mr. Smith, to remind you that
you are scheduled to see your picture proofs this
Friday at 7:30 p.m.

We are sure you are eagerly awaiting your lovely, pro-
fessional pictures. We look forward to showing them to
you, Mr. Smith.

Sincerely,


Distinctive Pictures
```

As with Search, *cursor position is important* when using Search/Replace.

DO: Be sure your cursor is at the top of the document (Home) (Home) (↑). Press (Alt) (F2) *Replace* or Search, Replace. Press (N) *No* to confirm.

DO: At the (→) *Srch:* prompt, key *Smith*. Press (F2) *Search*. At the *Replace with:* prompt, key *Smythe*. Press (F2) *Search* to perform the process. Check your document for three replacements.

DO: Return to the top of your document (*always*). Search for *pictures* and Replace with *portraits*. You decide whether to confirm or not.

DO: Print the document and save it as WPKEY9.1. Clear your screen.

QUICK QUESTIONS

1. Why is cursor position important for Search and Search/Replace?
2. What message signals you have ended the search?

3. If you want Search or Search/Replace to find all occurrences of a word or words regardless of case, how should you key the Search word(s)?
4. If you want Search or Search/Replace to find a specific word and not those letters within other words, how should you key the Search word(s)?
5. Give a Search/Replace shortcut alternative to keying "Clinical Psychology Section, Department of Psychiatry" five times in a document.

BLOCK (F12) OR (Alt)-(F4) ⊎ EDIT, BLOCK

The **Block** feature is an important command in any word processing package. Block allows you to set off a portion of text and perform a particular function on that block. The following is a list (WP9.2) of some of the block functions in WordPerfect.

FIGURE WP9.2

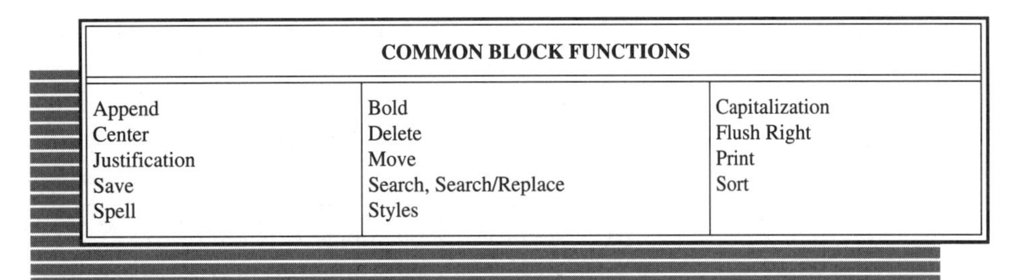

COMMON BLOCK FUNCTIONS		
Append	Bold	Capitalization
Center	Delete	Flush Right
Justification	Move	Print
Save	Search, Search/Replace	Sort
Spell	Styles	

KEYBOARD BLOCK. The steps to block text with the keyboard are:

1. Place your cursor at the beginning of the text to be blocked (you can also start the block at the end of the text and work toward the top.)
2. Press (F12) *Block* or (Alt)-(F4) *Block* or ⊎ Edit, Block. *Block on* flashes in the lower left corner of the screen.
3. Move your cursor to the end of the block. The entire block is highlighted using reverse video or a contrasting color.
4. *While* ***Block on*** *is flashing*, press the keys for the function you wish to perform on that text. The function is performed, and the highlight disappears.

MOUSE BLOCK. The steps to block text with the mouse are:

1. Position the mouse pointer on one end of the text to be blocked.
2. Press and hold down LMB while you move the mouse pointer to the other end of the text to be blocked (LMB drag).
3. Release LMB.
4. *While* ***Block on*** *is flashing*, use the mouse menu bar or press the keys to select the function you wish to perform on that text. The function is performed, and the highlight disappears.

If you begin the Block feature and change your mind, press (F1) *Cancel*, (F12) or (Alt)-(F4) *Block*, or ⊎ Edit, Block to toggle it off.

DO: Retrieve WPKEY7.4.

The activities below will use the keyboard method of blocking, but feel free to try the mouse method outlined above if you have a mouse available.

BOLD A BLOCK.

DO: Block the first sentence and make it bold. Place your cursor on the *T* in the first sentence. Press (F12) or (Alt)-(F4) *Block*. The message *Block on* is flashing on the lower left Status Line.

DO: To move your cursor quickly to the end of the block, press (.), the last character of the block. The entire sentence is highlighted. Press (F6) to *Bold* the block.

CENTER A BLOCK.

DO: Block and center the line *Jean Smith*. Place your cursor on the *J* in *Jean*. Press (F12) or (Alt)-(F4) *Block*. The message *Block on* is flashing.

DO: To move your cursor quickly to the end of the block, press (End). The entire line is highlighted. Press (Shift)-(F6) to *Center* it. You are prompted for verification: *[Just:Center]? No(Yes)*. Press (Y) for *Yes*.

SPELL CHECK A BLOCK.

DO: Use the Spell feature on the material from *Text that is justified on the right...* through the zip code. Place your cursor on the *T* in *Text*. Press (F12) or (Alt)-(F4) *Block*. The message *Block on* is flashing.

DO: To move your cursor quickly to the end of the material, press (4), the last character of the block. *The cursor moves to the **first** "4"*. Press (4) three more times to get to the *4* at the end in the zip code. Press (Ctrl)-(F2) *Spell* to check the block. (Correct any errors.)

DELETE A BLOCK.

DO: Delete the last sentence of the document. Place your cursor on the *Y* in *You*. What should you press now to begin the Block command?

DO: Highlight the entire sentence. What key should you press to do this?

DO: Press (Delete). You are prompted for verification: *Delete Block? No(Yes)*. Press (Y) for *Yes*.

SAVE A BLOCK.

DO: Save the first paragraph only with the block name (file name) PARAONE. Move to the *T* in *This* and block and highlight the entire first paragraph. Press (F10) *Save*. You are prompted for *Block name:*. Key PARAONE for the file name.

PRINT A BLOCK.

DO: Print the document *without the heading*. Move to the first paragraph, the *T* in *This* and press (Home) (Home) (Home) (←); this moves the cursor so the code for Left Justification is included in the block. Use Reveal Codes to see that your cursor is on the code, making the code part of the block.

DO: Activate the Block feature with (F12) or (Alt)-(F4). Highlight the entire document from that position by pressing (Home) (Home) (↓). Press (Shift)-(F7) *Print*. You are prompted for verification: *Print Block? No(Yes)*. Press (Y) *Yes*.

DO: Use (F10) to save the entire document, including the heading, as BLOKPRAC. Keep BLOKPRAC on your screen for the next feature.

MOVE (Ctrl)-(F4) EDIT, SELECT OR EDIT, MOVE

You can move one sentence, paragraph, or page to another location in the document by using the **Move** feature alone; you can move other amounts of text by blocking the text and then using the Move feature on the block.

DO: Move the first sentence of the first paragraph to the end of the paragraph. Place your cursor anywhere in the first sentence, *This text is left justified.* Press (Ctrl)-(F4) *Move*, (S) *Sentence* or Edit, Select, Sentence.

You have four choices for the sentence: **Move** it from its present location, **Copy** it to another location while it also remains where it is, **Delete** it, or **Append** (add) it to the end of a file that already exists on your disk.

MOVE A SENTENCE.

DO: Press (M) to *Move* the sentence. The sentence disappears, and a prompt appears at the lower left of the screen: *Move cursor; press* Enter *to retrieve.*

DO: Being careful not to press (↵Enter), move your cursor to the end of the first paragraph, the space after the period. Then press (Space) (Space) to insert additional space between the sentences. Press (↵Enter) to retrieve the sentence.

COPY A SENTENCE.

DO: Leave the sentence in its new position, but also put a copy of it in its previous location. Put your cursor anywhere in the sentence *This text is left justified.* Press (Ctrl)-(F4) *Move*, (S) *Sentence* or Edit, Select, Sentence. Press (C) to *Copy* the sentence. The text does not disappear this time because it is not moved, but merely copied.

DO: Reveal your codes. Place your cursor at the beginning of the first paragraph to the *right* of the [Just:Left] code so this sentence will remain in the left justification format. Press (↵Enter) to retrieve the sentence.

DELETE A PARAGRAPH.

DO: Delete the last paragraph of the document. Place your cursor anywhere within the last paragraph.

DO: Press Ctrl-F4 *Move*. Press P for *Paragraph*. Press D to *Delete* the paragraph.

MOVE A BLOCK.

DO: Use the Block command to highlight and move the text about Jean Smith, her address, city, state, and zip. Place your cursor on the *J* in *Jean*.

DO: Press Home Home Home ← to include the codes. The cursor does not look like it is at the beginning of the line, but Reveal Codes will show it is.

DO: Press F12 or Alt-F4 *Block* and then highlight the three lines that include the data about Jean.

DO: Press Ctrl-F4 *Move,* B *Block,* M *Move.*

DO: Place your cursor on the *T* in *Text that is justified...* right after *$9.98.* Press Home Home Home ← to move in front of all codes. Press ↵Enter to Retrieve the text.

COPY A BLOCK.

DO: Copy the three lines about Jean Smith; that is, leave them where they are and also put a copy at the bottom of the document. Place your cursor on the *J* in *Jean.*

DO: Press Home Home Home ←. Reveal Codes and find your cursor. Now *Jean* will be Center Justified when copied. Press F12 or Alt-F4 *Block* and then highlight the three lines that include the data about Jean.

DO: Press Ctrl-F4 *Move,* B *Block,* C *Copy.*

DO: Press Home Home ↓ to go to the bottom of the document. Cursor up if necessary to place your cursor right below the last line of the document. Press ↵Enter to retrieve the text.

DO: Print the document and save it as MOVEPRAC. Clear your screen.

QUICK QUESTIONS

1. What is the name of the feature that allows you to set off any portion of text and perform a particular function on it?
2. Looking at the list of block functions on page WP71, list the seven block functions that you did not do in this section.
3. Where should your cursor be before you activate the Block feature?
4. After you press F12 or Alt-F4 to activate the Block command,

what action should you perform before selecting the block function?

5. Should **Block on** be flashing when you press the keys for the desired function?
6. How can the Block feature be deactivated if you decide not to use it?
7. Why do you think you are prompted for verification when you attempt to delete a block?
8. What are four actions you can take in the Move feature?
9. When you use the Move command to move or copy text, how do you retrieve the text at the appropriate place?

Key the text below and save it as WPREV9. Use Flush Right before keying each rate.

River View Apartments
3390 North Vermont Street
Hollywood, CA 90028

Dear Mr. Wilson:

Thank you for your inquiry about our apartments.

We are highly respected for amenities such as fireplaces, whirlpool bathrooms, and mirrored bedroom doors. In addition, we have strolling security on the grounds 24 hours a day.

Our monthly rates are:

Studio	$550
One Bedroom	$625
Two Bedroom	$735
Three Bedroom Townhouse	$810

Please call or write if you would like more information or a tour of our excellent accommodations.

Sincerely,

Mary Kay Matthews, Rental Agent

P.S. A damage deposit of one month's rent is required at the time of signing a rental contract.

After saving the document as WPREV9, perform the operations listed below.

1. Search/Replace *apartments* with *condominiums*.
2. Search/Replace *respected* with *esteemed.*
3. Do the following Block functions:
   a. Move *security* before *strolling.*
   b. Move the entire second paragraph, *We are highly...*, to the end of the first paragraph, making one paragraph from two. (Delete any extra blank lines.)
   c. Delete the words *P.S.* and then move the text that was a P.S. to the end of the first paragraph. (You should end up with two paragraphs and a table in the letter.)
4. We just had to raise the rent on our studio apartments. Search for *550* and Replace with *575.*
5. Print the document. Save it as WPREV9A. Clear your screen.

ACTIVITY A - FINANCIAL REPORT 1

Key the following report. Clear all tabs and set new ones at 1 inch, 3 inches, and 5 inches. Save the document as WPRA9RPA and then make the changes listed below the report.

Page 1

JMC
1990 Widget Sales

Widget sales for JMC have grown this year, as you can see by the table below. Thanks to each and every one of you who has worked very hard in your sales territory!

	1989	1990
Period 1	1,334,887	1,299,345
Period 2	1,521,550	1,749,969
Period 3	1,499,745	1,792,442
Period 4	1,701,999	1,845,336

Although the year started out rather slowly, probably due to an uncertain manufacturing economy, by June JMC sales were 115% higher than the same time one year ago. This is really putting JMC on the map!

Your hard work and determination have paid off! You are JMC!

Make the following changes:

1. Search/Replace *Period* with *Quarter.*
2. Search/Replace *JMC* with *Jones-Miller Corporation.*
3. Move the second sentence in the first paragraph *Thanks to each...* so that it becomes the first sentence in that paragraph.
4. Block and delete the last sentence in paragraph two, *This is really....*
5. Search/Replace *1,499,745* with *1,592,335.*

Print the document and save it as WPRA9RPA.2. Clear your screen.

ACTIVITY B - FINANCIAL REPORT 2

Key the following report. Clear all tabs and set new ones at 1.8, 3.1, 4.3, and 5.7 inches on the tabline for the column headings. After keying the column headings, erase tabs and reset decimal tabs at 2.5, 3.7, 5.0, and 6.2 inches. Save the document as WPRA9RPB and then make the changes listed below the report.

BUDGET APPROVAL
FIRST QUARTER, 1993

	Advertising	Research	Salaries	Admin.
Region One	3,345.00	22,906.00	92,774.00	1,298.00
Region Two	6,488.00	-0-	234,946.00	5,773.00
Region Three	9,776.00	-0-	663,922.00	22,675.00
Region Four	-0-	150,000.00	220,500.00	27,899.00
TOTAL	19,609.00	172,906.00	1,212,142.00	57,645.00

These budget figures are subject to change prior to Dec. 1, 1992. Any changes will be forwarded to the finance officer in writing.

Make the following changes:

1. Search/Replace *Research* with *Develop*.
2. Search/Replace *663,922.00* with *663,229.00*.
3. Search/Replace *27,899.00* with *31,166.00*.
4. Change TOTALS: Salaries = 1,211,449 and Admin. = 60,912
5. Move the sentence, *Any changes will be forwarded...* so it becomes the **first** sentence following the table. (Switch the positions of the first and second sentences.)

Print the document and save it as WPRA9RPB.2. Exit from WordPerfect or clear your screen and continue to Section Ten.

10

ADVANCED DOCUMENT COMMANDS

OBJECTIVES

- Use the **Widow/Orphan** feature.
- Use the **Page Number** feature.
- Use a **Hard Page Break.**
- Use **Header**, **Footer**, and **Suppress** features.
- Use the **Outline** feature.
- Use the **Table** feature.

This section presents features that are very useful when preparing reports and other complex documents. First, the new commands will be presented and briefly practiced. Then you will follow step-by-step activities to complete a sample research paper, from the outline to the body of the report to the Works Cited page. The documentary style used, MLA, is common in high schools and colleges.

WIDOWS AND ORPHANS (Shift)-(F8) (L) (W) LAYOUT, LINE, WIDOW

A **widow** is the first line of a paragraph that is alone at the bottom of a page. An **orphan** is the last line of a paragraph that is alone at the top of a page. Widow and orphan lines are undesirable in formal documents and should be avoided in research papers.

To protect your document from widows and orphans, use the **Widow/Orphan** Protection feature in the Format command. This feature is in effect from the cursor position, so it is usually necessary to go to the top of the document to use the command.

DO: Press (Shift)-(F8) *Format,* (L) *Line,* (W) *Widow/Orphan Protection,* (Y) *Yes* (↵Enter). Press (F7) to exit the menu.

DO: Press (F11) or (Alt)-(F3) to *Reveal Codes.* If you see the code [W/O on], you have set the document to avoid widows or orphans. If you do not see this code, your WordPerfect program may have been set to avoid them by default.

PAGE NUMBERING Shift-F8 P N LAYOUT, PAGE, PAGE NUMBER

Page Numbering contains options that let you control how and where page numbers are placed. WP10.1 shows that several options are available:

FIGURE WP10.1

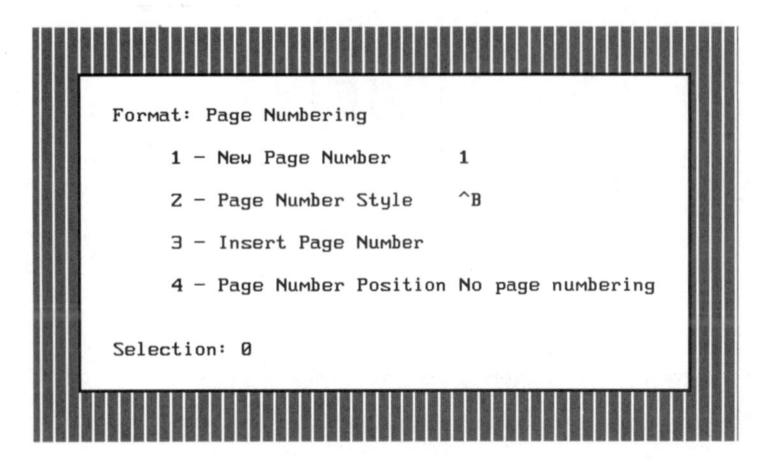

NEW PAGE NUMBER. This option allows you to begin page numbering with any number you desire. You can even key **i** or **I** for Roman numerals.

PAGE NUMBER STYLE. You can design a page number to appear in various styles. For example, you can place your name beside the page number, often required for the body of a research paper. To do this, key your name followed by Ctrl-B. **Ctrl-B is the code that will place a page number.** If you wish to change the page number style within a document, go to the page where the change should begin and set a new page number style.

INSERT PAGE NUMBER. You can set a page number at any place in a document with this option. Your cursor position is where the page number will appear.

FIGURE WP10.2

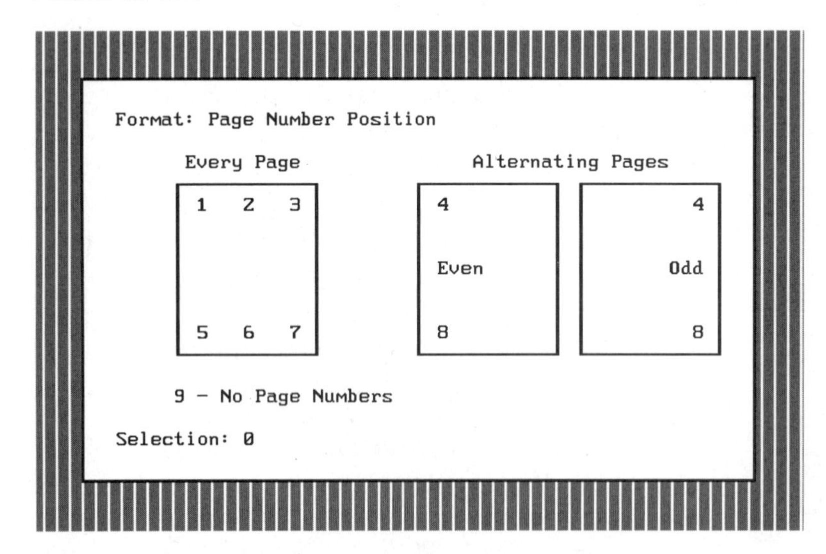

PAGE NUMBER POSITION. Use this option to begin page numbering from the cursor position forward. You may place the page number where you desire, on every page or alternating pages (WP10.2).

You will create a document several pages in length so you can see the page numbers on several pages. To force several pages, use Hard Page Breaks.

HARD PAGE BREAK Ctrl-Enter

Up to this point WordPerfect has counted your lines of text and decided where one complete page should end and a new page begin; this is called a Soft Page Break. You can force a new page yourself, called a **Hard Page Break**, at any location you desire. Press Ctrl-Enter where you want to end a page.

DO: On a blank screen, press (Shift)-(F8) *Format,* (P) *Page,* (N) *Page Numbering,* (P) *Page Number Position,* (6) (bottom center). This will place the page number at the bottom center of each page. Press (F7) to exit the menu.

DO: Press (Shift)-(F7), (V) *View,* (3) *Full Page* to see the blank page with a page number at the bottom center. Press (F7) to exit from View.

DO: Press (Ctrl)-(↵Enter) twice to create two new hard pages. Reveal codes to see [HPg] codes. [HPg] is the Hard Page Break code; [SPg] is the Soft Page Break code.

DO: View each page to see a page number at the bottom. Press (Shift)-(F7) (V) *View* (3) *Full Page.* If you can't read the page numbers, press (1) *100%* and then turn off Num Lock and press (+) on the numeric pad for Window Down. (Use (−) on the numeric pad for Window Up.)

DO: Press (Page Up) twice to view pages 2 and 1. Exit and clear the screen.

In the upper right hand corner of the page, make a page number that includes your last name followed by the page number:

DO: Press (Shift)-(F8) *Format,* (P) *Page,* (N) *Page Numbering,* (P) *Page Number Position* (3) (upper right corner). Press (S) *Page Number Style.*

KEY: *Your last name* (Space) (Ctrl)-(B).

DO: Press (F7) to exit the Page Numbering menu. Press (F11) or (Alt)-(F3) to *Reveal Codes.* Notice the two codes you placed in the document.

DO: Make two hard pages by pressing (Ctrl)-(↵Enter) twice.

DO: View the document (Shift)-(F7) (V) at 100%, using (Page Up) or (Page Down) to see each page. Exit View.

DO: Clear the screen.

QUICK QUESTIONS

1. What are some of the features in this section often used to make documents look more professional?
2. What is the word that refers to the last line of a paragraph that is alone at the top of a page?
3. What is the word that refers to the first line of a paragraph that is alone at the bottom of a page?
4. Which item on the Page Numbering menu allows you to design a page number's appearance?
5. Using Figure WP10.2, name six possible locations of a page number that appears on every page:
   a)
   b)

c)
d)
e)
f)
6. What two keys are pressed to place a page number code?
7. What two keys are pressed to force a hard page break?
8. What is a hard page break?

HEADERS AND FOOTERS (Shift)-(F8) (P) (H) LAYOUT, PAGE, HEADER

As you might guess, **Headers** appear at the top of pages, and **Footers** appear at the bottom of pages. Headers and footers are used when the same information should appear at the top or bottom of each page of a multiple-page document. One type of header or footer can be used for even pages, while a second type of header or footer can be used for odd pages. The same page can include both headers and footers.

Page numbering can be done in headers or footers instead of using the Page Numbering feature. We will create the same page numbering effect you just completed by using a header.

DO: Press (Shift)-(F8) *Format,* (P) *Page,* (H) *Headers,* (A) Header *A,* (P) *every Page.*

You have entered a special header screen—notice the status line both on the left and on the right. Although this is not your usual editing screen, you will key data in the same manner.

DO: Press (Alt)-(F6) to move to the upper right corner.

KEY: *Your last name* (Space) (Ctrl)-(B).

DO: Press (F7) to exit the header screen. Press (F7) again to return to your document screen.

Nothing appears on the screen. Headers and footers appear *only when you print or use View Document.*

DO: Press (F11) or (Alt)-(F3) to see the header code. Press (Shift)-(F7) and view the document. The page number looks like the one you created with the Page Number command.

DO: Create several new hard page breaks by pressing (Ctrl)-(↵Enter) twice.

DO: Use the View Document command to view the page with the 100% option. Press (Page Up) to see all pages. Exit view. Clear the screen.

Use Page Number Style if you want only a few words to appear with the page number. Use a header or footer if you want many words or several lines of text to appear with the page number.

Create a new header with three lines of text to appear at the upper right corner on every page.

DO: Press Shift-F8 *Format,* P *Page,* H *Headers,* A Header *A,* P *every Page.*

DO: Press Alt-F6 *Flush Right* and then *key your first and last name* Enter.

DO: Press Alt-F6 and then key the *name of your computer class* Enter.

DO: Press Alt-F6.

KEY: *Page* Space Ctrl-B Enter.

DO: Exit the header screen. Exit the Page Format menu.

DO: Reveal codes. Notice only a portion of the header text appears in the code.

DO: Press Ctrl-Enter to force two hard page breaks. View the document. Press Page Up repeatedly to see all pages. Exit View Document. Do *not* clear the screen.

The footer feature works just like the header feature, but the text will appear at the *bottom* of the page.

SUPPRESS Shift-F8 P U LAYOUT, PAGE, SUPPRESS

Often you do not want a page number on the first page of a research paper or business report. The **Suppress** command prevents page numbers and/or headers and footers from appearing on the *current* page.

DO: Press Home Home Home ↑ to go to the top of the document in front of all codes. *The suppress command must be at the top of the page, immediately after the Soft Page or Hard Page code if there is one.*

DO: Press Shift-F8 *Format,* P *Page,* U *sUppress.* The menu shown in Figure WP10.3 appears.

FIGURE WP10.3

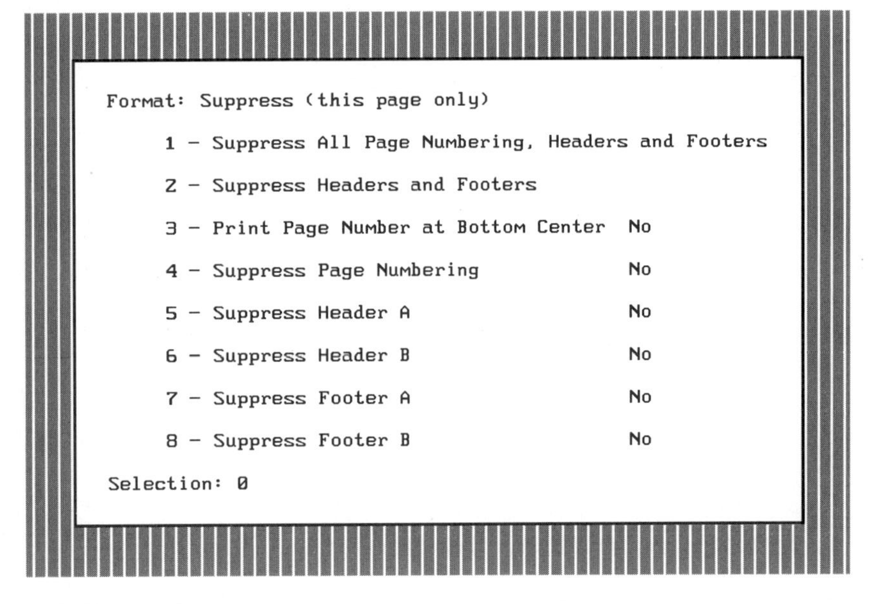

Format: Suppress (this page only)
1 - Suppress All Page Numbering, Headers and Footers
2 - Suppress Headers and Footers
3 - Print Page Number at Bottom Center No
4 - Suppress Page Numbering No
5 - Suppress Header A No
6 - Suppress Header B No
7 - Suppress Footer A No
8 - Suppress Footer B No
Selection: 0

The title at the top of the menu reminds you that options on this menu will suppress on the current page only.

Notice you may suppress headers, footers, and page numbers. You may select only one of these to be suppressed or a combination of them.

Option 3 is different from the other options. It allows the page number to be printed at the bottom center of the current page only. This is a standard procedure for the first page of some documents.

DO: Press (5) *Suppress Header A,* (Y) *Yes.* Then press (F7) to exit the Suppress Format screen.

DO: View all three pages to see if the header is suppressed on page one only. Exit View Document. Clear the screen.

OUTLINE (Shift)-(F5) (O) TOOLS, OUTLINE

Because outlines are commonly used to organize ideas prior to writing, WordPerfect provides an **Outline** feature. This feature automatically numbers the outline entries at each level. As you can see in WPCheck10.1 on page WP85, Roman numerals designate the highest level, uppercase letters the second level, and arabic numbers (1, 2, 3, etc.) the third level.

Figure WP10.4 illustrates which keys to press to stay in the same level or to move forward or backward one level. Press (Enter) at the end of an entry to remain at the same level. Press (Enter) at the end of an entry, followed by (Tab) to move ahead one level. Press (Enter) at the end of an entry, followed by (Shift)-(Tab) to move back one level. If you don't want to insert a level number, press (Ctrl)-(V) before pressing Enter. Press (F4), Indent, before keying an entry.

Create an outline using the guidelines in WP10.4. and the illustration of the completed document, WPCheck10.1.

DO: On a clean screen, center the heading and key it in all caps. Press (Shift)-(F6) *Center* and (Caps Lock).

KEY: GOAL SETTING (Enter) (Enter)

FIGURE WP10.4

OUTLINE MOVEMENT	
Keep the same level	Enter
Move one level ahead	Enter, Tab
Move one level back	Enter, Shift Tab
Before keying entries	F4

DO: Press (Shift)-(F5), *Date/Outline,* (O) *Outline,* (O) *On* to activate the Outline feature. Notice, the prompt *Outline* appears in the left corner of the Status Line.

DO: Press (Enter) to obtain the first level, Roman numeral I. Press (F4) to key the item for that level.

KEY: Determine Values (Enter) (Enter)

DO: Press (Tab) to move one level ahead (A).

KEY: (F4) Beliefs (Enter)

KEY: (F4) Principles (Enter)

KEY: F4 Ideals ↵Enter

DO: Press ↵Enter for a blank line. Press Shift-Tab to move back one level, to obtain a Roman numeral II.

KEY: F4 Determine Goals ↵Enter ↵Enter

DO: Press Tab to move one level ahead (A).

KEY: F4 Personal ↵Enter

DO: Press Tab to move one level ahead (1).

KEY: F4 Base on values ↵Enter

KEY: F4 Specific ↵Enter

KEY: F4 Realistic ↵Enter

DO: Press Shift-Tab to move back one level (B). Complete the outline using WPCheck10.1 as a guide. If you make a mistake, backspace to the last correct entry and redo from there. When you complete the last item, press Shift-F5, O outline, F off *before* you press ↵Enter.

WPCHECK10.1

```
                    GOAL SETTING

I.    Determine Values

      A. Beliefs
      B. Principles
      C. Ideals

II.   Determine Goals

      A. Personal
         1. Base on values
         2. Specific
         3. Realistic
      B. Work
         1. Base on values
         2. Specific
         3. Realistic

III. Discipline

      A. Personal
         1. Take control
         2. Start now
      B. Work
         1. Self-discipline
         2. A step at a time
         3. Time management
```

DO: Save the outline as WPOUTLN. Print it. Clear your screen.

QUICK QUESTIONS

1. What word is used to refer to information that appears at the top of each page of a multiple-page document?
2. Name two WordPerfect features that can be used to set page numbering.
   a)
   b)
3. Name the two times when you can actually see headers or footers.
   a)
   b)
4. When would you choose to use a header for page numbering rather than the Page Numbering feature?
5. What is the purpose of the Suppress command?
6. What is important about the placement of the Suppress code?
7. List the keys that will accomplish the desired movement in Outline.
   a) move one level back
   b) before keying entries
   c) keep the same level
   d) move one level ahead

TABLE (Alt)-(F7) (T) (C) LAYOUT, TABLES, CREATE

Use the **Table** feature to clearly present data without setting tabs. An example of a table is WP10.4 on page WP84. In essence, a table is a grid of rows and columns. Rows are *horizontal* elements, and columns are *vertical* elements. The rows and columns make it simple to key data, as you will see.

Recreate chart WP10.4 on page WP84.

DO: Press (Alt)-(F7) *Columns/Table*, (T) *Tables*, (C) *Create*.

You are asked for the number of columns:

KEY: 2 (Enter)

You are asked for the number of rows. Looking at WP10.4, the heading, four items, and the caption *WP10.4* each appear on separate rows.

KEY: 6 (Enter)

You are now in the **Table Edit** screen. You *cannot key data* in this screen. It is used only for *formatting* the table.

FIGURE WP10.5

```
Table Edit:  Press Exit when done          Cell A1 Doc 1 Pg 1 Ln 1.14" Pos 1.12"

Ctrl-Arrows Column Widths; Ins Insert; Del Delete; Move Move/Copy;
1 Size; 2 Format; 3 Lines; 4 Header; 5 Math; 6 Options; 7 Join; 8 Split: 0
```

Look carefully at your screen. (See WP10.5.) The table appears according to your column and row specifications.

Below the table you see an important message: *Table Edit: Press Exit when done.* Beside that message, you see the cell indicator, A1. It shows the cursor location in a table. Columns are referenced with letters, beginning with A. Rows are referenced with numbers, beginning with 1. The cell where Column A and Row 1 intersect is known as A1.

DO: Move the cursor bar from cell to cell, watching the cell indicator. Do you see how A and B refer to the two columns, while 1 through 6 refer to the six rows?

JOIN CELLS. Since the title is centered across the table, you will join the two cells in Row 1 so they become one cell. Still in the Table Edit screen:

DO: Move to Cell A1. Press F12 or Alt-F4 *Block. Block on* should be flashing on the left Status Line. Press → to move to Cell B1. Both A1 and B1 should be highlighted. Press J *Join,* Y *Yes* to verify the joining.

Next you will join both cells in Row 6 to simplify the caption line.

DO: Move down to A6. Press F12 or Alt-F3 *Block.* Press → to move to Cell B6. With both cells highlighted, press J *Join,* Y *Yes* to verify the joining.

After keying the text in the table, you will return to Table Edit for the finishing touches.

DO: Press F7 to exit from Table Edit. You are now in the editing screen and able to enter data into the table.

STATUS LINE. The Status Line has a new message listed: the current cell. If you do not see the "Cell" notation on the Status Line, your cursor has moved out of the table.

DO: To key the heading, place your cursor in Cell A1. Press (Shift)-(F6) *Center.*

KEY: OUTLINE MOVEMENT (do not Enter).

DO: Press (Tab) to move to the next cell, A2.

The cell positions are given in the directions below, as in [A2]; do *not* key them. Key the text and then press (Tab) to move to the next cell.

KEY: [A2] Keep the same level (Tab).

KEY: [B2] Enter (Tab).

KEY: [A3] Move one level ahead (Tab).

KEY: [B3] Enter, Tab (Tab).

DO: Complete the last two items in the table using the illustration on page WP85, pressing (Tab) to move to each cell. (Do not press Enter.)

DO: To key the caption at the right margin of the table in Cell A6, press (Alt)-(F6) *Flush Right.* (The lines around the caption will be erased soon.)

KEY: [A6] WP10.4.

COLUMN SIZE. To increase or decrease the size of a column, activate Table Edit with (Alt)-(F7). Then place your cursor on any cell in the column to be increased on decreased. Press (Ctrl) (→) to widen a column or (Ctrl) (←) to narrow a column.

DO: Press (Alt)-(F7) for Table Edit. At Cell A2 press (Ctrl) (→) 2 times to widen Column A. At Cell B2 press (Ctrl) (←) 10 times to narrow Column B.

ARRANGE LINES. You may change the appearance or remove some or all of the lines in a table with the Lines option of Table Edit.

DO: [A6] Still in Table Edit, press (L) *Lines,* (O) *Outside,* (N) *None.*

DO: Move to A5. Block A5 and B5. With both cells highlighted, press (L) *Lines,* (B) *Bottom,* (D) *Double.* Press (F7) to exit Table Edit.

DO: Press (Home) (Home) (↓) to move out of the table. Notice, the *Cell* position is gone from the Status Line. Use Reveal Codes to see that you are past the [Tbl Off] code.

DO: Save the document as WPTABLE. Print it.

DO: Either exit from WordPerfect or continue to the Reinforcement Activity.

QUICK QUESTIONS

1. What feature is used to clearly present data without setting tabs?
2. What does a table look like?
3. What row and column intersect when the Status Line indicates Cell B3?
4. What may and may not be done in the Table Edit screen?
5. What feature must be used before you can join two or more cells in a table?
6. What does it mean when the Status Line no longer has a *Cell* notation?
7. How can you increase or decrease the size of the columns in a table?
8. List the steps necessary to erase all the lines surrounding a cell.

Follow the steps below to complete a short sample research paper. The activities are very short, but representative of designing and keying a more complete paper. When preparing a research paper, you will follow a similar process. (Steps One and Two are illustrations only.)

STEP ONE: SELECT A TOPIC. For our sample, the topic is "Computer Monitors May Be a Health Hazard."

STEP TWO: GATHER DATA. When you do research, use notecards for data collection, preparing one bibliography card for each source of information. This sample report with two sources would have bibliography cards similar to those below. (Often the notecards and bibliography cards would be hand-written.)

SOURCE A BIBLIOGRAPHY CARD

Taylor, Wendy. "Don't Let Your Monitor Be the Death of You." PC Computing January 1991: 228-229.

A

SOURCE B BIBLIOGRAPHY CARD

Rosch, Winn L. "Monitor Emissions: Should You Worry?" PC Magazine July 1991: 106-107.

B

BIBLIOGRAPHY CARDS. Each bibliography card has the author's name, the name of the article, the name of the publication, the date, and the range of pages. Each bibliography source card is assigned a letter to simplify coding of associated notecards.

NOTECARDS. As data is gathered from the two sources, notecards with pertinent information are prepared. (See pages WP91-92.) The notecards are "coded" in the upper right corner. Notes taken from the first source are coded with "A," and notes taken from the second source are coded with "B." The page number is given after the code letter.

In addition to the source code and page number, a topic heading is recorded at the top of each card. This allows the cards to be arranged by category for logical placement in the outline and in the paper itself. Below the topic heading the important data is recorded, noting direct quotes.

NOTECARD 1

Define Danger *A-228*

Electromagnetic radiation is composed of electric and magnetic fields, both emitted at VLF (very low freq) and ELF (extremely low freq)

NOTECARD 2

Define Danger *B-106*

May be a link between monitor use and elevated cancer rates, eye stress, abnormal pregnancies, and miscarriages

NOTECARD 3

Define Danger *B-106*

The mechanism by which a VDT displays on-screen images generates electric and magnetic fields

VLF signals emitted by monitors, television sets

NOTECARD 4

Define Danger *B-106*

Associated with ELF fields in lab experiments & epidemiological surveys:
-cancer promotion
-changes in biological clocks
-alteration of nerve cells

NOTECARD 5

Scientific Evidence *A-228*

Not enough evidence to determine how much it threatens health

NOTECARD 6

Scientific Evidence *A-229*

Magnetic fields are chief hazard, but electric fields have been implicated, possibly with a combined effect more harmful than either one alone

(quote)

NOTECARD 7

Safety Products *A-228*

Only a handful of products reduce radiation exposure

Costly and incomplete

NOTECARD 8

Safety Products *A-228*

Antiglare/antiradiation screens intercept electric field radiation from front of monitor only

No device blocks both electric and magnetic radiation at both levels

NOTECARD 9

Safety Products *B-107*

Spurred on by increasing monitor-safety legislation in Europe & San Francisco, many monitor vendors have begun marketing models that claim to meet the stringent Swedish standards

NOTECARD 10

Safety Precautions *A-229*

-Work at least 28 inches from your monitor (arm's length)
-Stay 4 feet away from sides & back of monitors--electromagnetic fields are strongest there
-Turn off monitor when not using PC

STEP THREE: PREPARE AN OUTLINE.

A well-designed outline simplifies the writing of the report. The outline is based on the notecards, which are arranged by topic headings. When arranged in order, the notecards in our example could result in the outline shown on page WP93.

DO: *On a clean screen, key the following outline using these standard formatting instructions. (Print the outline and save it as MONITOR.OUT.)*

1. Top margin: 2 inches, bottom margin: 1 inch.
2. Left and right margins: 1 inch.
3. Linespacing: double.
4. No page number.

Reminders: Turn Outline feature on before you press Enter to activate it. Press (F4) before keying text.

Outline

Computer Monitors May Be a Health Hazard

I. What Is the Danger?

A. Electromagnetic radiation

B. Health risks

II. Scientific Evidence

A. Evidence inconclusive

B. Current testing

III. Solutions

A. Safety products

1. Limited number

2. Limited effectiveness

3. New standards

B. Safety precautions

STEP FOUR: WRITE THE PAPER.

The outline is followed to pull together the facts gathered on the notecards. Give credit to sources with imbedded notes in parentheses.

DO: *On a clean screen, key the following report using these standard formatting instructions. (Print the report and save it as MONITOR.RPT.)*

Page one only:

1. Top margin: 2 inches.
2. Linespacing: 2 (Quadruple space after the title).
3. Begin page numbering so this will be counted as page 1, but suppress page numbering so it does not appear on this page. Use the page number style described for the "Pages after page 1" below.

Pages after page one:

1. All four margins: 1 inch.
2. Linespacing: 2.
3. Page number in the upper right corner: **writer's last name(space)page no**. Key your name as the writer.
4. No widows or orphans.
5. Quotations of 4 lines or more: no quote marks, triple space before and after, indent 10 spaces from the left margin.

Reminders for the table: Single space; center the table using Table Edit's Option feature; use 1 column and 5 rows ("Table 1" is Row 1); block to remove lines or to add double lines; center headings with the Center command.

Computer Monitors May Be a Health Hazard

Cancer rates, eye stress, abnormal pregnancies, and miscarriages may be linked to computer monitor use (Rosch106.)

Both monitors and television sets generate electric and magnetic fields due to the way they display on-screen images (Rosch 106). This electromagnetic radiation is emitted at VLF (very low frequencies) and ELF (extremely low frequencies) (Taylor 228).

Lab experiments and epidemiological surveys with ELF fields have shown cancer promotion, changes in biological clocks, and alteration of nerve cells, according to Rosch (106).

Although it is stirring a lot of interest in research circles, the extent to which electromagnetic radiation threatens health has not been proven (Taylor 228). Taylor points out:

> While magnetic fields are considered the chief hazard, electric fields have been implicated as causing health problems in some studies. Some researchers even fear there may be some combined effect of the electric and magnetic fields that is more harmful than either one alone (229).

Spurred on by increasing monitor-safety legislation in Europe and San Francisco, monitor vendors have begun marketing models that claim to meet the stringent Swedish standards (Rosch 107). At this point, however, only a handful of products reduce radiation exposure, and they can be costly and incomplete (Taylor 228).

For example, antiglare/antiradiation screens intercept only electric field radiation and only from the front of the monitor (Taylor 228). No device blocks both electric and magnetic radiation at both VLF and ELF levels (Taylor 228). Significantly, these special screens do not block electromagnetic fields at the sides and back of a monitor, where they are strongest (Taylor 229).

Individuals can take some precautions to help protect themselves from electromagnetic radiation (Taylor 229), as shown in Table 1.

Table 1

Monitor Safety Precautions
Work at least 28 inches from your monitor (an arm's length).
Stay four feet away from the sides and back of monitors (and laser copiers and printers).
Turn off monitor when not using your PC.

Electromagnetic radiation may be a growing menace, as more people use computers both at work and at home. Research is ongoing, and vendors are likely to develop products that will block or greatly reduce these emissions. At present, computer users can take some simple precautions to diminish this possible health hazard.

STEP 5: PREPARE A WORKS CITED PAGE.

The Works Cited page is an alphabetic listing of your sources.

DO: *On a clean screen, key the Works Cited page using these standard formatting instructions. Print the page and save it as MONITOR.CIT.*

---

1. Top margin: 2 inches.
2. Left and right margins: 1 inch.
3. Linespacing: 2 (Quadruple space after the title).
4. No page number.
5. Press (F4) (Shift)-(Tab) to hang indent the first line of each source.

Works Cited

Rosch, Winn L. "Monitor Emissions: Should You Worry?" PC Magazine July 1991: 106-107.

Taylor, Wendy. "Don't Let Your Monitor Be the Death of You." PC Computing January 1991: 228-229.

STEP 6: PREPARE A TITLE PAGE.

The title page should have the following three lines centered horizontally and arranged in a pleasing vertical balance:

1. The title of the paper
2. The author's name
3. The instructor's name, name of the course, the date

DO: *On a clean screen, create and key a title page for the report you have been developing. Key your full name as the author, your instructor's name, and the name of your course. Print and save the title page as MONITOR.TPG.*

STEP 7: ASSEMBLE THE REPORT. Assemble the report in this order and turn in: Title Page, Outline, Report, Works Cited.

UNIT 4

Using Lotus 1-2-3

1

GETTING ACQUAINTED

OBJECTIVES

- Define spreadsheets.
- Recognize the type of keyboard to be used.
- Load the Lotus 1-2-3 program.
- Recognize the spreadsheet screen.
- Understand how to follow instructions in this unit.

SPREADSHEETS

Spreadsheets took the computer world by storm in the late 1970s. This type of program is very easy to use and has many functions that enable a Personal Computer to do serious "number crunching." Spreadsheets not only calculate, but they automatically update related figures when the user makes a change. This automatic update feature advances decision making; key in one number and see what effect it has on others.

Virtually all businesses today use some type of spreadsheet program. The spreadsheet standard of the industry is Lotus 1-2-3, the best-selling software package for IBM and compatible computers. Lotus is not only a spreadsheet, but also a data management and graphics program, hence the name "1-2-3"

THE KEYBOARD

Several configurations of keyboards are available. The keys on an enhanced keyboard are described first, but the keys on a standard keyboard are included. (See the "Hardware" section of *Using Computers* for an illustration of standard and enhanced keyboards.)

If you have an enhanced keyboard, use the cursor keys on the special key pad located between the alphabetic keyboard and the numeric keypad. It is a closer reach from the alphabetic keyboard, and it will free the numeric pad for the frequent keying of numbers in a spreadsheet when you use Num Lock.

If you have a standard keyboard, do not use Num Lock. Use the numeric pad for cursor movement. Then press Shift with a numeric pad key when you want a number.

FUNCTION KEYS AND THE TEMPLATE

When using Lotus, you will seldom be asked to use a function key. If a template is available, it is helpful but not necessary. Although Lotus makes use of ten function keys, only three of them will be used in this book.

THE MOUSE

Beginning with Version 2.3, Lotus 1-2-3 supports a mouse. The mouse can be used for pointer movement, command and help selection, and range specification. Section Two contains instructions for using the mouse for those who have one and prefer to use it.

LOADING LOTUS 1-2-3

The place where the Lotus program is stored varies among computer systems. One of the following may load the program for you; otherwise, ask your instructor.

1. *Two disk drives:*
   a) Start DOS.
   b) Insert the System Disk in Drive A.
   c) Insert your data disk in Drive B.
   d) Key **b:** (↵Enter) to set Drive b as the default for files.
   e) Key **a:123** (↵Enter) to start Lotus 1-2-3.
2. *Hard disk:*
   a) At the DOS prompt, key **cd\lotus** (↵Enter) (or the name of the directory where the Lotus system files are located).
   b) Insert your data diskette in the floppy drive.
   c) Key **123** (↵Enter).
3. *Networked system:*
   a) Log on to the computer system.
   b) Select Lotus 1-2-3 from the menu (or follow teacher directions).

THE SCREEN

When the Lotus 1-2-3 program is loaded, you see the worksheet screen. It displays a control panel at the top, a horizontal display of letters below that, and a vertical display of numbers at the left. An illustration of the worksheet screen and a detailed explanation is included in the next section.

FOLLOWING INSTRUCTIONS

In this book student actions such as data to be keyed, keys to be pressed, cells to be moved to, and options to be chosen will be between rules and specially marked as shown below. (DO NOT KEY now; just read and understand the following directions.)

- **Text to be keyed** will be indicated by the word **KEY:** and will be preceded by the cell at which it should be keyed. For example, you may see:

KEY: [C4] PRACTICE WORKSHEET

This direction means go to cell C4 and key the words PRACTICE WORKSHEET.

- **Keyboard actions other than keying** will be indicated by the word **DO:** and will be preceded by the cell at which it should take place.

  Command keys to press are shown in bold capital letters:

DO: [A6] / **W**orksheet **G**lobal **F**ormat **C**urrency **2** (↵Enter)

This means go to cell A6 and press the keys / W G F C 2 and strike Enter.

- **Other keys** to press are shown inside key caps: (End). If a key is to be held down while pressing another one, the keys will be "locked" together like this: (Ctrl)-(←).
- **File names** are shown in all caps but do not need to be keyed in all caps.

How computers calculate

When using a computer to solve mathematic operations, you must enter formulas correctly to receive an accurate solution. Only numeric values can be used in formulas, and the values must be arranged in the proper order for a correct solution.

The computer performs calculations from left to right, according to the order of operations shown below (LO1.1.) Expressions in parentheses are calculated first, followed by exponents. Multiplication and division are equal and are performed next. Finally addition and subtraction, which are equal, are performed.

Values in a formula must be separated by operators, but Lotus does not allow you to put spaces around the operators. The operators, + – * / ^, are shown with the type of calculation each performs in Figure LO1.1.

FIGURE LO1.1

ORDER OF OPERATIONS			
1) parentheses ( )	2) exponents ^	3) multiplication * or division /	4) addition + or subtraction –

A sample formula, the steps the computer will use to solve it, and the development of the solution are listed below.

Sample formula: 3 + (9 – 5) * 6 – 2^2

1. (9 – 5) = 4
   3 + 4 * 6 – 2^2
2. 2^2 (2 squared or 2 to the second power) = 4
   3 + 4 * 6 – 4
3. 4 * 6 = 24
   3 + 24 – 4
4. 3 + 24 = 27
   27 – 4 = 23

The solution: 23

The Review Exercise at the end of this section will give you practice calculating formulas like the computer does. Knowing how to compose formulas will help you when you work with a spreadsheet or other programs that use numbers.

QUICK QUESTIONS

1. What is a spreadsheet?
2. Do you have a standard or an enhanced keyboard?
3. Will you use the alphabetic keyboard or the numeric pad for numbers?
4. Do you have a template available?
5. What version of Lotus do you have? Does it support a mouse?
6. Write the steps you will use to get Lotus started each time you use it:
7. Name the three parts of the screen you will see when you load Lotus:
   a)
   b)
   c)
8. What does the following notation mean?

   DO: [B8] / **F**ile **S**ave SHEET1 (↵Enter)

9. What does the following notation mean?

   KEY: [F14] TOTAL PURCHASES

10. What does the following notation mean? (Alt)-(F5)
11. Must you key file names in all caps?

REVIEW EXERCISE

As a review for working with figures and formulas, calculate the solutions for the following problems. Follow the order of operations shown on page L4. Write your answers on the lines below. Use a calculator or scrap paper if you wish.

1) 50 – 2^2 * 4 – (22–14) = __________
2) 3^2 / 3 + (28 + 17) * 5 = __________
3) (5*4) + (36 + 41) – 4^2 – (16 / 8) = __________
4) 67 – (8 * 2.25) * 12.5 + (66.75 – 23.4) = __________
5) Find the difference between 3,655.27 and 2,897.82 __________
6) Find the sum: 782.88, 951.74, 68.22, 5,324.41 __________
7) Find the average of the following test scores: 78, 88, 90, 84, 82 __________
8) A business has sales of $621,890 and expenses of $495,339. What is the gross profit? __________
9) A sales person sells $860,000 of product and earns 7% commission on sales. What is the amount of the commission? __________
10) A new computer costs $3,500. With $300 down, a buyer can finance the remaining amount at a simple annual percentage rate of 14% for 4 years. What would the monthly payments be?

____

2

THE BASICS

OBJECTIVES

- Identify **rows** and **columns** that intersect as **cells.**
- Identify areas of the worksheet, including the **control panel.**
- Use various keys to move the **pointer.**
- Recognize that the worksheet is larger than the screen can display at once.
- **Enter data** in the form of labels, values, and formulas.
- Correct miskeying.
- Activate the command menu for Worksheet Erase and Quit.

THE BLANK WORKSHEET

If you have not loaded the Lotus 1-2-3 program, do so according to the steps listed on page L3 or the directions of your instructor. The Lotus worksheet will appear ready for data to be entered. The areas of the worksheet are shown in Figure LO2.1.

COLUMNS AND ROWS. The worksheet can be thought of as a grid of columns and rows, much like an accountant's ruled pad of paper. The worksheet uses vertical **columns** and horizontal **rows**.

BORDERS. Find the **Column Border**, a line of letters across the worksheet beginning with A and going through H. Each letter in the border refers to the column below it. The **Row Border** is a line of numbers going down the left edge of the worksheet, numbered from 1 through 20. Each number in the row border refers to the row beside it. There are many more letters in the column border and numbers in the row border than you can see on your screen at one time. The worksheet contains 256 columns and 8,192 rows.

CELLS. Data is keyed at the intersection of a column and a row, known as a **cell**. Each cell's **address** consists of the column letter and row number of the intersection point. For example, cell address B6 is the intersection of Column B and Row 6. Cell C2 is the intersection of Column C and Row 2. The column letter is always specified *first* in a cell address.

POINTER. The Lotus cursor is rectangular and called the **pointer**. The pointer fills a cell. Right now the pointer is in *Cell A1*, the place where Column A intersects with Row 1. The cell that the pointer is on is known as the **current cell**. The current cell, then, is A1.

ICON PANEL. Beginning with Version 2.3, an **icon panel** for mouse users is provided at the right edge of the screen. This panel contains pictures of screen scroll arrows (◀ ▶ ▲ ▼) and a question mark (?) as a symbol for Help. (Version 3.x also includes ⇧ ⇩ for Page Up and Page Down.)

FIGURE LO2.1
The Empty Worksheet

THE CONTROL PANEL

The three top lines of the Lotus screen, above the Column Border, are referred to as the Control Panel. The Control Panel keeps you informed of the current cell address, the contents and other characteristics of the current cell, and the current operating mode. When you use a Lotus command, the command menu will use the second and third lines of the Control Panel.

CONTENTS LINE. The current cell address (A1) appears in the top left corner of the Control Panel. This area is known as the Contents Line. The Contents Line also displays the contents and format of the current cell when the current cell contains data.

MODE INDICATOR. The current operating mode (READY) appears in the upper right corner. This area of the Control Panel is known as the Mode Indicator. You can enter new data only when the mode indicator displays *READY.*

STATUS LINE. At the bottom of your screen is the **Status Line**. It displays the date and time (not shown in LO1.1), and other items such as NUM when Num Lock is on, CAPS when Caps Lock is on, and SCROLL when Scroll Lock is on.

Watch the Control Panel as you move around the worksheet in the next topic.

QUICK QUESTIONS

1. What is the name for the line of letters across the Lotus worksheet?
2. What is the name for the line of numbers down the left edge of the worksheet?
3. What is the name for the intersection of a column and a row?
4. What is the cell address where Column D and Row 5 intersect?
5. What is the cell address where Row 7 and Column F intersect?
6. What is the name of the Lotus cursor?
7. What is the name that refers to the cell the pointer is on?
8. What is the name for the upper left area of the Control Panel?
9. Where would you look on the Control Panel to see the operating mode?

   What is the name for this area of the Control Panel?
10. What will the operating mode be when you can enter new data?
11. What two items of information are displayed in the lower left area of the worksheet?

MOVING THE POINTER

DO: Press (Home).

Home moves the pointer to the upper left corner, Cell A1, known as the home position. Look at the Contents Line to see the current cell.

DO: Press (→) 5 times.

Look at the Contents Line. What is the current cell (cell address)?

DO: Press (↓) 6 times.

What is the current cell? ____________

DO: Press (←) 3 times.

What is the current cell? ____________

DO: Press (Tab).

Tab moves the pointer *right* to the next screenful of cells. What is the current cell?

DO: Press (Shift)-(Tab).

Shift-Tab moves the pointer *left* to the next screenful of cells. What is the current cell? ________

DO: Press (Page Down).

Page Down moves the pointer *down* to the next screenful of cells. What is the current cell? ________

DO: Press (Page Up).

Page Up moves the pointer ________ (direction) to the next screenful of cells.

GOTO. **F5** is the **Goto** feature, allowing you to quickly move the pointer to any cell. When F5 is pressed, the Contents Line will ask for an address to go to, while it displays the current address. Key the desired cell address.

The current cell is A7. Go to M37.

DO: Press (F5).

KEY: [A7] (M) (3) (7) (↵Enter)

Now try the Goto feature yourself.

DO: Move your cursor to A1 *quickly.*

List two *quick* ways to move your pointer to cell A1: 1) ________ 2) ________

Quickly move to the last row in the worksheet.

DO: Press (End) (↓).

Move the pointer to the last column in the last row.

DO: Press (End) (→).

What is the cell address? ________ Then what is the last *row* of your worksheet? ________ What is the last *column* of your worksheet? ________

The first 26 columns of the worksheet are lettered from A to Z. The next 26 columns are lettered from AA to AZ, followed by columns BA to BZ, CA to CZ, etc. You have seen that only a small portion of the worksheet is visible at one time. You see only the portion of the worksheet that you are currently using.

DO: Press (Home) to return to A1.

THE MOUSE. (Ver 2.3 or newer.) When using a mouse, you have two pointers on your screen at one time. The cursor bar, which Lotus calls the cell pointer, is the size of the cell it occupies. A small square mouse pointer is also visible on the worksheet. In Figure LO2.1, the cursor bar is at Cell A1, and the mouse pointer is at Cell H9. You may move the pointer with the keys described in this book or with the mouse.

Chart LO2.2 shows how the icon panel allows you to use the mouse for pointer movement. For example, to move the pointer down, click the right mouse button on the ▼ symbol on the icon panel. Each time you click on it, the pointer will move down a cell.

FIGURE LO2.2
Moving the Pointer With a Mouse

POINTER MOVEMENT WITH A MOUSE	
Specific cell	Move mouse pointer to cell and click RMB.
Move pointer left	Click RMB on ◄ as many times as desired.
Move pointer right	Click RMB on ► as many times as desired.
Move pointer up	Click RMB on ▲ as many times as desired.
Move pointer down	Click RMB on ▼ as many times as desired.

QUICK QUESTIONS

1. What is the home position?
2. What key moves the pointer to A1?
3. Where will you find the cell address of the current cell?
4. Which key moves the cursor to the left one cell at a time?
5. Which key(s) will move the pointer to the left one screenful of cells?
6. Which key(s) will move the pointer up one screenful of cells?
7. What is the Goto key?
8. Write the 3 steps necessary to goto cell S88:
   a)
   b)
   c)
9. How many total columns does Lotus have?
10. How many total rows does Lotus have?
11. How many total cells are on the Lotus worksheet?

Correcting Errors

As you enter data, you may make errors of different kinds. Refer to chart LO2.3 when needed. It tells how to correct or cancel miskeying, cancel commands you have started, and make a cell blank. Notice, particularly, that (Esc) is used to correct many errors.

FIGURE LO2.3
Error Correction Chart

Error	Typing Status	Correction
miskeyed data	currently typing in that cell	1) backspace to erase and **rekey** or 2) press **Esc** to cancel the typing and then rekey
	have moved to a different cell	1) go back to the cell in error and **rekey** or 2) go back to the cell in error and press **F2** to edit
keyed data in a cell that should be blank	currently typing in that cell	press **Esc** to cancel the typing
	have moved to a different cell	go back to the cell in error and press **Delete** or use the **Range Erase** command
miskeyed a command	currently typing	press **Esc** to take one step back
	have moved on	go through the command again, choosing the correct option

DATA ENTRY

You will key a short party food list and then find the cost. Remember [C3] means move the pointer to Cell C3 and key. Watch the changes on the control panel as you key data. Use the chart above (LO2.3) to correct errors.

KEY: [A1] PARTY FOODS

After keying PARTY FOODS in cell A1, move the pointer to the cells given below for more data entry. Move down the columns using (↓). Key the data in initial caps as shown.

KEY: [A3] Chips

KEY: [A4] Cheese

KEY: [A5] Crackers

KEY: [A6] Punch

KEY: [A7] Cookies

LABELS. You have entered a heading and the food items. These text entries are known as **labels**.

DO: Check the accuracy of your keying; correct any mistakes.

KEY: [B3] 2.49

KEY: [B4] 3.99

KEY: [B5] 2.39

KEY: [B6] 4.99

KEY: [B7] 2.99

NUMBERS. The amounts you just entered are known as **numeric values**. Remember, only *numeric values* can be calculated.

Tell Lotus to calculate your total bill by adding the cost of the items. Be sure you key the entry at B9 exactly as shown, keying the + first, and *no spaces* within the formula. It is not necessary to key the formula in capital letters. (Later in this unit you will learn a much better way to add a group of numbers.)

KEY: [A9] TOTAL

KEY: [B9] +B3+B4+B5+B6+B7

Notice that the formula is displayed at the left on the second line of the Control Panel.

DO: Press ↵Enter

FORMULAS. You keyed a **formula** at B9 that added the amounts in Cells B3 through B7. Although you keyed a formula and it appears on the Contents Line of the Control Panel, Cell B9 in the worksheet shows the *answer* to the formula. Look at the Contents Line for the formula keyed and look at the worksheet for the answer to that formula.

Key a plus sign before a formula that starts with a cell address, even if the formula does a different arithmetic process like multiply or subtract. A plus sign (or a minus sign or parentheses) keyed as the first character in a cell will make the cell numeric. If you just keyed the *B* in *B3* first, Lotus would assume a label, and labels *cannot* be calculated. Only numeric values can be calculated!

Your worksheet should look like Figure LO2.4.

FIGURE L02.4
The Completed Worksheet

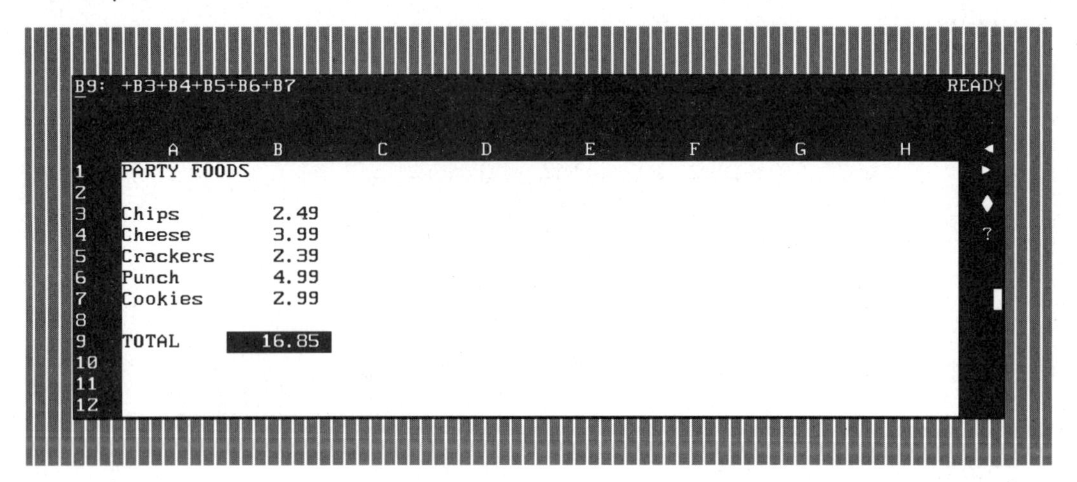

Command Menu

Special features, commands, and formatting are accomplished with the **Command Menu**. Using a tree structure, each command option will lead to another set of options until options are exhausted. Command menus are activated by pressing the slash key (/) or by moving the mouse to the Control Panel. When shown a command to key, *key the first letter of each word in the command*, shown in bold print. (Or click the right mouse button, RMB, on each command.)

Erase the Worksheet

To erase a worksheet, use the **Worksheet Erase** command. Clear the practice worksheet now by pressing / W E Y to complete the command **W**orksheet **E**rase **Y**es. Notice, the first letter of each word in the command is in bold print.

DO: Press / to activate the command menu.

DO: Press **W**orksheet **E**rase **Y**es. (**Y**es a second time if asked to verify the erasure.)

Quit

Use the **Quit** command to exit properly from Lotus 1-2-3 and return to the system prompt or program menu. Beginning in the next section, you must save your work before using this command.

DO: Press / **Q**uit **Y**es (**Y**es to verify if asked).

QUICK QUESTIONS

1. If you miskey data that you are currently entering in a cell, what are two methods to correct it?
   a)
   b)
2. If you keyed in a cell that should be blank and you have moved to a different cell, what should you do?
3. If you miskey the command you are currently entering, how can you go back a step in the command menu?
4. What is the name for alphabetic entries?
5. What is the name for numeric entries that can be calculated?
6. Can you have spaces between the elements in a formula?
7. Must a formula be keyed in capital letters?
8. Where on the screen should you look to see the actual formula as it was keyed?
9. Where on the screen should you look to see the answer to a formula?
10. What is the only type of data that can be calculated?
11. What character must be at the beginning of all formulas that have a cell address as the first value?
12. Which key activates the command menu?
13. What keys are pressed to exit from the Lotus program?
14. Does using the Quit command save your worksheet?

Follow these steps to practice entering data into a worksheet.

1. Load Lotus 1-2-3 or clear a worksheet on your screen with / **W**orksheet **E**rase **Y**es. (**Y**es if asked to verify.)
2. Key the following heading at [A1]: ALA CARTE.
3. Enter the following labels in Column A, beginning in Cell A3.
   [A3] Salad
   [A4] Soup
   [A5] Sandwich
   [A6] Drink
   [A7] Dessert

4. Enter the following numbers in Column B, beginning in cell B3. (Zeroes will not be displayed.)
   [B3] 2.25
   [B4] 1.80
   [B5] 2.50
   [B6] .75
   [B7] 1.25
5. Key the following at [A9]: TOTAL
6. Enter the formula to add all prices at [B9]: +B3+B4+B5+B6+B7 (Enter)
7. Check the accuracy of the worksheet and correct any errors. The sum **8.55** should appear in cell B9.
8. Clear the sheet. Press / **W**orksheet **E**rase **Y**es **Y**es.

REINFORCEMENT ACTIVITY

Follow these steps to practice entering data into a worksheet.

1. Enter the heading in cells A1 and B1:
   [A1] MONTHLY
   [B1] EXPENSES
2. Enter the following labels in Column A, beginning in Cell A3:
   [A3] Rent
   [A4] Electric
   [A5] Water
   [A6] Telephone
   [A7] Food
   [A8] Car Pmt.
   [A9] Gas & Oil
   [A10] Leisure
3. Enter the following numbers in Column B, beginning in Cell B3:
   [B3] 310
   [B4] 48.65
   [B5] 15.43
   [B6] 34.76
   [B7] 195.28
   [B8] 165.55
   [B9] 62
   [B10] 78.88
4. Key the following label at [A12]: TOTAL
5. Enter the formula to add all prices at [B12]: +B3+B4+B5+B6+B7+B8+B9+B10
6. Check the accuracy of the worksheet and correct any errors. The sum **910.55** should appear in Cell B12.
7. Quit Lotus 1-2-3.

3

DATA ENTRY

OBJECTIVES

- Select and cancel the **command menu.**
- Use **Help.**
- Determine when to use **labels** and **numbers.**
- Use **label prefix characters.**
- Set **column width.**
- Set **default drive.**
- **Save** a worksheet.
- **Quit** the program.

COMMAND MENU

Lotus 1-2-3 has easy-to-use commands that are displayed step by step on the screen. Once a command is chosen, the next set of choices appears. The illustration below shows how the command menus progress step by step, level by level. The command to widen a column is shown as an example:

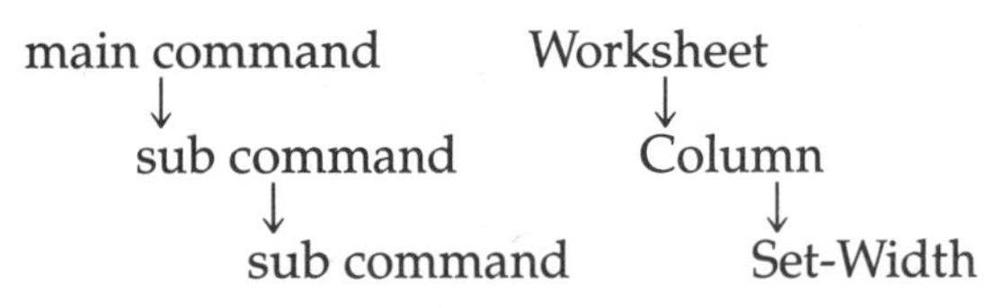

The **command menu** is activated by pressing the / key or moving the mouse to the Control Panel.

DO: Load the Lotus 1-2-3 program if necessary. A blank worksheet should appear on your screen.

DO: Press / to activate the command menu.

The command menu displays three lines of information on the Control Panel (LO3.1):

Top line: the current cell (A1) and the Mode Indicator (Menu).

Second line: the main command menu.

Third line: a sub command menu. (The sub commands shown are for the Worksheet command because it is highlighted at this time.)

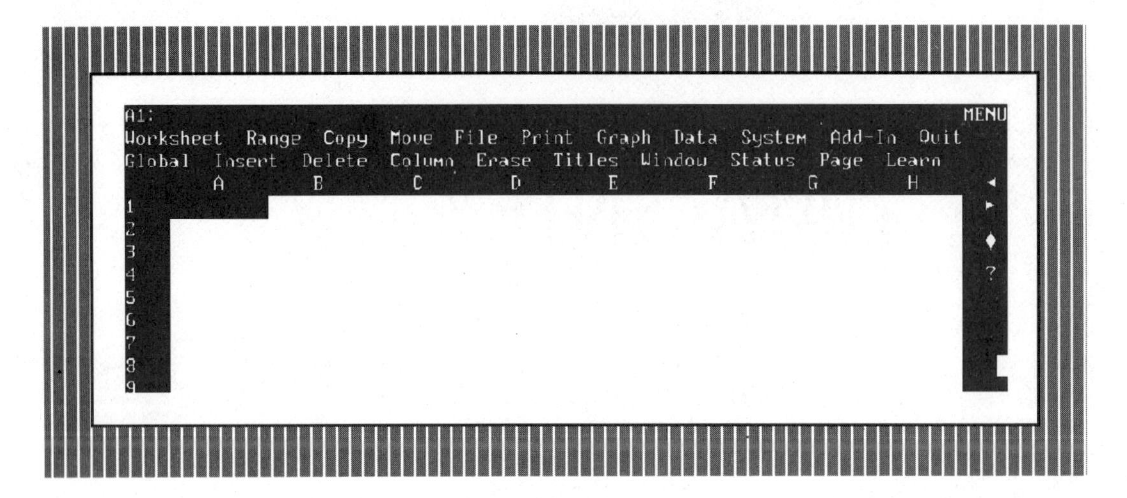

FIGURE L03.1
The Command Menu

SELECTING A COMMAND. A command may be selected by moving the pointer to the command and pressing Enter, by pressing the first letter of the command, or by clicking the left mouse button (LMB) on the command name. Pressing the first letter of the command is the preferred means of selecting commands because it is usually quicker.

COLUMN WIDTH. The default width of columns is *nine* spaces. If the default width is changed, a number in brackets on the Contents Line indicates the new size of the column. For example, [W12] indicates a column width of 12. If no width indication appears, the column still has the default size of 9 spaces. Use the **Worksheet Column Set-Width** command to widen all cells in a column. The pointer can be at any cell in the column when you use the command.

Change the width of Column A to 12 spaces.

DO: Check that the command menu shown in LO3.1 is displayed on your screen. If not, press / to activate it.

To complete commands, press the first letter of each word in the command; the letters are shown in bold. Press W C S 1 2 to complete the next command.

DO: [A1] **W**orksheet **C**olumn **S**et-Width 1 2 Enter. Notice the Contents Line shows [W12] for width of 12.

DO: Move the pointer to any cell in Column C. Use the steps above to set a column width of 16 spaces for all cells in Column C. Look for [W16] on the Contents Line.

BACK OUT OR CANCEL A COMMAND. If you start a command and change your mind or press the wrong key, you may back out one step at a time or entirely cancel the command you have started. Each time you press (Esc) or click the right mouse button (RMB) you will back out one command level. Pressing (Ctrl)-(Break) will cancel the entire command.

DO: Begin a command. Press / **W**orksheet **I**nsert.

DO: Back out of the command one level at a time. Press (Esc) 3 times or click RMB 3 times.

DO: Begin the command again. Press / **W**orksheet **I**nsert.

DO: Press (Ctrl)-(Break) to cancel the command.

HELP

To find out more about commands or other features of the program, get **Help** by pressing (F1) or clicking LMB on the question mark (?) on the icon panel.

DO: Look at the upper right corner of the Control Panel to be sure you are out of the Menu mode and in the Ready mode. If not, press (Ctrl)-(Break). Press (F1) or click LMB on the ? on the icon panel.

The 1-2-3 Help Index appears. The Help screen varies among the different versions of Lotus; however, it does improve with each version. Press (Esc) or RMB to exit help.

DO: Spend some time learning how to scroll through Help to get information about the various Lotus features. Press (Esc) to exit Help.

Activate the command menu to get Help about a command.

DO: Activate the command menu. Press (/) or move the mouse to the Control Panel.

The main command *Worksheet* is highlighted. Below the main command line are the sub commands, the options available if you choose Worksheet: Global, Insert, Delete, Column, Erase, Titles, Window, Status, Page, Learn.

Find out more about the Worksheet sub command *Window*.

DO: Press (W) for Worksheet or click on the command with LMB.

The sub commands have moved up to line two on the Control Panel and now have their own sub commands.

DO: Move the menu pointer to Window.

DO: Press (F1) or click LMB on the ? symbol for the Help screen.

What does the **W**orksheet **W**indow command do? ____________

After pressing / **W**orksheet **W**indow, what would occur if you chose *Vertical*? ______________________________

____

What would occur if you chose *Clear*? ______________________________

DO: Press (Esc) or click RMB to exit Help.

DO: Cancel the command menu by pressing (Ctrl)-(Break). You should be in Ready mode.

Use the Help feature when you have questions or are just curious about a command. Always use the Help feature before asking your instructor for help.

QUICK QUESTIONS

1. Why do many people think Lotus 1-2-3 commands are easy to use?
2. Name two ways to activate the command menu.
   a)
   b)
3. What is displayed on each line of the Control Panel when the command menu is activated?
   a) top line:
   b) second line:
   c) third line:
4. Name three ways to select a command.
   a)
   b)
   c)
5. What is the preferred means of selecting a command and why?
6. What key is pressed to back up one command level?
7. What keys are pressed to cancel an entire command?
8. What key is pressed for Help?
9. What key is pressed to exit Help?

Labels

Text entries are called **labels** in Lotus. When you key a letter as the first character in a cell, Lotus assumes you are keying a label and will display an apostrophe (') at the Mode Indicator on the Contents Line. Labels can never be used in calculations.

DO: As you key data, use the Error Correction Chart on page L12 in Lotus Section Two when needed.

DO: Press (Home) to go to A1.

KEY: [A1] G

DO: Look at the Mode Indicator. Lotus assumes you are keying a label.

KEY: [A1] eorge Washington (↵Enter)

SPILL OVER. The label you keyed at A1 extends beyond the cell. If the cells to the right of a label are blank, the label will *spill over* into those cells. If the cells to the right of a label contain data, the label will be *cut off* when it appears in the worksheet.

DO: Look at the Contents Line: A1 [W12] 'George Washington.

LABEL PREFIX CHARACTERS. The apostrophe in front of the *G* in *George* is the default **label prefix character**. A label prefix character determines where a label will be aligned in a cell. Every label has either the default label prefix character or one you select. Except for the left align, label prefix characters only align when the text entered is smaller than the cell width.

Numeric values should never have a label prefix character. If you get an error message when completing a formula, check for a label prefix character in the contents of cells used in the formula. (You may refer to illustration LOCHECK 3.1 on page L23 as you complete the worksheet.)

DO: Move to A4.

KEY: [A4] red (↵Enter)

DO: Look at the Contents Line. An apostrophe appears in front of the label.

The apostrophe as a label prefix character aligns the label at the *left* of the cell. This is the default alignment for labels. The label *red* is aligned at the left of Cell A4. Chart LO3.2 shows the label prefix characters and the positions they determine.

DO: Move to A6.

KEY: [A6] (") yellow (↵Enter)

Look at the Contents Line. Quote marks appear in front of *yellow*. The label is aligned at the *right* of the cell.

DO: Move to A8.

KEY: [A8] (^) blue (↵Enter)

Look at the Contents Line. The carat aligns *blue* in the center of the cell.

FIGURE LO3.2
Chart of Label Prefix Characters

LABEL PREFIX CHARACTERS	
'	Aligns at the left of the cell (default)
"	Aligns at the right of the cell
^	Aligns at the center of the cell

DO: Move your cursor to the cells shown in brackets below and key the labels. Do not press Enter; simply press (↓) to move to the next cell.

KEY: [C3] (^) center

KEY: [C5] (") right

KEY: [C7] (') left

Numbers

When you key a numeric digit or numeric symbol as the first character of a cell, Lotus assumes you are entering a **number or formula** and will display *Value* as the Mode Indicator. Numeric symbols include the plus sign, minus sign, decimal point, and parenthesis. Keying a number surrounded with parentheses gives the same effect as preceding the number with a plus sign.

DO: Watch the Mode Indicator as you key numbers. Notice which numeric symbols appear in the cell when the entry is completed.

KEY: [D1] 12345

KEY: [D2] .5531

KEY: [D3] +3792

KEY: [D4] –8888

KEY: [D5] (2706)

KEY: [D6] 44.55

KEY: [D7] 37

Except for necessary decimal points and minus signs for negative numbers, you *do not* control the appearance of numbers when you key them. A little later you will use commands to format numbers. Numbers must align on the right of the cell without a label prefix character.

KEY: [D8] 2,376,127 (↵Enter)

Lotus beeps at you (Ver 2.x) or ignores the commas (Ver 3.x) because you may not key *commas, spaces, or dollar signs* with a number. If the Mode Indicator displays *Edit*, you may make the following correction.

DO: Use the (←) cursor key to position the cursor on one of the commas. Press (Delete). Delete the second comma and then press (↵Enter).

A LABEL THAT BEGINS WITH A NUMBER. Occasionally you will want an entry that starts with a number to be accepted as a label. To do this, press the desired label prefix character before the number.

KEY: [D10] ' 372 W. 25

KEY: [D11] ^ 3D

KEY: [D12] " 5 mpg

A NUMERIC CELL THAT IS TOO NARROW. If a number or the result of a formula exceeds the width of the cell, asterisks (*) will appear across the cell or the number will be converted to scientific notation. (An example of scientific notation is 3.4E+09.)

DO: Press F5 and go to Cell F1.

KEY: [F1] 3447692364 ↵Enter

The number is displayed in scientific notation or asterisks because the cell has the default width of nine characters. Widen Cell F1 so the number can be shown in its entirety.

KEY: [F1] / **W**orksheet **C**olumn **S**et-Width 1 2 ↵Enter

Widen Column A. (This can be done at any cell in Column A.)

KEY: [A1] / **W**orksheet **C**olumn **S**et-Width

DO: Press → until the column is wide enough to display the entire label in A1, setting the width at 18. Press ↵Enter.

It is a common task to widen columns for both labels and numbers.

DO: Check your work with LOCHECK 3.1.

FIGURE LOCHECK3.1

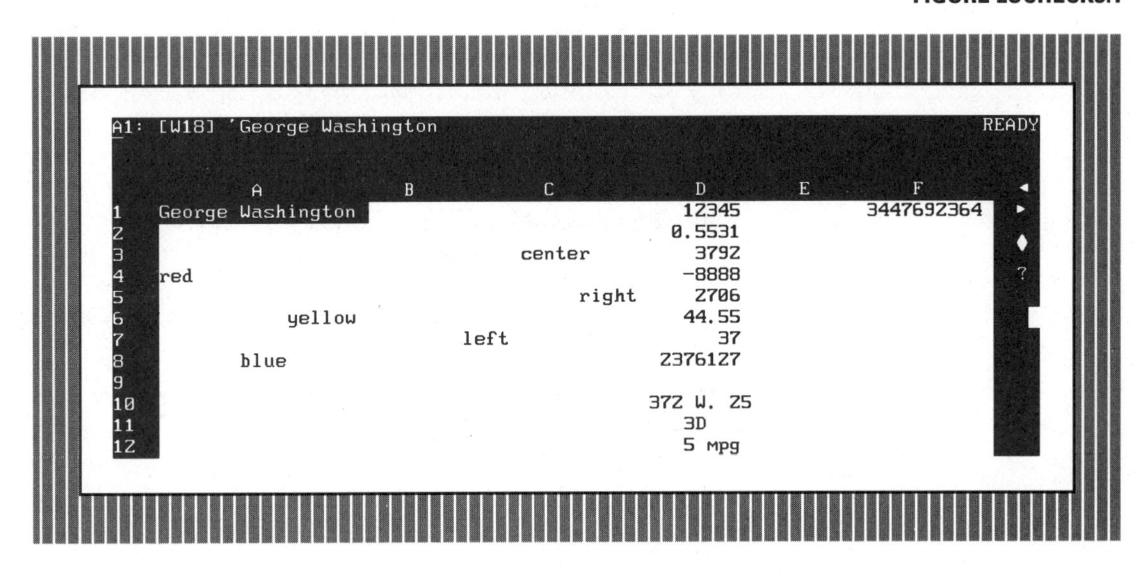

QUICK QUESTIONS

1. What are labels?
2. What does Lotus do if a label is longer than the cell and has blank cells to the right?
3. What does Lotus do if a label is longer than the cell and has data in the cells to the right?
4. Looking at the Contents Line, what is the meaning of an apostrophe in front of an entry?
5. How would you key the label *Week 1* if it was to be aligned at the center of a cell?
6. How would the label *"TOTAL* appear in a cell?
7. Could the entry *"3776* be used in a calculation? Why or why not?
8. If you press a plus or minus sign as the first character of a cell, what type of entry will it be?
9. Do numbers align at the right or the left of a cell?
10. Should you key dollar signs, commas, or spaces in a numeric entry?
11. What should you press before keying an address such as *6712 Eastern Avenue*?
12. What should you do if a number is changed to scientific notation or asterisks?
13. What is the default column width?
14. What command should you use to widen a column if the longest data is *Indianapolis, IN 46250*?

DEFAULT DRIVE

It will save you keying time if you designate the drive and path for storing your Lotus worksheets. This drive specification or directory can be a temporary one, or it can be a permanent one.

DO: Place a check mark in front of the directory specification your instructor wants you to use, and then key the correct directory command of the two shown below.

_____ Temporary Directory   _____ Permanent Directory

TEMPORARY DIRECTORY. Use the **File Directory** command to set a temporary directory each time you use Lotus.

/ **File** **Directory** *drive and path* (↵Enter)

PERMANENT DIRECTORY. Use the **Worksheet Global Default Directory** command to set a permanent directory that will remain in effect for your computer.

/ **Worksheet** **Global** **Default** **Directory** *drive and path* (↵Enter) **Update** **Quit**

SAVING LOTUS WORKSHEETS

Once the default drive is set, the **File Save** command is used to store the worksheet on the disk. When using Lotus 1-2-3, do *not* give files a file extension. Lotus automatically gives all worksheets the file extension **.WK1** in Ver. 2.x and **.WK3** in Ver. 3.x. This standard file extension makes Lotus worksheets recognizable both by computer users and the Lotus program itself when using the File Retrieve command.

Save the practice worksheet on your disk.

DO: / **File** **Save** LO3PRAC (↵Enter).

The program saves the file and the Mode Indicator displays *Ready*. The worksheet, however, remains on your screen.

After saving a worksheet, either use the Worksheet Erase command to get a new, clean worksheet or use the Quit command to exit from Lotus. Quit will return you to the system prompt or menu.

DO: Use either / **Worksheet** **Erase** **Yes** or / **Quit** **Yes**.

QUICK QUESTIONS

1. Compare the temporary directory command function to the permanent directory command function.
2. What sub command is used after keying the drive and path when setting the permanent directory?
3. Why is it important that you do not give worksheets a file extension?
4. What two commands should you use after you have completed a worksheet if you wish to save it on your disk and start a new worksheet?
   a)
   b)
5. What command will exit from Lotus and return you to the system prompt or menu?

REVIEW EXERCISE

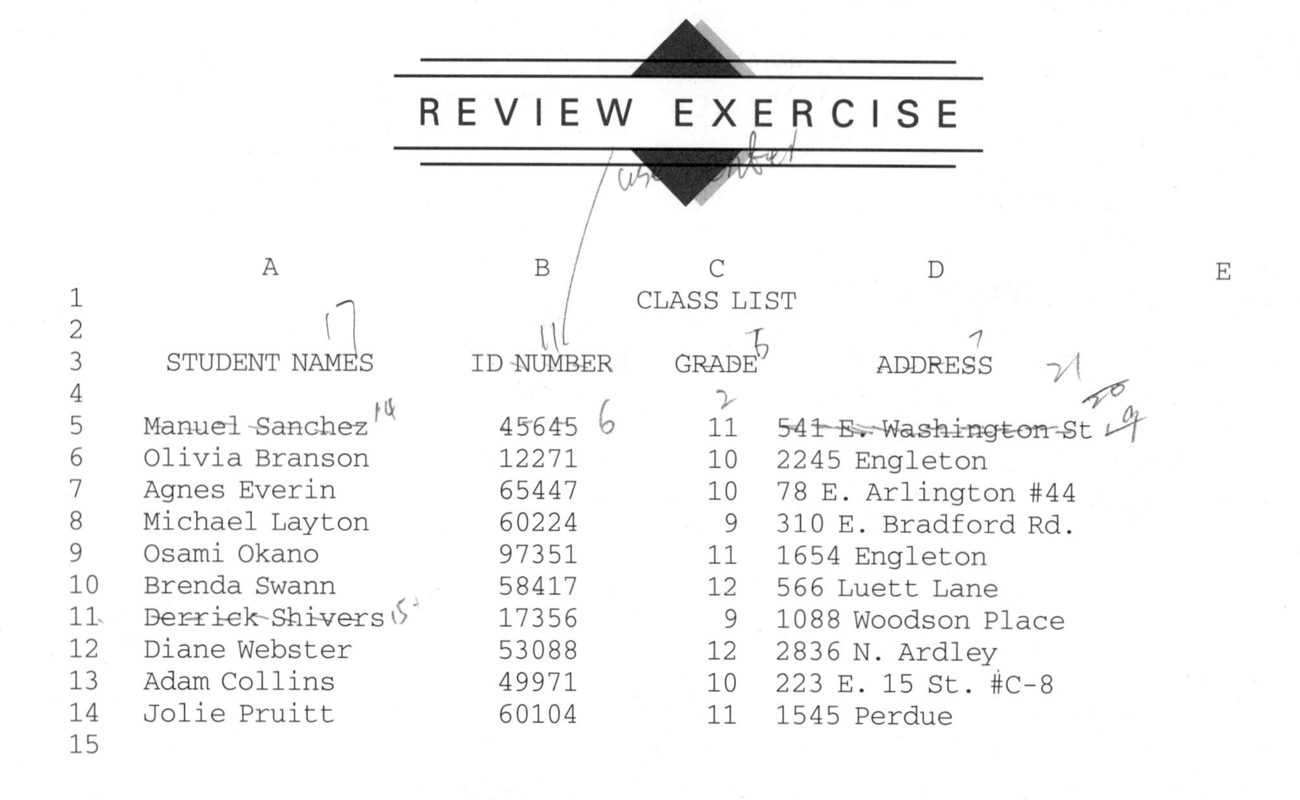

	A	B	C	D	E
1			CLASS LIST		
2					
3	STUDENT NAMES	ID NUMBER	GRADE	ADDRESS	
4					
5	Manuel Sanchez	45645	11	541 E. Washington St	
6	Olivia Branson	12271	10	2245 Engleton	
7	Agnes Everin	65447	10	78 E. Arlington #44	
8	Michael Layton	60224	9	310 E. Bradford Rd.	
9	Osami Okano	97351	11	1654 Engleton	
10	Brenda Swann	58417	12	566 Luett Lane	
11	Derrick Shivers	17356	9	1088 Woodson Place	
12	Diane Webster	53088	12	2836 N. Ardley	
13	Adam Collins	49971	10	223 E. 15 St. #C-8	
14	Jolie Pruitt	60104	11	1545 Perdue	
15					

Follow these steps to create the worksheet you see above.

1. Load Lotus if necessary, or clear an existing worksheet.
2. At C1 key the heading in all caps.
3. At A3 key the column heading STUDENT NAMES.
4. In Cells A5 through A14 key the student names.
5. Go to the longest name in Column A and widen the cell enough to leave one blank space after the name.
6. At B3 key the column heading in all caps ID NUMBER.
7. Key the numbers in Column B.
8. At C3 right align the heading GRADE.
9. Enter the grades in Column C.
10. At D3 center the heading ADDRESS.
11. Key the addresses in Column D, using the apostrophe label prefix character so they will be accepted as labels.
12. Widen Column D for the longest address.
13. Save the worksheet as LOREV3 and erase the worksheet.
14. If time remains, go on to the Reinforcement Activity. If not, quit Lotus 1-2-3.

ACTIVITY A - ACCOUNT BALANCES

	A	B	C	D	E
1			CUSTOMER ACCOUNT BALANCES		
2					
3	ACCOUNT		ACCOUNT		
4	BALANCE		NUMBER	CUSTOMER NAME	
5					
6	45.22		456-22-8874	Williams, Richard Mrs.	
7	105.33		656-85-9114	Tipton, Gladys	
8	-22.5		551-34-2782	Mendez, Oscar	
9	3.66		461-82-4645	Richardson, Luetta Ms.	
10	557.25		405-86-3622	Anderson, Brett	
11	53.78		386-42-6890	Crowder, Tom	
12	69.42		312-86-2448	Isobe, Reiko	
13	245.36		865-44-9074	Tramplin, Belinda Mrs.	
14	15.99		566-28-7671	Johnson, Elliott Mrs.	
15	37.98		389-65-4430	Johnson, Robin	
16					

Follow these steps to create the worksheet you see above.

1. Load Lotus if necessary, or clear an existing worksheet.
2. At C1 key the heading in all caps
3. At A3 and A4 center the column headings.
4. Key the numeric data in Column A.
5. At C3 and C4 center the column headings.
6. Key the remaining data in Column C, treating the numbers as labels.
7. Widen Column C to 14 spaces.
8. At D4 center the column heading.
9. Key the remaining data in Column D.
10. Widen Column D as much as necessary for the longest name.
11. Check for accuracy. Use the Error Correction Chart on page L12 if necessary.
12. Save the worksheet as LORA3A and erase the worksheet.
13. Go on to Reinforcement Activity B or quit Lotus 1-2-3.

ACTIVITY B - EMPLOYEE ROSTER

	A	B	C	D	E
1		EMPLOYEE ROSTER			
2					
3	SS#	NAME	DATE HIRED	DEPARTMENT	
4					
5	654-82-9644	Todd, Terri	02-07-89	Personnel	
6	455-95-1247	Dane, Aaron	11-24-78	Accounting	
7	657-11-8435	Bowman, Terry	11-05-82	Shipping	
8	514-12-6795	Liang, Chih	08-18-88	Accounting	
9	354-81-6849	Watson, Gayle	08-22-88	Admin	
10	654-97-1891	Allen, Harold	10-12-91	Shipping	
11	477-16-5843	Coyle, Alicia	02-06-92	Admin	
12	376-58-2208	Truett, Janey	04-19-91	Admin	
13					

Follow these steps to create the worksheet you see above.

1. At B1 key the heading in all caps.
2. At A3 key the column heading.
3. Key the remaining data in Column A as labels.
4. Widen Column A to 12 spaces.
5. At B3 key the column heading.
6. Key the remaining data in Column B.
7. Widen Column B as much as necessary for the longest name.
8. At C3 key the column heading.
9. Key the remaining data in Column C as labels.
10. Widen Column C by two spaces.
11. At D3 key the column heading.
12. Key the remaining data in Column D.
13. Widen Column D as much as needed.
14. Check for accuracy; correct errors.
15. Save the worksheet as LORA3B and erase the worksheet or exit from Lotus.

4

FORMULAS AND FUNCTIONS

OBJECTIVES

- **Retrieve** a worksheet.
- **Resave** a worksheet.
- Use **formulas.**
- **Edit** cells.
- **Point** to cells.
- Use @sum, @avg, @min, and @max **functions.**

RETRIEVE

An existing worksheet is brought into RAM with the **File Retrieve** command. When you use this command, all of the worksheet files on your disk with .WK1 or .WK3 file extensions are displayed on the Control Panel so you can select the one desired. (If you prefer, you may instead key the name of the file you want to retrieve.)

DO: Press / **F**ile **R**etrieve.

The third line of the Control Panel lists files with **.WK1** or **.WK3** file extensions. When you have more files than Lotus can display at once, press (→) to see other file names.

DO: Move the pointer through the file list to LO3PRAC. Press (↵Enter). The worksheet appears on your screen.

DO: Move the worksheet pointer to Cell A12. In the next step you will key the word *Edited* followed by the current date, as in *Edited 10/21/94.*

KEY: [A12] Edited (today's date) (↵Enter)

RESAVE A WORKSHEET

If you retrieve a worksheet, edit it, and save it a second time, you have a choice of giving the edited file a new name or the same name as the original. If you wish to save the file with the same name, you will be prompted to be sure you want to replace the original version with the edited version. This erases the original worksheet.

DO: Press / **F**ile **S**ave.

The original file name appears on the second line of the control panel. If you wish to save the file with a new name, just key it. You will give the file the new name LO4PRAC.

KEY: LO4PRAC (↵Enter)

The worksheet is saved as LO4PRAC, but it remains on your screen. In the next instruction, key the words *Second edit* followed by the current date.

KEY: [A14] Second edit (today's date) (↵Enter)

If you wish to save a worksheet under its original name, press (↵Enter) and then select *Replace.*

DO: Resave this file. Press / **F**ile **S**ave (↵Enter). (See LO4.1.)

FIGURE LO4.1
The Cancel or Replace Options

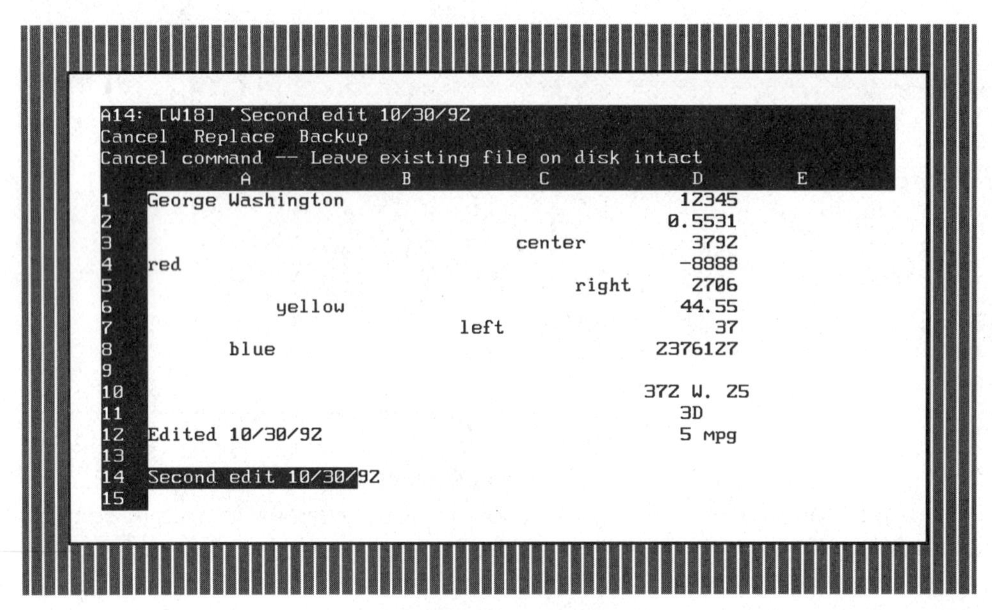

The choice of *Cancel* or *Replace* appears. (Some versions give an additional Backup choice.) If you choose *Cancel,* the file is not saved. If you choose *Replace,* the original file is overwritten on the disk.

DO: Select **R**eplace.

The worksheet is saved on your disk as LO4PRAC, but it remains on the screen.

DO: Erase the worksheet with / **W**orksheet **E**rase **Y**es.

Try the resave options again. Retrieve LOREV3.

DO: / **F**ile **R**etrieve (move the pointer to LOREV3 and then press (↵Enter)).

DO: Goto A16.

KEY: [A16] Your name, today's date, LOREV3A (↵Enter)

Save the worksheet with a different name, LOREV3**A**. The addition of the letter A makes a different file name.

DO: / **F**ile **S**ave.

KEY: LOREV3A

DO: Press (↵Enter) when you're sure you have spelled the file name correctly.

DO: Erase the worksheet, / **W**orksheet **E**rase **Y**es.

Retrieve and then save the worksheet with the same name, LOREV3A.

DO: Retrieve LOREV3A.

KEY: [A18] Second edit (↵Enter)

DO: Resave the file with the same name. Press / **F**ile **S**ave (↵Enter) **R**eplace.

DO: Erase the worksheet.

QUICK QUESTIONS

1. What file names does Lotus display when you use the File Retrieve command?
2. When you retrieve a worksheet and edit it, what are your two choices when saving it?
   a)
   b)
3. What prompt do you see if you try to resave a file with the original file name?
4. What command is used to erase a worksheet from the screen when it is no longer needed?

FORMULAS

Formulas perform calculations on numbers, other formulas, or on the contents of other cells. The following are examples of formulas:

- 1376.50*375
- (4627)-(50*.376)
- +D5/D1
- +B3-(B4*.7)
- +C12+$E$8

When you enter a formula in a cell, Lotus displays the *result* of the calculation in the cell. You can view the *formula* itself by looking at the Contents Line on the Control Panel.

CALCULATING WITH NUMBERS. The basic operators are: + for addition, – for subtraction, * for multiplication, and / for division.

DO: Have a clear worksheet. Use the numeric pad to key numbers and operators. DO NOT place *spaces* anywhere in the formulas.

DO: Widen Column A to 15.

KEY: [A1] 7689.352+8869.17563 (↵Enter)

Notice Cell A1 displays the result of the formula. The Control Panel cell contents, however, display the formula itself. What is the result of the formula? ___________

KEY: [A3] 3766.917-211.27 (↵Enter). What is the result of the formula? ___________

KEY: [A5] 476.175*7843.62 (↵Enter). What is the result? ___________

KEY: [A7] 4289.75/874.18 (↵Enter). What is the result? ___________

DO: Widen column C to 15.

KEY: [C2] 4781.44+(576.44*1.12) (↵Enter).

CALCULATING WITH CELL VALUES. When using cell values in a formula, move the pointer to each cell as you build the formula. This is called **pointing** to cells, and it is more accurate than keying cell addresses yourself. Begin the formula with + in the cell at which the result should appear. To get the result of the formula A5-C2 in Cell C4, key (+) in C4 and then point to the first cell of the formula.

KEY: [C4] (+)

DO: Move the pointer to A5. Notice the cell contents line on the Control Panel as you build the formula by *pointing* to cells.

KEY: [A5] (-)

DO: Move the pointer to C2. Look at the cell contents for the formula you have built. What is the formula? ___________

DO: Press (↵Enter). What is the result of the formula? ___________

Build another formula, A1/ (divided by) A3-A7, with the result in Cell C6.

KEY: [C6] (+)

DO: Point to A1.

KEY: [A1] /

DO: Point to A3.

KEY: [A3] -

DO: Point to A7. Press Enter. What is the formula at C6? ____________

Find the total of the numbers in Column A.

KEY: [A9] +

DO: Point to A7. Press +.

DO: Point to A5. Press +.

DO: Point to A3. Press +.

DO: Point to A1. Press Enter to complete the formula.

The result appears at A9, where the original plus sign was keyed. What is the result? ____________

DO: Total all the numbers in Column C using similar steps to those above. The result of the formula should appear at cell C8. What is the result? ____________

DO: Save the worksheet as LO4FORM and erase the worksheet.

EDIT CELLS

Take a few moments to review how to correct miskeyed data according to the Error Correction Chart on page L12. When you make an error while keying in a cell, just backspace and rekey. When you have moved on to another cell, use the **Edit** command to make corrections.

To use the Edit command, go to the cell in error and press F2 to display the cell contents on the Control Panel's edit line. Then use the cursor keys to move to the inaccurate character(s) and strikeover, insert, or delete.

Edit a cell with strikeover.

DO: Retrieve LO4FORM. (Don't forget to use → when needed to see more file names.)

DO: Move the pointer to cell A5. At A5 press F2 to edit the cell. The cell contents appear on the edit line.

DO: Use ← to place the cursor on the *1* in the first number. Press Insert to overstrike. Press 2 as the correct number.

DO: Use (→) to place the cursor on the *3* in the second number. You are still in overstrike mode, so just press (9).

DO: Check the formula: 476.275*7849.62. If correct, press (↵Enter) with the cursor at any position.

Edit another cell. The formula at A7 should be a subtraction formula instead of division. Also, an additional subtraction of 379.228 should be added at the end of the formula.

DO: Move the pointer to A7. Press (F2) to begin the Edit feature.

DO: Move the cursor to the division sign (/) and press (Insert) to overstrike. Key the minus sign ((−)). Press (Insert) again to end overstrike.

DO: Move to the right end of the formula using the (End) key.

KEY: [A7] (−) 379.225 (↵Enter). What is the new formula result? ____________

Edit a cell with Insert.

DO: Goto C4 and press (F2) to edit.

DO: Use (←) to move to the minus sign (–).

KEY: (+)(A) (7)

DO: The new formula should be +A5+A7-C2. Press (↵Enter) when the formula is correct.

Edit a cell with Delete.

DO: Goto C2. Press (F2) to edit.

DO: Press (←) to move to the far left of the contents, on the first *4* of 4781.44.

DO: Press (Delete) to delete 4781.44+.

DO: The new formula is (576.44*1.12). Press (↵Enter) when the formula is correct.

DO: Save the worksheet as LO4EDIT and then erase the worksheet.

QUICK QUESTIONS

1. What three values may be used in formulas?
   a)
   b)
   c)
2. Where will an actual formula be displayed?
3. Where will the result of a formula be displayed?

4. Write the operators used for addition, subtraction, multiplication, and division.
5. When building a formula by pointing to cells, where should you begin the formula and what should you key there?
6. How should you correct an error when you are still keying in the cell?
7. How should you correct an error when you have moved on to another cell?
8. Which key is used to activate Edit?
9. What three functions can you perform when editing?
   a)
   b)
   c)

FUNCTIONS

Lotus provides shortcuts called **functions** for complex formulas and other types of operations. Functions are used for mathematical, statistical, financial, and logical operations, among others. Because functions must be preceded with the @ sign, they are often called @functions or "at functions." The following are examples of the types of functions you will use in this book:

- @SUM(D5..G5)
- @AVG(B2..B12)
- @MIN(E5..J5)
- @MAX(C3..C22)

Functions are made up of several parts. After @ is the **function name**, like SUM for add, AVG for average, MIN for minimum, and MAX for maximum.

Some functions, like the ones shown above, require an argument. An **argument**, enclosed in parentheses, lists the data on which the function is to be performed. Many arguments are a range of cells. For example, the function @SUM(D5..G5) contains the argument (D5..G5). This function will add adjacent cells from D5 through G5.

What is the *function name* in @MAX(C3..C22)? ____________

What is the *argument* in that function? ____________

When keying a function, press [.] only once in the middle of the argument, even though Lotus will display two periods on the Control Panel. Do not key any spaces within the function. Press F1, Help, to get information about a function while you are keying it.

@SUM FUNCTION. The @SUM function adds the contents of cells.

DO: Retrieve LORA3A.WK1.

Column A of LORA3A.WK1 has the account balances of customers. To find the total of Column A, add all the account balances in cells A6 through A15. The following formula would total those cells: +A6+A7+A8+A9+A10+A11+A12+A13+A14+A15. A much better way to add the group of adjacent cells is by using the @SUM function; always use the @SUM function when appropriate. The argument is the list of cells to add, A6 through A15.

DO: Goto A17

KEY: [A17] @SUM(a6.a15) (↵Enter)

The *result* of the function appears in Cell A17. The function itself appears in the Control Panel on the Cell Contents line.

Identify the value at A17 by keying a descriptive label at B17.

KEY: [B17] TOTAL (↵Enter)

Key more data to be calculated with the @SUM function. As the worksheet gets larger, the screen may move, or **scroll**, as you move the pointer.

KEY: [E3] PREVIOUS

KEY: [E4] BALANCE

KEY:

[E6] 55.86
[E7] 34.40
[E8] 12.50
[E9] 3.66
[E10] 450.32
[E11] 53.78
[E12] 112.65
[E13] 371.55
[E14] 68.99
[E15] 37.98

POINT TO THE ARGUMENT. Since pointing to cells is more accurate than keying in cell addresses, point to the function argument. When pointing you can move up or down, left or right, whichever is most convenient.

KEY: [E17] @SUM(

DO: Use (↑) to point to E15. (Look at the Contents Line.)

The period is used as an **anchor** to establish the beginning of the range of cells to be added.

KEY: [E15] (.)

DO: Use ↑ to point to E6.

KEY: [E6]) ↵Enter

Look at the Contents Line. It should display: @SUM(E15..E6). If it is not correct, repeat the steps beginning at E17. Remember, Esc will cancel current keying.

KEY: [D17] " TOTAL

@AVG FUNCTION. The @AVG function averages the contents of a group of cells. It does this by totaling the contents of the cells and then dividing the total by the number of cells in the group.

Find the average account balance.

DO: Goto A18.

KEY: [A18] @AVG(

DO: Point to A15.

KEY: [A15] .

DO: Point to A6.

KEY: [A6]) ↵Enter

KEY: [B18] AVERAGE ↵Enter

Find the average previous balance.

KEY: [E18] @AVG(

DO: Point to E15.

KEY: [E15] .

DO: Point to E6

KEY: [E6]) ↵Enter

KEY: [D18] " AVERAGE

@MIN FUNCTION. The @MIN function displays the smallest or *minimum* value in a group of cells.

Find the minimum account balance.

KEY: [A19] @MIN(

DO: Point to A15.

KEY: [A15] .

DO: Point to A6.

KEY: [A6]) Enter

KEY: [B19] MINIMUM Enter

Find the minimum previous balance.

KEY: [E19] @MIN(

DO: Point to E15.

KEY: [E15] .

DO: Point to E6.

KEY: [E6]) Enter

KEY: [D19] " MINIMUM Enter

@MAX FUNCTION. The @MAX function displays the largest or *maximum* value in a group of cells.

Find the maximum account balance.

KEY: [A20] @MAX(

DO: Point to A15.

KEY: [A15] .

DO: Point to A6.

KEY: [A6]) Enter

KEY: [B20] MAXIMUM

Find the maximum previous balance.

KEY: [E20] @MAX(

DO: Point to E15.

KEY: [E15] .

DO: Point to E6.

KEY: [E6]) Enter

KEY: [D20] " MAXIMUM Enter

DO: Compare your completed worksheet to LO4.2. Save your worksheet as LO4ACBAL.

FIGURE L04.2
L04ACBAL File

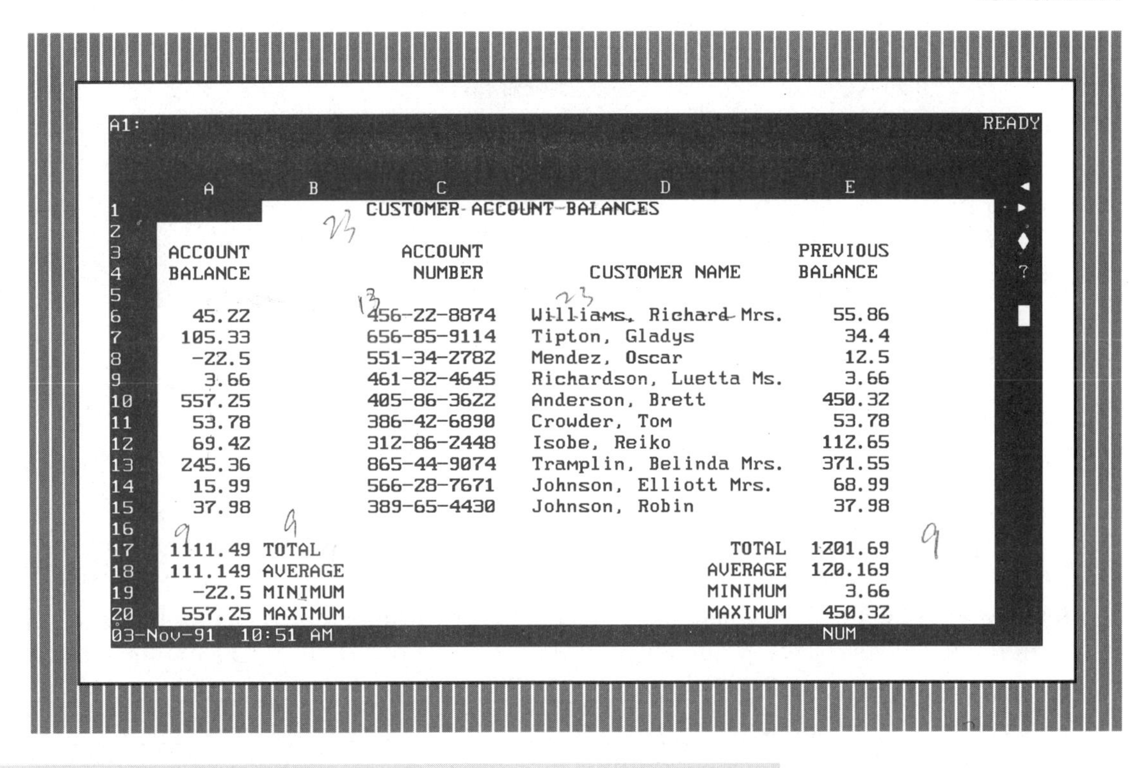

A1: READY

	A	B	C	D	E
1			CUSTOMER ACCOUNT BALANCES		
2					
3	ACCOUNT		ACCOUNT		PREVIOUS
4	BALANCE		NUMBER	CUSTOMER NAME	BALANCE
5					
6	45.22		456-22-8874	Williams, Richard Mrs.	55.86
7	105.33		656-85-9114	Tipton, Gladys	34.4
8	-22.5		551-34-2782	Mendez, Oscar	12.5
9	3.66		461-82-4645	Richardson, Luetta Ms.	3.66
10	557.25		405-86-3622	Anderson, Brett	450.32
11	53.78		386-42-6890	Crowder, Tom	53.78
12	69.42		312-86-2448	Isobe, Reiko	112.65
13	245.36		865-44-9074	Tramplin, Belinda Mrs.	371.55
14	15.99		566-28-7671	Johnson, Elliott Mrs.	68.99
15	37.98		389-65-4430	Johnson, Robin	37.98
16					
17	1111.49	TOTAL		TOTAL	1201.69
18	111.149	AVERAGE		AVERAGE	120.169
19	-22.5	MINIMUM		MINIMUM	3.66
20	557.25	MAXIMUM		MAXIMUM	450.32

03-Nov-91 10:51 AM NUM

QUICK QUESTIONS

1. What is the name for Lotus built-in formulas?
2. List the three parts of a function.
   a)
   b)
   c)
3. What is an argument?
4. Write the function that would add Cells B3 through B8.
5. Write the function to average Cells D2 through D9.
6. Write the function that would find the smallest value in Cells D5 through D12.
7. Write the function that would find the largest value in Cells A6 through A12.
8. After keying, where should you look to see the actual function used in a cell?
9. After keying, where should you look to see the result of a function?
10. What may be keyed to identify the result of a formula or function?
11. Why is it better to point to cells rather than key the cell addresses?
12. What is the purpose of the period when pointing to cells?

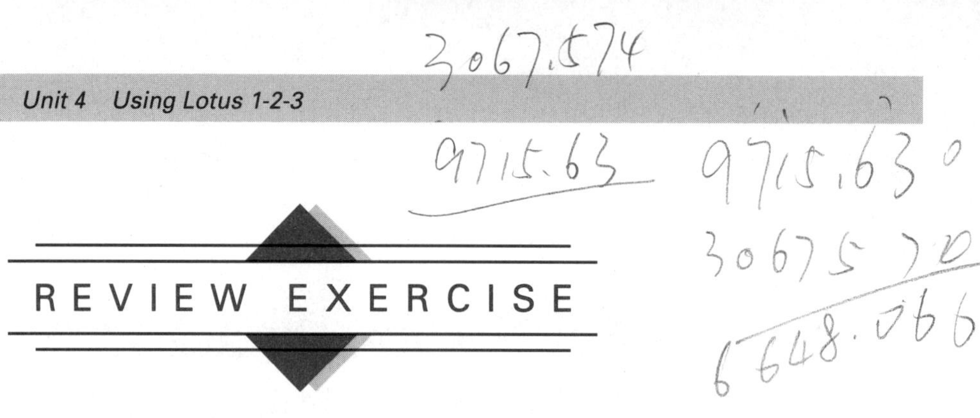

REVIEW EXERCISE

	A	B	C
1	42.85	576.15	
2	7733.24	99.08	
3	963.71	374.79	
4	66.22	53.47	
5	17.8	69.07	
6	59.35	0.37	
7	68.55	37.89	
8	967.43	6.32	
9	80.96	9715.63	
10			

1. On a clean worksheet, use the numeric keypad to key the figures in the worksheet above. Check for accuracy and edit as needed.
2. Key **Formulas** that will calculate the following at the designated cells. Point to cells rather than keying the cell addresses. Begin each formula with a plus. Write the formulas on the lines shown.

   [C1] The sum of A1 and B1. ____________

   [C2] The sum of A2 and B2. ____________

   [C3] The difference between A3 and B3. ____________

   [C4] The sum of A1 and B4. ____________

   [C5] Divide B5 by A5. ____________

   [C6] Divide A6 by B6. ____________

   [C7] Multiply B7 by B6. ____________

   [C8] Multiply A8 by B8. ____________

   [C9] Multiply A9 by B7 and then subtract the product from B9. Use parentheses to establish the order of calculations. ____________
3. Save the worksheet as LOREV4A and then erase the sheet.
4. Retrieve LOREV4A and key **Functions** that will calculate the following at the designated cells. Point to cells. Write the functions on the lines.

   [D1] The sum of A1, B1, and C1. ____________

   [D2] The sum of A1, B1, A2, and B21. ____________

   [D3] The average of A3, B3, and C3. ____________

   [D4] The average of A3, B3, A4, and B4. ____________

   [D5] The minimum value in all of Column A. ____________

   [D6] The minimum value in all of Column B. ____________

   [D7] The maximum value in Cells A1, B1, A2, B2, A3, and B3. ____________

[D8] The maximum value in all of columns A and B. ____________

[D9] The difference between the maximum and minimum values in all of Columns A and B.

____

5. Save the worksheet as LOREV4B and then erase the worksheet.

ACTIVITY A - GROUP GRADE STATISTICS

	A	B	C	D	E	F
1				STUDENT GRADES		
2						
3	STUDENT	TEST 1	TEST 2	TEST 3	TEST 4	
4						
5	Jones, L	88	86	79	89	
6	Kerr, G	100	78	90	100	
7	Slate, R	98	92	95	96	
8	Vance, P	87	75	72	80	
9	Cupp, R	77	67	71	80	
10	Mays, T	68	71	73	78	
11	Wilson, D	82	86	78	87	
12	Weeks, A	90	74	87	88	
13	Ruiz, L	94	88	86	92	
14	Goins, C	95	87	85	90	
15						

1. On a clean worksheet, key the data shown above. Key the main title STUDENT GRADES at D1. Center the column headings.
2. Key the following labels:
   [A16] AVERAGE
   [A17] MAXIMUM
   [A18] MINIMUM
3. At B16, C16, D16, and E16, key a function that will average the grades in each column.
4. At B17, C17, D17, and E17, key a function that will find the maximum value (highest grade) in each column.
5. At B18, C18, D18, and E18, key a function that will find the minimum value (lowest grade) in each column.
6. Save the worksheet as LORA4A and erase the worksheet.

ACTIVITY B - INDIVIDUAL GRADE STATISTICS

1. Retrieve LORA4A.
2. Add the following labels:
   [F3] AVERAGE
   [G3] MAXIMUM
   [H3] MINIMUM
3. At F5 through F14 key a function that will average each student's test scores.
4. At G5 through G14 key a function that will find the highest score for each student.
5. At H5 through H14 key a function that will find the lowest test score for each student.
6. Save the worksheet as LORA4B and erase the worksheet. Exit Lotus 1-2-3 or go on to the next section.

5

RANGES

OBJECTIVES

- Designate a **range.**
- **Print.**
- **Erase** a cell and a range.
- **Copy relative** and **absolute.**
- **Move.**

RANGE

A **range** is a rectangular group of *adjacent* cells, cells that border or touch each other. A range may be one cell, a horizontal group of cells (in a row), a vertical group of cells (in a column), or an arrangement of both horizontal and vertical cells (rows and columns). Figure LO5.1 shows the four ways cells can be grouped into a range.

Use a range command when you want to perform the same operation on several adjacent cells at once. Anchor the beginning of a range with a period, highlight the entire range with the cursor keys, and show the end of the range with Enter. Press (Esc) to cancel the anchor if necessary.

In this section you will learn to use commands that involve a range of cells.

PRINT

You have completed and stored many worksheets on your disk. Use the **Print** command to send a worksheet to the printer. Retrieve the worksheet and then use the steps in LO5.2 to print it.

DO: Retrieve LOREV4B from your disk. You will key the information needed to identify your printed spreadsheets, such as your name and the name of the file. Write on the line below the data your instructor wants you to key on every worksheet.

____

____

KEY: [A11] Your name, the name of the document LOREV4B, and the other data your instructor has asked you to include. Begin at A11 and key the data as one label; let the data spill over into the cells at the right.

Follow the steps shown in LO5.2 to print the LOREV4B worksheet.

FIGURE L05.1
Ranges May Be Horizontal, Vertical, or Both

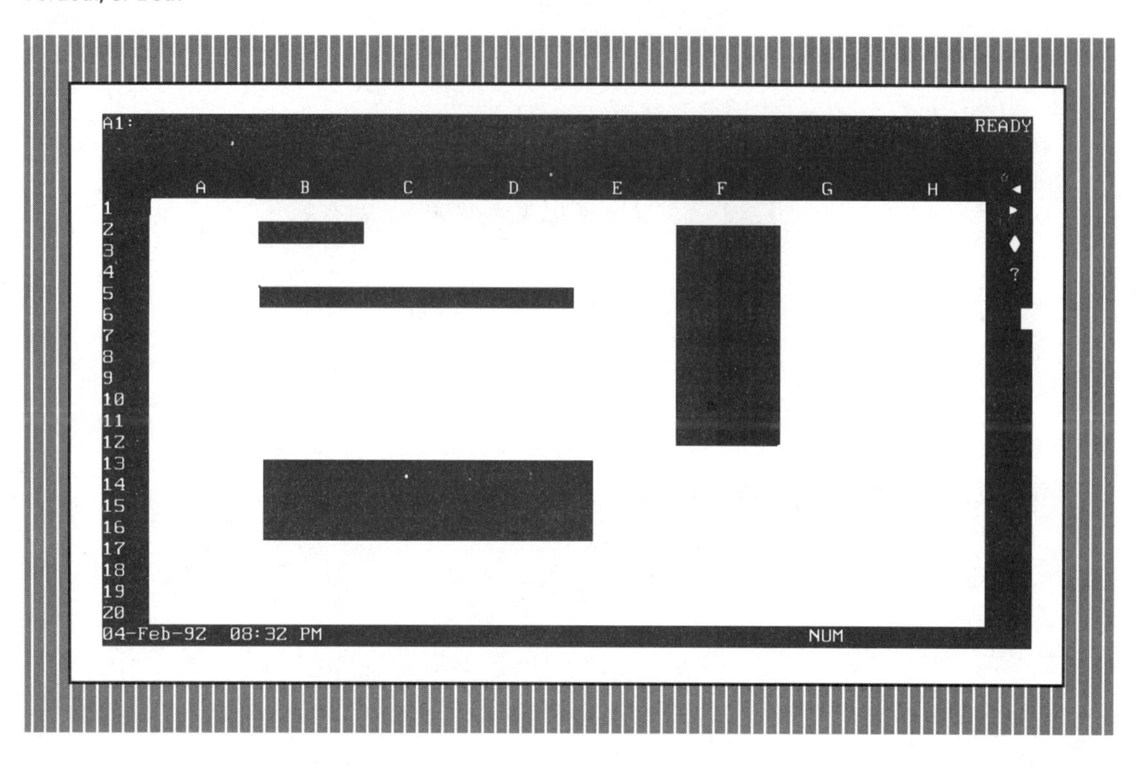

FIGURE L05.2

BASIC PRINTING	
1. Position the paper in the printer	Sets the top of form
2. Press (Home)	Moves the pointer to A1, the beginning of the print ranges in this book
3. **/P**rint	Begins the Print command
4. **P**rinter	Prints the file to the printer
5. **R**ange *highlight range* (↵Enter)	Allows you to set the range of cells to be printed
6. **A**lign	Tells Lotus the paper is correctly positioned
7. **G**o	Printing begins
8. **P**age	Advances paper for the completed document
9. **Q**uit	Quits the Print menu and returns to Ready mode

DO: Check the paper in the printer and set the top of a new sheet if necessary.

DO: Press (Home) to move the pointer to A1, the beginning of the print range.

DO: [A1] Press / **P**rint **P**rinter **R**ange.

DO: [A1] Press (.) to anchor A1 as the beginning of the print range. (If necessary to set a different anchor position, press (Esc).)

DO: Use (↓) to move to A11, the bottom row of the range, and then use (→) to move to D11 (or E11 if the line with your name extends beyond column D), the last column and row of the print range. (See LO5.3.)

FIGURE LO5.3
Setting the Print Range

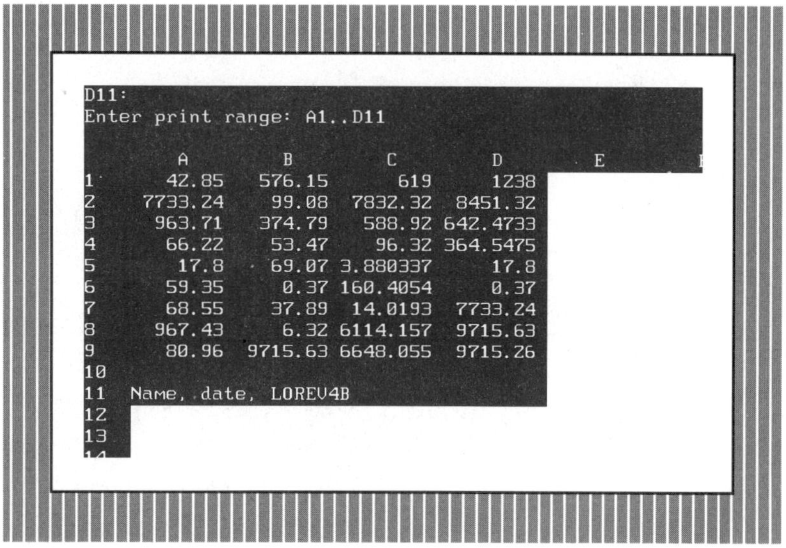

```
D11:
Enter print range: A1..D11

         A         B         C         D        E
1      42.85    576.15       619      1238
2    7733.24     99.08   7832.32   8451.32
3     963.71    374.79    588.92  642.4733
4      66.22     53.47     96.32  364.5475
5       17.8     69.07  3.880337      17.8
6      59.35      0.37  160.4054      0.37
7      68.55     37.89   14.0193   7733.24
8     967.43      6.32  6114.157   9715.63
9      80.96   9715.63  6648.055   9715.26
10
11  Name, date, LOREV4B
12
13
```

Once you anchor the start of the range, the worksheet is highlighted as you move toward the end of the range. The end of the range is the cell that is the *last row and last column used in the current worksheet*. This should include the line with your personal data. Press (↵Enter) to show the end of the range.

DO: [D11] Press (↵Enter) to designate the end of the range.

DO: Press **A**lign to clear for printing.

DO: Press **G**o to begin printing.

DO: Press **P**age to eject the paper in the printer. (Printing does not have to be completed.)

DO: Press **Q**uit to quit the print menu and return to Ready mode.

You do not have to clear the worksheet. A worksheet is automatically erased when you retrieve a new worksheet.

DO: Individually retrieve and print the spreadsheets directed by your instructor. Key your personal data including the name of each file before printing. You may mark the files to be printed below and on page L46 and then check them off after you print them.

	Filename	*Printing Complete*
____	LOREV3	____
____	LORA3A	____
____	LORA3B	____

_____ LO4PRAC _____

_____ LO4FORM _____

_____ LO4EDIT _____

_____ LOREV3A _____

_____ LO4ACBAL _____

_____ LOREV4A _____

_____ LOREV4B _____

_____ LORA4A _____

_____ LORA4B _____

QUICK QUESTIONS

1. What is a range in Lotus?
2. What are four ways cells can be grouped into a range?
   a)
   b)
   c)
   d)
3. When should you use a range?
4. What is the first step in basic printing of a worksheet?
5. Why did you press (Home) before using the Print command?
6. What is the purpose of Align when using the Print command?
7. What is pressed to anchor the beginning of a print range?
8. What cell should you designate as the end of a print range?
9. What key is pressed to show the end of a range?
10. What option is chosen when printing is complete?
11. Is it necessary to erase a worksheet before retrieving another worksheet?

ERASE

You may erase a cell or a range of cells by using the **Range Erase** command. (One or two cells may be erased in some versions of Lotus with the (Delete) key.) Be very careful with the Erase command because it is easy to accidentally erase the wrong values.

DO: Retrieve LO4FORM.

Erase the entries in Rows 8 and 9 of the worksheet. Go to the beginning of the range to be erased and then begin the Range Erase command.

DO: Goto A8.

DO: [A8] / **R**ange **E**rase

The message *Enter range to erase:A8..A8* appears (see LO5.4).

DO: [A8] Press (.) to anchor the pointer position, A8, as the beginning of the range.

DO: Use (↓) to move to A9 and then use (→) to move to the end of the range, C9.

Notice, the Control Panel shows you have designated A8 through C9 as the range. (See LO5.5.)

DO: [C9] Press (↵Enter) to end the range to be erased.

Rows 8 and 9 are blank; the cells have been erased.

FIGURE LO5.4
Beginning Range Erase

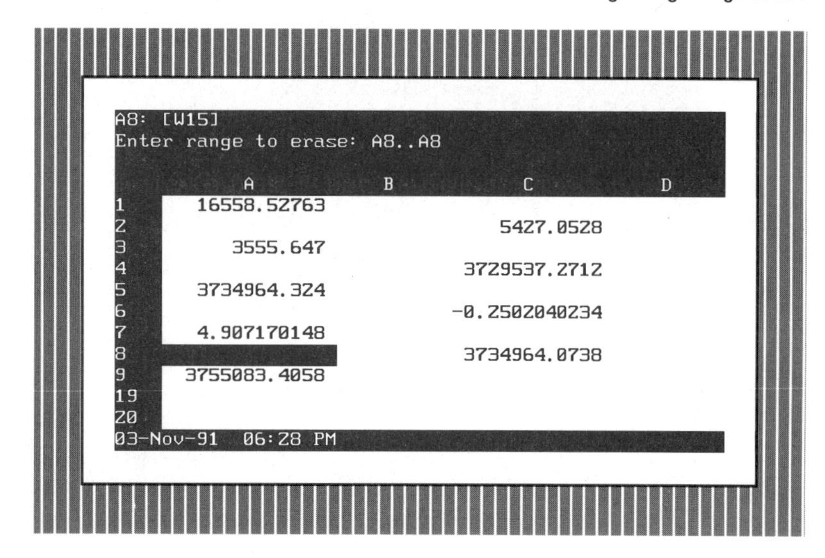

FIGURE LO5.5
Ending Range Erase

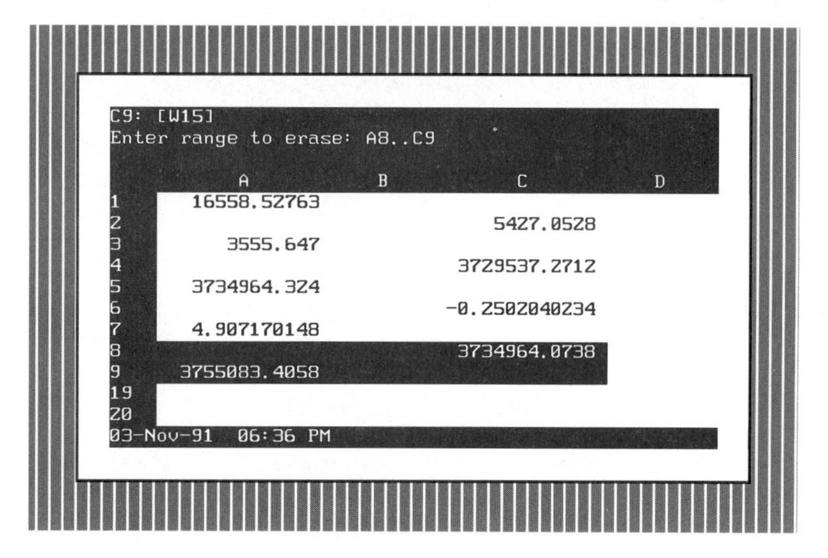

Erase Cells A3 through A7:

DO: [A3] / **R**ange **E**rase

DO: [A3] Press (.) to anchor A3 as the beginning of the range.

DO: Press (↓) to go to A7.

DO: [A7] Press (↵Enter) to end the range and erase the cells.

The message *ERR* appears at C6.

DO: Goto C6 and look at the Contents Line. Why might this cell show an error message?

____

DO: Use Range Erase to erase the remaining values in Column C.

DO: Use Range Erase to erase the value at A1.

The worksheet should be blank.

DO: / **W**orksheet **E**rase **Y**es to clear the worksheet.

QUICK QUESTIONS

1. What command is used to erase a single cell or a group of cells?
2. What is pressed to anchor the beginning of a range when using the Range Erase command?
3. What is pressed to show the end of a range when using the Range Erase command?
4. Why might you get an ERR message when erasing cells?

Copy

The **Copy** command copies data from one place to another, leaving the data in both places. Copy involves *two* ranges: **Copy what?** and **To where?** The *Copy what* or *From* range is the range of cells you want to copy. The *To where* range, also called the *To* range, is where you want to place them. Care must be taken when copying so that other data is not accidentally overwritten. Sometimes copying places zeros in blank cells; remove them with (Delete) or Range Erase.

COPY LABELS.

DO: Retrieve LO4ACBAL.

You will erase the labels at D17 through D20 and then copy the labels from B17 through B20 to the empty cells.

DO: Goto D17.

DO: [D17] / **R**ange **E**rase

DO: [D17] Press (.) to anchor D17 as the beginning of the range to be erased.

DO: [D20] Press (↵Enter) at the end of the range to be erased.

DO: Goto B17.

DO: [B17] /**C**opy

The message *Copy what? B17..B17* appears (LO5.6). Show where the cells to be copied begin and end.

DO: [B17] Press (.) to anchor the beginning of the *what* (from) range.

DO: [B20] Move the pointer to B20 and press (↵Enter) to end the *what* (from) range.

The *To where?* message appears. Show where the block of copied cells should be placed.

FIGURE LO5.6
"Copy what?" Message

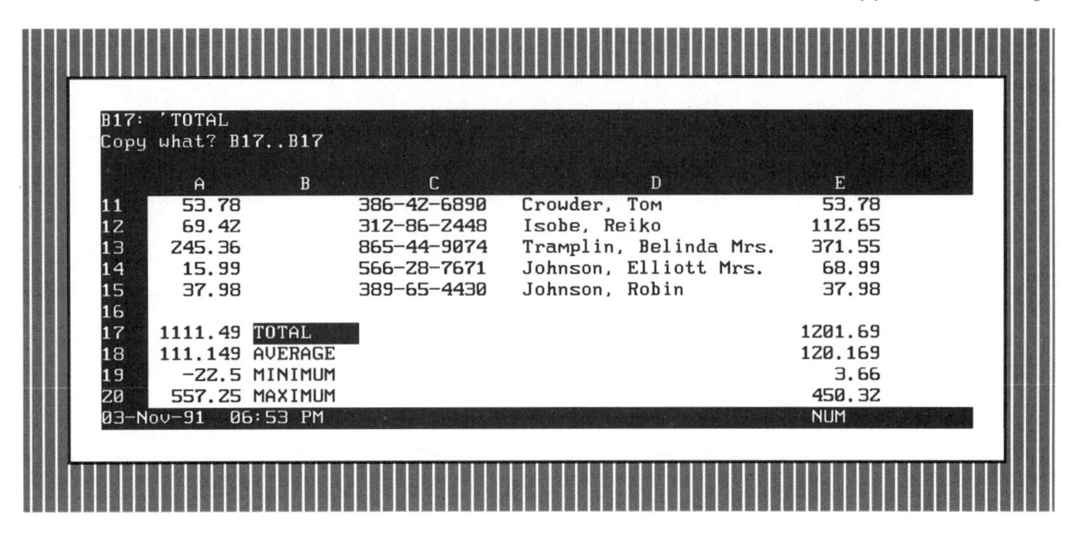

DO: Move to D17.

DO: [D17] Press period to anchor the beginning of the new *where* (to) location.

DO: Move to D20. Cells D17 to D20 are highlighted. (See LO5.7.)

DO: [D20] Press (↵Enter) to show the end of the new *where* location and the end of the copy.

COPY FORMULAS. Find the difference between the current account balance (column A) and the previous account balance (column E) for each customer. Key the formula once, and then copy it for all customers.

What formula would find the difference between A6 and E6?

____

FIGURE LO5.7
"To where?" Message

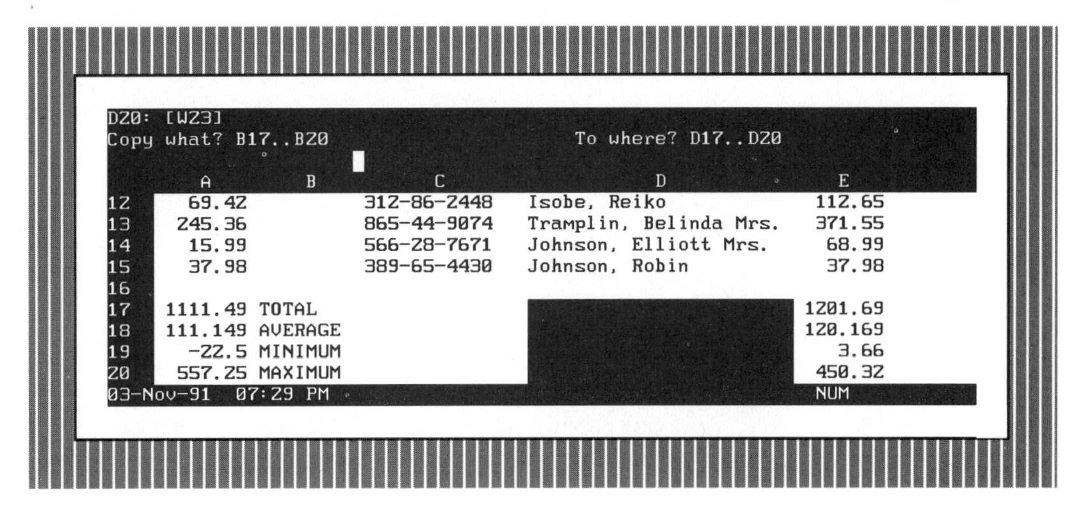

KEY: [F3] BALANCE

KEY: [F4] CHANGE

KEY: [F6] (+)

DO: Point to A6.

KEY: [A6] (-)

DO: Point to E6 and press (↵Enter).

The formula appears as the contents of F6, and the result of the formula appears in the cell. Since the current balance is smaller than the previous balance, there is a negative difference. This is shown as –10.64.

Copy the formula to Cells F7 through F15.

DO: [F6] / **C**opy.

Copy what? (from) is the formula at F6, which is shown as F6..F6, a one-cell range.

DO: Press (↵Enter) to accept F6..F6 as the *what* range.

To where? (to) appears. Since the pointer is there, F6 appears on the message line.

DO: Move to F7.

DO: [F7] Press (.) to anchor the beginning of the *where* range.

DO: Move to F15 and press (↵Enter) to end the *where* range, completing the copy.

DO: [F6] Look at the Contents Line. The formula in Row 6 has cell addresses A**6** and E**6**.

DO: [F7] Look at the Contents Line. When the formula was copied down one row to Row 7, the cell addresses changed one row, to A**7** and E**7**.

DO: [F8] The formula now has cell addresses of A**8** and E**8**, reflecting the copy one row down from A7 and E7.

RELATIVE COPY. When Lotus copies a function or a formula containing cell addresses, by default it copies **relative** to the new row or column in which it is placed. For example, if it is copied down, row numbers increase by one; if it is copied to the right, column letters increase by one.

Look frequently at the Cell Contents as you copy to see how the column letters and row numbers change as you copy.

QUICK QUESTIONS

1. What is the purpose of the Copy command?
2. What two ranges must be designated when using the Copy command?
3. What is used to anchor the beginning of a range when using the Copy command?
4. What is used to designate the end of a range when using the Copy command?
5. What is the meaning of the *Copy what?* message?
6. What is the meaning of the *To where?* message?
7. What does –10.64 mean as the result of a subtraction formula?
8. At C3 you have the following formula: +C3-B3. You copy the formula relative into Cells C4 through C10. What formula will appear at Cell C7?

COPY FUNCTIONS. Copy the functions at E17 through E20 into Cells F17 through F20.

DO: Goto E17.

DO: [E17] / **C**opy.

Copy what? (from) is the range of cells from E17 through E20.

DO: [E17] Press [.] to anchor E17 as the beginning of the *what* range.

DO: [E20] Press [↵Enter] for the end of the *what* range.

To where? (to) is the range of cells from F17 through F20.

DO: [F17] Move to F17, the first cell of the new location. Press [↵Enter].

If the *what* and *where* ranges are identical in size, it is not necessary to show the beginning and end of the *where* range when copying or moving. You can just move to the beginning of the *where* range and press Enter. The range will remain intact because Lotus must retain the same adjacent cell grouping.

DO: [E17] Move the pointer to E17. Look at the Contents Line. The function shows cell address E, the column the function is in.

DO: [F17] Look at the Contents Line. When the @SUM function was copied from Column E to Column F, the cell addresses changed to F, *relative* to the column where the function was placed.

DO: Move to the other functions in cells E18 through E20 and F18 through F20. You can see the functions were copied relative to their new locations.

DO: Save the worksheet as LO5COPY, but keep it on your screen for more practice.

COPY ABSOLUTE. As you have seen, by default Lotus copies functions and formulas with cell addresses relative to their new locations. Sometimes you don't want all of a formula to be relative because you don't want a cell address to change. You may override the relative default with an **absolute** (unchanging) cell address.

When a formula contains an absolute cell address, that address will remain intact if the formula is copied. An absolute cell address has a dollar sign *before* both the column letter and the row number. (You can also make just the row number absolute as A$3, or just the column letter absolute as $A3.)

Key a sample formula with an absolute address.

DO: Goto A26.

KEY: [A26] (+) $A$17 (-)

DO: Point to A6. Press (↵Enter).

The result of the formula is the difference between the total customer balance and the first customer's balance. Copy the formula to Cells A27 to A35, the cells for the other nine customers.

DO: [A26] / **C**opy (↵Enter).

DO: [A27] Press (.) and move to A35. Press (↵Enter) to end the copy.

DO: Press (↓) and look at the contents of each cell. The $A$17 absolute cell address did *not* change; it remains at all cells. The A6 relative cell address, however, did change by one row number (from 6 to 7, from 7 to 8, etc.) as the formula was copied down the column.

DO: At B26, key a formula that will subtract the first customer's current balance (relative) from the current maximum balance (absolute).

What formula did you key at B26? ____________

DO: On your own, copy the formula from B27 through B35.

DO: Look at the Contents Line. Did the cell address A20 remain absolute? Did the cell addresses for customers' current balances increase by one row number as they were copied down?

DO: [A26] Erase the sample formulas from A26 to B35. Press / **R**ange **E**rase.

DO: Press (.) to anchor A26 as the beginning of the range.

DO: Press (↓) to move to A35 and then (→) to move to B35. Press (↵Enter) to designate B35 as the end of the range to be erased.

DO: Press (Home) to move to the top of the worksheet.

Use a formula with an absolute cell address. Find the percentage each customer's previous balance is of the total previous balance.

What type of calculation is used to find a percentage? (Addition, subtraction, multiplication, or division) __________

KEY: [G3] PERCENT

KEY: [G4] OF TOTAL

KEY: [G6] (+)

DO: Point to E6 and press (/).

DO: Point to E17 and press (↵Enter). The percentage is shown as a decimal figure.

DO: [G6] Look at the Contents Line. Each customer's previous balance will be divided by the same figure, the total at E17. The cell address for E17 must be absolute.

DO: [G6] Press (F2) to edit the formula. Add a $ in front of the E and in front of the 17 in E17 ($E$17). Press (↵Enter).

DO: [G6] Press / **C**opy to copy the formula.

DO: [G6] Press (↵Enter) to accept one cell, G6..G6, as the *what* range.

DO: [G7] Press (.) to anchor G7 as the beginning of the *where* range and then move to the end of the *where* range.

DO: [G15] Press (↵Enter) to show the end of the *where* range.

DO: Press (↓) to view the contents of the cells.

The first cell address in the formula should have changed relative to its position, but the second cell address should not have changed. (See LO5.8.)

DO: Add the required line of personal data (name, file name, etc.) beginning in A22.

DO: Save the worksheet as LO5COPY.

When you set a print range, it remains with the file when it is stored on disk. The next time you print the worksheet, the range will already be set. Press (Esc) to cancel it if desired.

WIDE WORKSHEETS. Often a worksheet is wider than Lotus can print by default on one sheet of paper. LO5COPY is an example of a wide worksheet that will print on two pages. You may make several adjustments that will allow you to print more characters on each line.

FIGURE L05.8
L05COPY Worksheet After the Absolute Copy

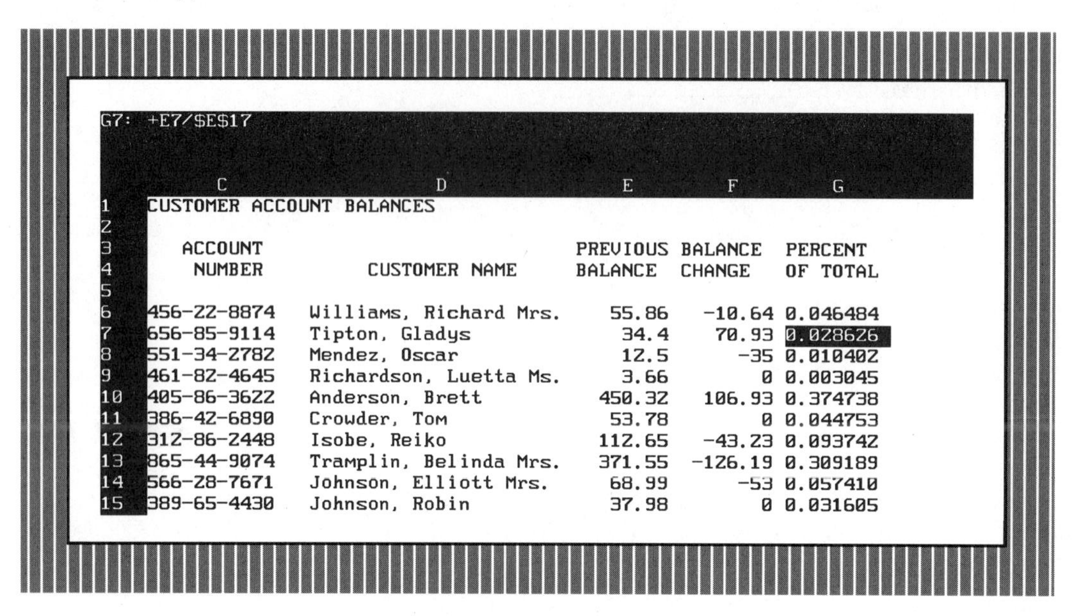
G7: +E7/$E$17

	C	D	E	F	G
1	CUSTOMER ACCOUNT BALANCES				
2					
3	ACCOUNT		PREVIOUS	BALANCE	PERCENT
4	NUMBER	CUSTOMER NAME	BALANCE	CHANGE	OF TOTAL
5					
6	456-22-8874	Williams, Richard Mrs.	55.86	-10.64	0.046484
7	656-85-9114	Tipton, Gladys	34.4	70.93	0.028626
8	551-34-2782	Mendez, Oscar	12.5	-35	0.010402
9	461-82-4645	Richardson, Luetta Ms.	3.66	0	0.003045
10	405-86-3622	Anderson, Brett	450.32	106.93	0.374738
11	386-42-6890	Crowder, Tom	53.78	0	0.044753
12	312-86-2448	Isobe, Reiko	112.65	-43.23	0.093742
13	865-44-9074	Tramplin, Belinda Mrs.	371.55	-126.19	0.309189
14	566-28-7671	Johnson, Elliott Mrs.	68.99	-53	0.057410
15	389-65-4430	Johnson, Robin	37.98	0	0.031605

Your instructor may want you to do one or more of the following to get a wide worksheet to fit on one sheet of paper:

- Use wide paper in a wide carriage printer.
- Reset the default margins using the / **P**rint **P**rinter **O**ptions **M**argins command.
- Use the control panel on the printer to select condensed print.
- Use a print setup code that is different for each type of printer.

DO: Press (Home) and then print the worksheet, setting the range as A1 through G22. If you have previously printed LO4ACBAL, you need only increase the size of the range.

MOVE. The **Move** command is used to place the values in a range of cells in a new location, leaving the former locations empty. When moving, care must be taken not to overwrite data or to move cells that would change formulas or functions in an undesirable way.

DO: Retrieve LO4PRAC.

Move the label *George Washington* from A1 to A10.

DO: [A1] / **M**ove.

Move what? (from) A1..A1 appears.

DO: Press (↵Enter) to accept cell A1 as the *what* range.

DO: [A10] (Notice the *To where?* indicator changes as you move.) At A10, press (↵Enter) to accept A10 as the new location.

Move Cells A4 through D4 to Cells B16 through E16.

DO: [A4] / **M**ove.

DO: [A4] Press [.] to anchor.

DO: [D4] Press [↵Enter] to end the range.

DO: [B16] Press [↵Enter] to accept B16 as the beginning cell of the new location.

Move the values in Column D to Column E.

DO: [D1] / **M**ove

DO: [D1] Press [.] to anchor.

DO: [D12] Press [↵Enter] to end the range.

DO: [E1] Press [↵Enter].

DO: Add your personal data line at A18. Save the worksheet as LO5MOVE.

DO: Print the worksheet.

PRINT CELL FORMULAS. It is often helpful to print cell formulas on the printer. The listing of cell formulas also shows column widths and format settings. The printed copy allows you to check the accuracy of a worksheet without being at the computer.

Print the cell formulas in the LO5MOVE worksheet using the Print command.

DO: / **P**rint **P**rinter **O**ptions **O**ther **C**ell-Formulas **Q**uit **A**lign **G**o **P**age **Q**uit [↵Enter]

DO: Turn in the cell formulas with your printout of the LO5MOVE worksheet.

DO: Clear the worksheet.

QUICK QUESTIONS

1. Besides a formula, what type of calculation can be copied with the Copy command?
2. During a copy with *what* and *where* ranges identical in size, why don't you have to designate the beginning and ending cells of the *where* range?
3. Where must dollar signs be placed to make a cell address an absolute value?
4. What is the purpose of an absolute cell address when using the Copy command?

5. What would you key to make D16 an absolute value?
6. If you print a worksheet before storing it, will the print range you set remain with the document?
7. What are some things you can do to get a wide worksheet to print on a single sheet of paper?
8. How is the Move command different from the Copy command?
9. List two mishaps that can occur when carelessly moving or copying data.
   a)
   b)

REVIEW EXERCISE

	A	B	C	D	E	F	G
1	STAMP-IT COMPANY						
2	INVENTORY SHEET						
3	March 31, 1993						
4					UNIT		
5	STOCK NO	QTY	UNIT	DESCRIPTION	PRICE	EXTENSION	
6							
7	340-374	15		MOV DATE #1	2.15		
8	340-484	20		MOV DATE #2A	2.15		
9	340-882	13		MOV DATE #3	2.35		
10	340-907	9		MOV DATE #2C	2.35		
11	72-237	16		MOV NUMBER	2.15		
12	72-563	27		MOV PRICE	2.15		
13	75-839	18		DATE AND TIME	19.55		
14	811-172	20		INKED FILE	4.15		
15	811-324	12		INKED AIRMAIL	4.15		
16	811-396	12		INKED COPY	4.15		
17	811-561	21		INKED FOR DEPOSIT ONLY	4.15		
18	811-776	8		INKED CONFIDENTIAL	4.15		
19							

On a clear worksheet, key the data shown above. Use label prefix characters for alphanumeric data that begins with a digit. Right align column headings in Columns B and E (numeric columns). The column heading UNIT is left aligned in Cell C5.

1. Enter data in Columns A, B, D, and E (Columns C and F have no data yet).
2. Copy a label. The value for Cells C7 through C18 in the UNIT column is *EA*. Because the same value is repeated, key the label *EA* at C7 and then copy it down the column through C18.

KEY: [C7] EA (↵Enter)

DO: [C7] / **C**opy (↵Enter)

DO: [C8] (.)

DO: [C18] (↵Enter)

3. Copy a formula. The extension value is QTY * UNIT PRICE. At F7 key the formula B7*E7 and then copy it.

KEY: [F7] (+)

DO: Point to B7 and key (*).

DO: Point to E7 and press (↵Enter).

DO: [F7] / **C**opy (↵Enter)

DO: [F8] (.)

DO: [F18] (↵Enter)

4. Enter a function and then copy it. Find the minimum value in Column B. At B19 enter the function @MIN(B7.B18) and then copy it to F19.

KEY: [B19] @MIN(

DO: Point to B7 and key (.).

DO: Point to B18 and press ()) (↵Enter)

DO: [B19] / **C**opy (↵Enter)

DO: [F19] (↵Enter)

5. Add a centered label for the minimum function.

KEY: [A19] (^) MINIMUM (↵Enter) maximum

6. Move a label. The label at A19 might look better centered between the two functions. Move the label to D19.

DO: [A19] / **M**ove (↵Enter)

DO: [D19] (↵Enter)

7. Complete the following actions on your own.

DO: [B20] Key the function that will find the largest Qty. in Column B.

DO: Copy the function at B20 to F20.

DO: [D20] Key a label appropriate for the values at B20 and F20.

DO: [F21] Enter a function to total the Extension values in Column F. At D21 key an appropriate label for the value at F21.

DO: Save the worksheet as LOREV5. Print the worksheet and then print the cell formulas.

DO: Clear your worksheet and go on to the next activity or quit Lotus.

ACTIVITY A - PURCHASE ORDER

	A	B	C	D	E	F
1	ALLEN AUDIO					
2	3744 East Lindley			PURCHASE ORDER #3724		
3	Berkeley, CA 94708					
4						
5		TO	DARRELL DISTRIBUTORS			
6			Box 7712			
7			Redmond, WA 98073			
8				UNIT		
9	QTY	STOCK NO	DESCRIPTION	PRICE	AMOUNT	
10						
11	2	778T6421	QUADRON T64 SPEAKER	55.25		
12	3	8804RS55	WOODKEN CASSETTE RECEIVER	260.99		
13	2	291L7299	QUADRON CAR AMPLIFIER	155.49		
14	4	4529GL88	ROC CD PLAYER	278.99		
15	3	9002HL52	ROC CASSETTE DECK	315.55		
16	2	723PN556	PLUM MOD 2 LOUDSPEAKER	445.99		
17						

On a clear worksheet, key the data shown on the purchase order above. Begin PURCHASE ORDER #3724 at D2. Right align TO in B5. Key DARRELL DISTRIBUTORS in C5. Right align column headings over numeric columns (A, D, E). Widen Column C to 26 spaces and Column D to 10.

1. At E11 key the formula that will multiply UNIT PRICE by QTY. Copy the formula from E12 to E16.
2. At E17 key a function to total the AMOUNT column. Key the label SUBTOTAL at D17.
3. At E18 key a formula that will calculate 5% sales tax on the order. Key 5% as .05. Key an appropriate label for the calculation at D18.
4. At E19 key a formula or function that will add the sales tax amount to the SUBTOTAL amount. Key the label TOTAL at D19.
5. Save the worksheet as LORA5A before you begin using the Move command. If you have trouble moving data, retrieve LORA5A and retry.

6. Move the values in the UNIT PRICE column, D8 through D19, to F8 through F19. (For the *what* range, anchor D8 as the beginning and D19 as the end.)
7. Move the values in the STOCK NO column, B9 through B16, to Cells D9 through D16.
8. Move the values in the QTY column, A9 through A16, to Cells B9 through B16.
9. Move the labels SUBTOTAL, SALES TAX, and TOTAL to D17 through D19, respectively.
10. Save the worksheet as LORA5A. (Replace if necessary.)
11. Print the worksheet and then print the formulas. Quit Lotus or clear your worksheet and go on to the next activity.

ACTIVITY B - INVOICE

x366.992

	A	B	C	D	E	F
1	DARRELL DISTRIBUTORS			INVOICE NO.		
2	Box 7712			1867		
3	Redmond, WA 9807					
4						
5	TO	ALLEN AUDIO				
6		3744 East Lindley				
7		Berkeley, CA 94708				
8				UNIT		
9	STOCK NO	QTY	DESCRIPTION	PRICE	AMOUNT	
10						
11	778T6421	2	QUADRON T64 SPEAKER *	58.55		
12	8804RS55	3	WOODKEN CASSETTE RECEIVER	260.99		
13	291L7299	2	QUADRON CAR AMPLIFIER *	165.49		
14	4529GL88	4	ROC CD PLAYER	278.99		
15	9002HL52	3	ROC CASSETTE DECK	315.55		
16	723PN556	2	PLUM MOD 2 LOUDSPEAKER	445.99		
17						

On a clear worksheet, key the data shown on the invoice above. Right align TO *at A5. Key* ALLEN AUDIO *at B5. Right align column headings over numeric columns. Widen Column C to 25.*

1. Key a formula at E11 that will multiply UNIT PRICE times QTY. Copy the formula into Cells E12 to E16.
2. At E18 key a function to total the AMOUNT column. Key the label SUBTOTAL at D18.
3. At E19 key a formula that will calculate a 5% sales tax on the subtotal. (The tax amount will have 3 decimal places.) Key an appropriate label at D19.
4. At E20 key a formula or function that will add the sales tax and subtotal amounts. Key the label TOTAL at D20.
5. Save the worksheet as LORA5B before you use the Move command below.
6. Move the STOCK NUMBERS, A9 through A16, to Cells F9 through F16. (Anchor A9 as the beginning of the *what* range and end the *what* range at A16.)
7. Move the values in the QTY column, B9 through B16, to Cells A9 through A16.
8. Move the STOCK NUMBER range to Cells B9 through B16.

9. At F9 key the label % TOTAL.
10. At F11 key a formula to find the percentage each amount (column E) is of the total (E20). Divide to calculate the percentage, and use an absolute value for the total ($E$20). Copy the formula to Cells F12 through F16.
11. Add a note in Cell A18.

KEY: [A18] * indicates price change.

---

12. Save the worksheet as LORA5B. (Replace if necessary.)
13. Print the worksheet and then clear it or Quit Lotus.

6

ENHANCING WORKSHEET APPEARANCE

OBJECTIVES

- **Insert** rows and columns.
- **Delete** rows and columns.
- **Repeat characters.**
- Use range and global **format** of numbers.
- **Scroll** a larger worksheet.
- Use **global column width.**

INSERT ROWS AND COLUMNS

To add entire columns or rows to a worksheet use the **Worksheet Insert** command.

DO: Retrieve LO4ACBAL.

Many business documents contain the name of the company in the heading. Insert one row at the top of the worksheet for the company name.

INSERT ONE ROW. To insert a row(s), place the pointer on the row that should *move down* to make room for the new row(s). The pointer may be at any cell in the row that will move down. Then use the Worksheet Insert command.

Insert a new row above Row 1. To do this, place the pointer on Row 1 so it will move down to make room for the new one. Since you will key a label at C1, begin the command there.

DO: [C1] / **W**orksheet **I**nsert **R**ow

DO: [C1] Press (↵Enter) to accept one row (C1..C1) for insertion.

KEY: [C1] PARKE'S DEPARTMENT STORE (↵Enter)

Insert a new Row 3 for the date. The Worksheet Insert command could be used at any cell in Row 3, but go to Cell C3 to begin the command because you will key the current date there.

DO: [C3] / **W**orksheet **I**nsert **R**ow

DO: Press (↵Enter) to accept one row (C3..C3) for insertion.

KEY: [C3] (Today's date, such as 12/14/94)

INSERT SEVERAL ROWS. Insert three new rows at Row 19. This will have the effect of moving TOTAL and the following lines down several rows. You may begin the insert at any cell in Row 19, but go to A19 for the following directions.

DO: [A19] / **W**orksheet **I**nsert **R**ow

DO: [A19] Set the range for 3 rows. Press [.] to anchor the start of the range.

DO: Press [↓] 2 times to highlight three rows in a downward direction.

DO: [A21] Press [Enter]. New rows at 19, 20, and 21 have been inserted.

Column B is blank except for some labels at B22 through B25. You will move the labels to C22 through C25 and then delete Column B.

DO: [B22] / **M**ove [.]

DO: Point to B25, the end of the range, and press [Enter].

DO: Specify *where* to put the cells. Point to C22.

DO: [C22] Press [Enter].

DELETE ROWS AND COLUMNS

Entire rows and columns may be deleted using the **Worksheet Delete** command. As you delete columns and rows, cell addresses in formulas will update automatically if those formulas include any cells not deleted but affected by the deletion. Because deleted rows and columns cannot always be restored, it is wise to save a worksheet before deleting in case you make an error. Save the file as LO6INDEL.

DO: / **F**ile **S**ave LO6INDEL [Enter]

DELETE ONE COLUMN. You may begin the column deletion at any cell in column B, but go to B22 for the directions below.

DO: [B22] / **W**orksheet **D**elete **C**olumn

DO: [B22] Press [Enter] to accept a one-column range (B22..B22).

DELETE SEVERAL ROWS. You will delete the three rows you previously inserted.

DO: Goto A19.

DO: [A19] / **W**orksheet **D**elete **R**ow

DO: [A19] Press [.] to anchor the beginning of the range.

DO: Point to A21 and press [Enter] to end the range.

DO: Save the worksheet as LO6INDEL. Select the Replace option. Leave the LO6INDEL worksheet on your screen.

MORE INSERT AND DELETE. For practice, complete the following steps to insert, delete, and move.

Insert a new column at D:

DO: At any cell in Column D, / **W**orksheet **I**nsert **C**olumn (↵Enter)

Move Column A, Account Balance data, to Column D.

DO: [A1] / **M**ove (.)

DO: Point to the end of the range, A22.

DO: [A22] (↵Enter)

DO: [D1] (↵Enter)

Delete the empty Column A.

DO: At any cell in Column A, / **W**orksheet **D**elete **C**olumn (↵Enter)

Delete labels no longer needed using the Range Erase command:

DO: [A19] / **R**ange **E**rase (.)

DO: Point to A22, the end of the range. Press (↵Enter).

DO: Check your worksheet with Figure LO6.1.

DO: Be sure your personal data line is at A24. Save the worksheet as LO6INDEL. Select the Replace option. Print the worksheet and then clear it.

FIGURE LO6.1
The LO6INDEL Worksheet

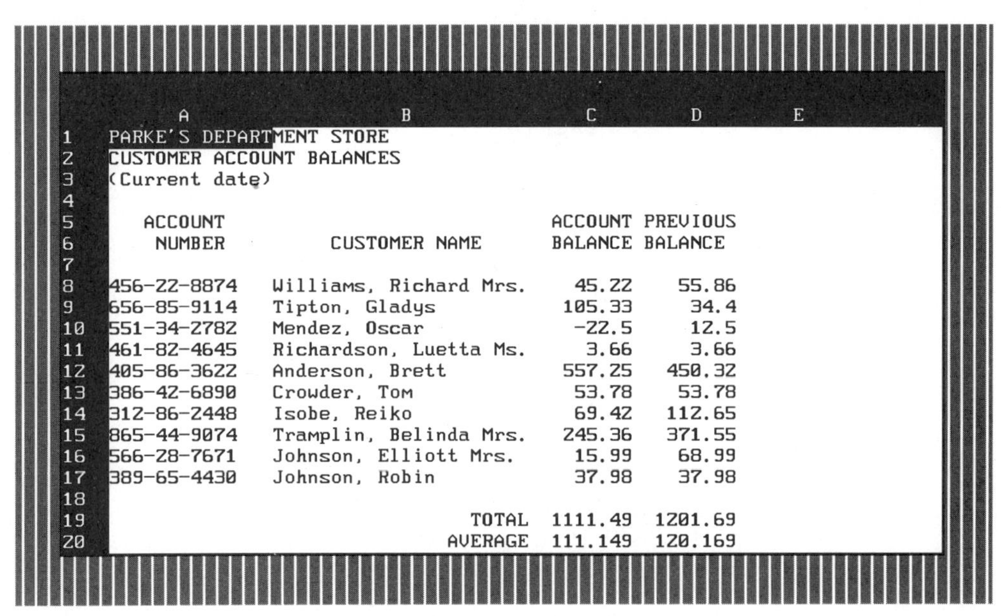

	A	B	C	D	E
1	PARKE'S DEPARTMENT STORE				
2	CUSTOMER ACCOUNT BALANCES				
3	(Current date)				
4					
5	ACCOUNT		ACCOUNT	PREVIOUS	
6	NUMBER	CUSTOMER NAME	BALANCE	BALANCE	
7					
8	456-22-8874	Williams, Richard Mrs.	45.22	55.86	
9	656-85-9114	Tipton, Gladys	105.33	34.4	
10	551-34-2782	Mendez, Oscar	-22.5	12.5	
11	461-82-4645	Richardson, Luetta Ms.	3.66	3.66	
12	405-86-3622	Anderson, Brett	557.25	450.32	
13	386-42-6890	Crowder, Tom	53.78	53.78	
14	312-86-2448	Isobe, Reiko	69.42	112.65	
15	865-44-9074	Tramplin, Belinda Mrs.	245.36	371.55	
16	566-28-7671	Johnson, Elliott Mrs.	15.99	68.99	
17	389-65-4430	Johnson, Robin	37.98	37.98	
18					
19		TOTAL	1111.49	1201.69	
20		AVERAGE	111.149	120.169	

QUICK QUESTIONS

1. What command is used to add entire rows or columns to a worksheet?
2. If you are going to erase Row 5, where should your pointer be when you begin the erase command?
3. What command is used to delete entire rows or columns in a worksheet?
4. What should be done before deleting rows or columns to possibly prevent a crisis?

REPEAT CHARACTERS

One of the simplest ways to enhance the appearance of a spreadsheet is by using **Repeat Characters**. Although it can be used to repeat any label, the Repeat Characters command is often used to underline or visually separate parts of the worksheet. To repeat characters, press \ (inverted slash), key the character(s), and press Enter. This will repeat the character(s) across one cell. After a cell is filled with repeat characters, you will often copy it to other locations.

It is important to remember that the inverted slash key (\) is used *only for repeat characters* in Lotus.

DO: Retrieve LORA5A.

Place a ruling above the SUBTOTAL amount.

DO: [E17] Insert a row for the ruling. Press / **W**orksheet **I**nsert **R**ow (Enter).

DO: [E17] (\) (-) (Enter)

Underline the column headings.

DO: [B10] (\) (-) (Enter)

Copy the characters in B10 to Cells C10 through F10.

DO: [B10] Press / **C**opy (Enter).

DO: [C10] (.)

DO: [F10] (Enter)

Place a decorative accent under the Allen Audio company name.

DO: [A4] (\) (*) (Enter)

Copy the *s to cell B4.

DO: [A4] Press / **C**opy [↵Enter].

DO: [B4] [↵Enter]

Place a decorative design at the bottom of the worksheet:

DO: [A21] [\] [*] [↵Enter]

DO: / **C**opy [↵Enter]

DO: [B21] [.]

DO: [F21] [↵Enter]

DO: Check the appearance of your worksheet with Figure LO6.2.

FIGURE LO6.2
The LO6PODEC Worksheet

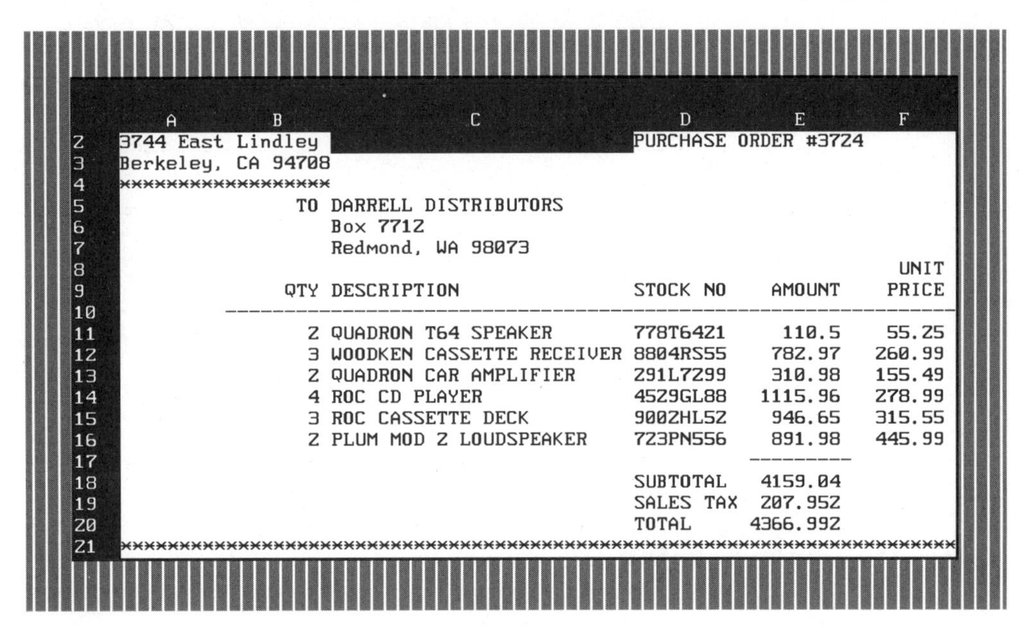

A B C D E F
2 3744 East Lindley PURCHASE ORDER #3724
3 Berkeley, CA 94708
4 ******************
5 TO DARRELL DISTRIBUTORS
6 Box 7712
7 Redmond, WA 98073
8 UNIT
9 QTY DESCRIPTION STOCK NO AMOUNT PRICE
10 --
11 2 QUADRON T64 SPEAKER 778T6421 110.5 55.25
12 3 WOODKEN CASSETTE RECEIVER 8804RS55 782.97 260.99
13 2 QUADRON CAR AMPLIFIER Z91L7Z99 310.98 155.49
14 4 ROC CD PLAYER 4529GL88 1115.96 278.99
15 3 ROC CASSETTE DECK 9002HL52 946.65 315.55
16 2 PLUM MOD 2 LOUDSPEAKER 723PN556 891.98 445.99
17 ---------
18 SUBTOTAL 4159.04
19 SALES TAX 207.952
20 TOTAL 4366.992
21 **

DO: Save the worksheet as LO6PODEC, print it, and erase it.

MORE REPEAT CHARACTERS. For practice, complete the following steps to enhance the appearance of an invoice, LORA5B.

DO: Retrieve LORA5B.

Add a ruling above the subtotal.

DO: [E17] [\] [-] [↵Enter]

Delete Column F.

DO: [F17] / **W**orksheet **D**elete **C**olumn [↵Enter]

Underline the column headings.

DO: [A10] \ ^ ↵Enter

DO: [A10] / **C**opy ↵Enter

DO: [B10] .

DO: [E10] ↵Enter

Place a border around the entire invoice. Insert two columns and a row and set a narrow column width.

DO: [A1] / **W**orksheet **I**nsert **C**olumn ↵Enter

DO: [A1] / **W**orksheet **C**olumn **S**et-Width 3 ↵Enter

DO: [A1] / **W**orksheet **I**nsert **R**ow ↵Enter

DO: [G1] / **W**orksheet **C**olumn **S**et-Width 3 ↵Enter

Center a character in Columns A and G and then copy down the columns.

DO: [A1] ^ • ↵Enter

DO: [A1] / **C**opy ↵Enter

DO: [A2] .

DO: [A22] ↵Enter

DO: [G1] ^ • ↵Enter

DO: [G1] / **C**opy ↵Enter

DO: [G2] .

DO: [G22] ↵Enter

Place characters in Rows 1 and 22:

DO: [B1] \ • ↵Enter

DO: / **C**opy ↵Enter

DO: [C1] .

DO: [F1] ↵Enter

DO: [B22] \ • ↵Enter

DO: [B22] / **C**opy ↵Enter

DO: [C22] .

DO: [F22] ↵Enter

DO: Check your worksheet with Figure LO6.3.

DO: Save the document as LO6INDEC.

DO: Print the worksheet. (You may have to press (Esc) to clear the previous print range.) Erase the worksheet.

FIGURE LO6.3
The LO6INDEC Worksheet

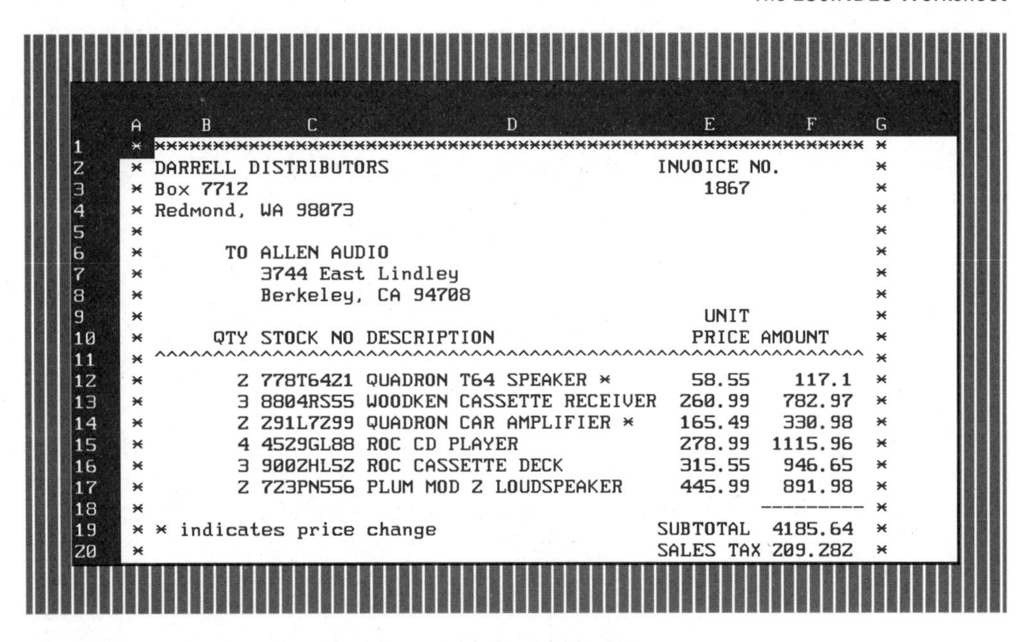

```
     A   B       C              D                 E        F     G
1    * ************************************************************ *
2    * DARRELL DISTRIBUTORS                   INVOICE NO.           *
3    * Box 7712                                   1867              *
4    * Redmond, WA 98073                                            *
5    *                                                              *
6    *      TO ALLEN AUDIO                                          *
7    *         3744 East Lindley                                    *
8    *         Berkeley, CA 94708                                   *
9    *                                            UNIT              *
10   *     QTY STOCK NO DESCRIPTION              PRICE AMOUNT       *
11   * ^^^^^^^^^^^^^^^^^^^^^^^^^^^^^^^^^^^^^^^^^^^^^^^^^^^^^^^^^^^^ *
12   *       2 778T6421 QUADRON T64 SPEAKER *     58.55    117.1    *
13   *       3 8804RS55 WOODKEN CASSETTE RECEIVER 260.99   782.97   *
14   *       2 291L7299 QUADRON CAR AMPLIFIER *  165.49    330.98   *
15   *       4 4529GL88 ROC CD PLAYER            278.99   1115.96   *
16   *       3 9002HL52 ROC CASSETTE DECK        315.55    946.65   *
17   *       2 723PN556 PLUM MOD 2 LOUDSPEAKER   445.99    891.98   *
18   *                                                   --------- *
19   * * indicates price change              SUBTOTAL   4185.64    *
20   *                                       SALES TAX  209.282    *
```

1. What are some uses for the Repeat Characters command?
2. List the three steps needed to use the Repeat Characters command.
   a)
   b)
   c)
3. For what features is the inverted slash key used in Lotus?
4. What keys would you press to fill a cell with hyphens (-)?
5. When preparing to print a worksheet, what should you press to cancel the previous print range when necessary?

QUICK QUESTIONS

FORMAT

As you have probably noticed, Lotus does not always display numbers exactly like you key them. For example, if you key 345.30, Lotus omits the ending zero. As a result, columns of numbers are not aligned on the decimal point. In addition, no dollar signs or commas for large numbers are displayed by Lotus. You may, however, format numbers to be more legible and attractive.

You can format all numeric cells in the worksheet to a particular format by using the Worksheet Global Format command. Or, you can format just some numeric cells to a particular format by using the Range Format command.

Frequently used formats include: comma, currency ($), fixed decimal places, and percent (%). If you choose currency or percent, every cell in the range will display the dollar sign or percent sign beside the value.

GLOBAL FORMAT. When most of the numbers on a worksheet should appear in a particular way, use the **Worksheet Global Format** command. This global command will change the default format for the entire worksheet. Then you can format individual areas of the worksheet that should have a different appearance by using the Range Format command. Range Format overrides Global Format!

DO: Retrieve LO5COPY.

SCROLLING. Since this worksheet is wider than the screen, the screen will **scroll** or *move* as you point from one side to the other. Press Tab to scroll one screenful to the right. Press Shift-Tab to move one screenful to the left.

Look at the worksheet to see how it should be formatted.

DO: [A1] Press (Tab) to move one screenful right.

Column F contains money amounts (dollars and cents). Column G contains percent amounts. (See the column heading and look at the cell contents at G6.)

DO: [G6] Press (Shift)-(Tab) to move one screenful left.

CURRENCY FORMAT. Columns A and E also contain money amounts. Since most of the worksheet contains money amounts, base the global format on that. Money amounts may be formatted as either currency with dollar signs and two decimal places, comma with two decimal places, or fixed with two decimal places. Currency and comma formats will place commas at appropriate places for thousands, millions, and billions.

Use a global currency format. The global format command can be used at any position in the worksheet.

DO: / **W**orksheet **G**lobal **F**ormat **C**urrency

Establish the number of decimal places.

DO: Press (↵Enter) to accept 2 decimal places.

COMMA FORMAT. Comma format looks similar to currency format, but no dollar signs are displayed.

FIXED FORMAT. Notice the entire sheet now has $ signs and two decimal places. Too many dollar signs can be confusing to read. Try the fixed format and see if the appearance is improved. Fixed format does not display dollar signs or commas.

DO: / **W**orksheet **G**lobal **F**ormat **F**ixed

DO: Press (↵Enter) to accept 2 decimal places.

The entire sheet now has 2 decimal places and no dollar signs.

RANGE FORMAT. Use the **Range Format** command to individually format one cell or a larger range of cells. Remember, Range Format *overrides* Global Format.

It is a common practice to place dollar signs at the first entry and at the total position in a column of dollar amounts. Use the Range Format command to format particular cells.

DO: [A6] / **R**ange **F**ormat **C**urrency 2 (↵Enter)

DO: [A6] Press (↵Enter) to format one cell, A6.

DO: [E6] / **R**ange **F**ormat **C**urrency 2 (↵Enter)

DO: [E6] Press (↵Enter) to format one cell, E6.

DO: [F6] On your own, key the command to assign the currency format with 2 decimal places to cell F6.

Column G has been formatted globally with 2 decimal places, just like the dollar amounts. However, it is important to show clearly that this is a different type of data. Format Column G for percent.

DO: [G6] / **R**ange **F**ormat **P**ercent 2 (↵Enter)

DO: [G6] Press (.) to anchor the beginning of the range.

DO: [G15] Press (↵Enter) to end the range.

DO: On your own, use **R**ange **F**ormat **C**urrency to have all three totals displayed with a dollar sign and 2 decimal places. If asterisks (*) appear across a cell when formatting it, widen the cell as much as needed to correctly display the number.

DO: Make a decorative row of periods (.) from A2 through G2.

DO: Make additional rows of periods across Rows 5, 16, and 21 in Columns A through G.

GLOBAL COLUMN WIDTH

Like the Global Format command, the **Global Column-Width** command will affect the width of every cell on the sheet. The Worksheet Column Set-Width command, however, overrides the Global Column-Width command. The Global Column-Width command can be used at any position on the worksheet.

DO: / **W**orksheet **G**lobal **C**olumn-Width 10 (↵Enter)

DO: Save the worksheet as LO6FORMT.

DO: Print the worksheet. Since it is wide, it will print on two sheets of paper unless you use techniques described in *Wide Worksheets* in Lotus Section Five.

DO: Erase the worksheet.

QUICK QUESTIONS

1. Which Lotus command is used to format all numbers in the worksheet to a particular format?
2. Which Lotus command is used to format just some cells to a particular format?
3. List four types of formats you may choose for numbers.
   a)
   b)
   c)
   d)
4. Why is it not a good idea to globally format numbers to have the currency format?
5. Which is the overriding command, Global Format or Range Format?
6. What should you press to scroll one screen to the right?
7. What should you press to scroll one screen to the left?
8. What command should be used to format one cell?
9. What should you do if asterisks appear across a cell when you format the cell?

	A	B	C	D	E	F
1	DESCRIPTION	JULY	AUGUST	SEPTEMBER	TOTAL	
2						
3	RECEIPTS					
4	SALES	4500	6800	6800		
5	SERVICE	6200	8500	8000		
6	TOTAL					
7						
8	PAYMENTS					
9	PRODUCT					
10	SALARIES	2000				
11	RENT	1000				
12	INSURANCE	123		130		
13	UTILITES	120				
14	SUPPLIES	55	90	90		
15	TOTAL					
16						

Key the worksheet shown above. The column heading DESCRIPTION is centered, and Column A is widened to 15. All other column headings are right aligned. Press the Space Bar to indent the DESCRIPTION items where shown. Follow the directions below and on page L72 to complete the worksheet.

1. Key @SUM functions at B6 and B15 to figure the total July receipts and the total July payments. Then copy the function to C6 through D6 and C15 through D15.
2. Key a formula for the product payment amounts (B9-D9), which are 50% of the sales figure for their respective months. To do this, key a formula at B9 that will multiply the sales amount for July (B4) by .5 (50%). Copy the formula to Cells C9 and D9.
3. Salaries, rent, and utilities are fixed amounts. Copy these fixed amounts in Column B into Columns C and D.
4. Copy the Insurance amount at B12 to C12.
5. Total each receipt and each payment for the 3-month period. At E4 key a function to total Cells B4, C4 and D4. Copy the function to Cells E5 through E15.
6. Delete the unwanted zeroes in Cells E7 and E8 with (Delete) or Range Erase.
7. Save the sheet as LOREV6A.
8. The worksheet needs some headings. Insert four rows at Row 1. (The range is Rows 1 to 4.) Key the following headings at A1, A2, and A3:
   QUALITY OFFICE SUPPLIES
   ESTIMATED RECEIPTS AND PAYMENTS
   FOR THE QUARTER ENDED SEPTEMBER 1993
9. Place quotes (") across Row 4. At A4 use Repeat Character and then copy it across to B4 through E4.

10. Insert a new row at Row 10. Then use Repeat Characters to place hyphens above the TOTAL amount at B10. Copy this to Columns C through E. Repeat these steps at Row 20.
11. Globally format for comma with two decimal places.
12. Globally widen cells to 12 places.
13. Use Range Format Currency to place dollar signs for all figures in Rows 8, 11, 14, and 21.
14. Save the worksheet as LOREV6B. Print it. Leave it on your screen for the next activity or erase it and quit Lotus.

ACTIVITY A - ESTIMATED RECEIPTS AND PAYMENTS

Retrieve LOREV6B.

1. Goto A23. Key the label: EST. INCOME.
2. At B23 key a formula to find the difference between July Total Receipts and Total Payments. Point to the cells (B11-B21) as you key the formula. Copy the formula to Cells C23 through E23. Format the cells for currency.
3. Use Repeat Characters to place equal signs (=) from B24 to E24.
4. At F8 key a formula that will calculate the percent of change from the beginning of the quarter (July) to the end of the quarter (September). To find the percent of change, subtract the July figure (B8) *from* the September figure (D8) and then divide by the July figure (B8). Point to the cells as you build the formula. Use parentheses around the subtraction part of the formula so it will be performed before the division. (The result of the calculation at F8 is .51.)
5. Copy the formula at F8 to Cells F9 through F23. Delete any cells that should be blank but instead display 0 or ERR.
6. Format Column F with the Range Format Percent command, using 2 decimal places.
7. Key at F5 a right-aligned label: % CHANGE.
8. Tidy the worksheet by copying from Column E quotes, rulings, and equal signs where needed in Column F.
9. Place quotes from A6 to F6 using Repeat Character and the Copy command.
10. Save the worksheet as LORA6A.
11. Print the worksheet and then erase it.

ACTIVITY B - TEST SCORES

GRADE	TEST 5
10	76
11	94
9	91
10	82
12	75
12	75
10	90
9	84
12	91
11	88

Retrieve LORA4A. Follow the directions below to enter the data shown at the appropriate places and to complete the worksheet.

1. Insert a new column at Column B. Center the column heading GRADE at B3. Beginning at B5, key the school grade data shown above.
2. Delete Row 1 with the main heading STUDENT GRADES, using the Worksheet Delete Row command. At D1 key a new main heading STUDENT TEST SCORES.
3. At G2 center the column heading AVERAGE. At G4 key the @AVG function that will average test scores 1 through 4. Copy it down column G through G17. Format the column for fixed, 1 decimal place. (Delete the 0 or ERR at G14.)
4. Set a global column width of 7. Use the Worksheet Column-Width to set Column A for a width of 10.
5. Add three new rows at Row 2.
6. Use Repeat Characters to put equal signs (=) across Cell A3. Copy the equal signs from B3 to G3. Follow the same procedure to put equal signs across Rows 5 and 16 to Column G.
7. Insert a new column at G. Center the label TEST 5 at G5. Beginning at G7, key the scores for Test 5 shown at the top of this page.
8. Look at the contents of H6. The average should be based on the scores in Columns C through G. Is it? If not, edit the function and then copy it down the column.
9. Copy the Average, Maximum and Minimum functions into Column G.
10. Delete Row 2.
11. Tidy the worksheet by adding missing equal signs.
12. Save the worksheet as LORA6B.
13. Print the worksheet and then erase it. Go on to the next section or quit Lotus.

7

SORTING

OBJECTIVES

- Recognize that a spreadsheet is a **database.**
- Distinguish between **ascending** and **descending** order.
- Set a **sort range**, both **primary** and **secondary.**
- Sort **alphabetically** and **numerically.**
- **Reset** data sort settings.

LOTUS AS A DATABASE

Before sorting data, it is helpful to know that Lotus is like a database because the worksheet is arranged by records and fields. For this reason, some people use Lotus as both a spreadsheet and a database.

Usually in Lotus, a *row is a record* and a *column is a field*. Figure LO7.1 shows part of the LO6INDEL worksheet. Each row, bounded by horizontal lines, contains a record of data about a customer.

The first row, data about Mrs. Richard Williams, is a record. The second row, data about Gladys Tipton, is a record, and so on. Always include the entire record (row) in the range of data to be sorted, otherwise you will separate data from the person or event it belongs with. For example, it would be an error to give Mrs. Williams's account number to Oscar Mendez through incorrect sorting.

Following is a part of the LO6INDEL worksheet (LO7.2). This time it is shown divided by vertical lines into fields, which are *types* of data such as account numbers, names, account balances, and previous balances. A column heading is a field *name*, like Account Number.

When you sort a worksheet, you select the field you want to **sort**, or arrange in order. For example, if the part of a worksheet shown in LO7.2 were sorted on the Customer Name field, Brett Anderson's record would be the first one; and Mrs. Richard Williams' record would be the last one.

FIGURE L07.1
Rows of Records

456-22-8874	Williams, Richard Mrs.	45.22	55.86
656-85-9114	Tipton, Gladys	105.33	34.4
551-34-2782	Mendez, Oscar	–22.5	12.5
461-82-4645	Richardson, Luetta Ms.	3.66	3.66
405-86-3622	Anderson, Brett	557.25	450.32

FIGURE L07.2
Columns of Fields

ACCOUNT NUMBER	CUSTOMER NAME	ACCOUNT BALANCE	PREVIOUS BALANCE
456-22-8874	Williams, Richard Mrs.	45.22	55.86
656-85-9114	Tipton, Gladys	105.33	34.4
551-34-2782	Mendez, Oscar	–22.5	12.5
461-82-4645	Richardson, Luetta Ms.	3.66	3.66
405-86-3622	Anderson, Brett	557.25	450.32

QUICK QUESTIONS

1. Why is Lotus like a database?
2. What part of a worksheet usually contains one record?
3. What part of a worksheet can usually be considered a field?
4. What part of a record should be included in the range of data to be sorted?
5. What part of the worksheet is a field name?

SORTING

Because it simplifies data entry, records are often entered into a spreadsheet in random order. Rearranging the records into alphabetic or numeric order, however, can make the data easier to read and analyze.

Use the **Data Sort** command to arrange records in alphabetic or numeric order.

DO: Retrieve the LO6INDEL worksheet.

DATA RANGE. When sorting, first set the **Data Range**, the range of records to be sorted.

DO: Go to the beginning of the range of records to be sorted. Go to A8.

Do not include headings, totals, etc. in a sort range. The sort range only includes complete records.

DO: [A8] / **D**ata **S**ort

DO: [A8] Select **D**ata-Range.

DO: [A8] Press (.) to anchor the beginning of the range

DO: [D17] Press (↵Enter) to end the range, including all records on the worksheet.

PRIMARY SORT KEY. After the Data Range has been set, select the **Primary Key**, the field on which the records will be sorted.

DO: [A8] Select **P**rimary-Sort.

You will sort on the Customer Name field, Column B.

DO: Go to Column B in any record and press (↵Enter) to set it as the primary sort key.

A new option appears on the Control Panel, *Sort order (A or D).*

ASCENDING ORDER. Ascending order (A) is the normal sort order, with letters going from A to Z and numbers from lowest to highest.

DESCENDING ORDER. Descending order (D) arranges letters from Z to A and numbers from highest to lowest. Descending is the default sort order.

Arrange the Customer Names in ascending order.

DO: Key (A) if necessary to set the Sort Order to ascending. Press (↵Enter).

DO: Select **G**o to perform the sort.

See if the customer names are arranged in order from Anderson to Williams. If the records are not arranged correctly, redo the sort.

The next sort will be on the Account Number field, arranged in ascending order.

DO: [A8] / **D**ata **S**ort **D**ata-Range

The previous data range should reappear, A8..D17. To reset a data range, press (Esc) and then set it where desired.

DO: If the data range A8..D17 appears, press (↵Enter) to accept it. (Otherwise, anchor the range at A8 and go to D17 and then press (↵Enter).)

DO: Select **P**rimary-Key.

DO: Move to any record in Column A, the Account Number field (↵Enter).

DO: Press (A) for ascending and (↵Enter).

DO: Select **G**o to sort.

The account numbers should be arranged in numeric order, from the lowest to the highest.

Sometimes it is helpful to see the largest values first. In the current situation, Parke's Department Store is very interested in how much money is owed them. Sort the Account Balance column in descending order so the largest balances are shown first.

DO: [A8] / **D**ata **S**ort (the previous data range is still in effect)

DO: Select **P**rimary-Key.

DO: Point to Column C, the Account Balance field, in any record. Press (↵Enter).

DO: Select **D** (descending) for the sort order. Press (↵Enter).

DO: Select **G**o to sort.

Check to see if the sorting is correct.

DO: On your own, sort in descending order on the Previous Balance field.

DO: Save the worksheet as LO7SORT1.

DO: Print the worksheet and then erase it.

MORE SORTING PRACTICE

DO: Retrieve LOREV5.

The Stamp-It Company wants to check for low quantity items so more can be ordered from the wholesalers. Arrange the LOREV5 worksheet in ascending order on the QTY field.

DO: [A7] At the first record, press / **D**ata **S**ort **D**ata-Range.

DO: [A7] Press (.) to anchor the data range.

DO: [F18] Press (↵Enter) to end the data range at the last record.

DO: Select **P**rimary-Key.

DO: Point to Column B, the QTY field, in a record. Press (Enter).

DO: Select A for ascending order (Enter).

DO: Select **G**o.

Analyze the sort. The quantities are listed from smallest to largest. There are two items with a quantity of 12 and two items with a quantity of 20. Stamp-It wants the duplicate quantities to be arranged by Stock No. Are the stock numbers of the items with quantities of 12 and 20 arranged in order (smallest to largest)? By coincidence, they are in order.

Stamp-It wants new information. They want the inventory items in order by Unit Price.

DO: On your own, sort the worksheet in ascending order on the Unit Price column.

Look at the result of the sort in Figure LO7.3.

SECONDARY SORT KEY. The **Secondary Sort Key** allows you to do a "sort within a sort." The Primary Sort Key determines the first field that will be arranged in order. Then, the records *within* that sort can be arranged on a second field by the Secondary Sort Key.

Looking at LO7.3, the Unit Prices are in order, lowest to highest, but many of the items have identical prices. To make data analysis simpler, sort on Stock No within Unit Price. Unit Price is the primary sort field, and Stock No is the secondary sort field.

FIGURE LO7.3
LOREV5 Sorted in Ascending Order on Unit Price

A1: 'STAMP-IT COMPANY R

	A	B	C	D	E	F
4					UNIT	
5	STOCK NO	QTY	UNIT	DESCRIPTION	PRICE	EXTENSION
6						
7	340-374	15	EA	MOV DATE #1	2.15	32.25
8	72-237	16	EA	MOV NUMBER	2.15	34.4
9	340-484	20	EA	MOV DATE #2A	2.15	43
10	72-563	27	EA	MOV PRICE	2.15	58.05
11	340-907	9	EA	MOV DATE #2C	2.35	21.15
12	340-882	13	EA	MOV DATE #3	2.35	30.55
13	811-776	8	EA	INKED CONFIDENTIAL	4.15	33.2
14	811-396	12	EA	INKED COPY	4.15	49.8
15	811-324	12	EA	INKED AIRMAIL	4.15	49.8
16	811-172	20	EA	INKED FILE	4.15	83
17	811-561	21	EA	INKED FOR DEPOSIT ONLY	4.15	87.15
18	75-839	18	EA	DATE AND TIME	19.55	351.9

DO: [A7] / **D**ata **S**ort

DO: It is not necessary to select the data range if it is still correct. If not correct, press (Esc) and then reset the range.

DO: [A7] Select **P**rimary-Key.

DO: Point to Column E, the Unit Price field. Press (↵Enter).

DO: Select **A**scending order (↵Enter).

DO: Select **S**econdary-Key.

DO: Point to Column A, the secondary sort field, Stock No. Press (↵Enter).

DO: Select **A**scending (↵Enter).

DO: Select **G**o.

Check the result of sorting on two fields. The four items with a unit price of 2.15 have their stock numbers arranged in order from the lowest to the highest stock number. The same is true for the items that have prices of 2.35 and 4.15.

DO: Save the worksheet as LO7SORT2 and then print it. Leave it on the screen.

RESET. Before sorting a worksheet a second time, it may be helpful to use the **Data Sort Reset** command. This clears the data range and the primary and secondary sort key settings from the previous sort.

DO: [A7] / **D**ata **S**ort **R**eset

All data sort settings are cleared. Make a new sort using Primary and Secondary keys.

DO: On your own, make Unit Price the primary sort field in *descending* order, and Qty the secondary sort field in *ascending* order.

DO: Save the worksheet as LO7SORT3.

DO: Print the worksheet and then erase it.

QUICK QUESTIONS

1. Why are records often arranged in alphabetic or numeric order?
2. What command is used to arrange records in order?
3. What is the data range?
4. What is the Primary Key?
5. Which sort order goes from Z to A and largest number to smallest?
6. When should you use the Descending order option?
7. How can you simplify data analysis when you sort on a field that has several records with identical data in the sorted column?
8. What command can be helpful before sorting a worksheet a second time?

	A	B	C	D	E	F
1	COLLEGE EXAM, INC					
2	EXAMINEES					
3	SATURDAY, MAY 8, 1993					
4	**					
5	NAME	SOCSEC NO	SEX	VERBAL	MATH	
6	**					
7	Crawford, Frank	454-88-5471	M	548	547	
8	Velez, Amelia	576-36-1873	F	457	483	
9	Tampps, LeGrand	312-74-7821	M	463	588	
10	Huff, Elaine	438-10-2372	F	548	547	
11	Runyan, Grace	610-29-8631	F	686	650	
12	Morales, Mario	357-72-5832	M	548	647	
13	Peterson, Kathy	574-20-3558	F	457	483	
14	Bancroft, Wayne	411-95-3264	M	463	407	
15	Forey, Harold	278-71-2239	M	575	516	
16	Toney, James	638-24-6684	M	548	483	
17	Honey, Ryan	584-33-4287	M	575	547	
18	Capps, Sandy	721-56-7328	F	457	461	
19	Prince, Amy	681-63-9005	F	389	588	
20						

Key the worksheet shown above. Align labels as shown and widen columns as needed. After saving the worksheet as LOREV7, complete the sorts described below.

1. Sort the worksheet in ascending order on the Name field. Save the sorted worksheet as LOREV7A. Print it.
2. Sort the worksheet on the Sex field as a primary sort (ascending) and the Name field as a secondary sort (ascending). Save the sorted worksheet as LOREV7B. Print it.
3. Sort the worksheet with Verbal as the primary sort (descending) and Name as the secondary sort (ascending). Save the sorted worksheet as LOREV7C. Print it.
4. Sort the math scores from highest to lowest; alphabetize names within the math score groupings. Save the sorted worksheet as LOREV7D. Print it.

1. Retrieve LORA6B.
2. Sort the worksheet alphabetically. Save the sorted worksheet as LORA7A. Print it.
3. Sort the worksheet on the Grade field with Grade 12 first and Grade 9 last. Save the sorted worksheet as LORA7B. Print it.
4. Sort the worksheet on the Average field, highest to lowest, but arrange the students alphabetically as a secondary sort. Save the sorted worksheet as LORA7C. Print it.

8

GRAPHS

OBJECTIVES

- Explain the **purpose** of graphs.
- Explain **data range.**
- Create **line, bar, multiple bar**, and **pie** graphs.
- Use graphical **elements.**
- **Name** and **Save** graphs.
- Use **PrintGraph** to print.

GRAPHS

The Lotus Graph commands translate worksheet data into a visual image of lines, bars, or segments of a circle. Because graphs show the *relationship* among numbers, data analysis is faster, easier, and more dramatic than with numbers alone.

Usually a graph depicts only some of the values on a worksheet. The series of rows or columns of data used for a graph is called the **data range**. Several different graphs may be created for the same worksheet. The graphs may be the same type but use different data ranges, or they may be different types of graphs. Some common types of graphs are line, bar, stacked bar, multiple bar, and pie.

Graphs can be viewed on screen or printed. If you have a color monitor, you can view the graphs in color. You can only print in color if you have a color printer.

The steps to create a graph are:

1. Create the worksheet.
2. Create the graph.
3. View and edit the graph.
4. Name the graph (and save the graph in Ver. 2.X).
5. Save the worksheet.
6. Print from the screen (Version 3.x) or enter the PrintGraph program (Version 2.x).

ELEMENTS OF A GRAPH

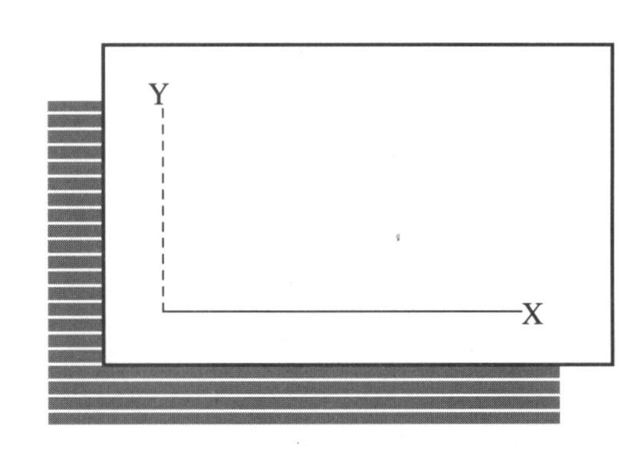

FIGURE LO8.1
Elements of a Graph

To understand how graphs are designed, it is necessary to understand the concept of the X-Y axis. As you can see, the X-axis is horizontal, and the Y-axis is vertical.

See how the graph in Figure LO8.1 is based on an X-Y axis. Study the elements of a graph.

Find the following graphic elements in LO8.1 (clockwise from the left):

The **Scale Indicator** shows the units, such as thousands or millions, of the y-axis.

Y Scale, set by Lotus according to the data range, describes the data points on the y-axis.

The **Y Axis** is a line along the left side of the graph with the vertical data points.

First and **Second Titles** identify the graph.

The **X Axis** is a line at the bottom of a graph with horizontal data points.

X-Axis Labels describe the data points on the x-axis.

The **Legend** is a caption that identifies each data range.

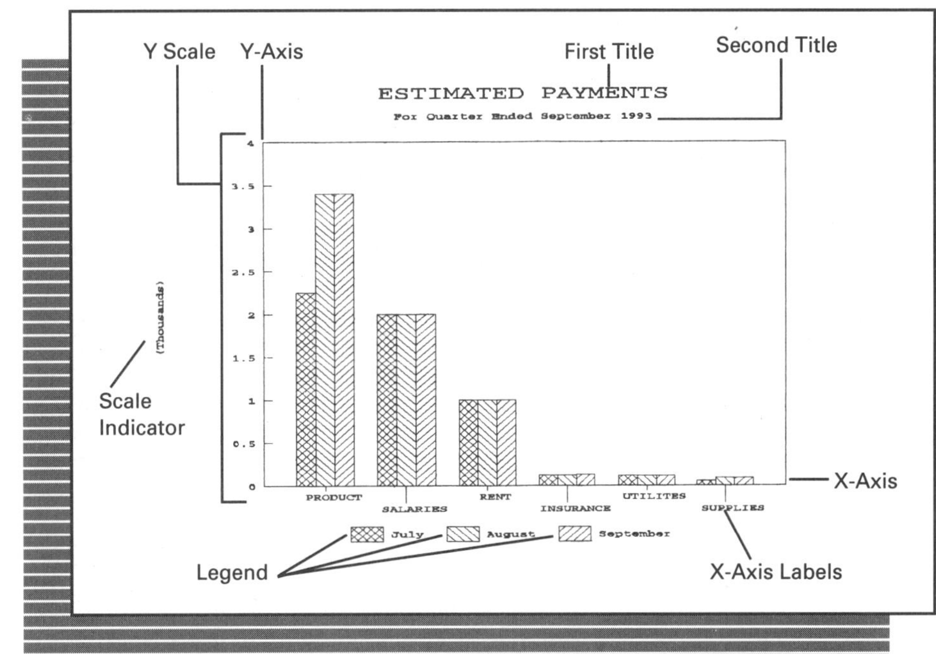

QUICK QUESTIONS

1. What is the purpose of the Lotus Graph command?
2. Why do graphs make data analysis faster and easier?
3. What is a data range?
4. What is the first step in creating a graph?
5. How will you print a graph?
6. What is the name for the horizontal axis of a graph?
7. What is the name for the vertical axis of a graph?
8. What is the purpose of the First and Second Titles of a graph?
9. Which graph element is automatically set by Lotus?
10. What is the purpose of the X-axis labels?
11. What is a legend?

LINE GRAPHS

As you can see from the chart below, LO8.2, **line graphs** are used to show change over time. Refer to this chart as you create line graphs; it guides you in making graph selections.

FIGURE LO8.2

LINE GRAPH
Purpose: Plots changes in data over time. Each line depicts a data range, each point on the line represents a value in the data range.
A-F: up to 6 data ranges or lines (one data range per line)
X: X-axis labels (identify the points on the lines)

DO: Retrieve the LOREV6B worksheet.

Because the LOREV6B worksheet shows change over a three-month period, use it to generate a line graph. Part of the LOREV6B worksheet is shown in LO8.3.

The data to be graphed is the July, August, and September Sales and Service Receipts figures. Data range A will consist of the Sales amounts, Cells B8, C8, and D8. Data range B will consist of the Service amounts, Cells B9, C9, and D9. Each data range will produce one line of this two line graph.

FIGURE LO8.3
LOREV6B Data Ranges A and B

	A	B	C	D	E
1	QUALITY OFFICE SUPPLIES				
2	ESTIMATED RECEIPTS AND PAYMENTS				
3	FOR THE QUARTER ENDED SEPTEMBER 1993				
4					
5	DESCRIPTION	JULY	AUGUST	SEPTEMBER	TOTAL
6					
7	RECEIPTS				
8	SALES	$4,500.00	$6,800.00	$6,800.00	$18,100.00
9	SERVICE	6,200.00	8,500.00	8,000.00	22,700.00
10					
11	TOTAL	$10,700.00	$15,300.00	$14,800.00	$40,800.00

Legends will identify the Sales and Service lines. The points on each line will be the months, so the X-axis labels will be July, August, and September. Figure LO8.4 shows the completed graph.

FIGURE LO8.4
Line Graph

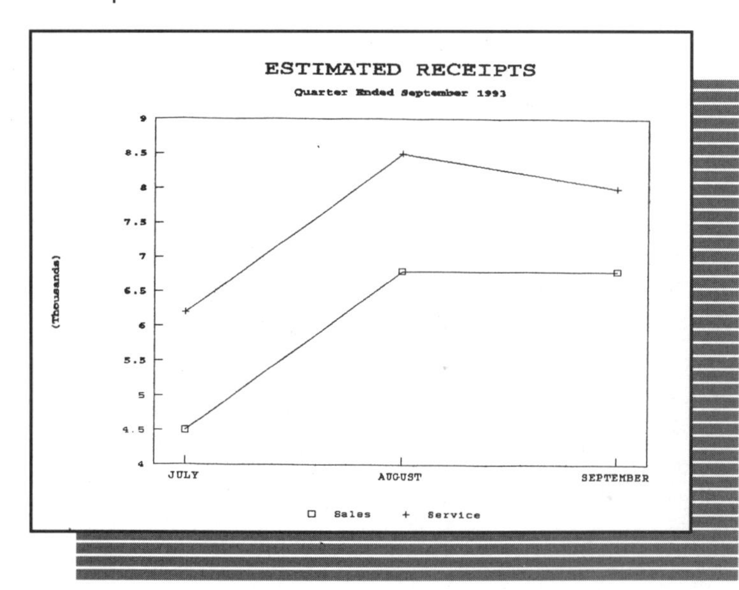

GRAPH MENU. Activate the Graph menu.

DO: / **G**raph

TYPE. Set the type of graph (line, bar, pie, etc.).

DO: Select **T**ype **L**ine

DATA RANGES. Set the data ranges, A and B.

DO: Press (A) for data range A.

DO: [B8] Goto B8 and press (.) to anchor the data range.

DO: [D8] Press (↵Enter) to end the data range.

DO: Press (B) for data range B.

DO: [B9] Press (.) to anchor the data range.

DO: [D9] Press (↵Enter) to end the data range.

X-AXIS LABELS. Set the X-axis labels to identify the data points.

DO: Press (X) for X-axis labels.

DO: Anchor B5 as the beginning of the range and D5 as the end of the range.

DO: Select **V**iew to view the graph.

LEGENDS. Two lines appear, with three data points for July, August, and September. However, the lines are not identified; both lines (ranges A and B) require legends. The Y scale has been set by Lotus.

DO: Press (Esc) to exit from the Graph View.

DO: Select **O**ptions **L**egend (A).

KEY: Sales (↵Enter)

DO: Select **L**egend (B).

KEY: Service (↵Enter)

DO: Select **Q**uit to quit the options menu.

DO: Select **V**iew.

FIRST AND SECOND TITLES. The data range lines are identified, but the purpose of the graph is not. Add a First and Second Title at the top of the graph.

DO: Press (Esc) to exit from the Graph View.

DO: Select **O**ptions **T**itles **F**irst.

KEY: ESTIMATED RECEIPTS (↵Enter)

DO: Select **T**itles **S**econd.

KEY: Quarter Ended September 1993 (↵Enter)

DO: Select **Q**uit to quit the Options menu.

DO: Select **V**iew. The completed graph should look like LO8.4. Analyze the graph to answer the following questions.

1. Which brings more receipts, sales or service? ____________
2. Is the difference between sales and service receipts about the same for each month? ____________
3. What is the *amount* of the lowest monthly receipt? ____________
4. What is the *amount* of the highest monthly receipt? ____________
5. What is the smallest scale indicator (Y scale)? ____________
6. What is the increment (amount of change) of the scale indicator? ____________

DO: Press (Esc) to exit View and return to the Graph menu.

NAME A GRAPH. When you enter new graph settings, previous settings are lost. To use several graphs within a worksheet, give each graph a name using the **Graph Name Create** command. Named graphs will remain with their worksheet and can be viewed when the worksheet is active with the **Graph Name Use** command. A graph name can be up to 15 characters in length.

Give the line graph you created the name REV6BLINE.

DO: Select **N**ame **C**reate.

KEY: REV6BLINE (↵Enter)

SAVE A GRAPH. A graph stored on disk by itself using the **Graph Save** command can be used with other programs or printed in Lotus versions prior to 3.0. Save the graph with a name that suggests the worksheet it was created from and the type of graph, such as pie or bar. Because this is a file, the file name can be up to eight characters; Lotus will add a .PIC (Ver. 2.x) or .CGM (Ver. 3.x) extension. .PIC and .CGM files cannot be retrieved into a Lotus worksheet; only .WK1 or .WK3 files can.

Save the file as REV6BLN1, because it is the first line graph based on the (LO)REV6B worksheet.

DO: Select **S**ave.

KEY: REV6BLN1 (↵Enter)

DO: Select **Q**uit to quit the graph menu.

SAVE THE WORKSHEET. After you name graphs you must save the worksheet that contains them. As usual, the worksheet will have a .WK1 or .WK3 extension.

DO: / **F**ile **S**ave

KEY: REV6BGR (↵Enter) and then erase the worksheet.

QUICK QUESTIONS

1. What is the purpose of line graphs?
2. What does each line represent on a line graph?
3. What does each line point represent on a line graph?
4. What is the purpose of X-axis labels?
5. What is the purpose of a legend?
6. What is added to a graph to identify the purpose of the graph?
7. What is pressed to exit from the Options menu?
8. What is the purpose of naming a graph?
9. What command is used to make a named graph the current graph?
10. Why is it necessary to save a worksheet when you have named its graphs?

BAR GRAPHS

Bar graphs are used to compare values to one another. A bar graph is shown in Figure LO8.1. The chart below shows that bar graphs may have one bar (**single bar**) or more than one bar (**multiple bars**). A stacked bar graph is a bar graph not used in this book.

FIGURE LO8.5

BAR GRAPH
Compares individual values or sets of values to one another. Each bar represents one value.
A: the range of bars for a single bar graph
A-F: multiple ranges for a multiple bar graph (one data range per bar)
X: x-axis labels identify the bars

SINGLE BAR GRAPH

The single bar graph you will create compares the verbal scores of all students. The file is sorted on verbal scores, so the bars should be in descending heights.

DO: Retrieve LOREV7C.

Activate the Graph menu and select the type of graph.

DO: / **G**raph **T**ype **B**ar

DATA RANGE. Use the verbal scores as Range A for the bars.

DO: Press (A) for data range A.

DO: [D7] Anchor the data range.

DO: [D19] End the data range.

View the graph.

DO: Select **V**iew.

There are 13 students in the worksheet; you should see 13 bars. The values on the Y-axis, the verbal scores, are automatically displayed by Lotus based on the values in the data range.

What is missing that would make the graph more meaningful? There are no titles describing the bars, and there is no title describing the purpose of the graph.

DO: Press (Esc) to return to the Graph menu.

X-AXIS LABELS. Add labels to describe the bars.

DO: Press (X) for X-axis labels.

DO: Set the label range from A7 to A19.

DO: View the graph.

The names are too long for the distance between the bars; reading them is difficult. To remedy this, return to the worksheet and rekey the last names only.

DO: Press (Ctrl)-(Break) to break out of the Command menu.

DO: Go to G7.

KEY: Runyan

DO: Press (↓) and key the last name only for each student through G19. Check the accuracy of your keying.

Generate the Graph menu again so you can reset the X-range. **The previous settings remain until you change them, reset them, or make a new graph**. The Type and A range are correct. Redo the X range of labels.

DO: / **G**raph

DO: Press (X) and then press (Esc) to cancel the old range.

DO: Set the range from G7 to G19.

DO: View the graph.

The graph is more informative now, but there is no indication that these are verbal scores or when the exam was taken. Add titles to the graph.

DO: Press (Esc) to return to the Graph menu.

FIRST TITLE.

DO: Select **O**ptions **T**itles **F**irst.

The first title is the most important one.

KEY: EXAM VERBAL SCORES [↵Enter]

SECOND TITLE.

DO: Select **T**itles **S**econd.

KEY: SATURDAY, MAY 8, 1993 [↵Enter]

DO: Select **Q**uit to quit the Options menu.

DO: View the graph.

The graph is clear and complete. See LO8.6. Name the graph to save it with the worksheet.

DO: Press [Esc] to exit View.

DO: Select **N**ame **C**reate.

KEY: REV7CSINGBAR [↵Enter]

Save the graph as a .PIC or .CGM file.

DO: Select **S**ave.

KEY: REV7CSBR [↵Enter]

DO: Select **Q**uit.

FIGURE LO8.6
Single Bar Graph

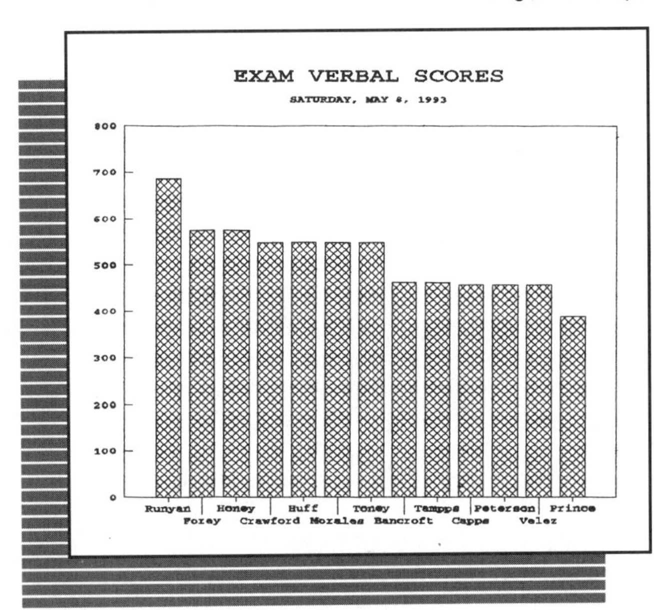

MULTIPLE BAR GRAPH

Multiple bar graphs compare several kinds of data. You will generate a graph to compare both the verbal and math scores for students. The verbal scores will be one data range, and the math scores will be a second data range.

DO: Refer to Chart LO8.5 to see the settings available for a multiple bar graph.

Previous settings remain in effect unless the Reset option is used. The type is still bar, and the A range is already set for the verbal scores. Set the next range, B, for the math scores.

DO: / **G**raph Ⓑ for the B range.

DO: Set the range from E7 to E19.

DO: View the graph.

The graph shows a double bar for each person. One bar is his or her verbal score. The other bar is his or her math score. But which is which? Create a legend that will show which bar design represents verbal scores and which bar design represents math scores.

DO: Press (Esc) to exit from View.

LEGEND.

DO: Press **O**ptions **L**egend.

Do you remember that range A is verbal and range B is math?

DO: Press Ⓐ for range A.

KEY: Verbal (↵Enter)

DO: Select **L**egend Ⓑ.

KEY: Math (↵Enter)

DO: Select **T**itles **F**irst to change the First Title to reflect the new data.

KEY: EXAM VERBAL & MATH SCORES (↵Enter)

DO: **Q**uit the Options menu.

DO: View the graph.

FIGURE LO8.7
Multiple Bar Graph

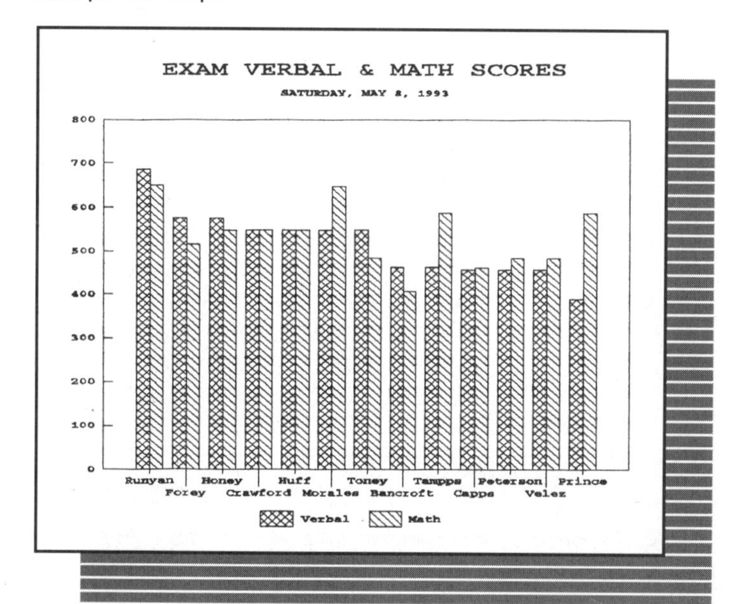

Data is displayed clearly and completely. Check your graph with LO8.7. Name the graph.

DO: Press (Esc) to exit from View.

DO: Select **N**ame **C**reate.

KEY: REV7CMULTBAR (↵Enter)

Save the graph as a .PIC or .CGM file.

DO: Select **S**ave.

KEY: REV7CMBR (↵Enter)

DO: Press **Q**uit to exit the Graph menu.

Save the worksheet so the named files will be stored with it.

DO: / **F**ile **S**ave

KEY: REV7CBAR (↵Enter) and then erase the worksheet.

QUICK QUESTIONS

1. What is the purpose of bar graphs?
2. How many data ranges can you have in a single bar graph?
3. How does Lotus determine the values on the Y-axis?
4. What can you do if X-axis labels are too long to be readable?
5. What graph option is used to cancel the previous graph settings?
6. What is the name of the second range in a multiple bar graph?

Pie Graphs

Pie graphs, used to show portions of a whole, involve only one data range. Chart LO8.8 shows some of the settings for pie graphs.

You will retrieve a worksheet that has used the @SUM function to total values. Graph the relationship of each cell in the @SUM argument (range) to the total.

DO: Retrieve LORA6A.

FIGURE LO8.8

PIE GRAPH
Identifies the relationship of each value in a data range to the entire data range.
A: the values in one data range that you want to show as pie slices
B: values that control hatch patterns, colors, or explosion of pie slices
X: the labels for the individual pie slices

To show the Estimated Sales Receipts for each month in relation to the total for the quarter, use Estimated Sales Receipts at B8 to D8 for the data range. Use the months at B5 to D5 as the X-axis labels for the pie slices.

DO: / **G**raph **T**ype **P**ie

DO: Press (A) to set the data range for the slices of pie.

DO: Set data range A from B8 through D8.

DO: Press (X) to set the labels for the slices of pie.

DO: Set label range X from B5 to D5.

DO: View the graph. It is informative, but it needs graph identification titles.

DO: Press (Esc) to exit View.

DO: Select **O**ption **T**itles **F**irst.

KEY: ESTIMATED SALES RECEIPTS BY MONTH (↵Enter)

DO: Select **T**itles **S**econd.

KEY: Quarter Ended September 1993 (↵Enter)

DO: Select **Q**uit to exit the Options menu.

DO: View the graph and then press (Esc) (Ctrl)-(Break) to return to the worksheet.

A pie graph can be enhanced by shading the pieces and/or **exploding** (separating) a piece or pieces. Range B, which controls these options, must be keyed into a blank area of the worksheet. The number of cells used for range B must equal the number of slices in the pie, in this case, three. The values to key in range B varies from 1 to 7 for shading and 8 for no shading. Add 100 to the shading value to explode a piece of pie.

KEY: [A30] 107 (↵Enter) (a shading value of 7 + 100 to explode the piece for B8)

KEY: [B30] 4 (↵Enter) (a shading value for C8)

KEY: [C30] 2 (↵Enter) (a shading value for D8)

Set the B range in the graph menu.

DO: / **G**raph **B** for range B

DO: Anchor A30 as the beginning of the range and C30 as the end of the range.

DO: View the graph.

FIGURE LO8.9
Pie Graph (RA6APIE2)

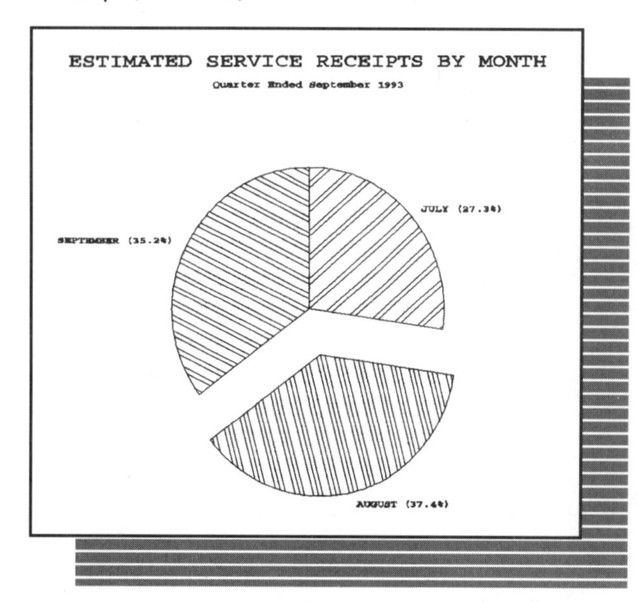

Name the graph.

DO: **N**ame **C**reate

KEY: RA6APIE1 (↵Enter)

RESET THE GRAPH SETTINGS. Use the Graph Reset command to cancel all previous graph settings.

DO: Select **R**eset **G**raph to cancel all settings.

DO: Begin a new pie graph. This time use the Estimated Service Receipts for the A range. Redo range, X-axis labels, and the Titles. Create a pie chart similar to that shown in LO8.9 (your shading may be different). Explode the August slice.

DO: View your completed graph.

Name the graph and then save the graph.

DO: Name the graph RA6APIE2.

DO: Save the graph as a .PIC or .CGM file called RA6APIE2.

DO: Exit the graph menu.

DO: Save the worksheet as LORA6AGR and then erase the worksheet.

PRINT GRAPHS

The method of printing graphs varies with the version of Lotus you are using. If you are using Version 3.0 or newer, use the directions below for *Version 3.x Printing*. If you are using Version 2, any release, begin with the directions under *Version 2.x Printing*.

VERSION 3.X PRINTING. Use **Print Image Current** to print the current graph or **Print Image Named-Graph** to print a graph you have named.

To print the line graph you named LOREV6BLINE that is a part of the REV6BGR worksheet, follow the steps below.

DO: / **F**ile **R**etrieve REV6BGR (↵Enter)

DO: / **P**rint **I**mage **N**amed-Graph REV6BLINE (↵Enter) **A**lign **G**o

Be patient; it may take a few minutes for your printer to begin printing the graph.

DO: When printing is complete, press (P) to eject the page and (Q) to quit the Print menu.

DO: Print the remaining named graphs: REV7CSINGBAR and REV7CMULTBAR (REV7CBAR worksheet), and RA6APIE1 and RA6APIE2 (LORA6AGR worksheet).

DO: If you have more time to work, go on to the Review Exercise at the end of this section. If your working time is over, exit from Lotus.

VERSION 2.X PRINTING. To print graphs you must exit from Lotus 1-2-3 and enter the Lotus PrintGraph program. The graphs are stored in the .PIC graphic files which you saved.

DO: / **Q**uit **Y**es (Yes to verify) to exit from Lotus

Next, you will enter the PrintGraph program, a separate utility program that comes with the Lotus 1-2-3 software. PrintGraph can only print .PIC files.

To enter PrintGraph, follow the step below that corresponds to what happens when you quit Lotus:

▶ If you return to the Lotus Access Menu:

DO: Select *PrintGraph.*

▶ If you return to the system prompt, remain in the Lotus 1-2-3 directory, or change to the Lotus 1-2-3 directory. You must be in the Lotus directory to enter PrintGraph.

DO: Key *lotus* (↵Enter) and select *PrintGraph.*

FIGURE LO8.10
The PrintGraph Screen

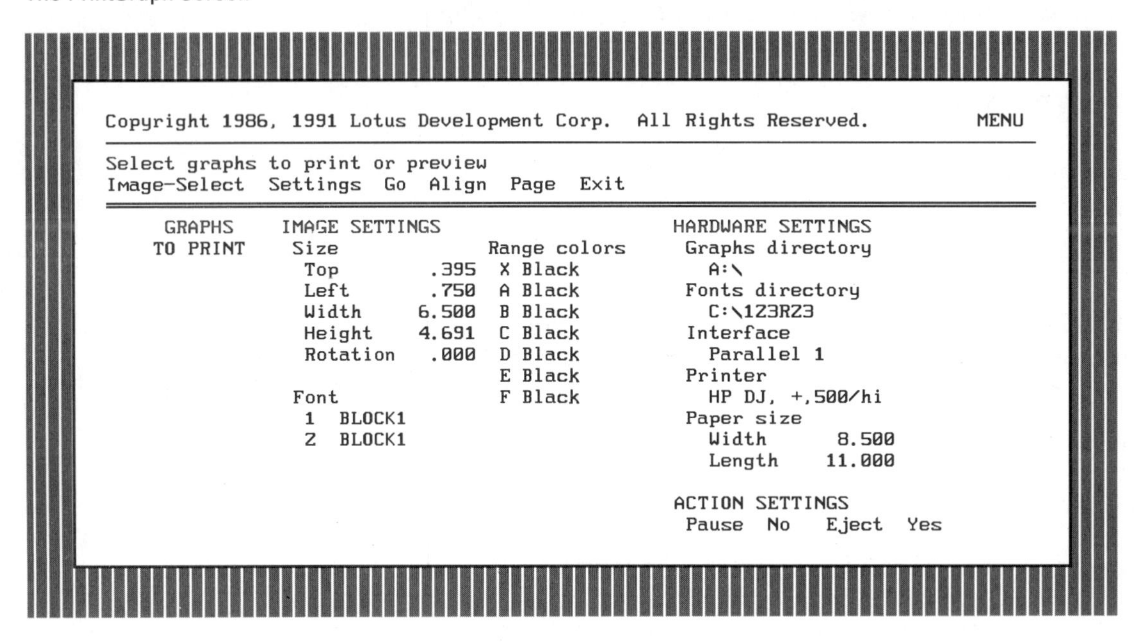

(Once in the Lotus directory, you can also key *pgraph* (↵Enter) to enter PrintGraph.)

The PrintGraph screen appears. It looks similar to LO8.10.

DO: Check the Hardware Settings for the current *Graphs directory.* This is where you have been saving all the files you create. If incorrect, select **S**ettings **H**ardware **G**raphs-Directory. Enter the path of your .PIC files.

DO: Select **Q**uit when done with the Graphs directory.

DO: Select **A**ction **E**ject to advance paper to the top of the next page after printing each graph. Select **Q**uit to exit the Action menu.

DO: Select **I**mage-Select to view the names of all .PIC files.

You may check the files to print below:

Graph Name

____ RA6APIE2

____ REV6BLN1

____ REV7CMBR

____ REV7CSBR

DO: From the Image-Select screen, press (↵Enter) on a single file you want to print or press (Spacebar) to mark or unmark a group of files for printing.

Selecting files to be printed returns you to the main PrintGraph menu.

DO: Select **A**lign **G**o.

DO: Press **E**xit **Y**es when you have completed printing.

DO: If you have time to continue, load Lotus 1-2-3 and go on to the Review Exercise.

1. What is the purpose of pie graphs?
2. How many data ranges can you use for a pie graph?
3. What command will cancel all previous graph settings?
4. List the steps you will follow to print a graph:
5. What file extension does Lotus give to a saved graph?
6. (Version 2.x users) What option should you choose from the PrintGraph main menu to see a list of your .PIC files for printing?
7. (Version 2.x users) When looking at all .PIC files on the Image-Select screen, what can you press to mark a group of files for printing?

Generate a single bar graph and then a multiple bar graph using the LOREV6B worksheet.

1. Retrieve LOREV6B.
2. Compare the amounts of the July Estimated Payments in Cells B14 to B19. This is range A.
3. Range X, the X-axis labels that identify the bars, are the labels in Cells A14 to A19.
4. The First Title is: ESTIMATED PAYMENTS. The Second Title is: July, 1993.
5. View the graph and make any necessary corrections. Name the graph REV6BSINGBAR. Save the graph as REV6BSBR.
6. Compare the amounts of the July, August, and September Estimated Payments by making a multiple bar graph. Range A remains from the single bar graph. Range B is the August values, Cells C14 to C19. Range C is the September values, Cells D14 to D19. Range X, the labels, remains.

7. Add appropriate First and Second Titles at the top.
8. Add a Legend for each bar. Legend A is July, B is August, and C is September.
9. View the graph. Name it REV6BMULTBAR. Save it as REV6BMBR.
10. Save the worksheet as REV6GR. Print the two graphs.

Create a pie graph and a line graph using the LOREV6B worksheet.

ACTIVITY A - PIE GRAPH

1. Use the **G**raph **R**eset command to clear the last graph.
2. Display the relationship of the three-month totals for the Product, Salaries, and Rent Payments, cells E14 to E16. This is the A Range.
3. Range X, the pie-slice labels, are the names of the Payment items. These are in cells A14 to A16.
4. The First Title is: TOTAL ESTIMATED PAYMENTS. The Second Title is: Quarter Ended September 1993.
5. In a blank area of the worksheet, key range B to shade the pie slices. Since there are three pie slices, range B should contain three cells. Explode the smallest pie slice.
6. Name the graph RA8APIE. Save the graph as RA8APIE. Save the worksheet as LORA8AGR.
7. Print the pie graph.

ACTIVITY B - LINE GRAPH

1. Use the **G**raph **R**eset command to clear the last graph.
2. This graph will have two lines. Range A is the changes in the estimated total Receipts for July, August, and September (B11.D11). Range B is the changes in the estimated total Payments for the three months (B21.D21).
3. The points on the line, the X-axis labels, are the months of July, August, and September.
4. Key appropriate First and Second Titles. Key a Legend for each line.
5. Name the graph RA8BLINE. Save the graph as RA8BLINE. Save the worksheet as RA8BLINE. Print the line graph.

UNIT 5

Using dBASE

1

GETTING ACQUAINTED

OBJECTIVES

- Define the term **database** and list advantages of computerized databases.
- Recognize the **Control Center** or **Access Menu.**
- List advantages of using **dot prompt commands.**
- **Load** the dBASE program.
- Understand how to follow instructions in this unit.

DATABASES

A **database** is a collection of data that can be accessed when needed. Most businesses cannot function without fast and accurate data about customers, employees, wholesalers, inventory, and billing, for example. Databases do not have to be on a computer; businesses keep many data files on paper or index cards.

Computerized databases, however, are simpler to update and can quickly sort, select, and print information. You will use the popular dBASE program to store and access data.

THE KEYBOARD

Several types of keyboards are possible. (See Unit 1, *Using Computers*, for an illustration of standard and enhanced keyboards.) The keys on an enhanced keyboard will be emphasized, but an attempt will be made to incude the keys on a standard keyboard as well.

THE TEMPLATE

Although the dBASE program includes a template, in this book you will rarely use the commands on it. A template could be helpful, but it is not necessary.

dBASE III AND dBASE IV

This unit is written for both dBASE III and dBASE IV users. Both versions of dBASE offer two methods for using the program: pull-down menus or a dot prompt. When you load either program, the pull-down menu screen appears first. dBASE III will display an Assist Menu, and dBASE IV will display a Control Center. (See DB1.1 and DB1.2.) Both programs look the same, however, when the dot prompt method is used. In this book you will bypass the pull-down menus and enter commands at the dot prompt.

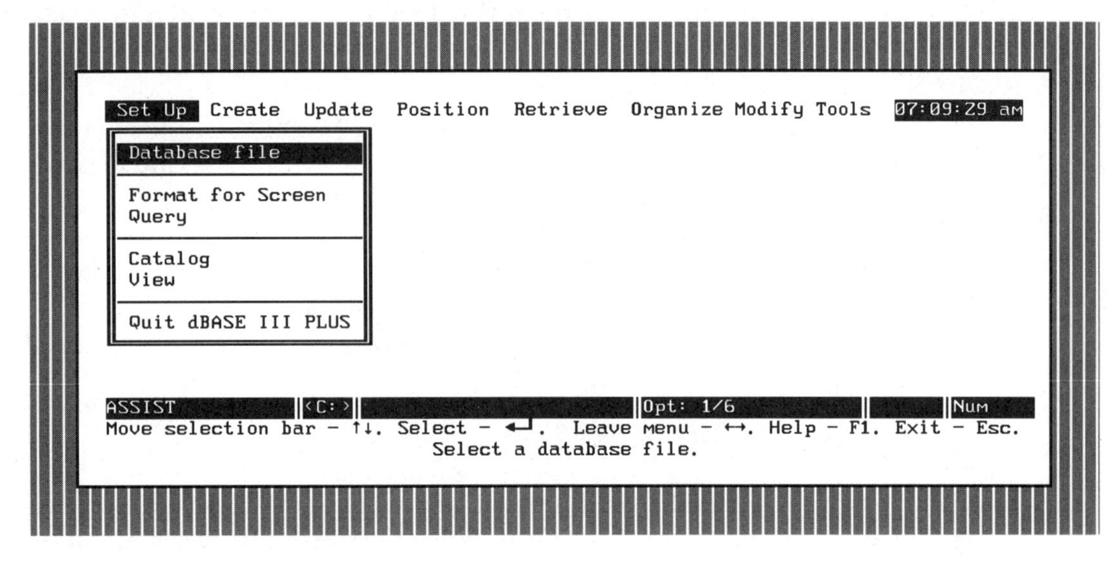

FIGURE DB1.1
dBASE III's Assist Menu

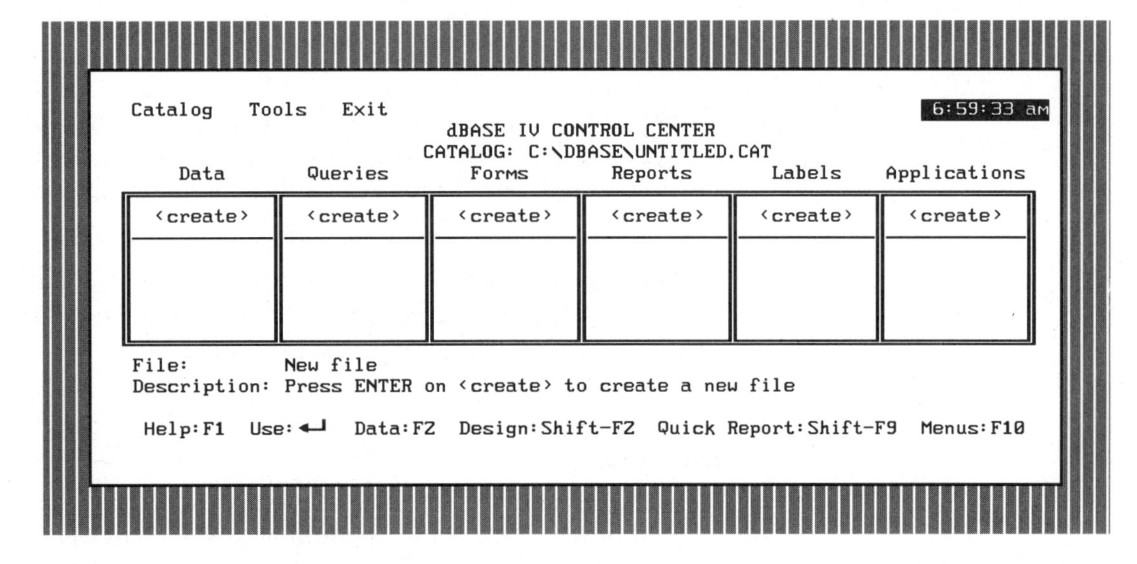

FIGURE DB1.2
dBASE IV's Control Center

Dot prompt commands

Entering dot prompt commands is very similar to entering DOS commands, as you did in Unit Two, *Using DOS*. There are several advantages to using the dot prompt commands instead of the pull-down menus: dot prompt commands can be simpler to learn and use, and they are the same in all recent versions of dBASE. The dot prompt commands are easily recognized throughout the sections by the [.] symbol. In addition, a list of dBASE dot prompt commands is included in the commands summary at the back of this text-workbook.

Loading dBASE

One of the following procedures may load the dBASE program for you. If not, your instructor will tell you how to load it in your particular situation.

1. *Hard disk:*
   a) At the DOS prompt, key CD\DBASE — (or the name of the directory where the dBASE system files are located).
   b) Insert your data diskette.
   c) Key **DBASE** (Enter).
2. *Networked system:*
   a) Log on to the computer system.
   b) Select *dBASE* from the menu (or follow instructor directions).

The Screen

After dBASE is loaded, you will see the copyright screen; press (Enter) to bypass this screen. When the dBASE III Assist Menu or the dBASE IV Control Center appears, dBASE is ready for your instructions. At that point, go to the dot prompt. To do this, press (Esc) in dBASE III or (Esc) (Y) in dBASE IV.

Following Instructions

In this unit, information about features will be presented flush at the left margin. Student actions such as data or commands to be keyed, keys to be pressed, and options to be chosen will be specially marked:

- **Data to be keyed** will be indicated by the word **KEY**.
- **Dot prompt commands** will be indicated by the symbol [.]. Used only in this section, the [.] symbol is used to make dot prompt commands stand out from the rest of the instructions for easy reference. Do not key the period or the brackets. Simply key the command.
- **Keyboard actions other than keying** will be indicated by the word **DO**.
- **Keys** to press are shown inside key caps, such as (Insert). If a key is to be held down while pressing another key, the keys will be "locked" together like this: (Ctrl)-(←)
- **File names** are shown in all caps but don't need to be keyed in all caps.

QUICK QUESTIONS

1. What is a database?
2. What are some advantages of computerized databases?
3. Do you have a template available?

4. What are the names for the pull-down menu screens in each version of dBASE?
   a) in dBASE III:
   b) in dBASE IV:
5. What are two advantages of using dot prompt commands rather than pull-down menus?
   a)
   b)
6. Write the steps you will use to get dBASE started each time you use it:
7. What is the first screen you will see when you load dBASE?
8. How will you recognize dot prompt commands when following instructions in this unit?

To prepare for working with databases, analyze data to see if it is numeric, alphabetic, or alphanumeric. Data usually falls into one of three categories:

- *Numeric data* - numbers, decimals, plus and minus signs
- *Alphabetic data* - letters only
- *Alphanumeric data* - combination of numbers, letters, and symbols

For each data item described in the table, decide whether it is numeric, alphabetic, or alphanumeric. Watch for symbols such as hyphens that would make the data alphanumeric. Place a check mark in the appropriate column. The first one has been done for you.

Data Item	Numeric	Alphabetic	Alphanumeric
Amount of payment	✓		
Last name			
Address			
Price			
Telephone number			
Test score			
ZIP code			
Gross profit			
Social security number			
City			
Hours worked			

2

THE BASICS

OBJECTIVES

- Define **DBMS** and its purpose.
- Identify **field, record, file,** and **database.**
- Identify the **Control Center** or **Assist Menu.**
- Locate the **dot prompt** and **status bar.**
- **Cancel** commands and menus.
- Identify command verbs and abbreviations.
- Use **Help, Clear, Set Default, List History,** and **Quit** commands.

ELEMENTS OF A DATABASE

DBMS. An information management program like dBASE III or IV is called a **database management system (DBMS)**. The purpose of a DBMS is for efficient storage, updating, and retrieval of data. Businesses of all sizes need to see how many units of a particular item they have in stock and when to reorder, the balance a particular customer owes, the date of an invoice, the address of a supplier, or the number of absences of an employee. These needs and many others can be met almost instantly by accessing data using a DBMS.

FIELD. A DBMS begins with a **field** of data. A field is one data item about a person, thing, or event. Examples of fields are: employee last name, name of inventory item, retail price, or date of last order.

RECORD. A *group* of fields related to one person, thing, or event is known as a **record**. An employee record might contain: last name, first name, social security number, date of birth, date of employment, wage rate, number of dependents, and department. An inventory record could include fields for name of item, quantity, date purchased, purchase price, and serial number.

FILE/DATABASE. All related records are known as a **file** or a **database**. All employee records would be in an "Employee File" or "Employee Database"; all furniture inventory records would be in a "Furniture Inventory File" or "Furniture Inventory Database"; all tax-deductible-item records would be in a "Tax Deductibles File" or "Tax Deductibles Database."

A file or database with five records is shown in DB2.1. Each database field and record is marked.

FIGURE DB2.1
Sample Database

Jackson	Norma	3322 Winding Way	Corona Del Mar	CA	35763
Peterson	George	8023 E Maryland	Thousandsticks	KY	41766
Tarryn	Suzanne	RR 2 Box 331	Pocono Lake	PA	18348
Samples	Duwan	2942 Eastern St	Pleasant Shade	TN	37145
Burge	Alissa	526 Kirkwood Dr	Myrtle Beach	SC	29577

The *fields* above are divided with heavy vertical lines. Fields appear as vertical *columns* in a database. Can you find the First Name field in all five records? Where is the State field?

The *records* above are divided by single horizontal lines. A record appears as a horizontal *row* in a database. Can you count all five records?

The *database* above is marked by double lines all around. If you keyed this database and stored it on your disk, what would be a good file name for it (maximum of eight characters)? ________________

Add a sixth record to the database. Fill in the blank record in DB2.1 with fields of data about *you*.

QUICK QUESTIONS

1. What word refers to an information management program like dBASE?
2. Why do businesses use DBMS programs?
3. What is the name for one data item about a person, thing, or event?
4. What is the name for a group of fields related to one person, thing or event?
5. What are two names for all related records?
   a)
   b)
6. Name three fields that might be contained in a Baseball Card Collection database.
   a)
   b)
   c)
7. When viewing data in a database, what appears as a **column**?
8. When viewing data in a database, what appears as a **row**?

The Dot Prompt Screen

If you have not loaded dBASE, do so according to the steps listed on page dB4 or the directions of your instructor.

When dBASE is loaded, the Control Center or Assist Menu is displayed. Since you will not use the pull-down menus, exit this screen.

DO: Press (Esc). If asked to verify, press (Y) for "yes" (dBASE IV).

The dot prompt screen appears, DB2.2.

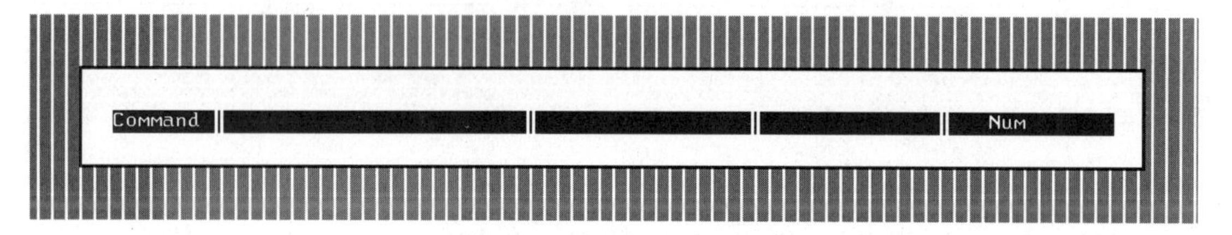

FIGURE DB2.2
The Dot Prompt

DOT PROMPT. The flashing cursor is beside a period, the **dot prompt**. This is where you key commands.

STATUS BAR. Below the dot prompt is the **Status Bar** where dBASE displays information about your database. The Status Bar also indicates when Num Lock or Caps Lock is on.

Keying Commands

CANCEL. Use (Esc) to cancel when keying commands or looking at menus.

SYNTAX. Designed to be like English, dBASE commands follow a specific structure, similar to English sentences. A dot prompt command must always begin with a *verb or action word*. Several dBASE commands are listed below; write the verb(s) in each command on the line.

.help set history ____________________

.clear ____________________

.set default to a ____________________

ABBREVIATION. To simplify keying of dot prompt commands, you may key only the first four letters of a command verb or its modifier. For example, you may key .DISP STRU for .DISPLAY STRUCTURE. DISP is a verb, and STRU is its modifier. This will be helpful when commands become longer.

Simple Dot Prompt Commands

Since you have not created a database yet, the commands you can use now are limited. The following commands, however, can be helpful ones to know. Key the command next to the dot prompt [.] and then press (Enter).

HELP. To receive information about commands, key **Help** followed by the name of the command in question.

Receive information on the Clear command by keying the following command.

[.] help clear (↵Enter)

What does the Clear command do? ______________________

____

DO: Press (Esc) to exit Help.

Get information on the Set Default command.

[.] help set default (↵Enter)

What does the Set Default command do? ______________________

____

DO: Press (Esc) to exit Help.

Find the purpose of the Directory (Dir) command.

[.] help dir (↵Enter)

What is the purpose of the Dir command? ______________________

____

DO: Press (Esc) to exit Help.

CLEAR. As you saw when using Help, the **Clear** command erases the screen. Erase your screen now using Clear.

[.] clear (↵Enter)

Any commands or menus that were on the screen have now been cleared. Use Clear if your screen becomes cluttered.

SET DEFAULT. A very important command in many computer situations, the **Set Default** command is used to set the default drive for saving database files.

The command .SET DEFAULT TO A will set Drive A as the default for saving files.

[.] set default to A (↵Enter)

Set the default drive to C.

[.] set default to C (↵Enter)

Set the default drive for your situation. Ask your instructor which drive letter you should use and then key the following command keying that drive letter where the blank appears.

[.] set default to ____ (↵Enter)

Ask your instructor if you should key this every time you begin to use dBASE. Yes ____ No ____

HISTORY. To save time, dBASE keeps a list or **history** of the dot prompt commands you key. This enables you to go to a previously keyed command and execute it without rekeying it. The history buffer contains the last 20 commands you keyed.

Look at your history of commands with the **List History** command.

[.] list history (↵Enter)

To execute one of the commands, press (↑) or (↓) to move through the list. When the command desired is at the dot prompt, press (↵Enter).

Execute the clear command.

DO: Press (↑) until *clear* appears at the dot prompt. Then press (↵Enter).

The screen is cleared.

DO: Press (↑) and (↓).

Your previously keyed commands are still available. You do not have to key .LIST HISTORY to use the commands in the history buffer, but only to display all of them at once.

QUIT. To exit from the dBASE program and return to the system level, key **Quit** at the dot prompt.

DO: Press (Esc) if necessary to clear the dot prompt command line.

[.] quit (↵Enter)

QUICK QUESTIONS

1. After loading the dBASE program, what key is pressed to go to the dot prompt?
2. What does the dot prompt look like?
3. What part of the screen will display information about your database?
4. Which key will cancel menus or commands being keyed?
5. Every dot prompt command must begin with what type of word?
6. How can you abbreviate the keying of commands?
7. Which command is keyed to receive more information about commands?
8. Which command is keyed to clear a cluttered screen?

9. What command will set A as the default drive?
10. What is the purpose of a command history?
11. Which commands are displayed in the history buffer?
12. What command will allow you to exit properly from the dBASE program?

ACTIVITY A - USE SIMPLE COMMANDS

1. Load dBASE and return to the dot prompt.
2. Key a command that will show you the purpose of the .LIST HISTORY command. What command did you key? ____________________

   ____
3. Key a command that will set your default drive. What is the command?

   ____
4. Key a command that will clear your screen. What is the command? ____________________
5. Without rekeying, how can you repeat the .HELP LIST HISTORY command? ____________________
6. Key the command to exit dBASE and return to the system level. What is the command? __________

ACTIVITY B - ARRANGE DATA IN FIELDS

Data for two records is shown below. See if you can complete each record in the chart by writing the data in the appropriate fields. Slashes are shown between data items.

Record #1: Johnson / Gary / 317 / 7881 Timber Trace / Cooper City / 247-8914

Record #2: Terry Town / 356 / Nancy / 781-3329 / Clark / 762-A Rose St

Last Name	First Name	Address	City	Area Code	Phone #

3

CREATE A DATABASE

OBJECTIVES

- State the purpose of a **needs assessment.**
- Define the term **database structure.**
- State the specifications for **file names** and **field definitions.**
- Identify the steps to **design a database.**
- **Save** a database structure.
- **Modify** a database structure.
- **Print** a database structure.
- Open a database and clear RAM with **Use.**

NEEDS ASSESSMENT

CONTENTS OF THE DATABASE. Before designing a database, it is important to determine what the contents of the database will be. Although dBASE files can be changed later, it is a complex computer task and may give undesired results. Determining the contents involves analyzing not only what data is needed now, but also data that may be needed in the future. This analysis can be called a **needs assessment**. To complete the needs assessment, many people may need to be interviewed and many questions may need to be answered.

For example, should fields for ZIP codes or area codes be included even though they are not needed now? Will the data be merged into letters or other correspondence? Will the data be imported into a spreadsheet? Will future growth require data not needed now but obtainable only at this time?

FORM OF THE DATA. Also, the form of the data is important. Should the last name be separate from the first name? Should the data be entered in all uppercase? Should the area code be in a separate field or included with the phone number? Will the ZIP code be five or nine digits in length or both?

DATABASE STRUCTURE

Once a thorough needs assessment has been completed, the **database structure** is designed. The database structure is a framework or foundation for storing and accessing data. It is designed when you define the fields in the database.

FILE NAME. The first step in creating a database is to give it a name. As with all DOS-based programs, dBASE allows a file name of up to 8 characters. Do not key a file extension; dBASE will add a .DBF file extension to database files. The .DBF file extension will help you and dBASE identify files.

FIELD DEFINITIONS. After the database is given a name, field definitions must be entered. Field definitions include field names, field types, field widths, and whether decimal places should be included for numeric fields. (In dBASE IV it must be determined if a field should be indexed; the answer is "No" in this book.)

Field Names may be up to 10 characters in length and must begin with an alphabetic character. No spaces are allowed, but the underscore can be used to give the appearance of a space (for example, PHONE_NO. for a telephone number field).

Field Type depends on the characters a field will contain. Each field must be designated as character, numeric, date, logical, or memo type. Chart DB3.1 shows how the field type is based on the field contents.

FIGURE DB3.1
Determining Field Types and Widths

Field Type	Field Contents	Field Width
Character	Contains alphanumeric data	Longest data item
Numeric	Contains numbers to be calculated	Number of digits + decimal point
Date	Contains month, day, and year	Eight
Logical	Contains either yes/no or true/false	One
Memo	A special field that contains informal text notes	Ten

A numeric field may contain decimals, but no dollar signs. A date field includes slashes between the date elements. A logical field may show T or F for true or false conditions.

Field Width is determined by the type of field or by the person structuring the database. Chart DB3.1 shows how widths are determined for different types of fields.

Character fields should be the width of the largest data item that could reasonably occur in that field. Fields that are too narrow will cut off characters. For example, when planning the size of a social security number field, the hyphens separating the numbers must be included. You also need to count periods, spaces, and commas when they are used. To determine the size of an address field, consider long addresses such as apartment numbers.

Numeric fields must be the width of the largest number of digits possible, plus the decimal point when it is used.

Date fields are eight characters in width to allow for the slashes (11/07/XX). Logical fields are only one character in width, for T or F. The memo field is given a default width of 10, but a memo may be much longer. The memo field will not be used in this book.

QUICK QUESTIONS

1. What is the purpose of a needs assessment?
2. What two factors should be considered in a needs assessment?
   a)
   b)
3. What is a database structure and when is it designed?
4. How many characters are allowed for a dBASE file name?
5. How many characters are allowed for a field name and what must the first character be?
6. Since spaces are not allowed in a field name, what character can be used to give the appearance of a space?
7. Would a social security number be a character or a numeric field?
8. What is used to separate the month, day, and year in a date field?
9. How wide should a numeric field be?
10. How wide is a logical field, and what data will appear in that type of field?
11. How do you determine the width for character and numeric fields?
12. What will happen to data in a field that is too narrow?

Design a Database

Follow the steps in the chart below, DB3.2, when designing a database.

FIGURE DB3.2

Designing a Database	
1.	Assess current and future needs.
2.	Name the database.
3.	Define the fields.
a.	field name
b.	field type
c.	field size

You will design a database using the steps given above. After a needs assessment, you decide to name the database CLASS because it contains data about a class of business students. Each record in the database will include the following fields: student ID number, name, grade, birthdate, and grade-point average (GPA).

The data that will be entered into the CLASS database is listed as shown.

Plan the field definitions. Look at the data shown and use chart dB3.1 on page dB13 to determine the type and width of each field.

Record the field types and widths of the CLASS database to the blanks in the box shown below. For the types, use C for Character, N for Numeric, and D for Date. Numeric fields that will not be calculated, such as ID_NO, should be made a character type field. For the GPA field, determine the number of decimal places needed. The first field has been done for you.

ID_NO	ST_NAME	GRADE	BIRTHDATE	GPA
81775	Lackey, Jill	12	03/17/76	2.7
83519	Troupe, Juan	12	10/22/76	2.22
88244	Pressman, Bill	12	12/12/75	3.45
79312	Withers, Erika	11	02/18/77	2.9
68823	Mendoza, Gloria	10	05/28/78	3.05
69007	Maxwell, Wally	10	11/04/78	1.89
74781	Seiffert, Janet	11	02/07/77	2.38
86607	Leon, Carmen	12	08/17/76	2.65
63770	Silvers, Pat	10	10/30/78	3.1
64349	Brooks, Glen	10	07/20/78	3.62

Field #	*Field Name*	*Type*	*Width*	*Dec*
1	ID_NO	C	5	
2	ST_NAME	______	______	
3	GRADE	______	______	
4	BIRTHDATE	______	______	
5	GPA	______	______	______

CREATE A DATABASE

DO: Load dBASE and go to the dot prompt. ALWAYS set the default drive as soon as you arrive at the dot prompt. Set the default for *your* data disk.

[.] set default to A (↵Enter) (use the drive letter of your drive).

Use the **Create** command to build the structure for a database called CLASS. You should already have set the default drive for your file.

[.] create class (↵Enter)

The Create command causes the file design screen to appear, allowing you to begin building the database structure.

FILE DESIGN SCREEN. Although the appearance of the file design screen differs in dBASE III and IV, the method of using the screen is the same. Figures DB3.3 and DB3.4 show the two file design screens.

Each screen provides a position for the **field name, type, width,** and **number of decimal places (Dec)**. (The dBASE IV screen also includes an **Index** column, in which you will key N for "No" for all fields in this book.)

Using the field information you recorded above, enter the first field into the database. The field name is **ID_NO** (use (Shift) to underscore), the type is **character**, and the width is **5**. Since it is not a numeric field, no decimal decision is available. (Index will always be N for dBASE IV users.) Press (↑) if it becomes necessary to change previously keyed fields.

FIGURE DB3.3
The dBASE III File Design Screen

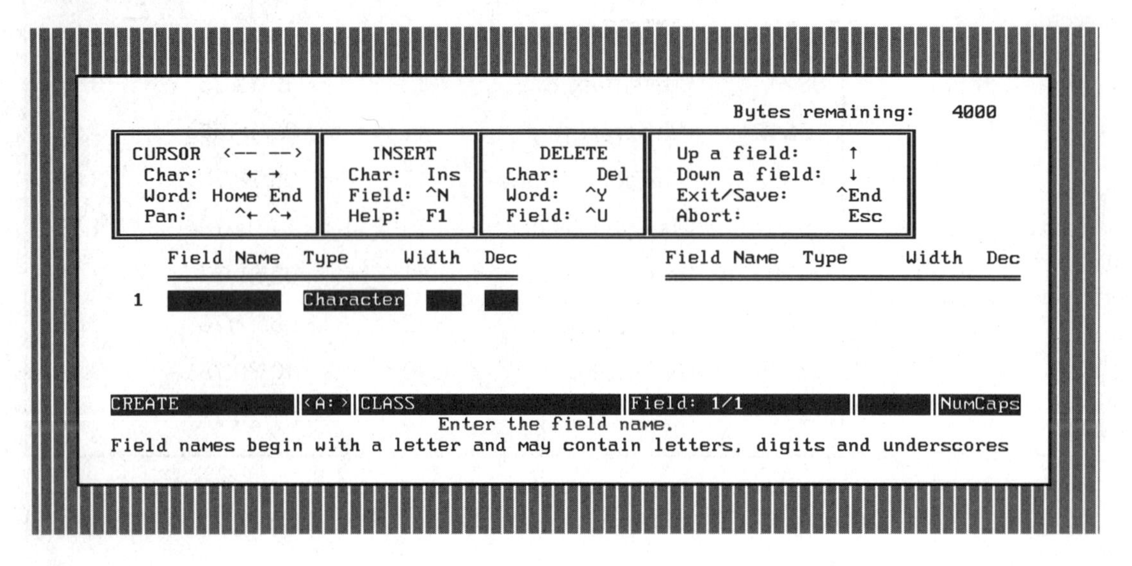

FIGURE DB3.4
The dBASE IV File Design Screen

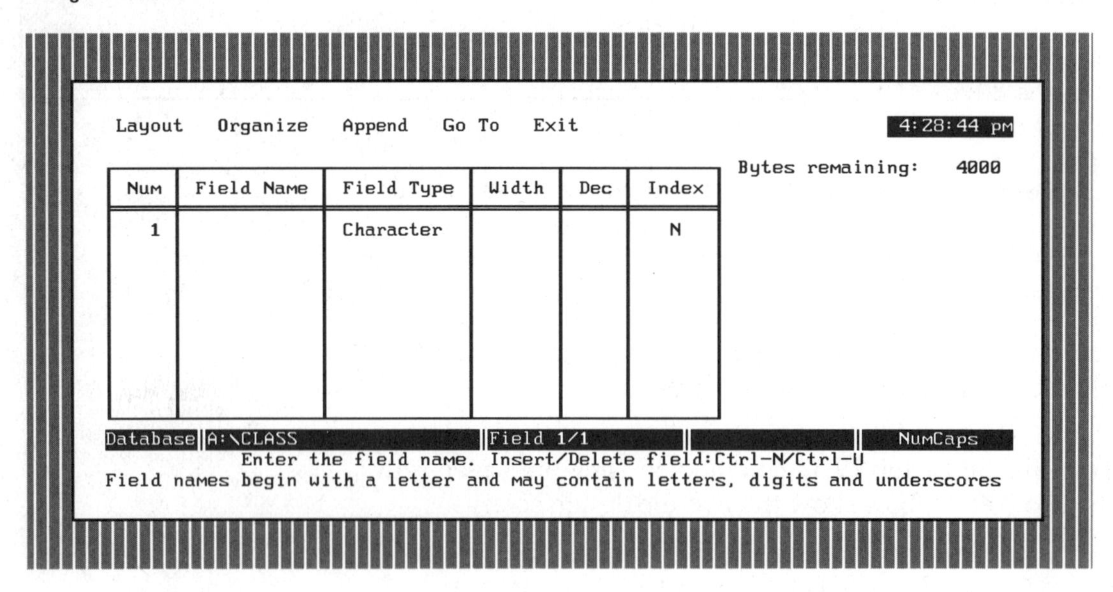

KEY: ID_NO (↵Enter)

DO: Press (↵Enter) to accept Character type.

KEY: 5 (↵Enter) (dBASE IV: also press (↵Enter) to accept N for Index.)

The cursor bar moves to the second field. The field name for field two is **ST_NAME**, the type is **character**, and the width is **15**.

KEY: ST_NAME (↵Enter)

DO: Press (↵Enter) to accept Character type.

KEY: 15 (↵Enter) (dBASE IV: also press (↵Enter) to accept N for Index.)

Complete field three. The field name is **GRADE**, the type is **character** (will not be calculated), and the width is **2**.

KEY: GRADE (↵Enter)

DO: Press (↵Enter) to accept Character type.

KEY: 2 (↵Enter) (dBASE IV: also press (↵Enter) to accept N for Index.)

DO: Complete field four on your own using the information you recorded on page dB15 to determine field name, type, and width. Press D for Date type.

Complete field five.

KEY: GPA (↵Enter)

KEY: n (↵Enter) (numeric type)

KEY: 4 (↵Enter) (width of 3 digits + a decimal point)

KEY: 2 (↵Enter) (2 decimal places) (dBASE IV: also press (↵Enter) to accept N for Index.)

SAVE THE STRUCTURE. Check the accuracy of the structure with fields one through five in Figure DB3.5 on page dB19. Then tell dBASE the structure is complete and to save it on your disk. Do this by pressing (↵Enter) twice on the first blank field. (You could press (Ctrl)-(End) instead.) When asked if you want to input data records now, you will always answer *No* to that question throughout this section.

DO: Press (↵Enter) on blank field six.

DO: Press (↵Enter) to confirm completion.

KEY: (N) (↵Enter) (*no*, you will not input data records now)

You are returned to the dot prompt. The Status Bar displays the name of the **active database** (the one currently in RAM) called CLASS, and that it currently has no records (Rec None).

LIST THE STRUCTURE. To see the structure you designed, use the **List** command. (Commands may be spelled out, or you may use four-letter abbreviations for verbs and modifiers.)

[.] list structure (↵Enter) (list stru)

The List command shows the desired output on the screen, the database structure. The structure shown is similar to DB3.5, but you only have the first five fields shown. The List command can be modified with TO PRINTER to show output on the printer.

DO: Be sure your printer is ready.

[.] list structure to printer (↵Enter) (list stru to prin)

DO: Press form feed on your printer to eject the paper.

MODIFY A DATABASE

Although an effort was made to completely plan the CLASS database before it was structured on the computer, it must be *modified*. A business club is now available to students, and those who have joined should be marked in the database.

Modifying a database allows you to change the structure. You may:

- add or delete fields
- change a field's name, type, or size.

Use the **Modify** command to return to the file design screen to make changes when necessary. Because modifying the structure is a complex task and you may lose data, try to avoid it if you can. However, you will modify databases in this section so you will know how to do so when it is necessary.

Modify the active database, CLASS, by adding another field called MEMBER. It will be a logical field, using True for members and False for nonmembers. The width of a logical field is automatically set at 1 character.

[.] modify structure (↵Enter) (modi stru)

The file design screen reappears.

DO: Press (↓) to move to field six.

KEY: MEMBER (↵Enter)

KEY: L (↵Enter) (logical type)

DO: Press (↵Enter) on blank field seven to end and save the modified structure.

The dBASE program asks, *Are you sure you want to save the changes?*

DO: Press (↵Enter) to confirm that you do want to save the changes.

See if the database has been modified.

[.] list structure (↵Enter) (list stru)

Print the new structure.

[.] list structure to printer (↵Enter) (list stru to prin)

Check your database structure for accuracy. It is shown in Figure DB3.5.

FIGURE DB3.5
CLASS.DBF File Structure

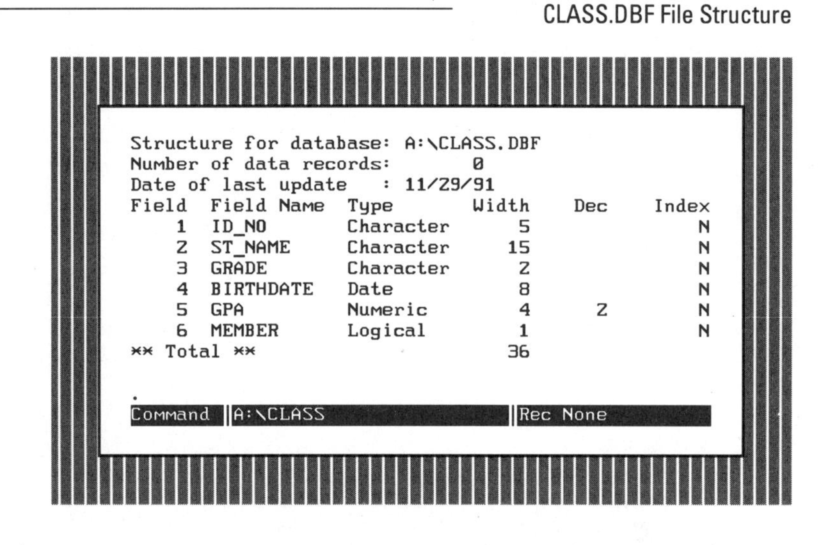

```
Structure for database: A:\CLASS.DBF
Number of data records:       0
Date of last update   : 11/29/91
Field  Field Name  Type       Width    Dec    Index
    1  ID_NO       Character      5               N
    2  ST_NAME     Character     15               N
    3  GRADE       Character      2               N
    4  BIRTHDATE   Date           8               N
    5  GPA         Numeric        4      2        N
    6  MEMBER      Logical        1               N
** Total **                      36
.
Command  ||A:\CLASS             ||Rec None
```

USE COMMAND

The **Use** command can be used to retrieve a database, called **opening** a database. The file that is opened becomes the active file, and the file name is displayed on the Status Bar. Look at the Status Bar to see the active file as you begin to use many files.

As you create more databases, you may open any one of them whenever you please. Key USE followed by the name of the database file you wish to open. You may then list the structure, modify the structure, or perform other dBASE operations.

The Use command will also **close** the active database, clearing RAM. Always key *Use* (↵Enter) to close an active database before opening another one.

Close the CLASS database.

[.] use (↵Enter)

The Status Bar does not display an active database name.

Open the CLASS database.

[.] use class (↵Enter)

Nothing new appears on the screen, but the Status Bar displays the name of the active database, CLASS. Any commands used now will affect the CLASS database.

[.] use (↵Enter)

The database is closed.

DO: If you have time to work, go on to the Review Exercise. If not, key QUIT at the dot prompt to exit from dBASE.

QUICK QUESTIONS

1. What are the three primary steps to follow when designing a database?
   a)
   b)
   c)
2. What is the width of a numeric field with four digits and a decimal point?
3. What type of field is birthdate?
4. What command would be keyed to build the structure for a database called ORDERS?
5. Which command will cause the file design screen to appear?
6. What four items of information about each field may be keyed in the file design screen?
   a)
   b)
   c)
   d)
7. How can you indicate to dBASE that you have completed the file design screen so it can be saved on disk?
8. What command will show the database structure on the screen?
9. What command will show the database structure on the printer?
10. List two changes you can make to an exisiting file structure:
    a)
    b)
11. Why should you avoid modifying a database if you can?
12. What command was used to modify the structure of the CLASS database?
13. What is the automatic width of a logical field?
14. What command should you key to make CLASS the active database file?
15. What command should you key to close an active database file?

REVIEW EXERCISE

After a needs assessment has been completed, the Happy Homemakers Club determines that they need the following fields of data about their members. A sample record with the largest fields possible is shown; use it to determine field widths.

Whitaker, Suzanne	356-7790	1618 West Nantucket	24541	05/09/90

1. Load dBASE and set the default drive if necessary.
2. Design the database. Use the following field names, but you determine the type and width of each field based on the record shown above and Chart DB3.1 on page dB13. Write the field types and widths on the lines.

Field#	*Field Names*	*Type*	*Width*
1	NAME	______	______
2	PHONE	______	______
3	ADDRESS	______	______
4	ZIP	*C*	______
5	DATE_JOIN	*D*	______

3. Use the Create command to create a database called CLUBMEM. Remember, data records will *not* be input at this time. (dBASE IV: the Index field is always N.)
4. List the file structure.
5. Modify the structure. It has become desirable to *calculate* the average age of the club members. Modify the database by adding an additional field called AGE. You decide the correct type and width of the field.
6. List the modified file structure to the printer and check with your instructor for accuracy. Modify the structure to make any corrections needed.
7. Close the active database file with *Use*.
8. Either go on to the next activity or quit the dBASE program.

ACTIVITY A - PRODUCT LIST

NoteBook, a small music bookstore in your neighborhood, has hired you to set up a product database. The data needed are: book number, book title, author of the book, year published, number of pages, and price. Design the database with the following field names. Some field definitions have been determined by NoteBook; you will make the remaining decisions.

Field#	*Field Name*	*Type*	*Width*	*Dec.*
1	BOOK_NO	C	5	
2	TITLE		30	
3	AUTHOR		10	
4	YR	C	2	
5	PG	C	3	
6	PRICE	N	5	2

1. Create a database called PRODUCTS. (Data records will not be input now.)
2. List the structure.
3. Modify the structure. NoteBook decides it would be helpful to have a field that designates whether the book is hardcover or paperback. Add a logical field called PB for Paperback. When the book is a paperback, the field will be true; when it is a hardcover book, the field will be false.
4. List the new structure to the printer and check with your instructor for accuracy. Modify the structure to make any corrections needed.
5. Close the active database file with *Use*.
6. Either go on to the next activity or quit the dBASE program.

ACTIVITY B - REAL ESTATE LISTINGS

Mrs. Burnes of Burnes Abodes, a real estate firm, wants to put her property listings on computer for easy access. From her needs assessment she concludes that the following fields are needed: address, price, number of bedrooms (BR) and baths (BA), whether it has a greatroom (GR), family room (FR), dining room (DR), central air (CA), or basement (BSMT), number-of-car garage (GAR), type of heat (HT), and the date the house was listed. Data that fits one of two conditions is placed in a logical field.

Complete the missing field definitions.

Field#	*Field Name*	*Type*	*Width*	
1	ADDRESS	______	20	
2	PRICE	______	6	(no dec.)
3	BR	C	1	
4	BA	C	3	
5	GR	L	1	
6	FR	L	______	
7	DR	L	______	
8	CA	L	______	
9	BSMT	L	______	
10	GAR	C	1	
11	HT	C	3	
12	LIST_DATE	D	______	

1. Create a database called LISTINGS. (Data records will not be input now.)
2. List the structure.
3. Modify the structure. Mrs. Burnes has decided that she would like to have the age of the home added to the database. Insert this field as Field 3. To do this, modify the database and use (↓) to move to Field 3 on the file design screen. Press (Ctrl)-(N) to insert a new field at this position. (The use of Ctrl-N to insert a field is displayed as a message on the file design screen.) Call this numeric field AGE with a width of 2. Arrow down to the first blank field and press Enter twice to save the structure.
4. Print the new structure to the printer and check with your instructor for accuracy. Modify the structure to make any corrections needed.
5. Close the active database file with *Use*.
6. Quit dBASE or go on to Section Four.

4

DATA ENTRY

OBJECTIVES

- Use the **Dir** command to see a list of database files, or all files.
- **Append** records.
- **Correct errors** while keying.
- **Move** within a record and to other records.
- **Save records.**
- **List** a file to screen and printer.

ADD RECORDS

In the previous section, you created several database files. Only the structure was saved on disk; you did not enter any data records, but you could have. After you created the structure, dBASE asked you if you wished to input data records. You responded with *No*.

In this section, you will add records to the structures you have created. To see the names of your database files, use the Dir command.

DIR COMMAND

The dBASE Dir command is similar to the DOS Dir command. With no additional parameters, however, the dBASE **Dir** command will display only the .DBF files. Close any active database, and then list the .DBF files you created in Section Three.

DO: If necessary, set your default drive or close an active database.

[.] dir (Enter)

You see a listing of all .DBF files. None of them are *active* right now because no file has been retrieved to RAM. Look at the Status Bar to see that no active file name is displayed.

You can list other types of files by keying the necessary parameters. To list all files on your disk, add wildcard parameters to the Dir command. (See the *Using DOS* unit for more information on wildcards.)

[.] dir *.* (Enter)

OPEN A DATABASE

When you used the Dir command to see the list of DBF files, you saw the CLASS file listed.

To open a database file, key the **Use** command followed by the file name. (Always be sure you have set the default drive before opening a database.) Open the CLASS database.

[.] use class (Enter)

The Status Bar indicates that the active file is CLASS. The commands you use now will affect the CLASS file.

To see more of the CLASS database, list its structure.

[.] list structure (Enter)

The name of the database, the number of records it contains (0), and the date of last update is shown. (See DB4.1.) You can also see the field names, types, widths, number of decimal places, and total width of records in the database. If you have questions about your database as you enter records, go to the dot prompt and list the structure.

FIGURE DB4.1
CLASS.DBF File Structure

```
Structure for database: A:\CLASS.DBF
Number of data records:       0
Date of last update   : 11/29/91
Field  Field Name  Type       Width    Dec    Index
    1  ID_NO       Character      5              N
    2  ST_NAME     Character     15              N
    3  GRADE       Character      2              N
    4  BIRTHDATE   Date           8              N
    5  GPA         Numeric        4      2       N
    6  MEMBER      Logical        1              N
** Total **                      36

.
Command ||A:\CLASS          ||Rec None          ||File ||
```

It is time to enter some records into the CLASS database.

FIGURE DB4.2
Edit Screen

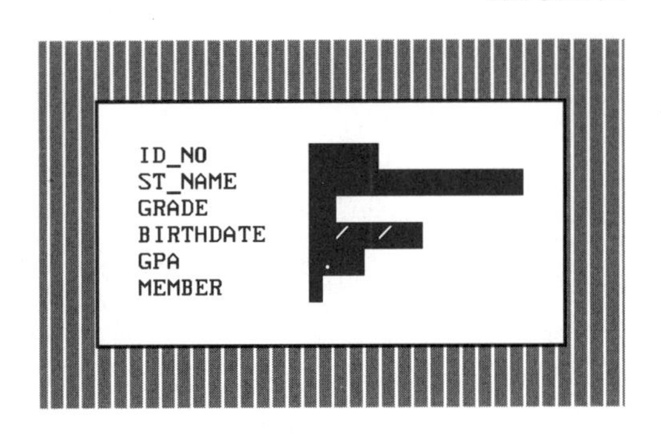

APPEND

Append means "add." To add records to a newly created database or at the end of existing records in the active database file, use the **Append** command.

[.] append (Enter)

Keying the Append command will display the Edit Screen shown in DB4.2.

A blank form for entering a record appears on the Edit Screen. Each field name is listed along the left side of the screen. Beside each field name is a data entry block that indicates the width of each field. For example, the ID_NO field is wide enough to hold 5 characters, the GRADE field is wide enough to hold 2 characters, and the GPA field is wide enough for 4 characters including the decimal point. These field widths were set when you created the CLASS database. The data entry blocks are empty, awaiting data to be keyed.

KEY DATA

As you key records for your databases, use upper and lower case where shown for the data. Press Enter only if the data entry block is not completely filled with characters. When a field is filled, the cursor automatically moves to the next field with a warning beep. When you key the decimal point at the appropriate position you will also hear a beep.

CORRECT ERRORS. Correct errors as you key, using ← Backspace and Delete. Use Insert to turn Typeover on and off.

MOVE WITHIN A RECORD. Use the four cursor keys, → ← ↑ ↓, to move within a record.

MOVE TO ANOTHER RECORD. Use the Page Up and Page Down keys to move to other records. Watch the Status Bar to see which records are completed. For example, the notation *EOF/2* means Record 2 is the End of the File (EOF). Thus, two records have been completed; you are ready to begin Record 3.

SAVE DATA. When you have entered all records, press Esc to exit the Edit Screen and save all changes.

DO: On the blank Edit Screen, key the data shown on page dB27 for Record 1. Do not key record numbers (R#). The directions will step you through the first record. Then key Records 2 through 10 on your own.

KEY: 81775 (Do not press Enter; this data fills the field.)

KEY: Lackey, Jill Enter (does not fill the field)

KEY: 12 (do not press Enter.)

KEY: 031776 (Do not key the slashes and do not press Enter.)

KEY: 2.7 Enter (This figure does not fill the field; dBASE adds a 0 so it will be filled.)

KEY: T (Do not press Enter; this character fills the field, automatically going on to the next record.)

DO: Using the following data, repeat the procedure above for Records 2 through 10.

When all records have been entered, your cursor is on a blank record. Pressing Esc on the blank record will save all records except the current blank one.

DO: Press Esc on Record 11.

You exit the Edit Screen and return to the dot prompt.

R#	ID_NO	ST_NAME	GRADE	BIRTHDATE	GPA	MEMBER
1	81775	Lackey, Jill	12	03/17/76	2.7	T
2	83519	Troupe, Juan	12	10/22/76	2.22	T
3	88244	Pressman, Bill	12	12/12/75	3.45	F
4	79312	Withers, Erika	11	02/18/77	2.9	T
5	68823	Mendoza, Gloria	10	05/28/78	3.05	T
6	69007	Maxwell, Wally	10	11/04/78	1.89	F
7	74781	Seiffert, Janet	11	02/07/77	2.38	T
8	86607	Leon, Carmen	12	08/17/76	2.65	F
9	63770	Silvers, Pat	10	10/30/78	3.1	T
10	64349	Brooks, Glen	10	07/20/78	3.62	T

LIST RECORDS

The records were saved as you proceeded through the data entry process. To see the records you entered, use the List command.

[.] list (↵Enter)

When used alone, the **List** command displays on screen all the records in the current database. Add the modifier **To Printer** to send the display of records to the printer. When using the List command, a database with many fields or wide fields will wrap part of each record to a second line on the screen or on the printer. Some printers will cut off characters when records are too wide. To avoid this problem, you can omit record numbers or print just certain fields of each record. You will learn how to do that in the next section.

DO: Prepare the printer.

[.] list to printer (↵Enter)

Use the Eject command to form feed the paper in the printer.

[.] eject (↵Enter)

ANALYZE THE PRINTED LISTING. Always check your printouts. If the structure is incorrect, modify the database. The records are shown with record numbers assigned by dBASE according to the order you entered the records. Zeros were added to fill the decimal places in the numeric field GPA. True is shown as .T. and False as .F. in the MEMBER field. Compare the printed listing with the data you were given. Circle any errors on the listing; in Section Six you will learn how to make changes to the records in a database.

The CLASS database is complete. Clear RAM with the Use command.

[.] use (↵Enter)

MORE PRACTICE. You will receive more practice entering records into a database in the Review Exercise and Reinforcement Activities at the end of this section.

QUICK QUESTIONS

1. What dot prompt command is keyed to see the names of all your database files?
2. What is an active file?
3. Where can you view the name of the active file?
4. Name two functions of the USE command.
   a)
   b)
5. What command would you key to open a .DBF file called INVOICES?
6. Which command is used to add records to the end of the active database file?
7. Which command will display the Edit Screen?
8. How does dBASE know the size of the data entry block to display beside each field name on the Edit Screen?
9. When appending records, should you press Enter as you complete each field of data? Explain.
10. Name two data entry situations in which you will hear a beep.
   a)
   b)
11. Which four keys are pressed to move within a record?
12. What two keys are pressed to move to other records?
13. What is the meaning of EOF/5 on the Status Bar?
14. During data entry, what does dBASE do if the decimal places in a numeric field are not filled with digits?
15. When data entry is complete, what is pressed to exit the Edit Screen and save all changes?
16. What command will display on the screen all the records in the current database?
17. What command will print all the records in the current database?
18. How does dBASE show true and false data in a listing?
19. What command may be used to clear RAM before beginning a new database?

Append the data shown below to the CLUBMEM database.

R#	NAME	PHONE	ADDRESS	ZIP	DATE_JOIN	AGE
1	Whitaker, Suzanne	356-7790	1618 West Nantucket	24541	05/09/90	25
2	Lowell, Rachel	354-7204	7391 Mariners Place	24536	10/12/88	32
3	Bridgman, Elaine	361-8523	2836 West Drake	24541	08/30/88	26
4	Lopez, Ruth	354-9935	1990 Bridgeport Ln	24520	11/14/91	44
5	Simpson, Carolyn	354-0821	3800 West Raymond	24520	02/25/89	37
6	Franklin, Terry	362-7873	7192 Red Brook Rd	24536	03/26/87	52
7	McMillan, Sandy	354-6096	8223 Lansing Ln	24536	08/22/88	37
8	Foxman, Alison	356-4149	3642 Belinda St	24541	01/13/90	45
9	Taylor, Beth	361-7839	2754 London Rd	24541	09/05/91	43
10	Crouch, Debbie	354-1256	7651 Leland	24536	08/22/88	27
11	Floyd, Martha	361-3878	2622 West Drake	24541	05/04/90	34
12	Franklin, Lori	362-7873	7192 Red Brook Rd	24536	03/08/91	23

1. Key the command .USE CLUBMEM.
2. Key the command .APPEND.
3. Key the data shown. Do not key the R# column, record numbers; dBASE will automatically give the records a number. Correct errors as you key.
4. After the data is entered, press (Esc) to exit the Edit Screen.
5. Key the command .LIST to see that the list of records is correct.
6. List the records to the printer; then use Eject to form feed.
7. Clear RAM before going to the next activity.

ACTIVITY A - PRODUCTS DATABASE

Add the following records to the PRODUCTS database. Do not key the R# column. List the records to the printer. A wide database may wrap part of a record to a second line either on the screen or on the printer; some printers will cut off characters when a record is too wide. This is acceptable in this section. When complete, clear RAM and continue to Activity B or quit dBASE.

R#	Book_No	Title	Author	Yr	Pg	Price	Pb
1	1340C	Contour Sound with Multitrack	Morris G	89	336	29.95	F
2	1400C	Construct a Recording Studio	Stone P	90	225	9.95	T
3	1332C	How To of Acoustics	Vergris L	92	366	22.95	F
4	1335E	Technology of Music	Porter G	88	290	39.95	F
5	1405C	Pro Guide to Live Sound	Anderson L	91	287	8.95	T
6	1407C	Pro Guide to Concert Sound	Anderson L	92	299	21.95	F
7	1419B	Art of Concert Lighting	Gillen S	93	257	25.50	F
8	1416B	Spectacular Light Effects	Madden R	91	191	27.95	F
9	3341D	Electronic Melody	Muench P	92	240	19.95	F
10	3622C	Synthesizer Source Book	Davis S	89	128	19.95	F
11	3582D	Composing on the Computer	Klenn B	91	225	21.95	F
12	3663C	Synthesizing Applications	Massey L	89	199	17.95	F
13	1819C	Audio Troubleshooting	Trailor D	88	325	10.95	T
14	1823C	Audio Repair	Trailor D	87	285	8.95	T
15	1556B	TV Sound Techniques	Akers R	91	299	25.95	F

ACTIVITY B - LISTINGS DATABASE

*Use the data shown below and on the following page to add records to the LISTINGS database. The records are listed vertically in this exercise. Press (↵Enter) to leave a field blank. In the logical fields, key **T** for true and press (↵Enter) for the blank (false) fields. dBASE will assume False for a blank logical field. Enter the current year in the LIST_DATE field.*

List the records to the printer. This database may wrap part of a record to a second line either on the screen or on the printer; some printers will cut off characters when a record is too wide. This is acceptable in this section. When complete, clear RAM and either go on to the next section or quit dBASE.

Field Name	Record #1	Record #2	Record #3
ADDRESS	621 Adams Court	3227 Sheffield	1529 Countrywalk
PRICE	79900	78900	87900
AGE	28	8	12
BR	3	3	3
BA	2	2	2
GR		T	
FR			T
DR			
CA	T	T	T
BSMT			
GAR		2	2
HT	Gas	Gas	El
LIST_DATE	10/12/xx	05/06/xx	03/04/xx

Field Name	Record #4	Record #5	Record #6
ADDRESS	1103 Lafayette Ln	6920 Desoto Ln	1654 West Wind Dr
PRICE	92900	121000	99900
AGE	8	3	5
BR	4	3	3
BA	2.5	2	2
GR		T	T
FR		T	
DR	T		T
CA	T	T	T
BSMT	T		T
GAR	2	2	2
HT	Gas	El	Gas
LIST_DATE	11/11/xx	09/25/xx	06/04/xx

Field Name	Record #7	Record #8	Record #9
ADDRESS	6420 W Royal St	6027 Patricia	7305 Hunters Run
PRICE	65900	45900	54900
AGE	28	27	11
BR	3	4	2
BA	1.5	1.5	1.5
GR			
FR			
DR			
CA	T	T	T
BSMT			T
GAR	1	1	1
HT	Gas	Oil	Gas
LIST_DATE	11/06/xx	09/14/xx	11/04/xx

5

DISPLAY RECORDS

OBJECTIVES

- **List** and **Display** records and fields.
- **Point** to a particular record.
- **Select** records.
- Identify the **relational operators.**
- Identify the **logical operators.**

In Section Four you keyed data records and learned how to list an entire database to the screen and to the printer. Your listings included all fields in all records, and this sometimes caused line scrolling and unattractive or incomplete printing. In some situations you want to view only records that meet a certain condition or only some fields in the records. This section will teach you how to "fine tune" your display of records.

LIST WITHOUT RECORD NUMBERS

Open the CLASS database and list the records. (Set the default drive if necessary.)

[.] use class (↵Enter)

[.] list (↵Enter)

All records are listed, and dBASE has added a column to display the record numbers. The records are numbered in the sequence they were entered into the database. If you did not save the records correctly you may see a record without data. In Section Six you will learn how to correct errors, including deletion of records.

If you have many fields or wide fields, you can reduce the displayed size of each record by listing them without the record number. To do this, use the **List Off** command.

[.] list off (↵Enter)

RECORD POINTING

As you move about a database, dBASE keeps track of the current (currently being used) record with a record pointer. The Status Bar will display the position of the record pointer.

You looked at the record pointer in the last section when you saw the *EOF/#* notation on the Status Bar. EOF (end of file) means that you are at the end of the database file, and the # represents the number of records in the file. When you are not at the end of the file, the Status Bar will show the record pointer as *n*/#, where *n* is the current record number and # is the number of records in the file.

GO. You can go to the first, last or any particular record by using the **Go** command. As you try the following Go commands on the CLASS database, watch the Status Bar to see that it is displaying the current record.

[.] go top (↵Enter)

The record pointer should display *1/10*. You are at the top of the file, on the first record.

[.] go bottom (↵Enter)

The record pointer should display *10/10*. You are at the bottom, on the last record.

[.] go 7 (↵Enter)

The record pointer should display *7/10*. You are on Record 7.

DO: Key a command that will point to Record 3.

What does the record pointer display on the Status Bar? __________

You can also just key the number of the record without Go.

[.] 8 (↵Enter)

DO: Key a command that will return the record pointer to Record 1.

List 3 commands you could have used above. ____________________

____

Display

Similar to the List command, the Display command will show on screen the records in the current database.

List and Display differ in two ways.

- **Display** will show only the current record unless you key *Display All*.
- **Display All** will show the entire database a screenful of records at a time to reduce scrolling.

Use the Display command to show the current record.

[.] display (↵Enter)

Only Record 1, the current record, is displayed. Now display Record 6 only.

[.] go 6 (↵Enter)

[.] display (↵Enter)

You may use Off with Display to suppress record numbers.

[.] display off (↵Enter)

Use Display All to view all records a screenful at a time. Press any key to continue to the next screenful when needed. The command **Display All to Printer** will print all records.

[.] display all (↵Enter)

List Fields

Sometimes a user wants to see only certain fields in the database. This can be done by keying the desired fields, separated by commas, with the List command. List the fields in the order you want them displayed. Field names must be spelled exactly as you spelled them when you structured the database. (It is an excellent idea to have a printed structure of each database so you can refer to it for field names and field types.)

List the database showing only the students' names and whether each is a business club member (member = true or false). Key the field names in all caps or initial caps; when listing field names, they will display in the case you key them. Check your display with DB5.1.

[.] list St_Name, Member (↵Enter)

FIGURE DB5.1
List St_Name, Member

```
Record#  St_Name          Member
     1   Lackey, Jill     .T.
     2   Troupe, Juan     .T.
     3   Pressman, Bill   .F.
     4   Withers, Erika   .T.
     5   Mendoza, Gloria  .T.
     6   Maxwell, Wally   .F.
     7   Seiffert, Janet  .T.
     8   Leon, Carmen     .F.
     9   Silvers, Pat     .T.
    10   Brooks, Glen     .T.
```

List the names and membership (member = true or false) to the printer. (To lessen keying, press (↑) to bring the last command to the dot prompt, press (End) to move to the right end of the command, and then add *to printer*.)

[.] list St_Name, Member to printer (↵Enter)

List the names and birthdates without record numbers.

[.] list off St_Name, Birthdate (↵Enter)

List the grade followed by the name with no record numbers.

[.] list off Grade, St_Name (↵Enter)

DO: List to the printer St_Name, Id_No, and GPA with no record numbers.

What command did you use? ____________________

Display Record 6 only with student name and GPA, no record number.

[.] go 6

[.] display off St_Name, GPA

QUICK QUESTIONS

1. How does dBASE number the records in a database?
2. Which command will allow you to reduce the displayed size of each record by listing them without record numbers?
3. What does dBASE use to keep track of the current record as you move through a database?
4. Where should you look to see the position of the current record?
5. Write a command to go to Record 26.
6. What should you key to see only the current record?
7. What should you key to see the entire database a screenful at a time?
8. Write a command that would list the Name, Address, and Phone fields of a database.
9. Write a command that would list the Name, Address, and Phone fields of a database without record numbers.

SELECT RECORDS

Often a user wishes to view only the records that meet a certain condition. This is called **selecting records**. For example, a baseball card collector with collection information in a computerized database may want to see a listing of only the shortstop cards or only the cards purchased since June of this year or only the cards that cost more than $5. The collector would select the records needed in each situation.

To select records, you must give dBASE the following information:

1) which field to consider
2) what value you want from the field
3) how you want the value compared

FIELD TO CONSIDER. The field name must be a valid field name in the active database, and it must be spelled the way it was entered into the database. (List structure if necessary.)

FIELD VALUE. The value will be either numeric or alphanumeric, according to the field type. (If necessary, list structure to see the types of fields.) Character fields have alphanumeric values, and both numeric and date fields have numeric values. Logical fields are handled differently.

If the value is numeric, simply key the value. However, alphanumeric data, called a **character string**, must be keyed with the value inside of quotes or apostrophes. Lack of quotes or apostrophes gives a *Data type mismatch* error message. Character data must also be keyed in the *case in which it was entered* into the database during record entry.

TYPE OF COMPARISON. The type of comparison is determined by the relational operator.

RELATIONAL OPERATORS

Chart DB5.2 shows the **relational operators** and the types of comparisons they perform.

FIGURE DB5.2

Relational Operators	
=	Equal
#	Not Equal
>	Greater Than
<	Less Than
>=	Greather Than or Equal To
<=	Less Than or Equal To

Do not key the two commands that follow; they are for illustration only. Note how the numeric and character values differ.

This command will show all records that have a net pay greater than or equal to 185.00 (numeric):

```
LIST FOR NETPAY >= 185.00
```

If the cities are keyed into a database with initial caps, this command will show all records that have Newark as the character data in the City field:

```
LIST FOR CITY = 'Newark'
```

SELECT CHARACTER AND NUMERIC DATA. You will select the records of all students who are in the 10th grade, or grade = 10. To do this, key the List command, the word FOR and then the field to select on, GRADE. (Key the selection field in upper or lower case; it is not displayed on the screen or paper.) The relational operator is the equal. Since *Grade* is a character type field, the value 10 must be enclosed in apostrophes or quotes.

```
[.] list for grade = '10' (Enter)
```

View the same records without record numbers.

```
[.] list off for grade = '10' (Enter)
```

View only the student name and ID number fields of the same records. (The field names to list should be keyed in upper case or initial caps because they will be displayed; the field to consider can be keyed in any case, as it will not be displayed.)

```
[.] list St_Name, Id_No for grade = '10' (Enter)
```

Select all of the students who are not in grade 10. (Use Shift-3 for the "not equal" character.)

[.] list for grade # '10' Enter

View the same records with student name and grade only fields, no record numbers.

[.] list off St_Name, Grade for grade # '10'

Select students who have a GPA of at least 2.5. The field is GPA (numeric field), the value is 2.5, and the comparison type is greater than or equal to (>=).

[.] list for gpa >= 2.5

View only the name, grade, and GPA of the same records, no record numbers.

[.] list off St_Name, Grade, GPA for GPA >= 2.5 Enter

DO: Key a command that will list the name, ID number, and GPA of students with a GPA of less than 3.0.

What command did you use? ____________________

DO: Key the same command, adding TO PRINTER to get a printed copy.

SELECT DATES. To select on a date field, you must add the **date function** you wish to use and place the date field name in parentheses. The date functions include year, month, and day. No space is allowed between the date function and the field name. Key the following commands to select on date.

Select the students born in 1976 or after, using the year function.

[.] list for year(birthdate) >= 1976 Enter

Select the students who have February birthdays using the month function.

[.] list for month(birthdate) = 2 Enter

Select students who were born on or after the 15th of the month, using the day function.

[.] list for day(birthdate) >= 15 Enter

SELECT LOGICAL FIELDS. Logical fields are handled in a different manner from the other types of fields. To see records with a true value, list the field to consider. To see records with a false value (not true), key .NOT. before the field name to consider.

[.] list for member (↵Enter)

To list nonmembers (MEMBER = .F.), key this command:

[.] list for .not. member (↵Enter)

LOGICAL OPERATORS

When selecting records, you occasionally want to see records that meet two or more conditions. For example, you may want to see records of 1) seniors 2) who have a GPA of 2.8 or higher. A command to select on two or more fields must include a logical operator between the fields.

The logical operators are: .AND., .OR., and .NOT. Use .AND. when two conditions must be true; use .OR. when either condition may be true; use .NOT. when neither condition may be true.

Select seniors (Grade 12) who have a GPA of 2.8 or higher.

[.] list for grade = '12' .and. gpa >= 2.8 (↵Enter)

Key a similar command to see juniors with a GPA of 2.0 or higher.

[.] list for grade = '11' .and. gpa >= 2.0 (↵Enter)

Select students with last names beginning with S through Z who are club members. The letter S must be uppercase, because all names start with a capital.

[.] list for st_name >= 'S' .and. member (↵Enter)

Select all seniors who are not club members.

[.] list for grade = '12' .and. .not. member (↵Enter)

Select all students who are seniors or who have a GPA between and including 2.5 and 3.5. (When allowing a data range, such as 2.5 through 3.5, you must use the field name both before and after the logical operator.)

[.] list for grade = '12' .or. GPA >= 2.5 .and. GPA <= 3.5 (↵Enter)

Select all sophomores and all seniors, but show only name and grade, with no record number.

[.] list off St_Name, Grade for grade = '10' .or. grade = '12'

Print without record numbers all sophomores who are club members.

[.] list off for grade = '10' .and. member to print

DO: Close the database.

QUICK QUESTIONS

1. What is "selecting records?"
2. What 3 items of information are needed to select records?
   a)
   b)
   c)
3. If a field value is alphanumeric, how should you key the character string?
4. What rule is important to remember about the case to use when keying character data?
5. What type of operator determines the type of comparison when selecting records?
6. Write a command that will select birthdays (a date field called BIRTHDATE) after 1975.
7. What is the purpose of logical operators?
8. What word surrounded by periods is used to select the records that are false in a logical field?
9. Which of the logical operators is used to select records when either of two conditions may be true?
10. Which of the logical operators is used to select records when neither condition may be true?

REVIEW EXERCISE

Open the CLUBMEM database. Display records as described below. Write the command used on the line.

1. List all records without displaying record numbers. ____________________
2. Go to Record 11. ____________________
   Display the current record. ____________________
3. List all records, but display only the NAME and PHONE fields. ____________________
4. List all records, but display only the DATE_JOIN and NAME fields with no record numbers.
   ____
5. List all records for members older than 35. ____________________
6. List all records for members whose last names start with M through Z. ____________________
7. List only the NAME and DATE_JOIN fields for those who joined before 1990 to the printer.
   ____
8. List only the members who are under age 40 and have a ZIP code of 24541 with no record numbers to the printer. ____________________
9. Close the database.

ACTIVITY A - PRODUCTS DATABASE

Open the PRODUCTS database. Display records as described below. Write the command(s) used on the line.

1. List all records without record numbers. ______
2. Go to Record 12. ______
3. Display only the TITLE and AUTHOR fields of the current record with no record number.
   ______
4. Display only the TITLE and AUTHOR fields of Record 8 with no record number.
   ______
5. List all records, but display only the PRICE and BOOK_NO fields. ______
6. List only the BOOK_NO and AUTHOR fields for books that cost $20 or more.
   ______
7. List only the YR, BOOK_NO, and TITLE fields of all books published in 1990 or later, no record numbers. (You may want to list structure to see the type of field for YR.)
   ______
8. List only the BOOK_NO, TITLE, and PRICE fields of all paperback books to the printer, no record numbers. ______
9. List only the BOOK_NO and PG fields of all books that were published prior to 1990 that have 250 pages or more.
   ______
10. List only the YR, BOOK_NO, PRICE, and PG fields of all hardcover books (not paperbacks) that cost $25 or more to the printer.
    ______

ACTIVITY B - LISTINGS DATABASE

Open the LISTINGS database. Mrs. Burnes, the owner of Burnes Abodes, has asked you to select records and give her ***printed copies of each****; write the number of the request on each printed listing. To save paper (and trees), Mrs. Burnes wants you to place several listings on the same sheet of paper if possible.*

1. List all records without record numbers.
2. List only the LIST_DATE, ADDRESS, and PRICE fields of Record 9.
3. List only the PRICE and LIST_DATE fields of all homes that cost less than $80,000.
4. A client wants a 3-bedroom house that costs between $60,000 and $90,000. What is available? List entire records without record numbers.
5. A client is looking for a 3-bedroom house with at least 1.5 baths. List entire records without record numbers.
6. A client is interested in finding a house that has 3-bedrooms, a two-car garage, and a basement. List only the ADDRESS and PRICE of each house that meets those needs, no record numbers.
7. Mrs. Burnes wants to know the price, number of bedrooms, number of baths, and type of heat of all homes $90,000 or more.
8. A client wants a house that has the following requirements: 3 or more bedrooms, 2 or more baths, a greatroom, and gas heat. Produce a listing showing the address and price only, no record numbers.
9. A client is searching for a home that is no older than 10 years, costs no more than $125,000, has at least 3 bedrooms and 2 baths, central air, a family room, and a 2-car garage. List entire records, no record numbers.
10. A client would like to find a home that costs less than $75,000, has at least 3 bedrooms and 1.5 baths, a garage, central air, and no oil heat. List the address, price, and age without record numbers.

6

UPDATE RECORDS

OBJECTIVES

- Explain the importance of updating records.
- **Edit** fields.
- Use **browse.**
- **Append** records.
- Use **Replace.**
- **Insert** records.
- **Delete** and pack records.
- **Recall** deleted records.

UP-TO-DATE RECORDS

Most of us have had at least one irritating experience with a business firm's inaccurate or out-of-date data. Perhaps you have sent a change-of-address form to a magazine publisher or a music club and waited two or three months for the company to mail the product to your new address. Have you ever notified a company several times of a change such as a misspelled name or incorrect phone number or ZIP code? Occasionally a company will keep billing you after you send a payment. Some people have reserved a hotel room over the phone to find that no such reservation exists when they arrive at their destination.

Most of these problems are a result of not keeping database records up to date. To keep satisfied customers, it is important that a business have a simple, timely procedure for updating records.

Updating records includes correcting data that has changed; adding new records; and erasing unneeded records. In this section you will learn to update the records in your database files.

EDIT RECORDS

Records may need to be **edited** or changed for a number of reasons, but this should always be done as soon as the new data is available. As you enter data, check that you are entering it in a similar manner to the data already in the database. It should be the same in case (all caps or initial caps or lower case), sequencing (last name comma first name, for example), and correct abbreviations if used. The **Edit** command will cause the Edit Screen to appear so data can be changed.

Open the CLASS database. (Set default if necessary.)

[.] use CLASS

GO TO A RECORD. The **Go** command is used to place the record pointer on the desired record, making it the current record. Use the Go and Edit commands to edit the record for Wally Maxwell, who has decided to join the business club. First list the records to see his record number.

[.] list (Enter)

FIGURE DB6.1
CLASS Listing

```
Record#  ID_NO ST_NAME          GRADE BIRTHDATE  GPA MEMBER
     1  81775 Lackey, Jill      12    03/17/76  2.70 .T.
     2  83519 Troupe, Juan      12    10/22/76  2.22 .T.
     3  88244 Pressman, Bill    12    12/12/75  3.45 .F.
     4  79312 Withers, Erika    11    02/18/77  2.90 .T.
     5  68823 Mendoza, Gloria   10    05/28/78  3.05 .T.
     6  69007 Maxwell, Wally    10    11/04/78  1.89 .F.
     7  74781 Seiffert, Janet   11    02/07/77  2.38 .T.
     8  86607 Leon, Carmen      12    08/17/76  2.65 .F.
     9  63770 Silvers, Pat      10    10/30/78  3.10 .T.
    10  64349 Brooks, Glen      10    07/20/78  3.62 .T.
```

As you can see, Wally is Record 6. Make Record 6 the current record.

[.] go 6 (Enter)

Look at the Status Bar to verify that you are pointing to Record 6. Edit the current record.

[.] edit (Enter)

Wally's record appears on the Edit Screen.

DO: Press (↓) to place the cursor on the Member field.

KEY: t

Wally's record is complete, so the cursor advances to the next record. When the cursor automatically advances to the next record, use (Esc) to save and return to the dot prompt.

DO: Press (Esc).

Make Record 6 the current record again and then display it to check if Wally's record has been edited and saved. Is the value for Member *true*?

[.] go 6 (Enter)

[.] display (Enter)

EDIT RECORD NUMBER. You can move the record pointer and edit a record with one command, **Edit Record**. You must include the record number with the command, but the Go command is eliminated.

Edit the record for Carmen Leon. She has informed us that the birthdate we have for her is incorrect. Her birthday is August 27, 1976. List the records to see her record number.

[.] list (↵Enter)

Carmen is Record 8. You can edit Record 8 by using the Edit Record command.

[.] edit record 8 (↵Enter)

The Edit Screen allows you to change Carmen's birthday.

DO: Press (↓) to place the cursor on the Birthdate field.

DO: Press (→) to place the cursor on the *1* in *17*.

KEY: 2

When you edit a record and the cursor remains on that record, press (Ctrl)-(End) to save the correction and return to the dot prompt.

DO: Press (Ctrl)-(End).

When saving an edited record from the Edit Screen, (Esc) saves the previous record, and (Ctrl)-(End) saves the record the cursor is on.

SELECT A RECORD. You can edit a record without knowing the record number if a field in the record has a unique value. Unique means "one of a kind." Unique values can include ID numbers, social security numbers, employee numbers, and other one-of-a-kind numbers.

You have been notified of another error in the database. The student with ID Number 74781 is in Grade 10. Use the EDIT FOR command.

[.] edit for ID_NO = '74781' (↵Enter)

DO: When you see the Edit Screen, change Janet's grade. Since the cursor remains on the edited record, press (Ctrl)-(End) to save it.

DO: On your own, go to the student record for *Lackey* using the Go, Edit Record, or Edit For command. Change the last name from *Lackey* to *Lacley*.

PAGE DOWN TO EDIT A GROUP OF RECORDS. When you edit a group of records, you often will not save until all records have been edited.

Grade cards have just been issued, and the students have new GPA figures.

DO: In the Edit Screen, begin at the top of the file and make the following changes. Press (Pg Dn) to advance to the next record when desired. Save appropriately with (Ctrl)-(End) or (Esc) when the last record is edited.

Lacley	2.85	Maxwell	2.02
Troupe	2.17	Seiffert	2.41
Pressman	3.48	Leon	2.64
Withers	3.13	Silvers	3.42
Mendoza	2.98	Brooks	3.85

Check for accuracy with DB6.2. Edit any incorrect data.

FIGURE DB6.2
Updated CLASS File

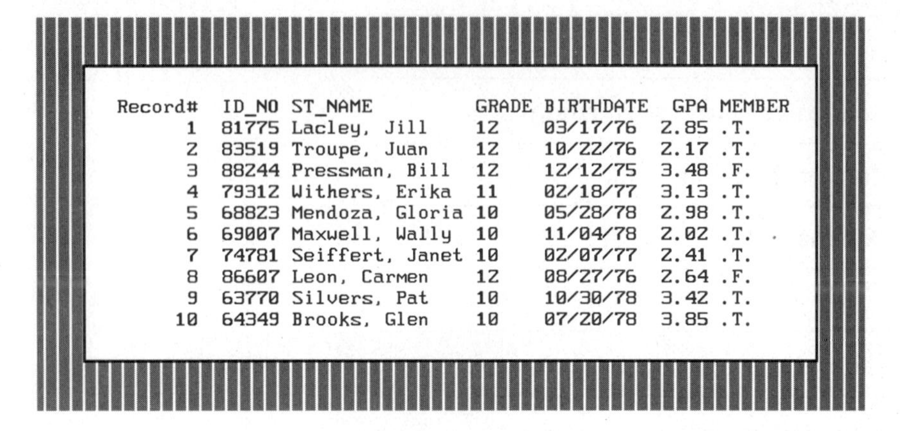

Record#	ID_NO	ST_NAME	GRADE	BIRTHDATE	GPA	MEMBER
1	81775	Lacley, Jill	12	03/17/76	2.85	.T.
2	83519	Troupe, Juan	12	10/22/76	2.17	.T.
3	88244	Pressman, Bill	12	12/12/75	3.48	.F.
4	79312	Withers, Erika	11	02/18/77	3.13	.T.
5	68823	Mendoza, Gloria	10	05/28/78	2.98	.T.
6	69007	Maxwell, Wally	10	11/04/78	2.02	.T.
7	74781	Seiffert, Janet	10	02/07/77	2.41	.T.
8	86607	Leon, Carmen	12	08/27/76	2.64	.F.
9	63770	Silvers, Pat	10	10/30/78	3.42	.T.
10	64349	Brooks, Glen	10	07/20/78	3.85	.T.

BROWSE TO EDIT A GROUP OF RECORDS. The **Browse** command offers a simpler way to edit a group of records. You may begin the browse at any record in the database; the Browse screen displays the current record and the next 17 records. Other records can be displayed by pressing (↑) or (↓).

Once the records are displayed on the Browse screen, press (↑) and (↓) to move from record to record. Use (Tab) to move right one field and (Shift)-(Tab) to move left one field. The records may be edited by using (Insert) or (Delete).

[.] go top (↵Enter)

[.] browse (↵Enter)

Another grading period has ended. Update the GPA field of the records once again.

DO: Use Browse to update the GPA field in each record.

Lacley	3.07	Maxwell	2.42
Troupe	2.61	Seiffert	2.39
Pressman	3.51	Leon	2.59
Withers	3.3	Silvers	3.48
Mendoza	3.16	Brooks	3.8

DO: Check the accuracy of the data. Correct any errors. Press (Ctrl)-(End) when done.

REPLACE. When many records contain the same data value that needs to be updated, the **Replace** command may be used to edit all of the records at one time. Because Replace makes all changes at once, it can be a dangerous command! Use the Replace command with caution.

For practice with the Replace command, change all 10th graders to 9th graders and then back to 10th graders.

[.] Replace grade with '9' for grade = '10' (↵Enter)

List the file to see the Grade 9 records. Next, change Grade 9 back to Grade 10.

[.] Replace grade with '10' for grade = '9' (Enter)

QUICK QUESTIONS

1. Why must a company have a simple, timely procedure for updating records?
2. Name three actions that update records.
   a)
   b)
   c)
3. What is meant by editing a record?
4. What are some precautions that should be taken to assure that new data is entered in a similar manner to existing data?
5. List three commands or combination commands that will allow you to edit a record.
   a)
   b)
   c)
6. When saving an edited record in the Edit Screen, what key(s) saves the record prior to the one the cursor is on?
7. When saving an edited record in the Edit Screen, what key(s) saves the record the cursor is on?
8. What key(s) will advance the cursor to the next record in the Edit or Browse screens?
9. List two ways to edit a group of records.
   a)
   b)
10. What is the purpose of the Replace command?

APPEND AND INSERT RECORDS

Sometimes new records must be added to a database file. If the records are added at the end of the existing file, they are appended. If the records are placed at some point within the database, they are inserted.

APPEND. The **Append** command adds records at the end of the database. Append records for two new students who have moved to our school. To append their records, use the following data:

79562	Brooks, Ryan	11	12/09/77	3.11	F
69112	Pratt, Alicia	10	03/23/76	2.74	F

[.] append (Enter)

DO: Enter the data shown above. Press (Esc) when complete so blank Record 13 is not saved.

INSERT. **Insert** is used when a new record is added to a file that has records arranged in order. Insert allows you to place a new record at any desired position in the arrangement, keeping the records in order. For example, a new employee is hired and must be added to the employee database, which is arranged in order by employee number. The new employee's record can be inserted at the appropriate position in the database according to his or her employee number.

Although the CLASS database is not arranged in any order, insert a record for practice. To insert, you must use the Edit Screen; you cannot use Browse to insert a record. Insert a new Record 4. Make Record 3 the current record, as Insert adds the new record *after* the current one. The record numbers of the records following the inserted one will change according to their new positions.

[.] go 3

[.] insert

DO: Key the following record. You will return to the dot prompt.

88568 Clackwell, June 12 02/04/76 3.2 F

DO: List the database to see if Clackwell is Record 4 and if Pratt, who was Record 12, is now Record 13.

DELETE RECORDS

Records should be deleted from the active database when they become obsolete, or outdated, for any reason. In the CLASS database, records should be deleted when a student permanently leaves the class.

Deleting records is a two-step process. First, records are *marked* for deletion using the **Delete** command. Records marked for deletion are indicated by the code *Del* on the Status Bar in the Browse or Edit Screen and by an asterisk beside the records when they are listed. The records are merely marked until the final step, called *pack*. The **Pack** command permanently removes all marked records. Before using Pack, however, you may "undelete" marked records by *recalling* them.

DELETE. To mark a record for deletion, use either the Delete command or delete from the Browse screen with Ctrl-U. Delete the records of two students who have moved from the school, June Clackwell and Pat Silvers.

DO: List the database to see Record 4. Delete it with the Delete command.

[.] delete Record 4 Enter

Delete the second record using Browse.

[.] browse Enter

DO: With your cursor on Pat Silvers's record, press (Ctrl)-(U). *Del* appears on the Status Bar. Press (Ctrl)-(End) to save the deletion and return to the dot prompt.

[.] list (↵Enter)

An asterisk should appear beside Records 4 and 10. Look at a deleted record in the Edit screen.

[.] edit 4 (↵Enter)

When in the Edit Screen, *Del* appears on the Status Bar.

DO: Press (Esc) to return to the dot prompt.

RECALL. To "undelete" a record marked for deletion, you may use the **Recall** command from the dot prompt or (Ctrl)-(U) from the Edit Screen. Ctrl-U is a toggle and deletes or undeletes records.

From the dot prompt, recall Pat Silvers's record, Record 10.

[.] recall Record 10 (↵Enter)

DO: List the file. Record 10 should no longer be marked for deletion.

PACK. The Pack command will remove the marked records from the database. Caution: before using the Pack command, always list the file and check that all records marked for deletion should be permanently removed. Any record listed with an asterisk will be erased when packed.

Remove Record 4 from the database.

DO: List and check for records marked for deletion. Only Record 4, Clackwell, should be marked with an asterisk; recall any others.

[.] pack (↵Enter)

DO: List the database. Since Clackwell has been removed, there should be 12 records.

[.] list to printer

DO: Close the database.

QUICK QUESTIONS

1. Explain the difference between appending and inserting records.
2. When you use the Insert command, where does dBASE place the new record?
3. When should records be deleted from a database?

4. Name two ways dBASE indicates that a record is marked for deletion.
   a)
   b)
5. What command will unmark a record marked for deletion?
6. What is the purpose of the Pack command?

REVIEW EXERCISE

1. Open the CLUBMEM database.
2. Use browse to make the following changes:
   a) Elaine Bridgeman has married. Her new name is Renfro.
   b) Alison Foxman's age was entered incorrectly. She is 43.
   c) Debbie Crouch has moved. Her new phone, address, and ZIP are: 356-7213, 1275 Royal Rd, 24541.
3. From the dot prompt, append a new member: Ginger Watkins, 361-1279, 3056 Brookside, 24541, 12-7-92, 38.
4. The post office has changed the ZIP code number for one area of the city. Use the Replace command to change 24541 ZIPs to 24551.
5. Insert a new Record 6: Marie Trenton, 361-5002, 1771 West Drake, 24551, 12-14-92, 34.
6. Delete two members who are moving out of town: Beth Taylor and Rachel Lowell.
7. Recall Beth Taylor's record; she is no longer moving.
8. Pack the records marked for deletion.
9. List the database to the printer.

ACTIVITY A - PRODUCTS DATABASE

1. Open the PRODUCTS database.
2. Use edit or browse to make the following changes:
   a) The author of "Electronic Melody" is Phillips A.
   b) Book numbers beginning with 140... should be changed to 139....
3. Replace books priced at 19.95 with 20.95.
4. Insert the following record after Book No. 1419B: 1415B, Concert Light Shows, Madden R, 92, 245, 31.50, F.
5. Delete three books which will no longer be carried: Nos. 1335E, 1390C, and 1556B.
6. Recall book No. 1556B.
7. Pack to remove marked records.
8. List the Book_No, Title, Author, Yr, and Price fields only to the printer.

ACTIVITY B - LISTINGS DATABASE

1. Open the LISTINGS database.
2. Use edit or browse to make the following changes:
   a) The home at 3227 Sheffield has Electric heat (El).
   b) The home at 6027 Patricia has an incorrect listing date. The date should be 11/14/XX.
   c) The prices on the following homes have decreased by $2000: 1529 Countrywalk, 6920 Desoto Ln, and 6420 W Royal St.
3. Two new homes have been listed. Add them to the database:
   a) 5622 Clayton Court, price=97500, age=15, BR=3, BA=2, FR=T, CA=T, GAR=2, HT=Gas, list_date=12/04/XX.
   b) 7868 Landon Drive, price=79900, age=21, BR=3, BA=2, DR=T, CA=T, BSMT=T, GAR=2, HT=Gas, list_date=12/10/XX.
4. One home has been sold and is no longer a listing. Mark 1103 Lafayette Ln for deletion.
5. Pack the marked records.
6. List the database without record numbers to the printer.

7

ARRANGE RECORDS

OBJECTIVES

- Compare **Sort** and **Index.**
- **Sort** records in **ascending** and **descending** order.
- **Sort** on **single** and **multiple fields.**
- Index on **single** and **multiple fields.**
- **View file names** for database and index files.

ORGANIZING RECORDS

The main purpose of having a database file is to easily access up-to-date information for on-screen display or written reports. When information is arranged in alphabetic, numeric, or chronological order, it is easier to locate records and to see relationships among the records.

The dBASE program provides two methods for arranging records, Sort and Index. The **Sort** command creates a copy of the original file, but the copy is arranged in order on a specific field or fields. The **Index** command makes the original database file *appear* sorted by creating a small record-sequencing file rather than a complete new file.

A sorted file is easier for a beginner to use, but most experienced database users prefer an indexed file. Sorted files take more disk space and are usually slower to use than indexed files, but indexed files cannot be arranged in descending order like sorted files. Indexed files can be automatically updated when the original file is updated, but sorted files must be updated separately.

Whether sorted or indexed, records are arranged on a specific field or fields called a **key**. The resulting file, arranged on the key, is called a **target** file.

SORT RECORDS

To sort records in a file, select the key field or fields on which you want the file arranged. Then, give a name to the new target file that will be created. The syntax for the sort command is: .SORT ON *key field* TO *target file name*. Sorted files are given a .DBF file extension by dBASE.

Give the target file a name that shows its relationship to both the original file and key field(s) on which it is arranged. You will sort the CLASS database on the field ST_NAME, making ST_NAME the sort *key*. The target file will be called CLASNAME, which indicates that the original file is CLASS, and the new file will be sorted on the ST_NAME field. When naming the sorted file, remember that a file name must be eight characters or less in length.

[.] use class (↵Enter)

[.] sort on st_name to clasname (↵Enter)

dBASE is sorting the records one by one, and the message *100% Sorted* will appear when the sorting is complete.

The sorted file CLASNAME is not the active file, as you can see by looking at the Status Bar; the original unsorted CLASS database is still active. **A sorted file is simply saved to disk when it is created; it must be opened to be active.**

Open the sorted file and list it to see that it is arranged in order. The records have been renumbered. See DB7.1.

[.] use clasname (↵Enter)

[.] list (↵Enter)

FIGURE DB7.1
CLASNAME Database

Record#	ID_NO	ST_NAME	GRADE	BIRTHDATE	GPA	MEMBER
1	64349	Brooks, Glen	10	07/20/78	3.80	.T.
2	79562	Brooks, Ryan	11	12/09/77	3.11	.F.
3	81775	Lacley, Jill	12	03/17/76	3.07	.T.
4	86607	Leon, Carmen	12	08/27/76	2.59	.F.
5	69007	Maxwell, Wally	10	11/04/78	2.42	.T.
6	68823	Mendoza, Gloria	10	05/28/78	3.16	.T.
7	69112	Pratt, Alicia	10	03/23/76	2.74	.F.
8	88244	Pressman, Bill	12	12/12/75	3.51	.F.
9	74781	Seiffert, Janet	10	02/07/77	2.39	.T.
10	63770	Silvers, Pat	10	10/30/78	3.48	.T.
11	83519	Troupe, Juan	12	10/22/76	2.61	.T.
12	79312	Withers, Erika	11	02/18/77	3.30	.T.

The ST_NAME field is arranged in alphabetic order on the last names. The last names are in *ascending order*, low (Brooks) to high (Withers). Ascending order is the default sorting order.

Arrange the original file again, this time on the sort key GRADE. Call the new sorted file CLASGRAD. First, open the original file, CLASS. It is best to sort and resort the original database file, which should be kept up to date.

[.] use class (↵Enter)

[.] sort on grade to clasgrad (↵Enter)

Open the sorted file and see the new arrangement of records. See DB7.2.

[.] use clasgrad (↵Enter)

[.] list (↵Enter)

FIGURE DB7.2
CLASGRAD Database

Record#	ID_NO	ST_NAME	GRADE	BIRTHDATE	GPA	MEMBER
1	69007	Maxwell, Wally	10	11/04/78	2.42	.T.
2	74781	Seiffert, Janet	10	02/07/77	2.39	.T.
3	69112	Pratt, Alicia	10	03/23/76	2.74	.F.
4	68823	Mendoza, Gloria	10	05/28/78	3.16	.T.
5	63770	Silvers, Pat	10	10/30/78	3.48	.T.
6	64349	Brooks, Glen	10	07/20/78	3.80	.T.
7	79312	Withers, Erika	11	02/18/77	3.30	.T.
8	79562	Brooks, Ryan	11	12/09/77	3.11	.F.
9	81775	Lacley, Jill	12	03/17/76	3.07	.T.
10	88244	Pressman, Bill	12	12/12/75	3.51	.F.
11	86607	Leon, Carmen	12	08/27/76	2.59	.F.
12	83519	Troupe, Juan	12	10/22/76	2.61	.T.

The records are arranged in numeric order according to grade (not to be confused with the fact that GRADE is a character type field). The new arrangement is useful, but it will be better if the student names are arranged in alphabetic order *within* the grades. In other words, group all of the 10th graders in alphabetic order by last name, group all of the 11th graders in alphabetic order by last name, and group all of the 12th graders in order by last name.

MULTIPLE FIELD SORT. Open the original database and sort it again, this time on two fields, GRADE and ST_NAME. GRADE is the primary, or first, sort key, and ST_NAME is the secondary sort key. Overwrite (replace) the CLASGRAD file with the new, improved sort.

[.] use class (Enter)

[.] sort on grade, st_name to clasgrad (Enter)

KEY: (Y) to overwrite clasgrad with the new sort.

Open the new sorted file and view the newly sorted records.

[.] use clasgrad (Enter)

[.] list (Enter)

The records are grouped by grade, and the students within each grade are in order by last name. See DB7.3.

FIGURE DB7.3
The CLASGRAD Database Sorted on Two Fields

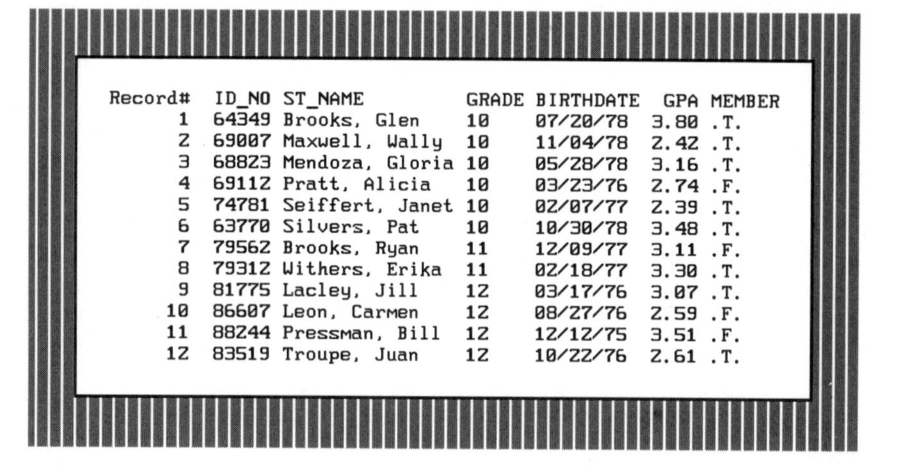

Record#	ID_NO	ST_NAME	GRADE	BIRTHDATE	GPA	MEMBER
1	64349	Brooks, Glen	10	07/20/78	3.80	.T.
2	69007	Maxwell, Wally	10	11/04/78	2.42	.T.
3	68823	Mendoza, Gloria	10	05/28/78	3.16	.T.
4	69112	Pratt, Alicia	10	03/23/76	2.74	.F.
5	74781	Seiffert, Janet	10	02/07/77	2.39	.T.
6	63770	Silvers, Pat	10	10/30/78	3.48	.T.
7	79562	Brooks, Ryan	11	12/09/77	3.11	.F.
8	79312	Withers, Erika	11	02/18/77	3.30	.T.
9	81775	Lacley, Jill	12	03/17/76	3.07	.T.
10	86607	Leon, Carmen	12	08/27/76	2.59	.F.
11	88244	Pressman, Bill	12	12/12/75	3.51	.F.
12	83519	Troupe, Juan	12	10/22/76	2.61	.T.

DESCENDING ORDER. Sort the CLASS file on the key field GPA, arranged in *descending order* (high to low) so that the highest GPA's will be listed first. The sort operation will be completed in descending order if you key **/D** after the field name. Perform the sort and then view the records.

[.] use class (Enter)

[.] sort on gpa/d to clasgpa (Enter)

[.] use clasgpa (Enter)

[.] list (Enter)

DATE SORT. A date type field is sorted just like as any other type of field. Sort the CLASS database on the BIRTHDATE field.

[.] use class (Enter)

[.] sort on birthdate to clasdate (↵Enter)

[.] use clasdate

[.] list (↵Enter)

LOGICAL FIELD SORT. Logical fields cannot be sorted like the other field types.

QUICK QUESTIONS

1. Why should data be organized?
2. List three sorting arrangements.
   a)
   b)
   c)
3. Which method of arranging records provides faster access to data?
4. Which method of arranging records can provide either ascending or descending order?
5. Which method of arranging records can update all related files when the main database file is updated?
6. What file extension is given to a sorted file?
7. What should be considered when naming a sorted file?
8. When sorting is completed, is the sorted file the active file?
9. What is the default sort order?
10. Write a command that would sort on two fields, GPA (primary sort) and ST_NAME (secondary sort), to create a file called GPANAME.
11. Compare sorting date fields and logical fields.

INDEX RECORDS

The command to index a file is similar to the Sort command. To index a file, select the key field or fields on which you want the file arranged. Then, give a name to the new target file that contains only key fields and record numbers. The syntax for the index command is: .INDEX ON *key field* TO *target file name*. Indexed files are given an .NDX file extension by dBASE.

Create an indexed file on the ST_NAME field. Name the indexed file CLASNAME. You already have a sorted file called CLASNAME.DBF, but the indexed file will be called CLASNAME.NDX.

[.] use class (↵Enter)

[.] index on st_name to clasname (↵Enter)

The message *100% indexed* appears when the indexing is complete. To see the effect of the indexed file, view the records.

[.] list (Enter)

DB7.4 shows a listing of the indexed file. Notice, the record numbers remain the same for each record; records are not renumbered with an indexed file like they are with a sorted file. (Compare record numbers in Figure DB7.4 with DB7.3.)

FIGURE DB7.4
CLASS Database Indexed on ST_NAME

```
Record#  ID_NO ST_NAME          GRADE BIRTHDATE  GPA MEMBER
     10  64349 Brooks, Glen     10    07/20/78  3.80 .T.
     11  79562 Brooks, Ryan     11    12/09/77  3.11 .F.
      1  81775 Lacley, Jill     12    03/17/76  3.07 .T.
      8  86607 Leon, Carmen     12    08/27/76  2.59 .F.
      6  69007 Maxwell, Wally   10    11/04/78  2.42 .T.
      5  68823 Mendoza, Gloria  10    05/28/78  3.16 .T.
     12  69112 Pratt, Alicia    10    03/23/76  2.74 .F.
      3  88244 Pressman, Bill   12    12/12/75  3.51 .F.
      7  74781 Seiffert, Janet  10    02/07/77  2.39 .T.
      9  63770 Silvers, Pat     10    10/30/78  3.48 .T.
      2  83519 Troupe, Juan     12    10/22/76  2.61 .T.
      4  79312 Withers, Erika   11    02/18/77  3.30 .T.
```

Return the database to its original order with the **Close Index** command. This will close all indexed files that are open.

[.] close index (Enter)

[.] list (Enter)

The database appears in its original order.

Once you have created an indexed file, it will remain with the main file, but it must be opened whenever you want to use it. Actually, all indexed files related to a database file should be opened every time you use the database so that any updates to the original database are automatically made to the indexed files as well. This will allow you to keep all indexed files current.

Open the indexed file you just closed so it becomes active once more. The **Set Index** command can be used to open one or many indexed files.

[.] set index to clasname (Enter)

Create a new indexed file using the index key BIRTHDATE. Call the indexed file CLASDATE.

[.] index on birthdate to clasdate.

[.] list (Enter)

The records are listed in chronological order by birthdate.

Two indexed files are now open, CLASNAME and CLASDATE. The last indexed file you created is the one in effect, called the **controlling index**. If no new indexed file is created when a database is open, the controlling index will be the first file keyed in the Set Index command. For example, when the command SET INDEX TO CLASDATE, CLASNAME is used, both the CLASDATE and CLASNAME indexed files are opened, but CLASDATE becomes the controlling index because it is the first file name listed. The controlling index is the record arrangement you see when you use the List command.

Close both indexed files. Then open both indexed files again with one command, making CLASDATE the controlling index. Then, view the records to see if they are in order on the BIRTHDATE field.

[.] close index (↵Enter)

[.] set index to clasdate, clasname (↵Enter)

[.] list (↵Enter)

Even though an indexed file is not the first one listed in the Set Index command, it can be made the controlling index by using the Set Order command. Make the CLASNAME indexed file the controlling index with the Set Order command. Since CLASNAME is the second file name in the Set Index command, it is File 2. After using the two commands below, see if the records are in order on ST_NAME.

[.] set order to 2

[.] list (↵Enter)

Create an indexed file using the key GPA. Since an index can arrange records only in ascending order, the GPAs will be listed from lowest to highest. Call the indexed file CLASGPA.

[.] index on gpa to clasgpa (↵Enter)

[.] list (↵Enter)

Now CLASGPA is the controlling index because it was the last one created. A newly created index overrides the Set Index or Set Order commands.

MULTIPLE FIELD INDEXING. Although an indexed file can have only one index key, you can use plus signs to join two or more fields together to get the appearance of a multiple index. The joined fields must be of the same type, all numeric or all character. Use an indexed file to display records arranged in order by grade, with student names in alphabetical order within the grades.

[.] index on grade+st_name to clasgrna (↵Enter)

[.] list (↵Enter)

Figure DB7.5 shows the file indexed on the GRADE and ST_NAME fields.

Close the indexed files and the active database.

FIGURE DB7.5
CLASS Database Indexed on GRADE + ST_NAME

Record#	ID_NO	ST_NAME	GRADE	BIRTHDATE	GPA	MEMBER
10	64349	Brooks, Glen	10	07/20/78	3.80	.T.
6	69007	Maxwell, Wally	10	11/04/78	2.42	.T.
5	68823	Mendoza, Gloria	10	05/28/78	3.16	.T.
12	69112	Pratt, Alicia	10	03/23/76	2.74	.F.
7	74781	Seiffert, Janet	10	02/07/77	2.39	.T.
9	63770	Silvers, Pat	10	10/30/78	3.48	.T.
11	79562	Brooks, Ryan	11	12/09/77	3.11	.F.
4	79312	Withers, Erika	11	02/18/77	3.30	.T.
1	81775	Lacley, Jill	12	03/17/76	3.07	.T.
8	86607	Leon, Carmen	12	08/27/76	2.59	.F.
3	88244	Pressman, Bill	12	12/12/75	3.51	.F.
2	83519	Troupe, Juan	12	10/22/76	2.61	.T.

[.] close index (↵Enter)

[.] use (↵Enter)

VIEW FILE NAMES

To view the names of all files on your disk including database and indexed files, use the DOS command DIR *.*. Then look for DBF and NDX file extensions.

[.] dir *.* (↵Enter)

A better way to see just .DBF files is to key the Dir command by itself or with the DBF file extension.

[.] dir (↵Enter)

[.] dir *.dbf (↵Enter)

To see just indexed files, key the Dir command with the NDX file extension.

[.] dir *.ndx (↵Enter)

DO: Quit dBASE or go on to the Review Exercise.

QUICK QUESTIONS

1. What are the contents of an indexed file?
2. What file extension is given to an indexed file?
3. What does an indexed file do with the record numbers of the main file?
4. What command will return an indexed database to its original order?
5. Why should you open all indexed files related to a database every time you use the database?
6. If two indexed files are created, which is in effect?
7. What is a controlling index?
8. For the following command, circle the name of the controlling index:
   SET INDEX TO CLASGPA, CLASDATE, CLASNAME
9. Circle the name of the controlling index after the following two commands have been keyed:
   SET INDEX TO CLASGPA, CLASDATE, CLASNAME
   SET ORDER TO 3
10. What character is keyed between two or more field names to join them as one key field for indexing?
11. What command will display all database and indexed file names?

1. Open the CLUBMEM database.
2. Sort on the NAME field. Call the sorted file CLUBNAME.
3. Open the CLUBNAME file and list to check for proper sorting.
4. Open CLUBMEM. Sort using ZIP as the primary sort key and NAME as the secondary sort key. Call the sorted file CLUBZIP.
5. Open the CLUBZIP file. List it to the printer, displaying only the 24551 ZIP codes.
6. Open CLUBMEM. Index on the NAME field. Call the indexed file CLUBNAME.
7. List the records to see if they are indexed properly.
8. Index on the DATE_JOIN field. Call the indexed file CLUBDATE.
9. List the CLUBDATE.NDX records to the printer, without record numbers.
10. Make an index that appears arranged first by ZIP and then by ADDRESS. Call the indexed file CLUBZPAD.
11. List the CLUBZPAD.NDX records to the printer with the record numbers and the ZIP and ADDRESS fields only.

ACTIVITY A - PRODUCT DATABASE

1. Open the PRODUCTS database.
2. Sort on the TITLE field. Call the sorted file PRODTITL.
3. Open the PRODTITL file and use the Display All command to check for proper sorting.
4. Open PRODUCTS. Sort using AUTHOR as the primary sort key and TITLE as the secondary sort key. Call the sorted file PRODAUTH.
5. Open the PRODAUTH file and list it to the printer, displaying only the authors whose names begin with A through M, without record numbers.
6. Open PRODUCTS. Index on the BOOK_NO field. Call the indexed file PRODBKNO.
7. Index on the YR field. Call the indexed file PRODYR.
8. Index on the PRICE field. Call the indexed file PRODPRI.
9. Use the PRODBKNO, PRODYR, and PRODPRI indexed files. Make PRODBKNO the controlling index. List the records to the printer without record numbers.
10. Make an index that appears arranged first by YR and then by BOOK_NO. Call the indexed file PRODYRNO.

11. List the PRODYRNO.NDX records to the printer with the YR, BOOK_NO, and TITLE fields displayed with the record numbers.

ACTIVITY B - LISTINGS DATABASE

1. Open the LISTINGS database.
2. Sort on the PRICE field in descending order. Call the sorted file LISPRICE.
3. Open the LISPRICE file and display all records to check for proper sorting.
4. Open LISTINGS. Sort using HT as the primary sort key and PRICE in descending order as the secondary sort key. Call the sorted file LISHTPRI.
5. Open the LISHTPRI file and list it to the printer with the HT, PRICE, and ADDRESS fields displayed, with the record numbers.
6. Open LISTINGS. Index on the ADDRESS field. Call the indexed file LISADD.
7. Index on the AGE field. Call the indexed file LISAGE.
8. Index on the PRICE field. Call the indexed file LISPRI.
9. Index on the BR field. Call the indexed file LISBR.
10. Index on the BA field. Call the indexed file LISBA.
11. Using all five of the indexed files, make LISBR the controlling index. List only the three-bedroom records to the printer with the BR, BA, PRICE, and ADDRESS fields displayed only, with record numbers.
12. Using all five of the indexed files, make LISPRI the controlling index. List only the homes with a price less than 90,000 to the printer. Display the PRICE, AGE, and ADDRESS fields only, no record numbers.
13. Make an index that appears to be arranged first by BR and then by BA within the BR groups. Call the indexed file LISBRBA.
14. List the LISBRBA.NDX records to the printer with the BR, BA, LIST_DATE, and ADDRESS fields displayed; include record numbers.

8

CREATE REPORTS

OBJECTIVES

- Create reports with **page number, date,** and **title.**
- Report on **specific fields.**
- **Modify reports** when needed.

REPORT FORM

To prepare reports that appear more professional than the listings you have printed in earlier sections, use the Report Generator (dBASE III) or the Report Writer (dBASE IV). The Report Generator and the Report Writer create attractive report forms that may include report titles, page numbers, and the date, as well as totals for numeric fields. (See Figures DB8.1A and DB8.1B.)

When you create a report form with the Report Generator/Writer, it is based on the structure of the active database. Since the report form will be stored as a file on your disk, you may use it repeatedly with the original database and its sorted files. The dBASE program gives report forms an .FRM file extension. (dBASE IV gives additional extensions to report files.)

CLASNAME REPORT

In this section you will create a report based on the CLASNAME database, a sorted version of the CLASS database. Once the report form is created, you can use it with the CLASS database or any of its sorted files because they all have the same structure (contain the same fields).

If you are using dBASE III, you will create the report in shown in DB8.1A. If you are using dBASE IV, you will create the report shown in DB8.1B. Notice, the report is double spaced, has a page number, the date, and a title or main heading. Each column that was chosen for the report has a column heading, and the data listed in the columns is from the database records.

DBASE III OR IV. Although you will begin the report form creation at the dot prompt, you will design the report using special design screens. Because the report design screens are very different in the two versions of dBASE, this section is divided into two parts. If you are using dBASE III, use the directions that start below. If your version is dBASE IV, turn to page dB70 and follow the directions beginning there.

FIGURE DB8.1A
Report on CLASNAME for dBASE III

```
Page No.       1
MM/DD/YY                             BUSINESS CLASS STUDENTS


STUDENT NAMES         GRADE  ID NO   BIRTHDATE    GPA   CLUB


Brooks, Glen          10     64349   07/20/78     3.80   .T.
Brooks, Ryan          11     79562   12/09/77     3.11   .F.
Lacley, Jill          12     81775   03/17/76     3.07   .T.
Leon, Carmen          12     86607   08/27/76     2.59   .F.
Maxwell, Wally        10     69007   11/04/78     2.42   .T.
Mendoza, Gloria       10     68823   05/28/78     3.16   .T.
Pratt, Alicia         10     69112   03/23/76     2.74   .F.
Pressman, Bill        12     88244   12/12/75     3.51   .F.
Seiffert, Janet       10     74781   02/07/77     2.39   .T.
Silvers, Pat          10     63770   10/30/78     3.48   .T.
Troupe, Juan          12     83519   10/22/76     2.61   .T.
Withers, Erika        11     79312   02/18/77     3.30   .T.
```

THE dBASE III REPORT GENERATOR

CREATE REPORT. To create a new report form, first open the database that will be used for the report and then use the Create Report command. You will then be prompted for a name for the report. dBASE will add an .FRM extension to the report file name.

[.] use clasname (Enter)

[.] create report (Enter)

The message *Enter report file name:* appears. Name the report CLASS; it will be saved as CLASS.FRM, a different file name from CLASS.DBF, the original database file.

KEY: class (Enter)

The Report Form menu screen appears, DB8.2. *Options* is highlighted, and the Options menu is pulled down.

FIGURE DB8.1B
Report on CLASNAME for dBASE IV

BUSINESS CLASS STUDENTS

Page No. 1
MM/DD/YY

STUDENT NAMES	GRADE	ID NO	BIRTHDATE	GPA	CLUB
Brooks, Glen	10	64349	07/20/78	3.80	Y
Brooks, Ryan	11	79562	12/09/77	3.11	N
Lacley, Jill	12	81775	03/17/76	3.07	Y
Leon, Carmen	12	86607	08/27/76	2.59	N
Maxwell, Wally	10	69007	11/04/78	2.42	Y
Mendoza, Gloria	10	68823	05/28/78	3.16	Y
Pratt, Alicia	10	69112	03/23/76	2.74	N
Pressman, Bill	12	88244	12/12/75	3.51	N
Seiffert, Janet	10	74781	02/07/77	2.39	Y
Silvers, Pat	10	63770	10/30/78	3.48	Y
Troupe, Juan	12	83519	10/22/76	2.61	Y
Withers, Erika	11	79312	02/18/77	3.30	Y

FIGURE DB8.2
The Report Form Menu Screen

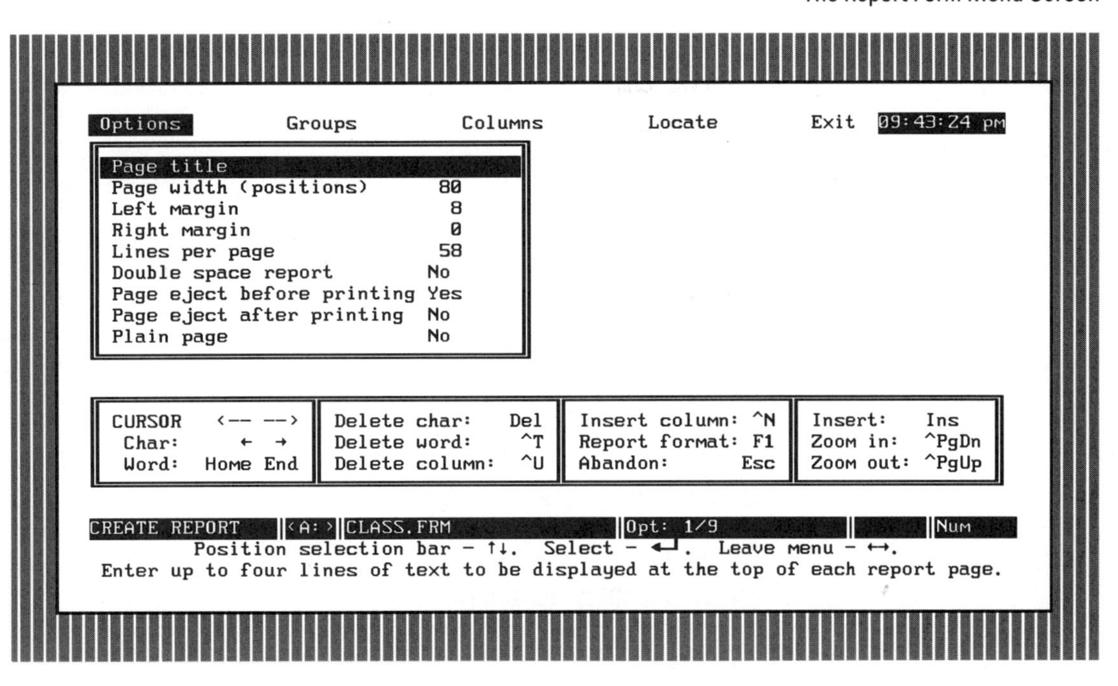

OPTIONS MENU. This menu is used to specify the title, margins, and spacing of the report. You will key a title and make the report double spaced. Press ↓ to highlight the item desired, and then press ↵Enter to select it.

DO: Highlight *Page title* and then press ↵Enter.

A white box (black in the figure below) appears in which you can key the title(s) of the report. See DB8.3. The title may contain up to four lines which will be centered between the margins.

FIGURE DB8.3
Page Title Box

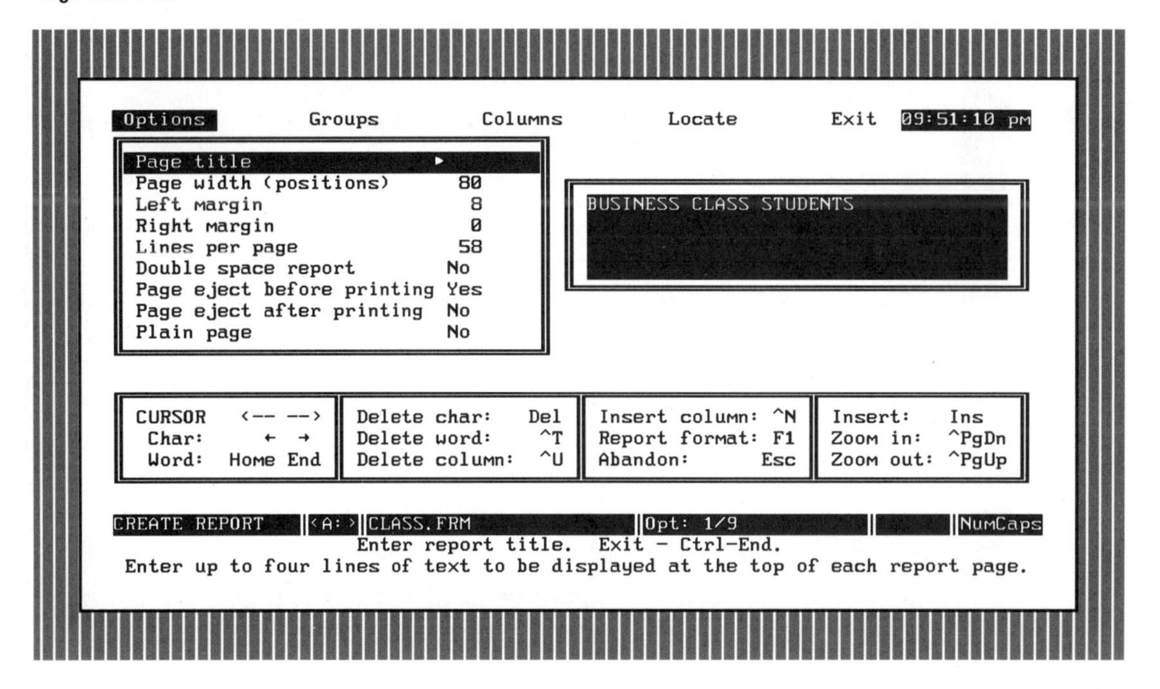

KEY: BUSINESS CLASS STUDENTS

DO: Press Ctrl-End to exit the Page Title entry box.

DO: Highlight *Double space report.*

Items that have the value *Yes* or *No* can be toggled to the opposite value by pressing ↵Enter.

DO: Press ↵Enter to toggle double spacing to *Yes.*

Toggle Page Eject After Printing to *Yes* so the report will eject in the printer.

DO: Highlight *Page eject after printing.*

DO: Press ↵Enter to toggle *Yes.*

None of the other items on the Options menu will be selected. To move to other menus, press →.

DO: Press → to move to the Groups menu.

GROUPS MENU. This menu enables you to arrange the report records in groups according to data in a specific field. You will not group data on this report.

DO: Press (→) to move to the Columns menu.

COLUMNS MENU. This important menu defines how the fields of data in the body of the report will appear. The arrangement of the fields is displayed in the Report Format window. See DB8.4.

FIGURE DB8.4
The Columns Menu

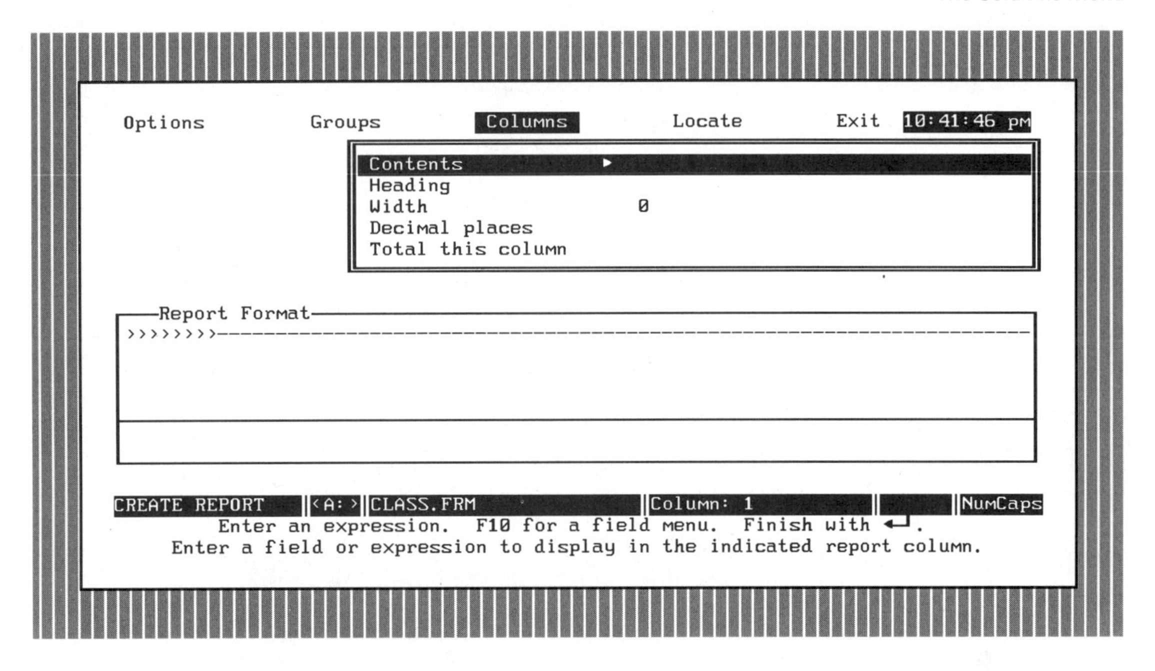

The *Contents* option is used to select the data for a column. Contents must contain a field name that is in the active database.

DO: Highlight *Contents*. Press (↵Enter) to select it.

When you select items in the Columns menu, an arrow appears beside the cursor. (See DB8.4.) You cannot proceed with this option until the arrow appears. Beside the arrow enter the data field wanted as column one of the report. To do this, press (F10) for a field list. (Below the Status Bar is a reminder to press *F10 for a field menu.*)

DO: Press (F10).

When the list of fields appears, select the ST_NAME field as the first column of the report. See DB8.5.

DO: Highlight *ST_NAME*. Press (↵Enter) to select it.

ST_NAME appears as the Contents of Column 1. Look at the Status Bar to see that you are on Column 1.

DO: Press (↵Enter) to complete the contents entry.

FIGURE DB8.5
Field List

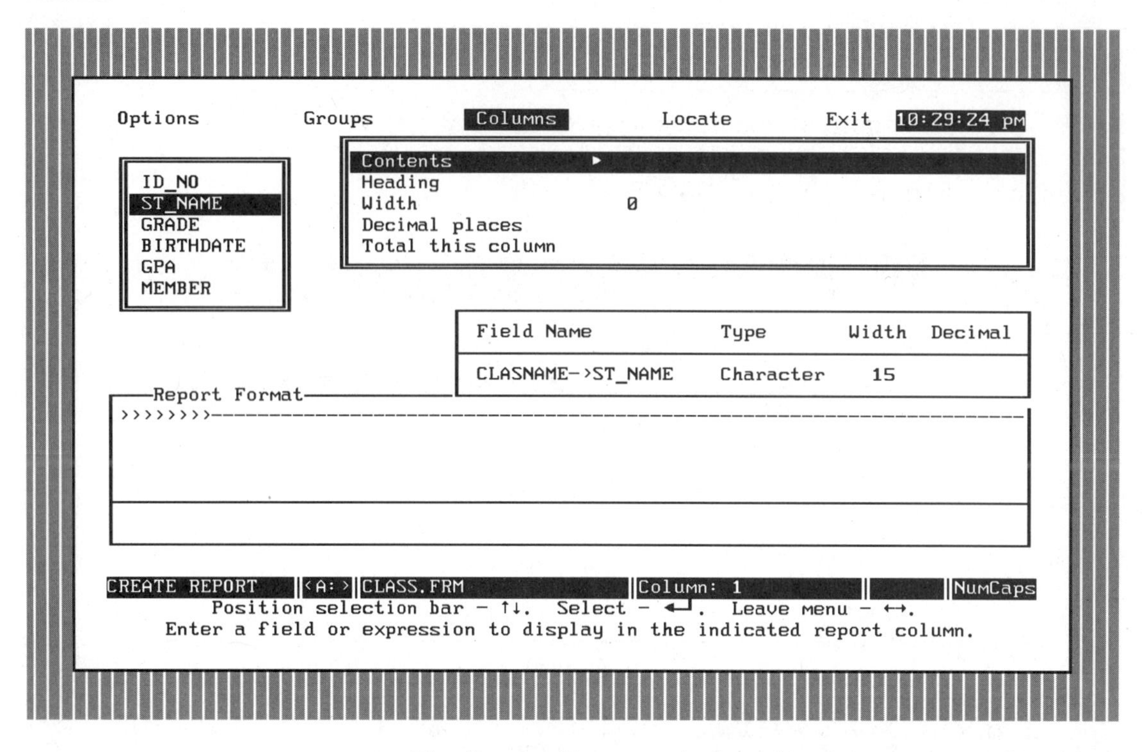

FIGURE DB8.6
Heading Box

The Report Format window displays a string of Xs for Column 1 because it is a character type field. See DB8.6.

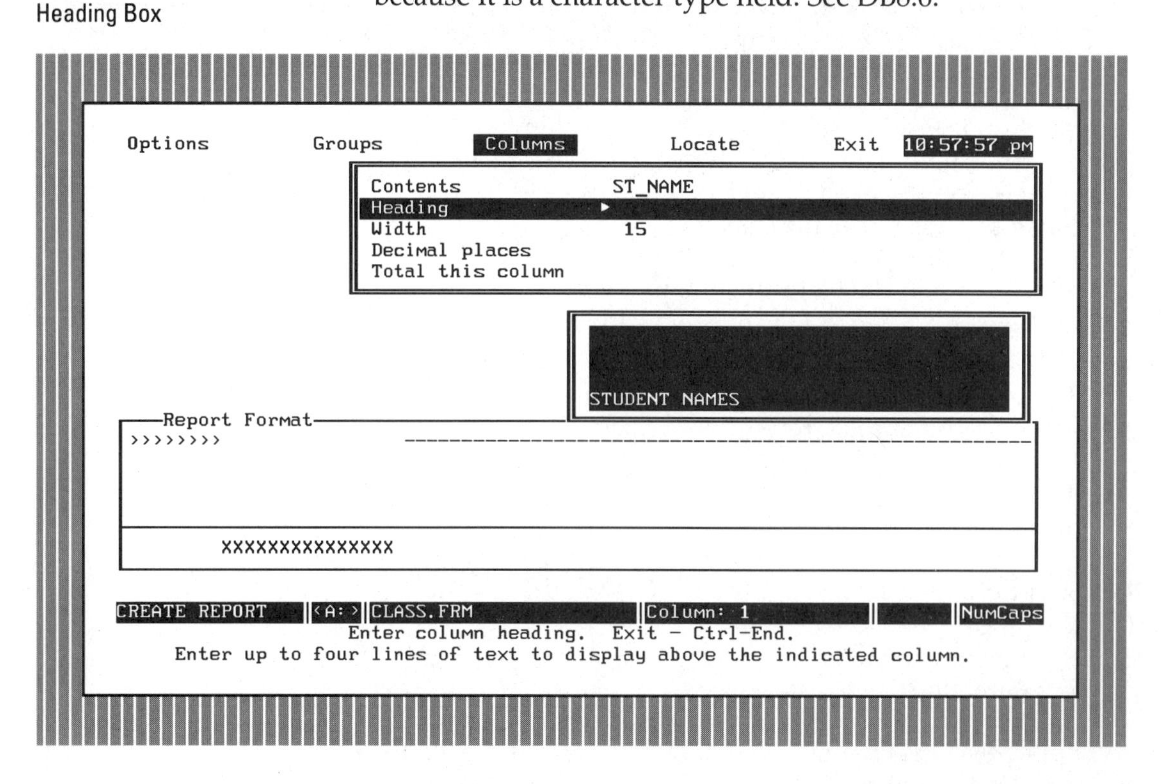

DO: Press ↓ to move to the Heading option. Press ↵Enter to select it.

HEADING. The Heading option enables you to key exactly what you would like for the column heading. The heading does not have to be a field name and can be of almost any length, but a long column heading over a narrow column is usually not desirable.

When you select Heading, a box appears for you to key the column heading. See DB8.6. The box allows a four-line column heading. Press Enter three times to move to the bottom line; otherwise three blank lines will appear below the column heading.

DO: Press (↵Enter) three times to move to the last line in the box.

KEY: STUDENT NAMES

DO: Press (Ctrl)-(End) to exit the heading box.

The three semicolons that appear in front of the heading in the pull-down menu will not print but will suppress the three blank lines.

WIDTH. dBASE will automatically assume the column to be the width of the field you chose for the Contents of the column, unless the column heading is wider. You may change the width if desired.

DO: Leave the width at 15.

Since the column is set for a width of 15, 15 Xs for Column 1 are shown in the Report Format window.

DECIMAL PLACES AND TOTAL THIS COLUMN. These options are colored gray and cannot be selected unless the field is numeric type.

Column 1 is complete. Refer to DB8.1 to see how Column 1 will appear when printed.

ENTER ADDITIONAL COLUMNS. To format additional columns, press Page Down. The Status Bar will display the column number as you continue. You can press (Page Up) to return to previous columns to make changes if necessary.

DO: Press (Page Down) to move to Column 2.

Column 2 will contain data from the GRADE field, which is 2 characters in width and character type. The column heading will be GRADE.

DO: Highlight *Contents* and press (↵Enter) to select it.

DO: Press (F10) to get a field list.

DO: Highlight *GRADE* and press (↵Enter) to select it.

DO: Press (↵Enter) to end the Contents entry.

DO: Press (↓) to move to *Heading*. Press (↵Enter) to select it.

DO: Press (Enter) three times.

KEY: GRADE

DO: Press (Ctrl)-(End) to complete the heading entry.

DO: Leave the width at 5.

Column 2 is complete. It is shown as 2 Xs in the Report Format window.

DO: Press (Page Down) to move to Column 3.

Column 3 will contain data from the ID_NO field, which is 5 characters in width and character type. The column heading will be ID NO.

DO: Select *Contents.*

DO: Press (F10) for a field list. Select *ID-NO*. Press (Enter).

DO: Press (Enter) to complete the Contents entry.

DO: Press (↓) and select *Heading.*

DO: When the heading entry box appears, press (Enter) three times.

KEY: ID NO

DO: Press (Ctrl)-(End) to complete the heading entry.

DO: Leave the width at 5.

Column 4

DO: Press (Page Down) to move to Column 4.

DO: Select *Contents.*

DO: Press (F10) for a field list. Select *BIRTHDATE*. Press (Enter).

DO: Select *Heading.*

KEY: BIRTHDATE at the appropriate place. Press (Ctrl)-(End) when complete.

The width of the field is shown as 9 because the column heading BIRTHDATE has 9 characters; the field itself is only 8 characters in width because it is a date type field. Date fields are shown as *mm/dd/yy* in the Report Format window.

DO: Move to Column 5.

Column 5

DO: Look at Column 5 in DB8.1. Complete the Contents and Heading for Column 5. Remain on Column 5.

NUMERIC FIELD. Because Column 5 is a *numeric* field, the *Decimal places* and *Total this column* are white, and you may choose them. The decimal places should remain at 2, but *Total this column* defaults to *Yes.* There is no purpose in totalling GPA's, so toggle it to *No.*

DO: Press (↓) to move to *Total this column.*

DO: Press (↵Enter) to toggle to *No.*

Numeric fields are shown as 9s with optional decimal places in the Report Format window.

DO: Move to Column 6.

Column 6

DO: Look at Column 6 in DB8.1. Complete the *Contents* and *Heading* options.

Look at the Report Format window above the Status Bar. The logical field appears as .L. Check that all fields look correct. You can press (Page Up) to return to previous columns to make changes if necessary.

You have completed the report form. Exit the Report Form menu screen.

DO: Press (→) to highlight Exit. Press (↵Enter) to select *Save.*

REPORT COMMAND. The Report command can be used to perform the following actions:

Dot Prompt Command	*Produces This Result*
.report form *form name*	displays the entire report
.report form *form name* for *field = value*	displays selected records in the report
.report form *form name* to print	displays the report on the printer
.report form *form name* for *field = value* to print	displays selected records on the printer

PRINT. First, print the entire report. Then, print only selected records.

[.] report form class to print (↵Enter)

[.] report form class for GPA > 3.0 to print (↵Enter)

MODIFY REPORT. If the report is not correct, you can correct it at any time with the Modify Report command. To modify a report, at the dot prompt key the command MODIFY REPORT and press (↵Enter). When you are prompted, key the name of the report to be modified. When the Report Form menu screen appears, choose the appropriate menu and make corrections. When done, choose *Exit* and *Save.* (If you don't want to save corrections, choose *Abandon.*)

This is the end of the instructions for the dBASE III Report Generator.

DO: Exit dBASE or go to the Review Exercise at the end of Section Eight.

THE dBASE IV REPORT WRITER

CREATE REPORT. To create a new report form, first open the database that will be used for the report and then use the Create Report command. You will then be prompted for a name for the report. dBASE IV will add an .FRM extension to the report file name, as well as create special .FRG and .FRO report files. This book will refer only to the .FRM report file.

[.] use clasname (Enter)

[.] create report (Enter)

The message *Enter report file name:* appears. Name the report CLASS; it will be saved as CLASS.FRM, a different file name from CLASS.DBF, the original database file.

KEY: class (Enter)

DO: If the Layout menu is pulled down, press (Esc).

Menus are accessed with (F10) and canceled with (Esc).

The Reports Design screen appears, DB8.7. This screen is divided into *bands* or report sections. A ruler is displayed above the first band.

FIGURE DB8.7
The Reports Design Screen

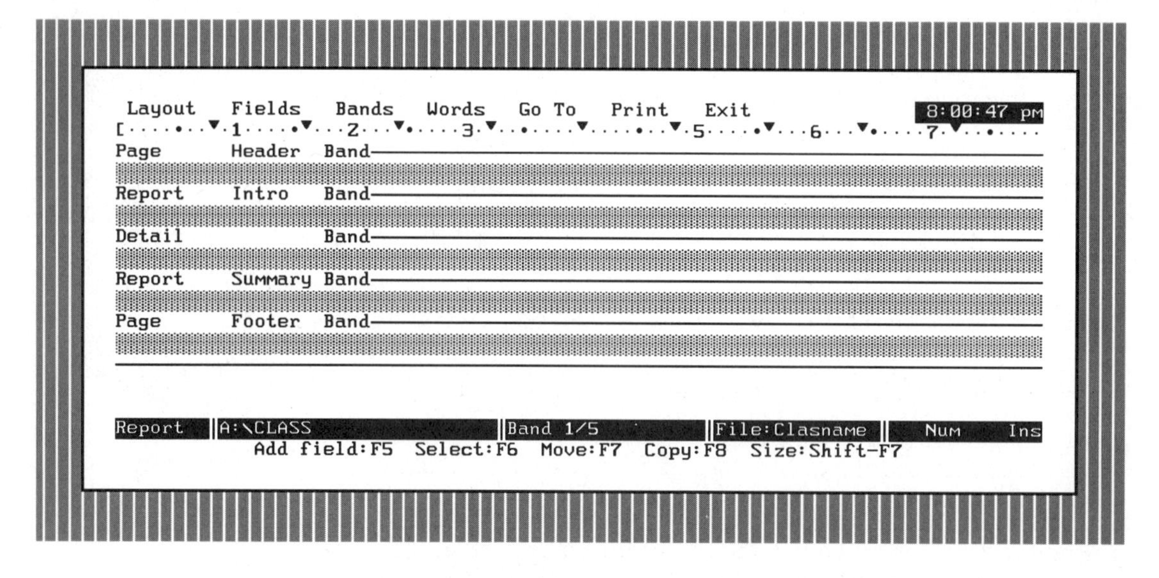

BANDS. Each band includes the name of the band, such as Page Header Band, and below that a line of small blocks that correspond to the positions on the ruler. (The blocks may not be clearly visible in Figure DB8.7 but should be clear on your screen.) The first block is position 0, the next one is .1, then .2, etc. The Status Bar displays the current Line number and Column number; use the Line and Column numbers for correct placement of items. (Use Ctrl-U to insert additional band lines, and Ctrl-Y to delete band lines.)

THE RULER. The ruler, shown in DB8.8, is marked in inches; each dot marks .1 inch. The ruler shows the right margin as [, the left margin as] , and tabs with ▼. The default margins are set at 0 and 254; tabs are set every .8 inches.

FIGURE DB8.8
The Ruler

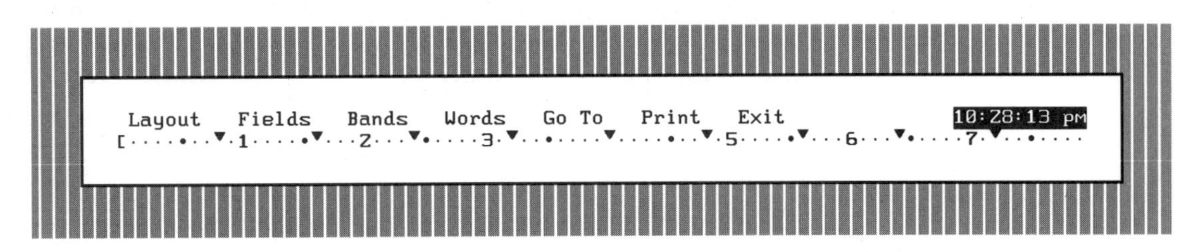

RESET MARGINS.

DO: Press ↓ to place the cursor on the first block in the Page Header Band, Line 0, Column 0, on the Status Line.

DO: Press F10 to activate the menus.

DO: Use → to select *Words.*

DO: Use ↓ to select *Modify Ruler* ↵Enter.

The cursor appears on the ruler line. Set the left margin at 1 inch.

DO: Press → until the cursor is on Position 1. Press [.

Set the right margin at 7 inches.

DO: Press → or Tab until the cursor is on Position 7. Press].

DO: Press Ctrl-End to save the settings.

FIGURE DB8.9
Page Header Band

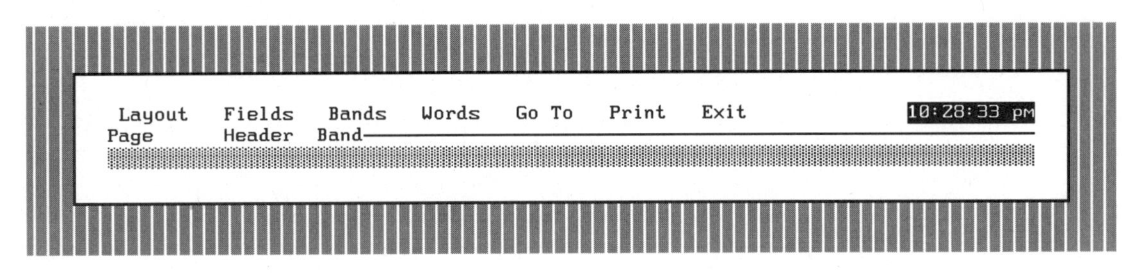

PAGE HEADER BAND. The first band is the Page Header Band, and it prints at the top of every page. See DB8.9. The Page Header Band can contain the page number, date, and column headings.

DO: Press (Enter) to place the cursor on the block at the 1 inch position in the Page Header Band, Line 1, Column 10, on the Status Bar.

KEY: Page No

Below the Status Bar is a list of function keys to use for several features. Included in the list is *Add field: F5.*

DO: Press (F5) for a list of fields.

The picklist shown in DB8.10 appears. The picklist shows four types of entries that you can include in a report, such as Predefined entries (those supplied by dBASE). The page number and date are predefined fields to dBASE. You have keyed the words *Page No;* now, select the page number itself.

DO: Press (→) to move to the Predefined column. Use (↓) to select *Pageno* (Enter)

FIGURE DB8.10
Field Picklist

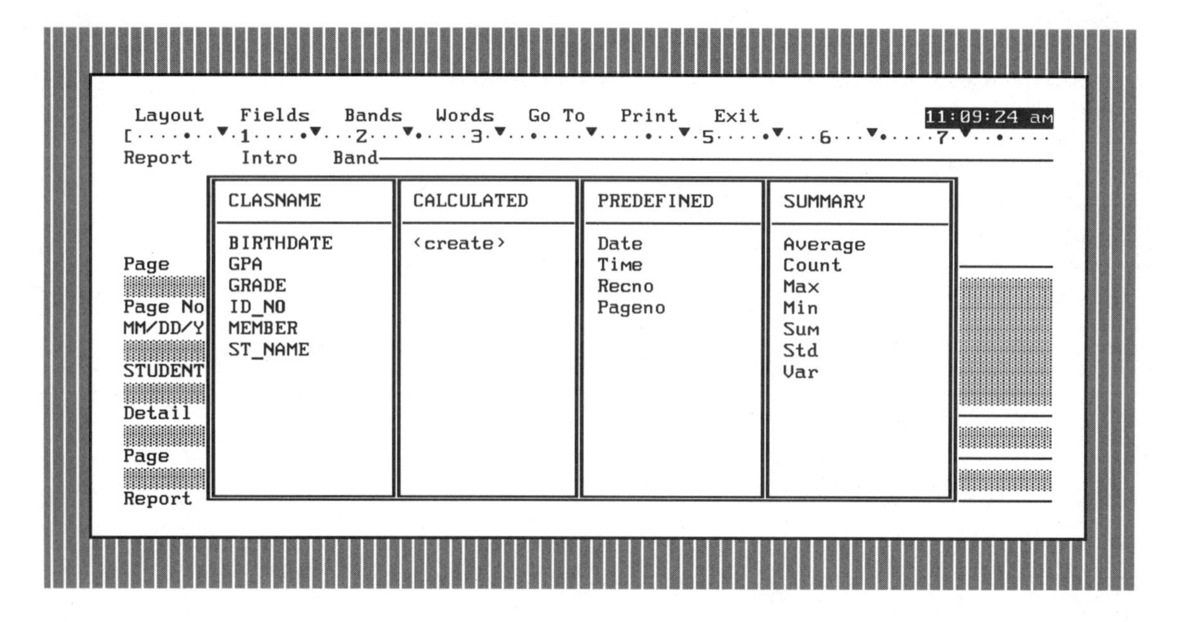

DO: Press (Ctrl)-(End) to accept the predefined field.

DO: Press (Enter) to move the cursor to the next line.

The cursor is now on Line 2, Column 10. Place date information using the format MM/DD/YY.

DO: Press (F5) for a field list.

DO: Press (→) to select *Predefined, Date* (Enter).

DO: Press (Ctrl)-(End) to accept the predefined field.

DO: Press (Enter) two times to leave a blank line.

KEY: STUDENT NAMES

DO: Press (→) to move to Line 4, Column 27.

KEY: GRADE

DO: Press (→) to move to Line 4, Column 33.

KEY: ID NO

DO: Press (→) to move to Line 4, Column 39.

DO: BIRTHDATE

DO: Press (→) to move to Line 4, Column 49.

KEY: GPA

DO: Press (→) to move to Line 4, Column 54.

KEY: CLUB (↵Enter)

The blank line below the column headings will separate the column headings from the data in the columns.

REPORT INTRO BAND. The Report Intro Band, shown in DB8.11, is used to place a title or main heading on the report. The heading BUSINESS CLASS STUDENTS should be centered between the margins.

FIGURE DB8.11
Report Intro Band

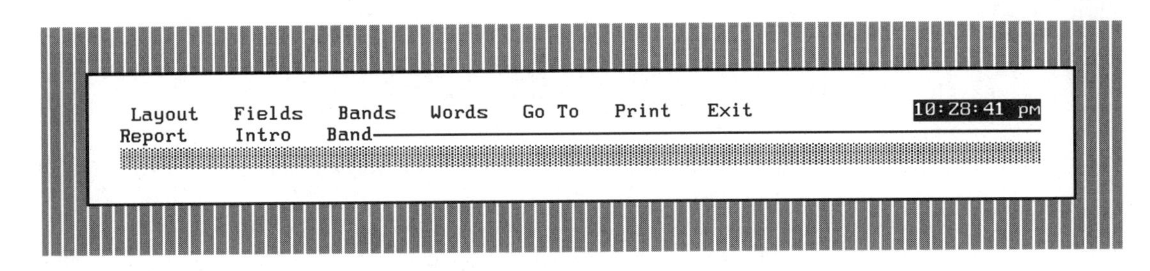

DO: Press (↓) to move the cursor to the first block on the Report Intro Band, Line 0, Column 10.

DO: Press (↵Enter) two times to leave two blank lines.

DO: Press (F10) to access the menus.

DO: Use (→) to select *Words* (if not already selected).

DO: Select *Position* (↵Enter).

DO: Select *Center* (↵Enter).

The cursor moves to the center, Column 40.

DO: Press (← Backspace) once for every two letters in the heading BUSINESS CLASS STUDENTS (11 times).

KEY: BUSINESS CLASS STUDENTS (↵ Enter)

Move the Report Intro Band so it appears before the Page Header Band; otherwise, the column headings will appear before the main heading.

DO: Press (F10) to access the menus.

DO: Select *Bands.*

DO: Select *Page heading in report intro.*

DO: Press (↵ Enter) to toggle *No.*

The Report Intro Band now appears above the Page Header Band.

DETAIL BAND. The detail band, shown in DB8.12, is used to place the fields of data in the report. The detail band shows the columns as *field templates.* A field template displays the width and type of a column. A character field with a width of five, for example, would be displayed with five X's. Character type fields are shown as *Xs,* numeric fields as *9s,* date fields as *MM/DD/YY,* and logical data as *Ys.*

FIGURE DB8.12
Detail Band

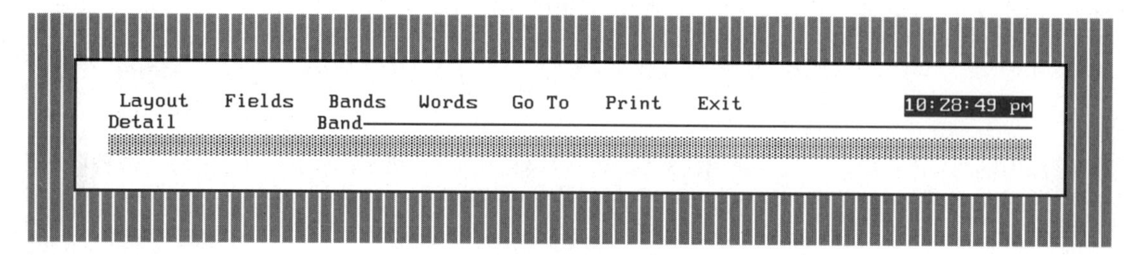

Each field will begin on the same ruler position as its corresponding column heading.

DO: Move the cursor to the block at the 1 inch position on the Detail Band, Line 0, Column 10.

Looking at Figure DB8.1B on page dB63, the first column contains student names, the ST_NAME field. Add the ST_NAME field as the first field in the Detail Band.

DO: Press (F5) to add a field.

The left column of the picklist has the file name CLASNAME at the top, with the field names listed below.

DO: Press (↓) to select ST_NAME (↵ Enter).

A new pop-up menu appears, as shown in DB8.13. The field name, type, and length are displayed. The field template is shown as 15 *Xs,* the width of the character type field. The template can be changed if desired. Leave the default template as shown; place it on the Detail Band.

DO: Press (Ctrl)-(End) to complete the placement of Field 1.

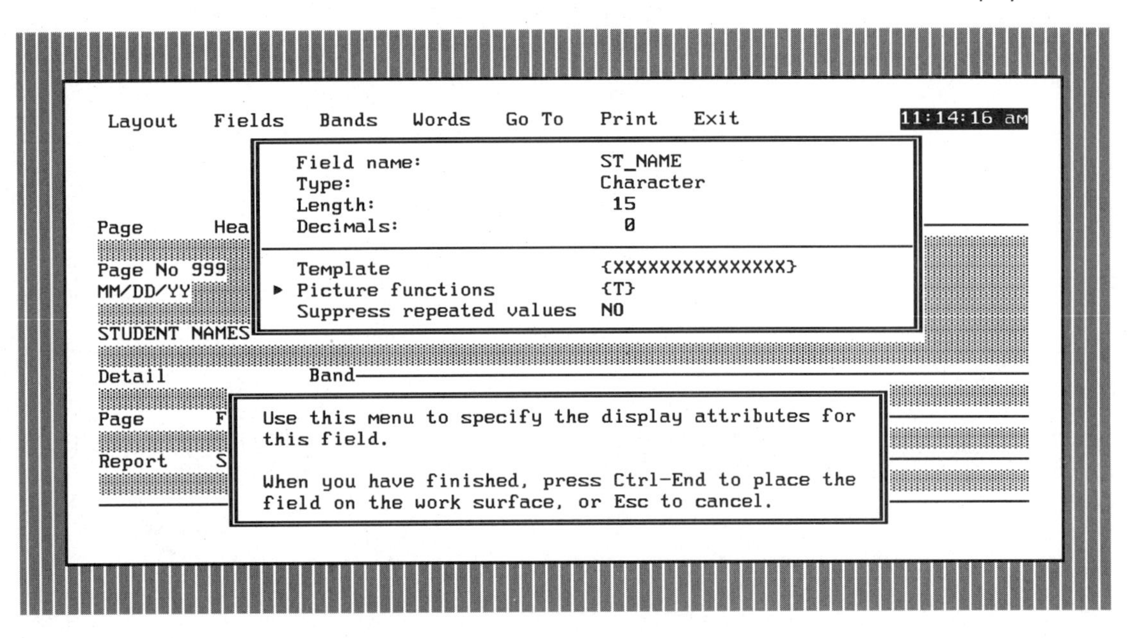

FIGURE DB8.13
Display Attribute

DO: Press (→) to move to Line 0, Column 27.

Design the template for Field 2, GRADE.

DO: Press (F5).

DO: Press (↓) to select GRADE (↵Enter).

Accept the default template, XX.

DO: Press (Ctrl)-(End) to place the field.

DO: Press (→) to move to Line 0, Column 33.

DO: Press (F5).

DO: Select *ID_NO* (↵Enter).

DO: Press (Ctrl)-(End) to place the field.

DO: Press (→) to move the cursor to Line 0, Column 39.

DO: Press (F5).

DO: Select *BIRTHDATE* (↵Enter).

DO: Press (Ctrl)-(End) to place the field on the work surface.

DO: Press → to move the cursor to Line 0, Column 49.

DO: Press F5.

DO: Select *GPA* ↵Enter.

DO: Press Ctrl-End to place the field.

DO: Press → to move to Line 0, Column 54.

DO: Press F5.

DO: Select *MEMBER* ↵Enter.

DO: Press Ctrl-End to place the field.

DO: Compare your bands to DB8.14. Make any corrections that are needed.

FIGURE DB8.14
The Report Design

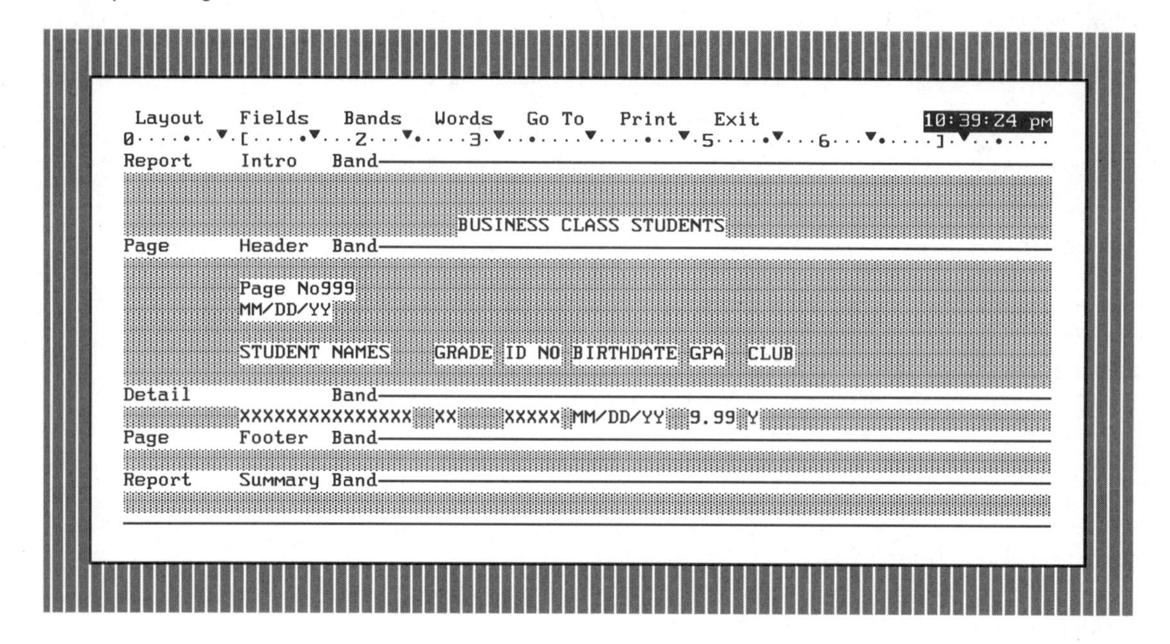

With your cursor still on the *Detail Band*, make the detail lines double spaced.

DO: Press F10 to activate the menus.

DO: Select *Bands.*

DO: Select *Spacing of lines for band.*

DO: Press ↵Enter two times to toggle spacing to *Double.*

DO: Press Esc.

PAGE FOOTER BAND. A page footer will print at the bottom of each page. The page footer may contain any type of data or text. You will not have a page footer in this report.

REPORT SUMMARY BAND. The report summary prints on the last page only, showing totals of numeric fields. You will not have a report summary in this report.

SAVE. Save the report form and exit the report form screen.

DO: Press (F10) to activate the menus.

DO: Press (→) to select *Exit*.

DO: Press (↵Enter) to select *Save changes and exit*.

REPORT COMMAND. The Report command can be used to perform the following actions:

Dot Prompt Command	*Produces This Result*
.report form *form name*	displays the entire report
.report form *form name* for *field* = *value*	displays selected records in the report
.report form *form name* to print	displays the report on the printer
.report form *form name* for *field* = *value* to print	displays selected records on the printer

PRINT THE ENTIRE REPORT.

[.] report form class to printer (↵Enter)

MODIFY REPORT. If the report is not correct, you can correct it with the Modify Report command. Move to the appropriate band and make corrections. When done, choose *Exit* and *Save*. (If you don't want to save corrections, choose *Abandon*.)

PRINT SELECTED RECORDS. Print only the records where GPA is greater than 3.0.

[.] report form class for GPA > 3.0 to print (↵Enter)

DO: Exit dBASE or go on to the Review Exercise.

Create a report form that will produce reports similar to the ones shown below. Use the CLUBNAME file (names arranged in order), and call the report form CLUB. First, print the entire report. Second, print only the records where the ZIP is 24551.

HOMEMAKERS CLUB

Page No 1
MM/DD/YY

NAME	PHONE	ADDRESS	ZIP
Crouch, Debbie	356-7213	1275 Royal Rd	24551
Floyd, Martha	361-3878	2622 West Drake	24551
Foxman, Alison	356-4149	3642 Belinda St	24551
Franklin, Lori	362-7873	7192 Red Brook Rd	24536
Franklin, Terry	362-7873	7192 Red Brook Rd	24536
Lopez, Ruth	354-9935	1990 Bridgeport Ln	24520
McMillan, Sandy	354-6096	8223 Lansing Ln	24536
Renfro, Elaine	361-8523	2836 West Drake	24551
Simpson, Carolyn	354-0821	3800 West Raymond	24520
Taylor, Beth	361-7839	2754 London Rd	24551
Trenton, Marie	361-5002	1771 West Drake	24551
Watkins, Ginger	361-1279	3056 Brookside	24551
Whitaker, Suzanne	356-7790	1618 West Nantucket	24551

HOMEMAKERS CLUB

Page No 1
MM/DD/YY

NAME	PHONE	ADDRESS	ZIP
Crouch, Debbie	356-7213	1275 Royal Rd	24551
Floyd, Martha	361-3878	2622 West Drake	24551
Foxman, Alison	356-4149	3642 Belinda St	24551
Renfro, Elaine	361-8523	2836 West Drake	24551
Taylor, Beth	361-7839	2754 London Rd	24551
Trenton, Marie	361-5002	1771 West Drake	24551
Watkins, Ginger	361-1279	3056 Brookside	24551
Whitaker, Suzanne	356-7790	1618 West Nantucket	24551

ACTIVITY A - PRODUCTS DATABASE

Create a report form that will produce reports similar to the ones shown below. Use the PRODTITL file (titles arranged in order), and call the report PRODUCT. First, print the entire report. Second, print only the records where the price is greater than or equal to 25.00.

Page No 1
MM/DD/YY

NOTEBOOK MUSIC BOOKSTORE
TITLE LISTING

BOOK TITLE	BOOK NO	AUTHOR	PRICE
Art of Concert Lighting	1419B	Gillen S	25.50
Audio Repair	1823C	Trailor D	8.95
Audio Troubleshooting	1819C	Trailor D	10.95
Composing on the Computer	3582D	Klenn B	21.95
Concert Light Shows	1415B	Madden R	31.50
Contour Sound with Multitrack	1340C	Morris G	29.95
Electronic Melody	3341D	Phillips A	20.95
How To of Acoustics	1332C	Vergris L	22.95
Pro Guide to Concert Sound	1397C	Anderson L	21.95
Pro Guide to Live Sound	1395C	Anderson L	8.95
Spectacular Light Effects	1416B	Madden R	27.95
Synthesizer Source Book	3662C	Davis S	20.95
Synthesizing Applications	3663C	Massey L	17.95
TV Sound Techniques	1556B	Akers R	25.95

Page No 1
MM/DD/YY

NOTEBOOK MUSIC BOOKSTORE
TITLE LISTING

BOOK TITLE	BOOK NO	AUTHOR	PRICE
Art of Concert Lighting	1419B	Gillen S	25.50
Concert Light Shows	1415B	Madden R	31.50
Contour Sound with Multitrack	1340C	Morris G	29.95
Spectacular Light Effects	1416B	Madden R	27.95
TV Sound Techniques	1556B	Akers R	25.95

ACTIVITY B - LISTINGS DATABASE

Create a report form that will produce reports similar to the ones shown below; see if you can make the two-column headings, using two band lines. Use the LISPRICE file (arranged in order by price), and call the report LISTINGS. First, print the entire report. Second, print only the records where the age is 10 years or less.

```
Page No 1
MM/DD/YY
                        LISTINGS ARRANGED BY PRICE

   LIST                                          DATE
  PRICE  ADDRESS              AGE   BR    BA     LISTED

 119000  6920 Desoto Ln         3    3    2      09/25/XX
  99900  1654 West Wind Dr      5    3    2      06/04/XX
  97500  5622 Clayton Court    15    3    2      12/01/XX
  85900  1529 Countrywalk      12    3    2      03/04/XX
  79900  621 Adams Court       28    3    2      10/12/XX
  79900  7868 Landon Drive     21    3    2      12/10/XX
  78900  3227 Sheffield         8    3    2      05/06/XX
  63900  6420 W Royal St       28    3    1.5    11/06/XX
  54900  7305 Hunters Run      11    2    1.5    11/04/XX
  45900  6027 Patricia         27    4    1.5    11/14/XX
```

```
Page No 1
MM/DD/YY
                        LISTINGS ARRANGED BY PRICE

   LIST                                          DATE
  PRICE  ADDRESS              AGE   BR    BA     LISTED

 119000  6920 Desoto Ln         3    3    2      09/25/XX
  99900  1654 West Wind Dr      5    3    2      06/04/XX
  78900  3227 Sheffield         8    3    2      05/06/XX
```

UNIT 6

Integration

1 Sharing Files

2 WordPerfect as a Destination File

3 Lotus as a Destination File

4 dBASE as a Destination File

1

SHARING FILES

OBJECTIVES

- Define **stand-alone** and **integrated** software packages.
- Explain why stand-alone packages are popular.
- Recognize Windows as a **consistent user interface.**
- Define **integration** and why it is important.
- Differentiate **source** and **destination** files.

WHY AND WHEN FILES ARE SHARED

This text-workbook has taught the fundamental features of the most widely sold software packages in three application areas: word processing, spreadsheet, and database. These packages, WordPerfect, Lotus 1-2-3, and dBASE, have obtained an enormous customer base because people feel they outperform similar programs. Each of the programs was written by a different software company working independently to write a single effective product. As a result, these **stand-alone software** packages vary in appearance and operation.

Some companies have written software packages that include word processing, spreadsheet, and database in one package called **integrated software**. Integrated software may also include telecommunications and/or graphic programs. These packages are often easier to learn and use because all of their applications have a consistent user interface, that is, they operate similarly. Most people, however, find that integrated software does not have the powerful features available from the best stand-alone packages.

In the future, stand-alone packages will probably look more alike and operate more consistently with a user interface program called Windows. (For more information about Windows, see *Section Two* of the *Using Computers* Unit.)

At the present time, however, several operations are necessary to share files between stand-alone programs. The software companies that write programs like WordPerfect, Lotus, and dBASE have met this need to share data between programs, called **integration**, in various ways. In this unit you will learn how to integrate data to produce complex documents.

SOURCE AND DESTINATION FILES

A **source file**, also called **foreign** or **imported file**, is a file created in another program that will be brought into the current program. The file that receives the source file is the **destination** or **target** file, and the source file must be changed to a form the destination file program can use.

For example, the text of an annual report could be created in WordPerfect. Statistical data and graphs could be created in Lotus 1-2-3 and then retrieved into the report. The Lotus files would be considered source files because they would be imported into WordPerfect. The WordPerfect text receives the source files, so it is considered a destination file.

The original manuscript for this text-workbook was keyed using the WordPerfect program. Almost all illustrations are source files because they were created using other programs. Figure IN1.1 below shows part of a page in the Lotus section of this book. Here a Lotus graph is the source file, with WordPerfect as the destination file.

In this unit you will have the opportunity to use WordPerfect, Lotus, and dBASE as both source and destination files.

FIGURE IN1.1
WordPerfect as Destination File with Lotus as Source File

DO: Begin a new pie graph. This time use the Estimated Service Receipts for the A range. Redo range, X-axis labels, and the Titles. Create a pie chart similar to that shown in LO8.9 (your shading may be different). Explode the August slice.

DO: View your completed graph.

Name the graph and then save the graph.

DO: Name the graph RA6APIE2.

DO: Save the graph as a .PIC or .CGM file called RA6APIE2.

DO: Exit the Graph menu.

DO: Save the worksheet as LORA6AGR.

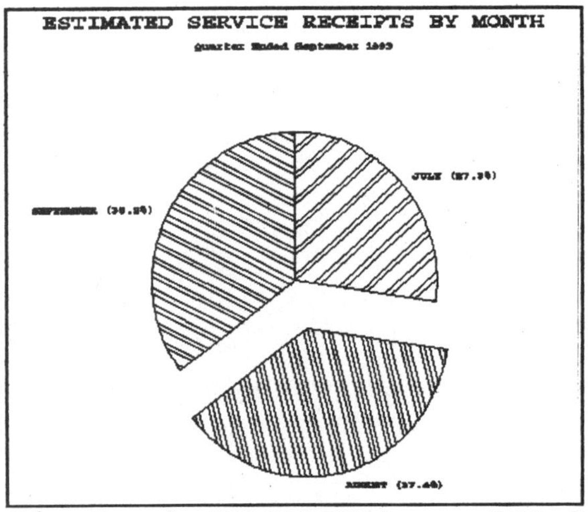

Pie Graph (RA6APIE2) LO8.9

★ **PRINT GRAPHS**

The method of printing graphs varies with the version of Lotus you are using. If you are using

QUICK QUESTIONS

1. What is a stand-alone software package?
2. What is an integrated software package?
3. Why are integrated software packages easy to use?
4. Why do people like stand-alone packages?
5. What is the name of the user interface that will probably make stand-alone packages look more alike and operate more consistently in the future?
6. What word refers to the sharing of data between programs?
7. Why is it necessary to integrate data between stand-alone packages?
8. What is a source file?
9. What are some other names for a source file?
10. What is a destination file?

WORDPERFECT AS A DESTINATION FILE

OBJECTIVES

- **Import a worksheet** as a **Table** or using **Text In/Out.**
- Use **Table Edit** to change an imported worksheet.
- **Import a graph** using a graphic box.
- **Center** and **set the size** of a graph.
- Recognize that the format of a graphic is determined by its **file extension.**
- Define **merge letter, primary file** and **secondary file.**
- Create a **delimited database file.**
- **Convert** a delimited database file to a WordPerfect merge file.
- Place **merge codes** in primary and secondary files.
- **Merge documents.**

FILES TO BE USED

The files used in this section were created and stored in previous units of this book. The files are also stored on the Solution Disk available from the publisher. The files used here are: LOREV7C.WK1 (.WK3), REV7CMBR.PIC (.CGM), CLASS.DBF, LOREV6B.WK1 (.WK3), REV6BLN1.PIC (.CGM), and CLUBMEM.DBF.

LOTUS WORKSHEET AS A SOURCE FILE

Lotus worksheets may be imported directly into WordPerfect if the worksheet was created with a release of Lotus prior to 3.0. For Release 3.0+, see page INT9. When a worksheet is directly imported, it takes the form of a WordPerfect Table, with lines separating the cells. The worksheet may then be manipulated as any WordPerfect table, including removal of lines if desired.

To directly import a worksheet into WordPerfect, retrieve the file as you would any WordPerfect file. Use Retrieve Shift-F10 or List Files F5, followed by the name of the file, at the position you want the source file to appear.

DO: To prepare the destination file, load WordPerfect.

DO: If possible, set the Font for Courier 10 cpi, as the worksheet will have a better appearance. Press Ctrl-F8 F *font* and select Courier 10 cpi or similar font.

KEY: On a clean screen, key the short note shown in Figure IN2.1, keying today's date where indicated.

FIGURE IN2.1
WordPerfect Destination File

```
(Current date)

Dear Examinee

The College Exams taken on Saturday, May 8, 1993, have
been scored. The data below shows the verbal and math
scores of all examinees on May 8, and a graph compares
the verbal and math scores.
```

DO: Press Enter two times to leave a blank line after the text.

DO: Save the file before beginning integration. Press F10.

KEY: SCORES.INT Enter

DO: Use a disk containing the LOREV7C.WK1 (.WK3) worksheet completed in the Lotus section of this book.

DO: Press Shift-F10.

KEY: (include any path needed) LOREV7C.WK1 (.WK3) Enter

The worksheet appears with lines around the cells. Delete the four rows at the top of the worksheet and the names and gender of the examinees. Then remove the lines. Changes will be made using Table Edit. Remember, press Tab to move a cell to the right, and Shift-Tab to move a cell to the left in the table.

Erase the top four rows of the worksheet.

DO: Place your cursor on Cell A1 (see the Status Line).

DO: [A1] Press Alt-F7 for Table Edit.

DO: [A1] Press F12 or Alt-F4 to Block. Use → and ↓ to block Cells A1 through E4.

DO: [E4] Press Delete and then select **R**ows.

Still in Table Edit, erase the Name and Sex columns.

DO: [A1] Press F12 or Alt-F4 to Block. Use ↓ and → to block Cells A1 through B15.

DO: [B15] Press Delete and then select **C**olumns.

Erase all lines.

DO: [A1] Press F12 or Alt-F4 to Block. Use → and ↓ to block Cells A1 through C15.

DO: [C15] Select **L**ines **A**ll **N**one.

Center the table between the left and right margins.

DO: At any position in the table, select **O**ptions, **P**osition of Table, **C**enter. Press F7 to exit Table Options.

DO: Press F7 to exit Table Edit.

Now, view the entire document.

DO: Press Shift-F7 V 3 (Full Page). Then press F7 to leave the View Document screen.

DO: Save the document as SCORES.INT, using F10 (Yes, Replace).

You will now place a graph in the document. When viewing the current document, you can see that there is about a 3-inch area below the worksheet in which the graph can be placed.

LOTUS GRAPH AS A SOURCE FILE

Graphics can only be imported into WordPerfect as the contents of a graphic box. Create a box, and then retrieve the REV7CMBR graphic into the box.

DO: Leave a blank line after the end of the worksheet.

DO: Press Alt-F9 for Graphics.

DO: Select **F**igure **C**reate.

The Figure Definition menu shown in IN2.2 appears.

DO: Use the disk with the Lotus .PIC or .CGM graph files.

DO: Select **F**ilename from the Figure Definition menu.

KEY: (include any path needed) REV7CMBR.PIC (.CGM) ↵Enter

DO: Select **H**orizontal Position, **C**enter.

FIGURE IN2.2
Figure Definition Menu

```
Definition: Figure

     1 - Filename

     2 - Contents              Empty

     3 - Caption

     4 - Anchor Type           Paragraph

     5 - Vertical Position     0"

     6 - Horizontal Position   Right

     7 - Size                  3.25" wide x 3.25" (high)

     8 - Wrap Text Around Box  Yes

     9 - Edit
```

DO: Select **S**ize, **H** for Set **H**eight/Auto Width.

KEY: 2.8 (Enter) for height

DO: Select **E**dit to see the graphic. Press (F7) to exit Edit.

DO: Press (F7) to exit the Figure Definition menu.

View the completed document.

DO: Press (Shift)-(F7), (V), (3). Press (F7) to exit the view.

Make any needed changes and then print the document.

DO: Press (Shift)-(F7) (F).

Check the completed document with IN2.3.

DO: Save the document as SCORES.INT (Yes, Replace), and clear the screen.

OTHER GRAPHIC SOURCE FILES

Many graphic files other than Lotus graphs may be imported into WordPerfect. Another type of graphic file frequently used in WordPerfect documents is **clip art**. Clip art refers to pictures that have been scanned into a computer or drawn on a computer using special graphics programs.

Some clip art may be directly retrieved into WordPerfect graphic boxes, but some will not be accepted in its original format. To determine the format of a graphic image, look at its file extension. WordPerfect has its own graphic format known as .WPG, so any

(Current date)

Dear Examinee

The College Exams taken on Saturday, May 8, 1993, have been scored. The data below shows the verbal and math scores of all examinees on May 8, and a graph compares the verbal and math scores.

SOCSEC NO	VERBAL	MATH
*********	*******	*****
610-29-8631	686	650
278-71-2239	575	516
584-33-4287	575	547
454-88-5471	548	547
438-10-2372	548	547
357-72-5832	548	647
638-24-6684	548	483
411-95-3264	463	407
312-74-7821	463	588
721-56-7328	457	461
574-20-3558	457	483
576-36-1873	457	483
681-63-9005	389	588

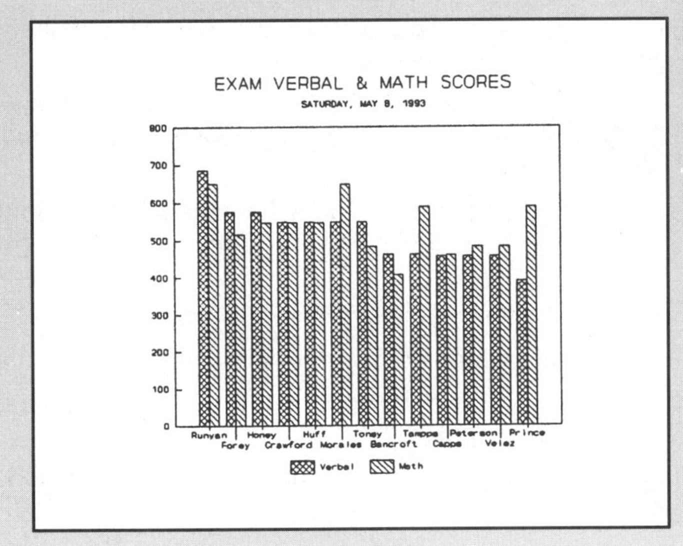

FIGURE IN2.3
Completed SCORES.INT File

graphic with the .WPG file extension can easily be imported. Several .WPG graphic images are included with the WordPerfect program.

Another common graphic format has the .PCX file extension, and it may directly imported into a box. Other graphic formats directly supported by WordPerfect are: .CGM, .DHP, .DXF, .EPS, .GEM, .HPGL, .IMG, .MSP, .PIC, PNTG, PPIC, and TIFF. Graphics files not directly supported may be changed to a compatible format by using a file conversion program.

Lotus Release 3 as a Source File

A Lotus Release 3.0+ worksheet cannot be directly imported as a table. It must either be translated with the Lotus Translate utility to .WK1 format or imported into WordPerfect with the **Text In/Out** command. Text In/Out may be used to import an entire worksheet, or just a portion of one, in any release format. After importing the worksheet, go to page INT7 to import the graph as a source file.

Follow these directions to import a worksheet using the Text In/Out command:

1. Press Ctrl-F5 for Text In/Out.
2. Select **S**preadsheet, **I**mport.
3. Select **F**ilename and then key the name of the worksheet, LOREV7C.WK3. (For a portion of a worksheet, you would select **R**ange and then key the range of cells.)
4. Select **P**erform Import.

QUICK QUESTIONS

1. How is a Lotus worksheet (prior to Release 3.0) retrieved into WordPerfect?
2. What form is taken by a directly imported worksheet?
3. How can the lines be removed from an imported worksheet?
4. How are graphics imported into WordPerfect?
5. Which option on the Figure Definition menu (IN2.2) allows you to select the graphic file to be imported?
6. Which Figure Definition menu option allows you to place the graphic between the left and right margins?
7. Which Figure Definition menu option allows you to set the height and/or width of the graphic image?
8. How can you determine the format of a graphic image?
9. What is the file extension of WordPerfect's graphic clip art images?
10. How can a graphic image not directly supported by WordPerfect be imported?
11. Which WordPerfect feature may be used to import a worksheet created in any version of Lotus 1-2-3?

MERGE DOCUMENTS

While database files can be used to bring data into any type of WordPerfect document, they are frequently used to provide the data for merge letters. **Merge letters** are computerized form letters that are combined, or merged, with personal data to make the letters look personalized.

The body of the form letter is keyed into WordPerfect and saved as a **primary file**. The **primary file** is the basic document, so all formatting should be done in this file. The primary file is saved by itself on disk.

A **secondary file** is the file that contains the data that will be inserted into the letters. The secondary file contains one record for each form letter to be sent. The fields in each record are the data to be placed into a letter. The secondary file is saved by itself on disk.

When both the primary file and the secondary file have been saved, the two files are merged using the **Merge/Sort** command.

You are to prepare short form letters to be given to all students in a class. The purpose of the letter is to inform each student of his or her current GPA.

DBASE AS A SOURCE FILE

First, prepare the secondary file, which is the source file. The records for the secondary file will be imported from the database file called CLASS. The fields to be used for the secondary file are: ID_NO, ST_NAME, GRADE, and GPA.

Integrating a database file with WordPerfect is not as simple as the previous imports. First, the database file must be made into a **delimited file**, one that separates or delimits the fields and records. Second, the delimited file must be **converted** to a secondary merge file using the WordPerfect Convert program, replacing the delimiter characters with merge code delimiters. These two steps are performed outside of the WordPerfect program.

DELIMITING THE DATABASE FILE. Use the dBASE Copy command to place the desired CLASS database fields in the order needed for the secondary file. The Copy command will also save the data fields to a special delimited file called CLASS.SEC.

DO: To prepare the delimited source file, load dBASE and go to the dot prompt.

[.] use class (↵Enter)

[.] copy fields st_name, id_no, grade, gpa to class.sec delimited (↵Enter)

[.] quit (↵Enter) (Quit the dBASE program and remain at or go to the system prompt.)

CONVERSION OF THE DELIMITED FILE. The delimited file can be converted to a WordPerfect secondary merge file called CLASS2.SEC by using a special conversion utility included with the WordPerfect program. To access the conversion program, you must be at the system prompt, not in the WordPerfect program.

DO: Make the current directory the one that contains the delimited file called CLASS.SEC. Remain at the system prompt.

KEY: c:\wp51\convert ↵Enter (specify the path of *your* Convert program)

FIGURE IN2.4
The Convert Menu

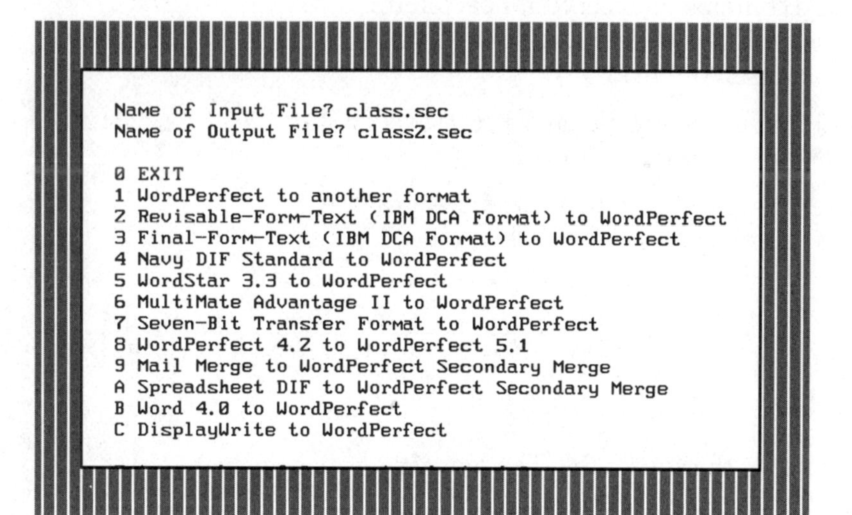

Name of Input File? class.sec
Name of Output File? class2.sec
0 EXIT
1 WordPerfect to another format
2 Revisable-Form-Text (IBM DCA Format) to WordPerfect
3 Final-Form-Text (IBM DCA Format) to WordPerfect
4 Navy DIF Standard to WordPerfect
5 WordStar 3.3 to WordPerfect
6 MultiMate Advantage II to WordPerfect
7 Seven-Bit Transfer Format to WordPerfect
8 WordPerfect 4.2 to WordPerfect 5.1
9 Mail Merge to WordPerfect Secondary Merge
A Spreadsheet DIF to WordPerfect Secondary Merge
B Word 4.0 to WordPerfect
C DisplayWrite to WordPerfect

KEY: class.sec ↵Enter (input file/delimited file)

KEY: class2.sec ↵Enter (output file/file name of new merge file)

The Convert Menu shown in Figure IN2.4 appears.

DO: Select 9 Mail Merge to WordPerfect Secondary Merge.

The file is now in mail merge form with appropriate merge codes, but the convert program must be told that commas separate fields and that Hard Returns and a Line Feed separate records.

The Convert program prompts: *Enter Field delimiter characters or decimal ASCII values enclosed in { }.* You will enter a comma as the field delimiter character.

KEY: , ↵Enter

The next prompt states: *Enter Record delimiter characters or decimal ASCII values enclosed in { }.* The ASCII value for carriage return/line feed as record delimiters is {13}{10}. Press Shift-[and Shift-] to get the braces (curly brackets).

KEY: {13}{10} ↵Enter

The last prompt is: *Enter character to be stripped from file or press Enter if none.* Since dBASE placed quotes between records, they need to be stripped from the file. The ASCII code for quotes is {34}.

KEY: {34} ↵Enter

The file should be converted. To see this file, load the WordPerfect program and then retrieve the converted file, CLASS2.SEC.

DO: Load WordPerfect.

DO: Press Shift-F10.

KEY: class2.sec Enter (include any path needed)

Part of the converted file is shown in IN2.5. The code {END FIELD} appears at the end of each field except the last one in each record. Field #1 is last name and first name; Field #2 is ID Number; Field #3 is grade; and Field #4 is GPA. These field numbers are important. When the primary file is designed, the position for data to be inserted is indicated by a merge code with field number.

The code {END RECORD} signals the end of each record.

The secondary file is already saved on your disk as CLASS2.SEC. Clear the screen to begin the primary file on a blank screen.

DO: F7 N N

FIGURE IN2.5
Part of the Converted File

```
Lacley, Jill{END FIELD}
81775{END FIELD}
12{END FIELD}
3.07{END RECORD}
Troupe, Juan{END FIELD}
83519{END FIELD}
12{END FIELD}
2.61{END RECORD}
Pressman, Bill{END FIELD}
88244{END FIELD}
12{END FIELD}
3.51{END RECORD}
Withers, Erika{END FIELD}
79312{END FIELD}
11{END FIELD}
```

THE PRIMARY FILE. Prepare the primary file, which is the destination file. The primary file is the form letter, with merge codes where the secondary data is to be inserted. Each primary merge code includes the number of the field in the secondary file that will supply the missing data at that position.

Key the form letter shown in IN2.6. To obtain the {FIELD}# code, press Shift-F9 F *ield* and then the number of the field to be placed at that position. (The merge codes cannot be keyed using the keyboard; they must be obtained by using the Merge Code command.) The directions on page INT14 will help you begin the form letter.

FIGURE IN2.6
Primary File

```
STUDENT ID NUMBER: {FIELD}2~
GRADE: {FIELD}3~

(Current Date)

Dear {FIELD}1~
Congratulations! Your GPA for this grading period is
{FIELD}4~!
Sincerely,

George Winger
Principal
```

KEY: STUDENT ID NUMBER: (Space) (Space)

DO: Press (Shift)-(F9) (F) (2) (↵Enter).

KEY: GRADE: (Space) (Space)

DO: Press (Shift)-(F9) (F) (3) (↵Enter) (↵Enter).

DO: Press (↵Enter) three times.

KEY: Today's date

DO: Press (↵Enter) four times.

KEY: Dear (Space)

DO: Press (Shift)-(F9) (F) (1) (↵Enter) (↵Enter) (↵Enter).

DO: Complete the body of the letter on your own, including the Field 4 code shown in Figure IN2.6.

Save the primary file as CLASS.PRI, obtaining a blank screen.

DO: Press (F7) (Y) CLASS.PRI (↵Enter) (N).

MERGE THE PRIMARY AND SECONDARY FILES. Once the primary and secondary files reside on disk, the two can be merged. With a blank screen, use the MERGE command; the merge will take place on the screen, where the merged document can be checked for correctness.

DO: Press (Ctrl)-(F9) and select **M**erge.

KEY: CLASS.PRI (↵Enter) (primary file)

KEY: CLASS2.SEC (↵Enter) (secondary file)

If the merge is not correct, you have made an error in the primary file. To correct an error:

1. Clear the merge from the screen.
2. Retrieve the file in error (CLASS.PRI).
3. Correct the error(s) and save the file, replacing the incorrect one.
4. With a blank screen, use the Merge command again and check the result.

Common errors in the primary file include keying the merge codes instead of using the Merge Codes command, and placing the wrong field number.

Print the merged letters from the screen.

DO: Press (Shift)-(F7) (F).

The merged letters may be saved as a merged file, but this is not necessary. The Merge command can always be used to merge the primary and secondary files if needed in the future.

DO: Clear your screen.

QUICK QUESTIONS

1. What is a merge letter?
2. What is a primary merge file?
3. What is a secondary merge file?
4. List the two steps necessary to import a dBASE file into WordPerfect.
   a)
   b)
5. What code appears at the end of each field in a secondary file?
6. What code appears at the end of each record in a secondary file?
7. Why does each merge code in the primary file have a number?
8. What command is used to obtain the {Field} # codes in a primary file?
9. Is it necessary to save merged letters? Why or why not?

Create the integrated document shown on page INT16. Set the font for Courier 10cpi or a similar font.

1. Key the headings and paragraph for the memo in WordPerfect.
2. Import the LOREV6B.WK1(.WK3) worksheet.
   a. Remove all rows and columns except those shown.
   b. Erase all lines.
   c. Center the table between the left and right margins.
3. Import the REV6BLN1.PIC(.CGM) graph.
   a. Place the graph into a figure box.
   b. Center the box horizontally.
   c. Set the box size for a width of 4 inches and a height of 3 inches.
4. View the document. Make any corrections needed.
5. Print the document. Then save it as INREV2.

TO: Dora Scottman
Advertising Director

FROM: Lee Handel
Finance Director

DATE: (Current Date)

SUBJ: Estimated Receipts for the Third Quarter

Here is the data you requested on estimated receipts for both Sales and Service for the Third Quarter. Let me know if you need additional information.

DESCRIPTION	JULY	AUGUST	SEPTEMBER
RECEIPTS			
SALES	$4,500.00	$6,800.00	$6,800.00
SERVICE	6200.00	8500.00	8000.00
	----------	----------	----------
TOTAL	$10,700.00	$15,300.00	$14,800.00

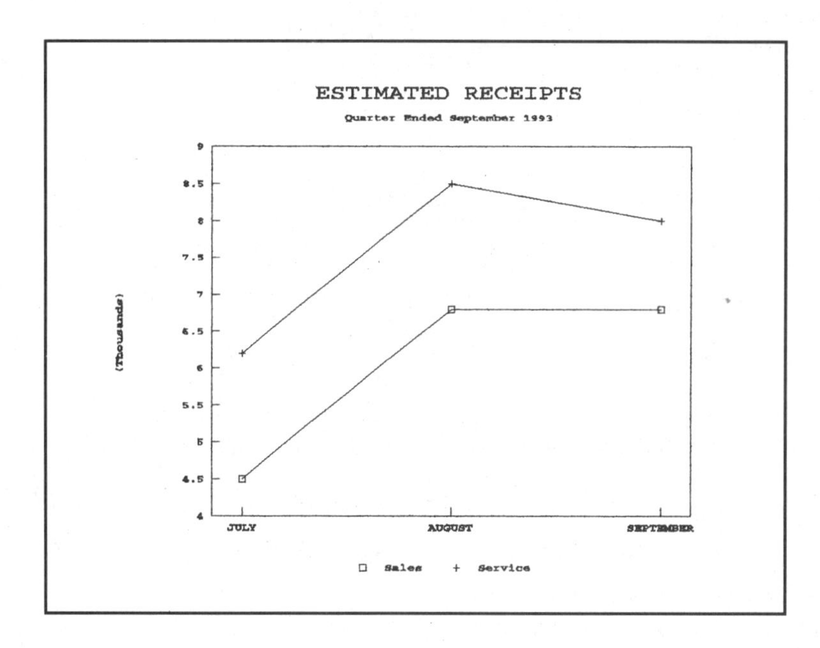

A sample merge letter is shown below. Key the primary file and then use the CLUBMEM database for the secondary file. Merge the files to create 13 letters.

1. Create a delimited file.
   a. When dBASE is loaded, use the CLUBMEM file.
   b. Delimit the file using the following dot prompt command:
      COPY FIELDS NAME, ADDRESS, ZIP TO CLUBMEM.SEC DELIMITED
   c. Quit the dBASE program.
2. Convert the delimited file to a WordPerfect merge file.
   a. Access the WordPerfect conversion program.
   b. Follow the conversion steps given in Section Two, calling the Input File CLUBMEM.SEC and the Output File CLUBMEM2.SEC
3. Load WordPerfect and on a clean screen, key the primary file shown on page INT18. Save the file as CLUBMEM.PRI.
4. Merge the CLUBMEM.PRI primary file and the CLUBMEM2.SEC secondary file. Check for accuracy on screen.
5. Print the first six letters. To do this, press (Shift)-(F7), select (M)ultiple Pages, key (1) (-) (6) (Enter).
6. Save the file as INRA2.

ONE OF THE INRA2 MERGED LETTERS

(Current Date)

Whitaker, Suzanne
1618 West Nantucket
Old Oak, VA 24551

Dear Whitaker, Suzanne:

This is just a reminder about our next meeting. We will meet at 7 p.m. at the Harbor Branch Library. Our guest speaker will be Frances Parke, well-known dietitian and home economist. See you there!

Sincerely,

Martha Floyd
Corresponding Secretary

CLUBMEM.PRI PRIMARY FILE

```
(Current Date)

{FIELD}1
{FIELD}2
Old Oak, VA {FIELD}3

Dear {FIELD}1:

This is just a reminder about our next meeting. We will meet at 7 p.m. at the
Harbor Branch Library. Our guest speaker will be Frances Parke, well-known
dietitian and home economist. See you there!
Sincerely,

Martha Floyd
Corresponding Secretary
```

3

LOTUS AS A DESTINATION FILE

OBJECTIVES

- Change a WordPerfect file to **ASCII format.**
- **Import a text file.**
- **Parse** a text file.
- Save an **extracted file.**
- **Translate** a database file.

FILES TO BE USED

The files used in this section were created and stored in previous units of this book. The files are also stored on the Solution disk available from the publisher. The files used here are: WPRA8TB, PRODTITL.DBF, WPRA9RPB.2, and LISPRICE.DBF.

WORDPERFECT TEXT AS A SOURCE FILE

Text from WordPerfect may often be directly imported into Lotus 1-2-3 using the File Import Text command as long as each line of the text file ends with a carriage return (HRt) and is no longer than 240 characters. However, to avoid possible version problems with direct import, you will: 1) change a WordPerfect text file to ASCII format from within WordPerfect; 2) import the ASCII file to Lotus; and 3) parse the ASCII text. (**ASCII** format uses standard codes to represent characters and symbols, allowing communication between programs.)

The source file will be a small list created in the WordPerfect section of this book, WPRA8TB. Once the file is changed to ASCII format and imported into Lotus, it will have to be parsed to convert lines of data into separate cells.

CHANGE TEXT TO ASCII FORMAT.

DO: Load WordPerfect.

DO: Use the disk with the WPRA8TB file.

DO: Retrieve WPRA8TB.

Use the Text In/Out feature to save the file in ASCII format.

DO: Press Ctrl-F5, Text In/Out.

DO: Press Ⓣ DOS **T**ext, Ⓢ **S**ave.

KEY: WPRA8TB.TXT (↵Enter) (key a path if necessary)

DO: Press (F7) Exit, Ⓝ no do not save, Ⓨ yes to exit WordPerfect.

IMPORT THE TEXT FILE. Import the WPRA8TB.TXT file into Lotus.

DO: Load Lotus 1-2-3.

DO: / **F**ile **I**mport **T**ext

KEY: WPRA8TB.TXT

DO: [A1] Look at the Contents Line.

Although the column headings appear to be in separate cells, a look at the Contents Line shows all headings are one long label at Cell A1. (See the Contents Line of IN3.1.)

FIGURE IN3.1
The Contents Line for Column Headings

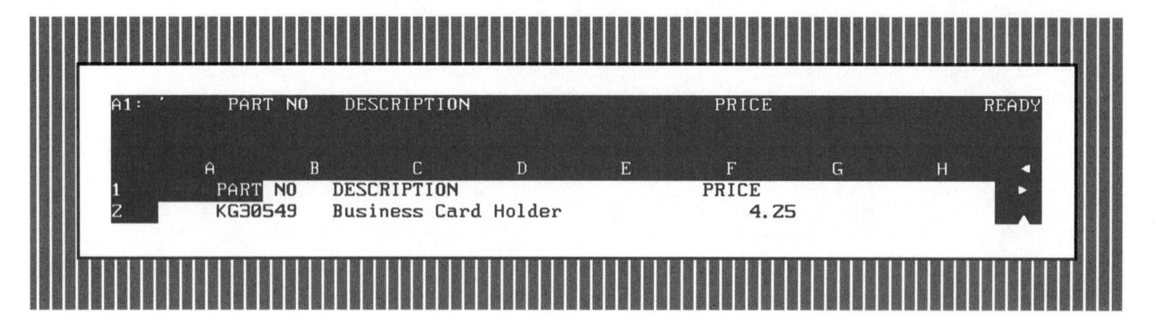

The Import command makes each *line* of text a single *cell* in Lotus.

DO: [A2] Look at the Contents Line.

Again, all data in each *line* has been imported as a single cell of labels. You cannot calculate with the numbers since they have become labels.

CREATE A FORMAT LINE. Use the Data Parse command to separate the headings and data into individual cells. Then numbers can be used for calculating. Begin at the first cell with a long label, Cell A1, the column headings.

DO: [A1] / **D**ata **P**arse **F**ormat-Line **C**reate

DO: Press (F6) to deactivate the dialog box for a simpler screen (if needed).

Lotus inserted a format line in Row 1 that displays parsed column heading words. Figure IN3.2 shows the format line. Look at Row 1 closely. Row 1 shows an L above the first letter of each word in Row 2. There is a > shown above the remaining letters in each word. There is an * above each blank space between words. Lotus will separate words (labels) into cells where there is a blank space.

FIGURE IN3.2
Default Headings Format Line

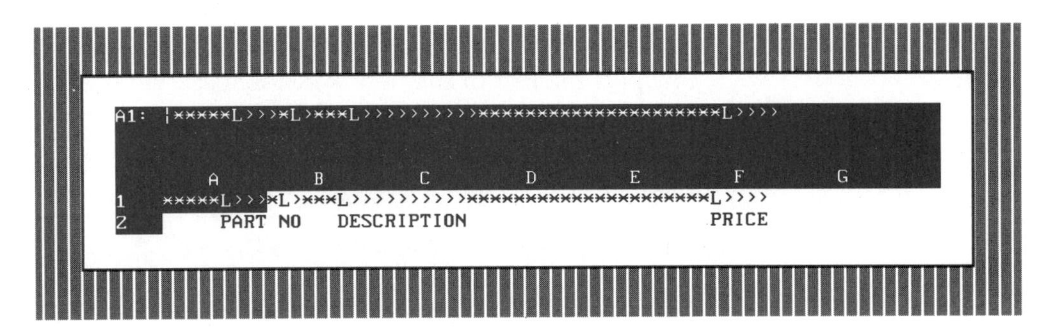

EDIT THE HEADINGS FORMAT LINE. The column heading PART NO will be separated into two cells because of the space between the words. This must be edited.

DO: Select **F**ormat-Line **E**dit.

When editing a format line, you are in overstrike mode, as indicated at the bottom of the screen.

DO: Press (→) to place the cursor on the 10th character in the format line, an * above the space between PART and NO.

KEY: >>

Now the first label is formatted as *****L>>>>>> as shown in IN3.3. This will make PART NO one cell instead of two.

The remainder of the format line looks correct except the last column. The format for the last heading is L>>>>, for a width of five characters. Add three *s to give it a width of eight characters.

FIGURE IN3.3
Edited Heading Format Line

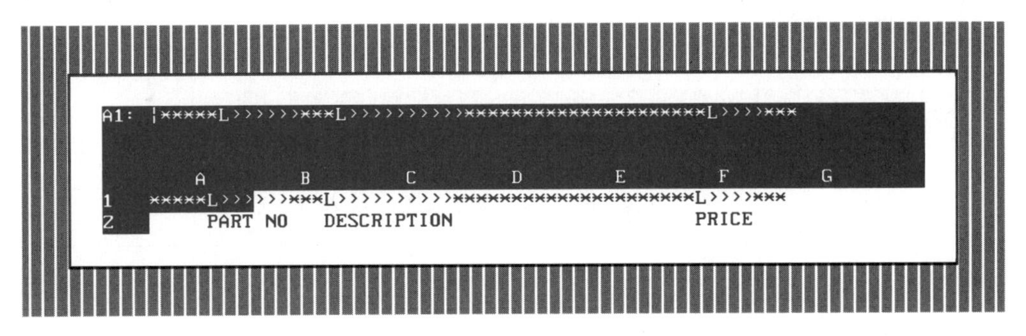

DO: Press (→) to move to the end of the format line.

KEY: ***

The format line is complete. (See IN3.3.) Quit the format edit.

DO: Press (↵Enter).

DO: Select **Q**uit.

CHECK FOR ADDITIONAL FORMAT LINES. It is important to inspect the rest of the new spreadsheet. Will the formatting for the headings be correct for the data? Create a new data format line for the data in the worksheet. Go to where the first row of data is displayed, Cell A3.

DO: [A3] / **D**ata **P**arse **F**ormat-Line **C**reate

DO: Press (F6) to deactivate the dialog box (if needed).

Lotus inserted a new format line at Row 3 with the data parsed into separate cells. Figure IN3.4 shows the default format line.

EDIT THE DATA FORMAT LINE. The data in the Description column has been separated into three separate cells and will have to be edited. The numeric field PRICE does have a V for value, so the data can be calculated, but the width of the field is only five characters indicated by V>>>>, and must be widened.

DO: Select **F**ormat-Line **E**dit.

DO: Press (→) to move to the middle of the Description column, right above the space between *Business* and *Card.*

FIGURE IN3.4
Default Data Format Line

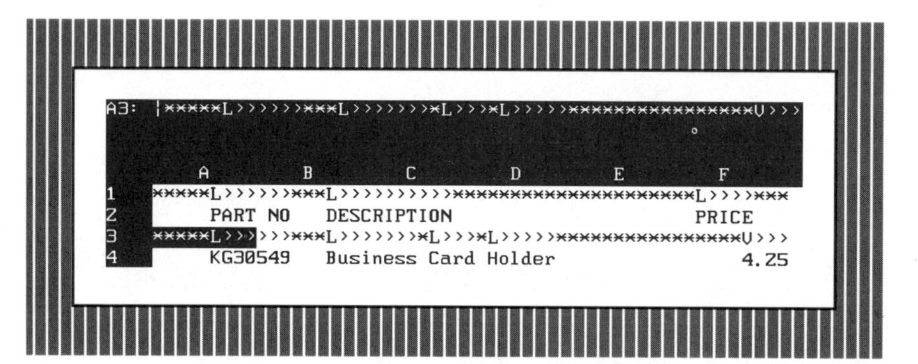

KEY: >>>>>>> (seven times)

Now the data *Business Card Holder* is formatted with an L followed by 19 >s, for a column width of 20 characters. (See IN3.5.)

Change the Price column format to a width of six characters by placing the V that begins the column two spaces to the left of its present position.

DO: Key over the last two *s in the format line and the V with V>>.

Check your format line with IN3.5. Make any needed changes.

DO: Press (↵Enter) and select **Q**uit.

Save the formatted worksheet as a safety precaution.

DO: / **F**ile **S**ave WPRA8TB.WK1 (.WK3)

CREATE THE OUTPUT RANGE. The column to be parsed is Input. The Input-Column is only one column because all the data is still long labels in Column A, from A1 through A12.

FIGURE IN3.5
Edited Data Format Line

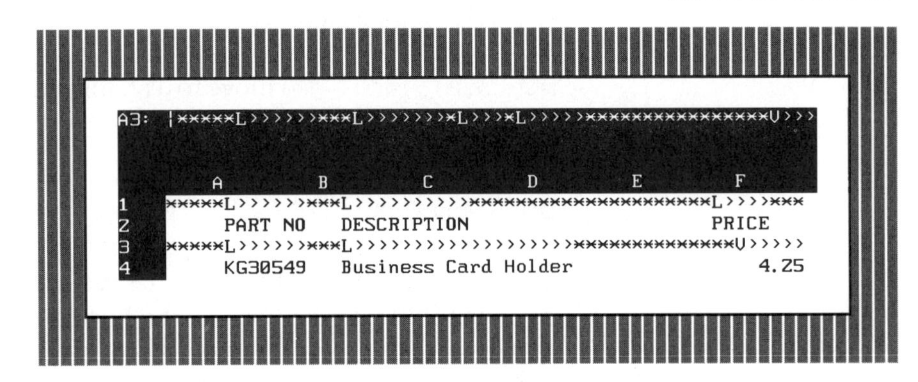

DO: [A1] / **D**ata **P**arse **I**nput-Column

DO: Press ⓘ. Move to A12 (↵Enter).

The Output is the final parsed worksheet. Set the Output Range to be the first cell in a blank range large enough to hold the parsed rows and columns. Begin the new worksheet at Cell H1.

DO: Select **O**utput-Range.

DO: Move to H1.

DO: [H1] Press (↵Enter).

DO: Select **G**o.

VIEW THE PARSED WORKSHEET. Move to Cell H1 and move the cursor around the worksheet to see that the column headings and data are in separate cells. The labels have the label prefix character ' in front of them, and the numbers do not. The Description column must be widened, as parsing ignores blanks within a column. (Instead, additional >s could have been added to widen the Description column before it was parsed.)

COMPLETE THE WORKSHEET.

DO: Anywhere in Column I, select / **W**orksheet **C**olumn **S**et-Width and press (→) until the column is wide enough to display the widest value (↵Enter).

Insert three rows to add headings and then include a total line.

DO: [H1] / **W**orksheet **I**nsert **R**ow (.) and move to H3 (↵Enter).

KEY: [H1] ITEMS REQUESTED FOR CONFERENCE ROOM

DO: Move to H2 and key the current date with the month spelled out.

KEY: [I15] TOTAL

DO: At J15 key an @SUM function that will add all values in Cells J5 through J13.

KEY: [H17] Your name and the filename WPRA8TB.WK1 (.WK3)

PRINT THE WORKSHEET.

DO: [H1] / **P**rint **P**rinter **R**ange (.)

DO: Press (→) and (↓) to move to J17, the end of the range, and press (↵Enter).

DO: Select **A**lign **G**o **P**age.

DO: Select **Q**uit.

SAVE AN EXTRACTED FILE. Save only the final worksheet that is in Cells H1 through J17 using the File Extract command. This command will save parts of a worksheet as individual files; adding the Formulas option will keep the formulas with the worksheet. The newly saved file will be named WPRA8TB.WK1 (WPRA8TB.WK3).

DO: [H1] / **F**ile **X**tract **F**ormulas

KEY: WPRA8TB.WK1 (.WK3)

Set the range for the extracted file.

DO: [H1] Press (.).

DO: Press (→) and (↓) to move to J17, the end of the range, and press (↵Enter).

A file called WPRA8TB.WK1 (.WK3) was saved before, so select Replace to save the current version of the file.

DO: Select **R**eplace (↵Enter).

Retrieve the WPRA8TB worksheet, verifying clearing of the old worksheet.

DO: / **F**ile **R**etrieve

DO: Select WPRA8TB.WK1 (.WK3).

The completed worksheet appears.

DO: Quit Lotus or go on to the next topic.

QUICK QUESTIONS

1. What is the purpose of the Lotus Data Parse command?
2. Which WordPerfect command is used to save a file in ASCII format?
3. What is a format line?

4. What does a space mean to Lotus when it parses a line?
5. What command is used to change a format line?
6. Name two types of changes you may want to make to a format line.
   a)
   b)
7. What is the Output-Range when parsing?
8. What is the purpose of the File Extract command?

DBASE AS A SOURCE FILE

As you have probably discovered, database files and spreadsheets are similar because horizontal rows are records and vertical columns are fields. Because of their similar structures, either can be translated for easy import to the other.

To convert the PRODTITL database file into a Lotus worksheet, use the Lotus Translation Program.

DO: Use the disk with the PRODTITL.DBF file.

DO: Make the Lotus directory the current directory.

KEY: trans (↵Enter) (or select *Translate* from the Lotus Access Menu)

The source program menu similar to IN3.6 appears. Select the source program.

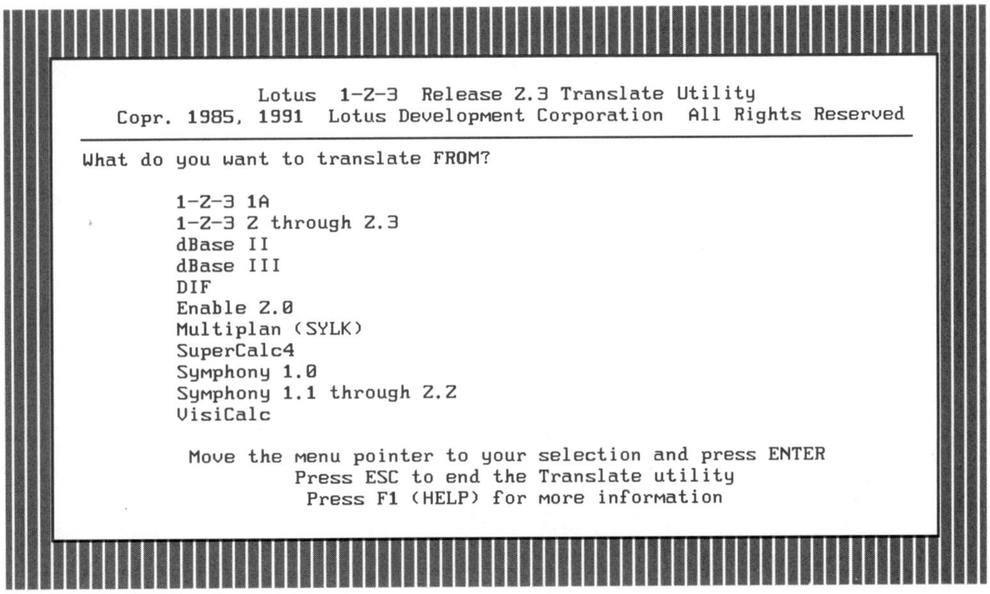

FIGURE IN3.6
The Source Program Menu

```
              Lotus  1-2-3  Release 2.3 Translate Utility
   Copr. 1985, 1991  Lotus Development Corporation  All Rights Reserved

What do you want to translate FROM?

        1-2-3 1A
        1-2-3 2 through 2.3
        dBase II
        dBase III
        DIF
        Enable 2.0
        Multiplan (SYLK)
        SuperCalc4
        Symphony 1.0
        Symphony 1.1 through 2.2
        VisiCalc

         Move the menu pointer to your selection and press ENTER
                  Press ESC to end the Translate utility
                   Press F1 (HELP) for more information
```

FIGURE IN3.7
Destination Program Menu

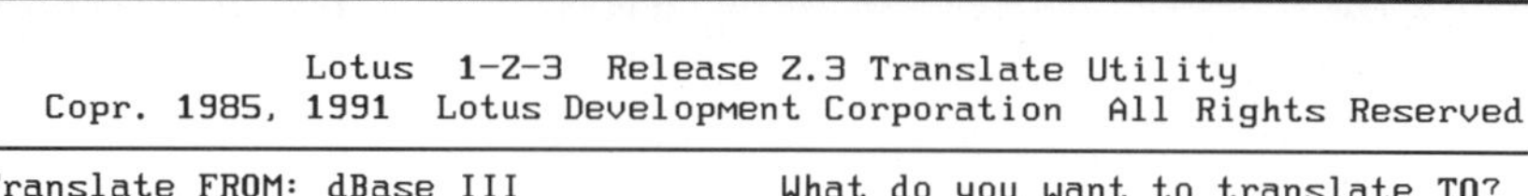
Lotus 1-2-3 Release 2.3 Translate Utility
Copr. 1985, 1991 Lotus Development Corporation All Rights Reserved
Translate FROM: dBase III
What do you want to translate TO?
1-2-3 1A
1-2-3 2 through 2.3
Symphony 1.0
Symphony 1.1 through 2.2
Move the menu pointer to your selection and press ENTER
Press ESC to return to the source product menu
Press F1 (HELP) for more information

DO: Highlight *dBASE III* and press Enter (even if you are using dBASE IV).

In Lotus 2.x, the destination program menu shown in IN3.7 appears. In Lotus 3.x, there is only one destination program, *1-2-3 Release 3*. Select the destination program.

DO: Highlight *1-2-3 2 through 2.x in Lotus 2.x* or *1-2-3 Release 3* in Lotus 3.x. Press Enter.

A list of limitations to translating from dBASE III to 1-2-3 appears. None of the limitations applies to the PRODTITL.DBF file.

DO: Press Esc to continue.

DO: If the file you wish to translate appears on the screen, use ↓ to highlight it and then press Enter. If not, press Esc two times and then key the *path* of the PRODTITL.DBF file Enter.

A list of .DBF files appears. (See IN3.8.) Select PRODTITL.DBF.

DO: Use ↓ to highlight *PRODTITL.DBF* and press Enter.

DO: Press Enter to accept PRODTITL.WK1 (.WK3) as the Target (destination) file.

DO: Highlight *Yes* Enter to proceed with the translation.

DO: Press Esc Esc to exit the Translate utility.

DO: Highlight *Yes* Enter to leave Translate.

Retrieve the source file into the Lotus program.

FIGURE IN3.8
List of .DBF Files

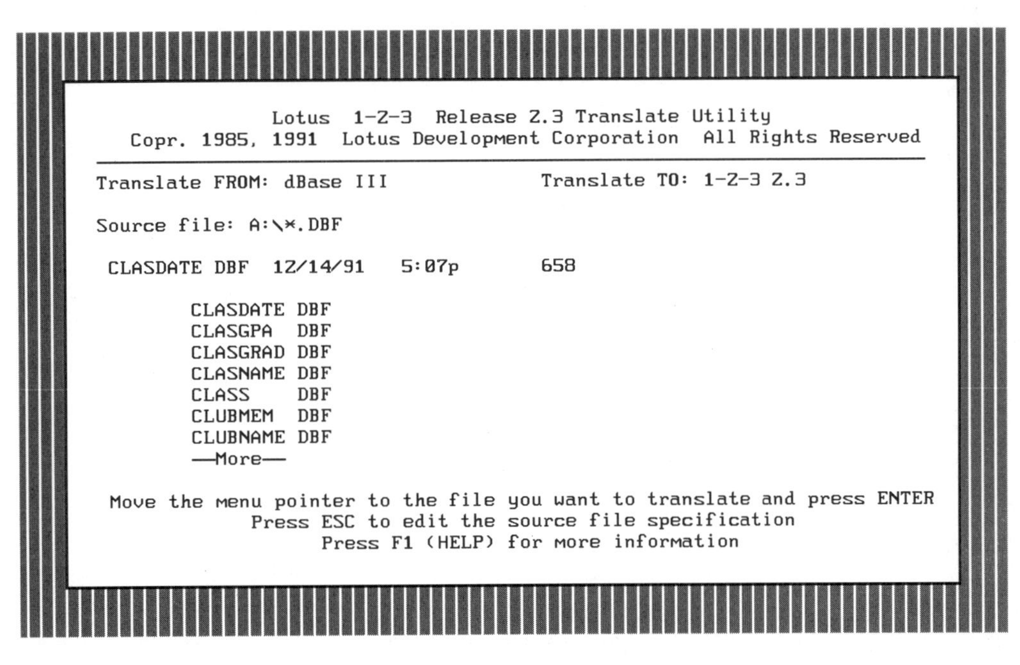

DO: Load Lotus 1-2-3.

DO: / **F**ile **R**etrieve

DO: Select PRODTITL.WK1 (.WK3) (↵Enter).

The imported file appears, IN3.9.

COMPLETE THE WORKSHEET. All data is already in separate cells, but some fields are too narrow. Use the Column Set-Width command to widen columns where needed.

FIGURE IN3.9
The Imported PRODITITL.WK1 File

```
     A                 B                      C         D  E   F   G
1   BOOK_TITLE                               AUTHOR    YRNO_PRICE PB
2   1419BArt of Concert Lighting             Gillen S  9325725.50 0
3   1823CAudio Repair                        Trailor D 87285 8.95 1
4   1819CAudio Troubleshooting               Trailor D 8832510.95 1
5   3582DComposing on the Computer           Klenn B   9122521.95 0
6   1415BConcert Light Shows                 Madden R  9224531.50 0
7   1340CContour Sound with Multitrack       Morris G  8933629.95 0
8   3341DElectronic Melody                   Phillips A9224020.95 0
9   1332CHow To of Acoustics                 Vergris L 9236622.95 0
10  1397CPro Guide to Concert Sound          Anderson L9229921.95 0
11  1395CPro Guide to Live Sound             Anderson L91287 8.95 1
12  1416BSpectacular Light Effects           Madden R  9119127.95 0
13  3622CSynthesizer Source Book             Davis S   8912820.95 0
14  3663CSynthesizing Applications           Massey L  8919917.95 0
15  1556BTV Sound Techniques                 Akers R   9129925.95 0
```

DO: [A1] / **W**orksheet **C**olumn **S**et-Width

DO: Press (→) until Column A is wide enough for the longest data item plus one space (8) (↵Enter).

DO: [C1] Widen the column to leave one space between the longest data item in Column C and the first character in Column D.

DO: Widen Columns D and E.

Notice that the data in the logical field PB (Paperback) has been changed to 0 for False and 1 for True.

Find the average price of the books and key an appropriate label.

DO: [F17] Key an @AVG function to find the average of Cells F2 through F15.

KEY: [D17] AVG PRICE

KEY: [A19] Your name and the filename PRODTITL

PRINT THE WORKSHEET.

DO: [A1] / **P**rint **P**rinter **R**ange (.)

DO: [G18] (↵Enter)

DO: Select **A**lign **G**o **P**age.

DO: Select **Q**uit.

SAVE THE WORKSHEET. Save the worksheet as PRODTITL.WK1 (PRODTITL.WK3), replacing the previous version.

DO: / **F**ile **S**ave

DO: Press (↵Enter) to select PRODTITL.WK1 (PRODTITL.WK3) as the filename.

DO: Select **R**eplace.

DO: Quit Lotus or continue to the Review Exercise.

QUICK QUESTIONS

1. How are database files and spreadsheets similar?
2. What is the purpose of the Lotus Translation Program?
3. What is another name for the Destination file?
4. How is the translated database data arranged when it is retrieved into a blank worksheet?
5. What does the Translation program do to logical fields?

Follow the directions in Section Three to integrate a WordPerfect file into a Lotus worksheet.

1. Load WordPerfect and retrieve the WPRA9RPB.2 file. Use Text In/Out to save it in ASCII format as WPRA9B.TXT.
2. Load Lotus and use File Import Text to retrieve WPRA9B.TXT. Use the Data Parse Format-Line Create and Edit commands to make and edit format lines for each of the three heading lines and the first data line. The correct format lines are shown below in Figure IN3.10.

FIGURE IN3.10

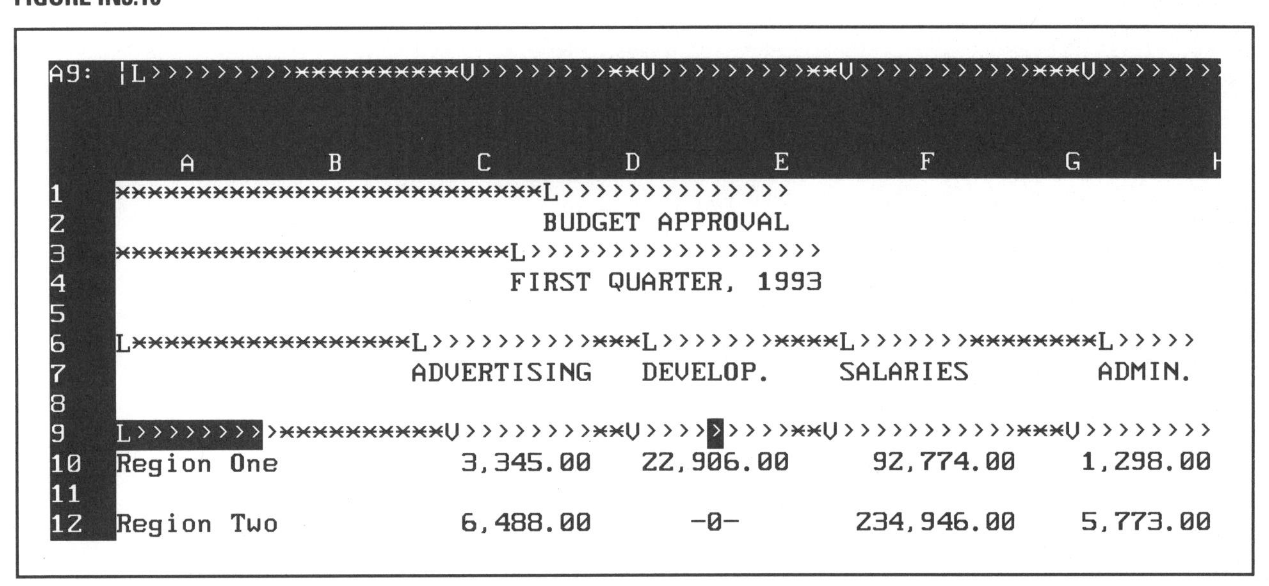

The Input-Column is A1 through A18 (omit the two lines of text in Rows 19 and 20). The Output-Range is I1.

3. Edit the worksheet.
   a. Key the number *0* where the -0- labels are so they can be calculated.
   b. Globally format the figures to be comma (,) format with two decimal places.
   c. Widen necessary cells.
   d. Insert a blank row above the TOTAL line.
   e. At J12 key an @AVG function to obtain the average value in Cells J5 through J8. Copy the function to K12 through M12. Key the label AVERAGE at I12.
   f. At I14 key your name and the filename WPRA9B.WK1 (.WK3).
4. Print the new worksheet only (I1 through M14).
5. Save the Extracted file, I1 through M14, as WPRA9B.WK1 (.WK3).

Follow the directions in Section Three to use the Lotus Translation Program to import the LISPRICE.DBF database file into Lotus. Then follow the directions below.

1. Edit the worksheet.
   a. Delete Columns F through L.
   b. Widen Columns C, D, and E for better appearance.
   c. Insert 2 rows at Row 1. At A1 key BURNES ABODES LISTINGS.
   d. Use an @MIN function at B15 to find the smallest price in Column B. Key the label LOWEST at A15.
   e. Use an @MAX function at B16 to find the largest price in Column B. Key the label HIGHEST at A16.
   f. At A18 key your name and the filename LISPRICE
2. Print the worksheet.
3. Save the worksheet as LISPRICE.WK1 (.WK3).

4

dBASE AS A DESTINATION FILE

OBJECTIVES

- Prepare a document for import to dBASE.
- **Translate** a spreadsheet to database format.

FILES TO BE USED

The files used in this section were created and stored in previous units of this book. The files are also stored on the Solution disk available from the publisher. The files used here are: WPRA8TB.WK1 (.WK3), LOREV7A.WK1 (.WK3), and WPRA9B.WK1 (.WK3). Integration Section Three must be completed before beginning this section.

WORDPERFECT AS A SOURCE FILE

WordPerfect text cannot be directly imported into dBASE. A WordPerfect file must first be altered using the WordPerfect Convert program. The WordPerfect file can either be put in secondary merge form, converted to spreadsheet .DIF and then converted to .WK1 (.WK3) format; or the WordPerfect file can be converted to ASCII format, converted to spreadsheet .WK1 (.WK3), and parsed.

After the former WordPerfect file has become a Lotus worksheet, it can be translated by the Lotus Translation utility to dBASE III format. The dBASE III format can be used by dBASE IV as well.

Because the WordPerfect file must be changed to Lotus format first, this section will consider only conversion of a Lotus file to a dBASE file. You will use the WPRA8TB.WK1 (.WK3) file that you converted from WordPerfect format to Lotus format in Section Three of Integration. You will prepare the worksheet for database compatibility and then use the Lotus Translate program to make the conversion.

LOTUS AS A SOURCE FILE

Before a spreadsheet can be translated to a database file, it must look just like a database. Load Lotus and retrieve the worksheet.

DO: Use the disk with the WPRA8TB.WK1 (.WK3) file.

DO: Load Lotus and retrieve the WPRA8TB.WK1 (.WK3) file.

CRITERIA FOR TRANSLATION. When using the Lotus Translate program to convert a worksheet to a database, certain criteria need to be followed for successful translation. Look at the WPRA8TB worksheet to see that all appropriate criteria are met. Make necessary changes.

1. **The entire file must be a database**. This means that only field names and records can be contained in the worksheet. Delete rows not a part of the database. Delete the three rows above the field name row; and delete the blank, total, and name lines.

   DO: [A1] / **W**orksheet **D**elete **R**ow (.)

   DO: [A3] (↵Enter)

   DO: [A11] / **W**orksheet **D**elete **R**ow (.)

   DO: [A14] (↵Enter)

2. **The first row of the file must consist of field names that begin with a letter**. This is correct.
3. **Field names longer than ten characters will be truncated (cut off)**. The field name DESCRIPTION will be truncated to DESCRIPTIO. Since this is an awkward spelling, change the field name to DESCRIPTN.

   KEY: [B1] DESCRIPTN

4. **The second row must be the first data record, and each cell in that row must contain data or be formatted**. This is correct.
5. **The format found in the first data record is used for the entire database**. Columns A and B contain labels, which are character type in dBASE; and Column C contains numeric data. This is correct.
6. **Columns must be wide enough to display the data or the data will be truncated**. The columns are wide enough that all characters are visible.
7. **Numeric columns should allow for dBASE to add a decimal point and two digits to whole numbers**. Column C, the only numeric one, already has a decimal point and two decimal places.

The worksheet is made up of field names and data records only and is ready for translation to .DBF format. Check IN4.1 for accuracy.

Make a printed copy of the worksheet.

DO: [A1] / **P**rint **P**rinter **R**ange (.)

DO: [C10] (↵Enter)

DO: Select **A**lign **G**o **P**age.

DO: Select **Q**uit.

Save the worksheet with a different name, REQITEMS.WK1 (.WK3), and then exit the program.

DO: / **F**ile **S**ave

KEY: REQITEMS.WK1 (.WK3) (↵Enter)

DO: / **Q**uit **Y**es

TRANSLATE THE WORKSHEET TO .DBF FORMAT. To translate the worksheet, use the Lotus Translation utility.

FIGURE IN4.1
Worksheet Edited to Database Compatibility

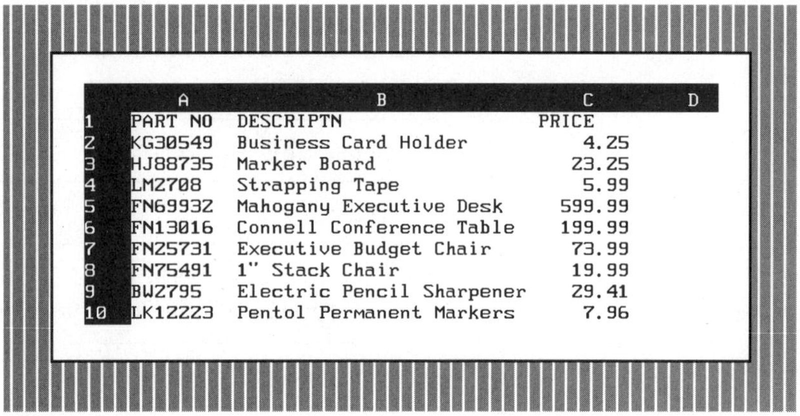

	A	B	C	D
1	PART NO	DESCRIPTN	PRICE	
2	KG30549	Business Card Holder	4.25	
3	HJ88735	Marker Board	23.25	
4	LMZ708	Strapping Tape	5.99	
5	FN69932	Mahogany Executive Desk	599.99	
6	FN13016	Connell Conference Table	199.99	
7	FN25731	Executive Budget Chair	73.99	
8	FN75491	1" Stack Chair	19.99	
9	BW2795	Electric Pencil Sharpener	29.41	
10	LK12223	Pentol Permanent Markers	7.96	

DO: Make the Lotus directory the current directory.

KEY: trans (↵Enter) (or select *Translate* from the Lotus Access menu)

Select the source program.

DO: Highlight *1-2-3 through 2.x* and press (↵Enter).

Select the destination program.

DO: Highlight *dBASE III* and press (↵Enter) (even if you are using dBASE IV).

A screen with the translation criteria is displayed. Since you have already considered the criteria, continue.

DO: Press (Esc).

Select REQITEMS.WK1 (.WK3) as the source file.

DO: Press (Esc) (Esc).

KEY: (The drive letter/directory where REQITEMS.WK1 (.WK3) is located) (:) (↵Enter) (for example, A: (↵Enter) or C:\lotus: (↵Enter))

DO: Select *REQITEMS.WK1* (.WK3) from the list (↵Enter).

DO: Press (↵Enter) again to verify the REQITEMS filename.

DO: Select *Worksheet* (↵Enter).

DO: Select *Yes* (↵Enter) to proceed with the translation.

The translation is complete.

DO: Press (Esc) (Esc).

DO: Select *Yes* (↵Enter) to leave Translate.

USE THE NEW TRANSLATED DATABASE. Load dBASE and retrieve and list the new REQITEMS.DBF database file.

DO: Load dBASE.

[.] use REQITEMS (↵Enter)

[.] list (↵Enter)

Check to see if Fields 1 and 2 (previously Columns A and B) are character type and Field 3 (previously Column C) is numeric.

[.] list structure (↵Enter)

Print the new database and then exit the dBASE program.

[.] list to print (↵Enter)

[.] quit (↵Enter)

QUICK QUESTIONS

1. What two steps are necessary to integrate a WordPerfect file into dBASE?
   a)
   b)
2. What must be done to a WordPerfect file before it can be changed to worksheet .DIF format?
3. What must be done to a spreadsheet before it can be translated to a database?
4. What will happen to field names longer than ten characters and to columns that are not wide enough to display the data when translated to .DBF format?
5. What must be in the first row of the worksheet to be translated?
6. What must be in the second row of the worksheet to be translated?
7. How does the Translate program know which fields in the database should be numeric and which should be character?
8. What criteria must be followed for the width of numeric columns?
9. What dot prompt command would be used in dBASE to retrieve a translated file called NEWFILE.DBF?
10. When listing the structure, compare the type and width of the fields in the database to the fields that were in the worksheet.

1. Use the criteria listed in this section to prepare the LOREV7A.WK1 (.WK3) worksheet, prepared in Lotus Section Seven, for translation to a database file. Call the edited worksheet EXAMSCOR.
2. Use the Lotus Translation program to produce an EXAMSCOR.DBF file.
3. In dBASE, list the structure to print.
4. List to print.

In Integration Section Three Review Exercise, you converted the WPRA9RP.2 file to WPRA9B.WK1 (.WK3).

1. Use the criteria listed in this section to prepare the WPRA9B worksheet for translation to a database file. Don't forget to assign a field name to the data in Column A, such as AREA. Save the edited worksheet as BUDGQTR1.
2. Use the Lotus Translation program to produce a BUDGQTR1.DBF file.
3. In dBASE, list the structure to print.
4. List to print.

APPENDIX

Command Summaries

1 DOS Commands

2 WordPerfect Commands

3 Lotus Commands

4 dBASE Commands

DOS COMMANDS

Cancel a command: (Ctrl)-(Break)

Change directory: CD *directory name* (↵Enter)

Change to root directory: CD\ (↵Enter)

Clear the screen: CLS (↵Enter)

Copy a file: *COPY drive\directory\sending-file* (Space) *drive\directory\receiving-file* (↵Enter)

Date set: DATE (↵Enter)

Delete a file: DEL *file name* (↵Enter)

Directory list with wide display: DIR/W (↵Enter)

Directory list: DIR (↵Enter)

Directory list with pause: DIR/P (↵Enter)

Erase a file: ERASE *file name* (↵Enter)

Format a disk: FORMAT *drive letter*: (↵Enter)

Log drive: key the drive desired followed by a colon and (↵Enter) (ex: A: (↵Enter))

Prompt to display current directory: PROMPT PG (↵Enter)

Prompt to return to original appearance: PROMPT (↵Enter)

Rename a file: RENAME *current-file new-file* (↵Enter)

Time set: TIME (↵Enter)

Version of Dos: VER (↵Enter)

Wildcards: * and ?

2

WORDPERFECT COMMANDS

Block: F12 or Alt-F4 Ⴘ Edit Block

Bold: F6

Cancel: F1

Center: Shift-F6 Ⴘ Layout Align Center

Clear tabs: Ctrl-End

Clear the Screen: F7 N N

Control printer: Shift-F7 C Ⴘ File Print C

Count: Ctrl-F2 C Ⴘ Tools Spell Count

Double indent: Shift-F4 Ⴘ Layout Align Indent

Exit/save: F7 Y filename ↵Enter N or Y

Flush right: Alt-F6

Footer: Shift-F8 P F Ⴘ Layout Page Footer

Hang Indent: F4 Shift-Tab

Hard page break: Ctrl-↵Enter

Header: Shift-F8 P H Ⴘ Layout Page Header

Help: F3 Ⴘ Help

Justification: Shift-F8 L J Ⴘ Layout Justify

Left indent: F4 Ⴘ Layout Align Indent

Line spacing: Shift-F8 L S Ⴘ Layout Line Line Spacing

List files: F5 Ⴘ File List Files

Look: F5 L Ⴘ File List Files L

Lookup: Ctrl-F2 L Ⴘ Tools Spell Look Up

Margin (top/bottom): Shift-F8 P M Ⴘ Layout

Margin release: Shift-Tab Ⴘ Layout Align Margin

Margin (left/right): Shift-F8 L M Ⴘ Layout Line Margin

Move: Ctrl-F4 Ⴘ Edit, Select

Orphan: Shift-F8 L W Ⴘ Layout Line Widow

Outline: Shift-F5 O ⊎ Tools Outline

Page number code: Ctrl-B

Page number: Shift-F8 P N ⊎ Layout Page Page Number

Print: Shift-F7 ⊎ File Print

Rename a file: F5 M ⊎ File List Files M

Resave a File: F7 Y ↵Enter Y N or Y

Restore deleted text: F1 R ⊎ Edit Undelete

Retrieve a File: Shift-F10 ⊎ File Retrieve

Retrieve from List Files: F5 R ⊎ File List Files R

Reveal Codes: F11 or Alt-F3

Save: F10 ⊎ File Save

Search/replace: Alt-F2 F2 F2 ⊎ Search Replace

Search: F2 F2 ⊎ Search Forward

Spell: Ctrl-F2 ⊎ Tools Spell

Suppress: Shift-F8 P U ⊎ Layout Page Suppress

Table: Alt-F7 T C ⊎ Layout Tables Create

Thesaurus: Alt-F1 ⊎ Tools Thesaurus

Underline: F8

View Document: Shift-F7 View ⊎ File Print V

Widow: Shift-F8 L W ⊎ Layout Line Widow

WORDPERFECT CURSOR COMMANDS

Bottom of document: Home Home ↓

Down one screenful: + (on numeric pad)

Down one page: Page Down

Go to specific page: Ctrl-Home *page #*

Left on the typing line: Home Home ←

One word right: Ctrl →

One word left: Ctrl ←

Previous position of cursor: Ctrl-Home Ctrl-Home

Right on the typing line: End

Top of document before all codes: Home Home Home ↑

Top of document: Home Home ↑

Up one page: Page Up

Up one screenful: − (on numeric pad)

LOTUS COMMANDS

Cancel a command: (Esc) or (Ctrl)-(Break)

Column width: / Worksheet Column Set-Width

Column width global: / Worksheet Global Column-Width

Copy: / Copy *what range* (↵Enter) *to range*

Default drive (permanent): / Worksheet Global Default Directory drive/path (↵Enter) Update

Default drive (temporary): / File Directory *drive/path*

Delete column: / Worksheet Delete Column *set range*

Delete row: / Worksheet Delete Row *set range*

Edit a cell: (F2)

Erase a cell: / Range Erase or (Delete)

Erase a range of cells: / Range Erase *set range*

Erase worksheet: / Worksheet Erase (Yes)

Format global: / Worksheet Global Format

Format range: / Range Format

Go to a cell: (F5)

Go to A1: (Home)

Graph commands: / Graph

Graph print (ver 2.x): / Quit Yes (Yes) *PrintGraph program* Image-Select (↵Enter)

Graph print (ver 3.x): / Print Image Current or Named-Graph

Graph name: / Graph Name Create

Graph save as .pic or .cgm file: / Graph Save

Graph use: / Graph Name Use

Graph view: / Graph View

Help: (F1)

Insert column: / Worksheet Insert Column *set range*

Insert row: / Worksheet Insert Row *set range*

Margins: / Print Printer Options Margins

Move: / Move *from range* (Enter) *to range*

Print: / Print Printer Range *set range* (Enter) Align Go (Page) Quit

Print cell formulas: / Print Printer Options Other Cell-Formulas

Quit: / Quit Yes (Yes)

Repeat characters: \ character (Enter)

Retrieve a worksheet: / File Retrieve file name

Save a second time: / File Save (Enter) Replace

Save a worksheet: / File Save *file name*

Sort (ascending): / Data Sort Data-Range *set data range* (Enter) Primary-Key *set sort column* (Enter) A (Enter) Go

Sort (descending): / Data Sort Data-Range *set data range* (Enter) Primary-Key *set sort column* (Enter) D (Enter) Go

Sort reset: / Data Sort Reset

POINTER MOVEMENT

Move to A1: (Home)

Right a screenful: (Tab)

Left a screenful: (Shift)-(Tab)

Down a screenful: (Page Down)

Up a screenful: (Page Up)

Go to a specific cell: (F5)

LABEL PREFIX CHARACTERS

' Aligns at the left of the cell (default)

" Aligns at the right of the cell

^ Aligns at the center of the cell

DBASE COMMANDS

Abbreviation for commands: first 4 letters

Add records: APPEND (↵Enter)

Browse: BROWSE (↵Enter)

Cancel commands or menus: (Esc)

Clear RAM: USE (↵Enter)

Clear screen: CLEAR (↵Enter)

Close database: USE (↵Enter)

Close indexed file: CLOSE INDEX (↵Enter)

Create database structure: CREATE (↵Enter) or CREATE *file name* (↵Enter)

Default drive: SET DEFAULT TO *drive letter* (↵Enter)

Delete: DELETE RECORD *record number* (↵Enter) or (Ctrl)-(U) from Edit or Browse screen

Display database by screenful: DISPLAY ALL (↵Enter)

Display current record: DISPLAY (↵Enter)

Dot prompt: Control Center: (Esc) (Y) or Access Menu: (Esc)

Edit screen: EDIT (↵Enter)

Edit record: EDIT RECORD *record number* (↵Enter) (ex: EDIT RECORD 12 (↵Enter))

File names of indexed files: DIR *.NDX (↵Enter)

File names of databases: DIR (↵Enter) or DIR *.DBF (↵Enter)

File names of all files on disk: DIR *.* (↵Enter)

Find record to be edited: EDIT FOR *field name = value* (↵Enter)

Form feed printer paper: EJECT (↵Enter)

Go to a specific record: *GO record number* (↵Enter)

Help: (F1) or HELP *command* (↵Enter)

Index on multiple fields: INDEX ON *key field+key field* TO *target file name* (↵Enter)

Index on one field (ascending only): INDEX ON *key field* TO *target file name* [↵Enter]

Insert record: INSERT [↵Enter] (adds record after the current record)

List structure (for field names, types, widths): LIST STRUCTURE [↵Enter]

List commands: LIST HISTORY [↵Enter]

List records: LIST [↵Enter]

List records with no record numbers: LIST OFF [↵Enter]

List certain fields: LIST *field name, field name...* [↵Enter]

Modify structure of database: MODIFY STRUCTURE [↵Enter]

Move to another record (edit screen): [Page Up] or [Page Down]

Move within a record (edit screen): [→], [←], [↑], or [↓]

Move pointer to first record: GO TOP [↵Enter]

Move pointer to last record: GO BOTTOM [↵Enter]

Move pointer to record: GO *record number* [↵Enter]

Open database: USE *file name* [↵Enter]

Open indexed file: SET INDEX TO *index file name* [↵Enter]

Print records: LIST TO PRINTER [↵Enter]

Print structure: LIST STRUCTURE TO PRINTER [↵Enter]

Quit dBASE: QUIT [↵Enter]

Recall deleted record: RECALL RECORD *record number* [↵Enter] or [Ctrl]-[U] from Edit or Browse screen

Remove deleted records: PACK [↵Enter]

Save records: [Esc] on a blank record or [Ctrl]-[End] on a filled record

Select a condition: LIST FOR *field name* =,#, >,<,>=,<= *value* [↵Enter] (ex: LIST FOR AREA='317' [↵Enter])

Select conditions: LIST FOR *field name* =,#, >,<,>=,<= *value* .and.,.or.,.not. *field name* =,#, >,<,>=,<= *value* (ex: LIST FOR AREA = '317'.AND. AGE < 30)

Select false logical fields: LIST FOR .NOT. *field name*

Select true logical fields: LIST FOR field name

Select certain dates: LIST FOR *day, month, or year(field name)* =,#, >,<,>=,<= *value* (ex: LIST FOR YEAR(BIRTHDATE)>=1975)

Set controlling index: SET ORDER TO *position of file name in prior multiple SET INDEX TO command* (ex: SET ORDER TO 3)

Sort a file (ascending): SORT ON *key field* TO *target file name*

Sort a file (descending): SORT ON *key field*/D TO *target file name*

Structure a database: CREATE

GLOSSARY

A

Active file: The file currently in RAM

Address: The column letter and row number of a cell on a worksheet or in a WordPerfect Table

Align Character: The character on which WordPerfect will align numbers or text when a decimal tab is encountered

Alphanumeric: Compared to alphabetic and numeric data, alphanumeric data is a combination of numbers, letters, and symbols

Application program: A program that will obtain the desired output for the person using the computer

Arithmetic-Logic Unit (ALU): The part of the system unit that performs calculations and logical operations on data

Ascending order: Arrangement of data from low to high: A - Z and 1 - 9

ASCII: A file format that uses standard codes to represent characters and symbols, allowing communication between programs

ASCII code: A standardized coding system for data representation among computers

Assist menu: The opening pull-down menu screen in dBASE III

Auxiliary storage device: A device, such as a disk drive, that stores programs and information received from RAM

B

Backup: An extra copy of a program or file for emergencies

Bands: The report screen sections in the dBASE IV Report Writer

Bar graph: A Lotus graph that compares values to one another through different sized bars

Binary code: Refers to stored data as a series of only two digits, 0 and 1

Bit pattern: The set of binary digits that represent a particular character

Block: Feature that allows any portion of text to be set off for performance of a particular function, such as moving

Boot up: Load operating system programs that prepare the computer for use

Bulletin board system (BBS): Computer communication center often set up by a computer hobbyist so other hobbyists can send and receive messages and software

Byte: One character stored in a computer or on a disk

C

CD-ROM: See *Compact disk*

Cell: The intersection of a column and a row on a worksheet or in the WordPerfect Table feature

Central processing unit (CPU): Processor inside the computer that follows the instructions of a computer program to change incoming data to the desired output

Character: The smallest size of data, such as the letter "M" or the digit "8"

Character string: A group of characters that will not be used in calculations

Chip: A tiny wafer with electronic circuits used in computerized devices

Click: Press a mouse button

Clip art: Pictures that have been scanned into a computer or drawn on a computer using a special graphics program

Cold boot: Turn on the computer so it can activate DOS

Column: One vertical portion of a spreadsheet, identified by a letter

Column border: A line of letters across the top of a worksheet that identifies each column

Command menu: The Lotus menu bar that is activated by pressing the slash key

Commercial software package: An off-the-shelf program usually written by a software company to meet general needs for that type of program

Communications software: Programs that tell the computer how to use a modem

Compact disk: Also known as CD-ROM and optical disk, it has data stored as microscopic pits and smooth areas that create different reflective properties when read by a laser beam

Computer: An electronic device that is programmed to receive data, change the data to information, present the information, and store the information

Computer program: A series of instructions telling the computer what actions to take

Computer system: The computer and all of its devices

Contents line: The top left corner of the Lotus screen that displays the current cell address and the contents and format of the current cell

Control center: The opening pull-down-menu screen in dBASE IV

Control panel: The three top lines of the Lotus screen that displays the current cell contents and format, the current operating mode, and command options

Controlling index: The indexed file that is in effect in dBASE

CPU: See *Central processing unit*

CRT: Name for the computer screen

Current cell: The cell that the pointer is on in a worksheet

Current directory: The directory on which DOS will perform all commands unless instructed otherwise

Current drive: The drive on which DOS will perform all commands unless directed otherwise

Cursor keys: Keys with arrows on them that move the cursor up, down, left, and right

D

Daisy wheel printer: A printer that prints much like an electronic typewriter; it has a print wheel and can only print text

Data: Raw facts entered into a computer

Database: Application software that enables a person to enter data, arrange it alphabetically or numerically, select only certain pieces of data, and print the data in the desired form; *also:* a collection of related information about a subject organized in a useful manner that provides a foundation for retrieving information and making decisions

Data item: See *Field*

Data range: A series of rows and/or columns to be included in a worksheet operation

Database Management System (DBMS): An application program with data storage, organization, and retrieval capabilities for multiple databases

Database structure: A framework or foundation for storing and accessing data that is designed when you define the fields in the database

DBMS: See *Database Management System*

Decimal Tab: Type of WordPerfect tab that lines up data in each column at the decimal point

Default: An option set in the software package that can usually be reset by the user

Delete key: Erases the character your cursor is on

Delimited file: A database file that has the fields and records separated for import to another program

Descending order: An arrangement of data from high to low: Z - A and 9 - 1

Desktop publishing: Application software that arranges text and graphics to produce flyers, brochures, and newsletters

Destination file: The file that receives the source or foreign file

Directory: A specially named area of a disk set aside to contain its own files and subdirectories; *also:* a record of each file's position on a disk

Disk operating system: System programs that manage the computer hardware and the operation of application programs

Diskette: Small plastic computer storage disk

Display: See *screen*

Documentation: Materials that accompany a program, including a user's manual, instructions, and reference information

DOS: Abbreviation for disk operating system

Dot matrix printer: A printer that prints text and graphics as a series of dots

Dot prompt: The line preceded by a period where dBASE commands are keyed

Double click: Press a mouse button two times in quick succession

Double Indent: A word processing feature that indents all lines of a paragraph from both the left and right margins

Double-sided diskette: A diskette that can have data recorded on both the top and bottom surfaces

Drag: Press and hold a mouse button while moving the mouse

Drive specification: The current drive or any drive specified in a command

E

Edit: Make changes to a document

Editing screen: The WordPerfect typing screen

Electronic mail (E-Mail): The sending of text to another computer which stores the message until the user reads his or her on-computer mail

Extension: Three characters preceded by a period that may be added to a file name

F

Field: A related set of words; a data item

Field definition: The name, type, width, and optional decimal places for a field in a database

File: A document created on a computer and stored on disk; *also:* All related records about a specific group of people or events

File name: A name of up to eight characters given to a file

File server: A computer that allows LAN users to share data and programs. It usually has a large hard disk

Fixed disk: See *Hard disk*

Floppy: A diskette

Floppy Disk Drive: A device that records data to and reads data from diskettes

Font: Variable size and design of printed characters

Footer: Text that appears consistently at the bottom of multiple pages

Foreign files: Files created in a program other than the current one

Format: Prepare a diskette to be used by a particular type of disk drive; also erases all files from a disk

Formula: A calculation of numbers, other formulas, or the contents of cells in Lotus

Full-feature program: An expensive application program that can perform numerous operations and usually takes hours to learn

Function: Shortcuts for complex formulas and other types of operations in Lotus, preceded by the @ sign

Function keys: Special keys used to perform operations in computer programs

G

Global command: A command that affects the entire document

Graphic: Pictorial illustration of data, as a spreadsheet graphic

GUI: Abbreviation for graphical user interface, a screen display that shows pictures of user options

H

Hard copy: The display of computer information on paper

Hard disk: A storage medium that is made of one or more metal platters that pack data very tightly

Hard disk drive: A storage device that is permanently located inside the system unit of some computers

Hard drive: See *Hard disk drive*

Hard page break: A new text page forced by the user at a desired location

Hardware: Computers and their related devices

Headers: Text that appears consistently at the top of multiple pages

High-density: Refers to a diskette that packs more data per inch than double-density diskettes

History: A list of the dot prompt commands keyed in dBASE

Home position: Cell A1 in Lotus

I

Icon panel: A Lotus screen panel containing pictures of scroll arrows and a question mark for mouse users

Impact Printer: A printer that strikes the paper with an inked ribbon

Import: Retrieve a file created in another program

Imported file: See *Source file*

Index: dBASE command to make the original database file appear sorted by creating a record-sequencing file

Information: The result of data processing

Ink jet printer: A printer with a nozzle that sprays ink onto paper in the shape of a character or design

Input: Send data to RAM for processing

Input Hardware: A device that sends data to RAM

Installation: The process of copying a program to a hard drive or file server that includes identifying the hardware the program will use

Integrated software: Software packages that usually include word processing, spreadsheet, and database functions in one large package

Integration: Sharing data between programs

Interactive videodisc: Read-only disk designed for the storage of images that can be input to RAM from a videodisc player

J

Justification: Alignment of a group of text lines in relation to the left and right margins

Justification, Center: Centers text between the margins

Justification, Full: Aligns text at both right and left margins

Justification, Left: Aligns text at the left margin only

Justification, Right: Aligns text at the right margin only

K

Key: A specific field or fields on which records are arranged or selected

Kilobyte (K): Approximately one thousand bytes

L

Label: A text entry in Lotus

Label prefix character: A character in Lotus that determines where a label will be aligned in a cell

LAN: See *Local Area Network*

Laptop: A microcomputer small enough to be portable

Laser printer: A printer that uses a version of the reproduction technology of copy machines to fuse text and graphic images to the page

Lease agreement: A contract that comes with many software packages that states the rights purchasers have when they buy the package

Left indent: WordPerfect feature that indents all lines of a paragraph from the left margin

Left tabs: Type of WordPerfect tab that aligns data on the left in each column

Legend: A caption that identifies each data range of a Lotus graph

Limited-feature program: An inexpensive application program that is easy to use and performs only a few operations

Line graph: A Lotus graph that uses data plotted on lines to show change over time

Local Area Network (LAN): Computers linked within a limited area so users can share data and programs, exchange information, andshare hardware such as printers and a massive hard disk

Log drive: Change to another drive by keying the letter of the drive followed by a colon

Logical operation: An operation by which the computer determines if a character is greater than, less than, and/or equal to another character

Logical operator: A special word used in dBASE to link multiple fields for record selection; the logical operators are .AND., .OR., and .NOT

M

Magnetic spots: Method of storing data on the tracks of a disk

Main memory: The storage unit inside a computer, called RAM in microcomputers

Margin Release: Feature that permits keying or moving text into the left margin

Main frame: A large computer system, usually made up of one or more large processors, many terminals, and several large storage devices

Megabyte (MB): Approximately one million bytes

Menu: A list of options or commands on screen

Menu bar: A pull-down listing of commands in WordPerfect and other programs

Merge letter: A personalized letter produced through an application program that will alternate the body of the letter with the personal data for each receiver of the letter

Microcomputer: A computer that is small enough to sit on a desktop and is controlled by a microprocessor; also called a PC (personal computer)

Microprocessor: The CPU in a microcomputer

Minicomputer: Mid-sized computer system with a powerful processor (CPU) that is traditionally accessed through keyboard-and-screen non-processing terminals that look like computers

Mode indicator: The upper right corner of the Lotus screen that displays the current operating mode

Modem: A device used to send data from one computer to another

Modify a database: Change the structure of a database by adding or deleting fields or changing a field name, type, or size

Monitor: A name for the computer screen

Monochrome screen: A display screen in a single color against a contrasting background

Motherboard: The main circuit board of a microcomputer which contains RAM, ROM, and the microprocessor

Mouse: An input device that is used to select options from a program menu or to draw on the computer screen

MS-DOS: The operating system software for IBM and compatible computers

N

Needs analysis: The process of analyzing present and future data needs before creating a database

Number: A numeric value, it may contain only digits and numeric symbols

Numeric operators: The basic operators are + for addition, – for subtraction, * for multiplication, and / for division

Numeric symbol: A symbol allowed in a numeric field: a plus sign, minus sign, decimal point, or parenthesis

O

On-line data service: A company that provides computer services to subscribers

Open a database: Retrieve a database file

Operating system program: See *Disk operating system*

Optical Disk: See *Compact disk*

Orphan: The last line of a paragraph that is alone at the top of a page

Output hardware: A device that receives information from RAM and usually presents it in a readable form, either on a computer screen or on paper

P

Pack: dBASE command to remove records marked for deletion

Parameters: Qualifiers that make a DOS command more precise

Parity bit: The bit the computer uses for data accuracy

Parse: A command to separate an imported file's headings and data into individual cells in Lotus

Path: Drive and/or directory where a file is stored or is to be stored

PC (personal computer): See *Microcomputer*

Peripheral device: Any computer device except the CPU and main memory

Picklist: A menu that shows the types of entries that can be included in a dBASE IV report, such as field names and predefined fields

Pie graph: A circular Lotus graph divided to show portions of a whole

Point to cells: Move the pointer to the cells involved in building formulas or functions in Lotus

Pointer: The name for Lotus 1-2-3's rectangular cursor; *also:* the name for the mouse cursor in any program

Port: A socket in the system unit for attachment of a peripheral device

Primary file: The basic document that will be used in a merge operation

Primary sort key: The first field that will be arranged in order when sorting in Lotus

Print: Place a computer document on paper

PrintGraph: The Lotus utility program that enables printing of graphs (prior to Lotus 3.0)

Printout: The display of computer information on paper

Process: Change input data to output information

Process hardware: A device which changes data into information

Processor: See *Central processing unit*

Program: See *Computer program*

Programmer: A person who writes computer programs

Prompt: See *System prompt*

Proportional typefaces: Characters designed to vary in width so that wide letters like *M* are given more printing space than narrow letters like *I* for a more attractive appearance

Public domain software: Software that has been written by professional or amateur programmers who want to share their products with others at no charge

Pull-down menu: On-screen list of options or commands that can be activated when needed

R

RAM: See *Random access memory*

Random access memory: Internal microcomputer storage for the active program and data

Range: A rectangular group of adjacent cells in Lotus

Read-only storage device: A special device that uses disks purchased with data already on them; the user cannot record on them (compact disk, videodisc)

Receiving file: The new file that will exist when a file copy command is completed

Record: All related fields about an individual or an event

Record pointer: The marker used by dBASE to keep track of the current record

Recording density: Refers to how much data can be stored on a diskette

Relational operator: An operator such as > < = # that determines the type of data comparison to be performed

Release number: The number that indicates minor changes to a software package

Repeat characters: A string of characters used to underline or visually separate parts of a worksheet

Report Generator: The dBASE III program that provides user-defined report forms

Report Writer: The dBASE IV program that provides user-defined report forms

Resolution: The sharpness of image on a computer screen

Restore: Recover deleted text

ROM: Read-only memory inside the computer that contains special programs that power up the computer

Root directory: The main directory on a disk

Row: One horizontal portion of a spreadsheet, identified by a number

Row border: A line of numbers going down the left edge of a worksheet that identifies each row

S

Scale indicator: Shows the units, such as thousands or millions, of the Y Scale on a graph

Scanner: Hardware that can "read" data and send it to RAM, eliminating the need for human entry of data

Screen: A device that displays data entered from the keyboard as well as instructions and information from the computer program

Scrolling: Screen movement to allow viewing a part of the document that is not visible

Secondary file: The file that contains the variable data that will be inserted into a merge document

Secondary sort key: The field that will be arranged in order within the primary sort field

Sector: The pie-shaped storage unit of a disk

Select records: To view only the records that meet a certain condition

Sending file: The file to be copied during a file copy command

Shareware programs: Programs available for a small registration fee that are often written by a computer hobbyist who has developed a useful program to share with others

Shell: A user-friendly interface that presents an on-screen list of commands

Shutter: Metal slide on a 3 ½-inch diskette that is opened by the disk drive so it can access the recording surface

Soft page break: Where WordPerfect decides one complete page should end and a new page begin through use of a line count

Software: A series of instructions telling the computer what actions to take

Sort: To arrange records into alphabetic, numeric, or date order

Source file: A file created in another program that will be brought into the current program; foreign file

Special-purpose software: Software written for a specific type of business

Spreadsheet: Application software that calculates and automatically updates figures and usually provides graphical images of numeric data

Stand-alone software: A software package developed by a private company to perform specific operations independent of any other program

Status line: The portion of the screen where a program displays information about the current file

Storage: The storing of computer data or information on an auxiliary storage device

Storage hardware: A device that provides auxiliary storage for programs and data, usually in the form of a disk drive

Subdirectory: A secondary directory within a primary directory

Suppress: A command that prevents page numbers and/or headers and footers from appearing on the current page

System prompt: The symbol displayed by DOS that indicates it is ready for a command

System software: Programs that boot up, operate, and maintain the computer system

System unit: A computer device which includes a motherboard, storage, a power supply, and expansion slots

T

Table: A grid of rows and columns in WordPerfect

Target file: See *Destination file*

Telecommunication: Technology that requires a sending device that will change data into telephone signals, a receiving device that will change the telephone signals back into the original data, and a telephone line linking the two

Template: A strip of material positioned above or around the function keys for quick reference of program commands

Title: A heading that identifies a Lotus graph

Toggle: An on/off feature or key

Track: The circular portion of a disk on which data is stored

Trackball: An input device similar to a mouse that is used to select options from a program menu or to draw on the computer screen

U

User interface: A bridge between the user and the operating system designed to make using a computer easier

Utility: A program that performs computer housekeeping tasks such as formatting a disk and erasing files

V

Version number: The number that indicates major changes to a software package since initial marketing

Virus: A computer program that will spread by copying itself, causing unusual, and sometimes serious, problems for users

W

Warm boot: With the computer on, DOS is activated by pressing Ctrl-Alt-Delete

Widow: The first line of a paragraph that is alone at the bottom of a page

Wildcard: The wildcards ? and * enable a computer user to perform actions on a group of files at once

Windows: A program that creates a more user-friendly DOS environment by providing a graphical user interface (GUI) which is similar in all programs

Word: A related set of characters

Word processing: Application software that uses the computer to enter and arrange text in an attractive, easily read form

Wordwrap: A word processing feature where the software makes line ending decisions

WPG: WordPerfect's own graphic format

Write-protect notch: A small cut-out on a 5 ¼-inch diskette that a user can cover with tape to prevent data on the disk from being altered or deleted

Write-protect switch: A small plastic slide on a 3 ½-inch diskette that a user can open to prevent the disk from being written on

X-axis: The line at the bottom of a Lotus graph with horizontal data points

X-axis labels: Words that describe the data points on the x-axis of a Lotus graph

Y-axis: The line along the left side of a Lotus graph with vertical data points

Y scale: The range of values on the Y-axis of a graph set by Lotus according to the designated data range

INDEX

D